DOWN TO EARTH

*The Territorial Bond
in South China*

DOWN TO EARTH

The Territorial Bond in South China

EDITED BY DAVID FAURE

AND HELEN F. SIU

STANFORD UNIVERSITY PRESS

Stanford, California 1995

Stanford University Press
Stanford, California
© 1995 by the Board of Trustees of the
Leland Stanford Junior University

Printed in the United States of America

CIP data appear at the end of the book

Stanford University Press publications are
distributed exclusively by Stanford
University Press within the United States,
Canada, Mexico, and Central America;
they are distributed exclusively by
Cambridge University Press throughout
the rest of the world.

Acknowledgments

This book is another step on a long track to the roots of Chinese social history. Its collective authors have had the pleasure of sharing their discoveries for a decade while pursuing diverse agendas in the Pearl River delta and Hong Kong. Captivated by the intricate making of local society with regional identities and state cultural symbols, we strive to give theoretical and historical imaginations an ethnographic grounding.

Wolfram Eberhard, Maurice Freedman, Fu Yiling, Liang Fangzhong, Leong Sow-theng, Lo Hsiang-lin, G. William Skinner, and Barbara Ward blazed the trail. Tanaka Issei and Hamashita Takeshi added inspiration and companionship in the field. However, our guides have to be the villagers and outsiders in south China who cared to talk to us, often for no other reason than that it might be meaningful for them to do so. Their hospitality, mixed with healthy doses of understanding and humor, has always been appreciated.

The generosity of many institutions made our quest possible. In particular, the Committee on Scholarly Communications with the People's Republic of China, the Institute of Chinese Studies at the Chinese University of Hong Kong, the Freemasons Fund for East Asian Studies, the Wenner-Gren Foundation for Anthropological Research, the Yale Center for International and Area Studies, the Whitney Humanities Center, and the Cheng Yu-tung and Lee Shau-kee Fund for Yale-CUHK South China Studies supported fieldwork by various contributors from 1986.

James Watson and Jerry Dennerline kindly added their comments when some of the chapters published here were presented at a meeting of the Association for Asian Studies in 1990. Too See Lou of the Chinese University of Hong Kong prepared the maps for publications. Muriel Bell of Stanford University Press persisted when publication was nowhere in sight. Our manuscript editor, Suzanne Schafer, waded through our details on top of

British and American spellings and five different ways of romanizing Chinese. Margaret Everett prepared the Index. Liz Kyburg and Wing-hoi Chan, without fail, ordered the reluctant computer at Yale to print out the necessary pages.

To them all, the editors are grateful

D.F.
H.F.S.

Contents

Photo sections follow pages 82 and 160

Maps, Figures, and Tables

Units of Measurements and Ming and Qing Reign Names and Dates

UNITS OF MEASUREMENTS

1 *mu* = ⅙ acre

1 *qing* = 100 *mu* = 16.7 acres

1 catty = 1.33 lb.

1 tael = 1.33 oz. of silver

MING AND QING REIGN NAMES AND DATES

Ming

Hongwu	1368–98	Hongzhi	1488–1505
Jianwen	1399–1402	Zhengde	1506–21
Yongle	1403–24	Jiajing	1522–66
Hongxi	1425	Longqing	1567–72
Xuande	1426–35	Wanli	1573–1620
Zhengtong	1436–49	Taichang	1620
Jingtai	1450–57	Tianqi	1621–27
Tianshun	1457–64	Chongzhen	1628–44
Chenghua	1465–87		

Qing

Shunzhi	1644–61	Daoguang	1821–50
Kangxi	1662–1722	Xianfeng	1851–61
Yongzheng	1723–35	Tongzhi	1862–74
Qianlong	1736–95	Guangxu	1875–1908
Jiaqing	1796–1820	Xuantong	1909–11

Contributors

CHAN WING-HOI holds an M.A. in Social Anthropology (Ethnomusicology) from the Queen's University, Belfast, Northern Ireland, and is currently enrolled in graduate research in the Department of Anthropology at Yale University.

CHOI CHI-CHEUNG obtained the Ph.D. in History from the University of Tokyo and is currently a lecturer at the Division of Humanities, Hong Kong University of Science and Technology. He has published articles on Cheung Chau in Japanese and Chinese, and is currently studying the business history of south China.

DAVID FAURE holds a Ph.D. from Princeton University and is University Lecturer in Modern Chinese History and a fellow of St. Antony's College at the University of Oxford.

PATRICK HASE is a civil servant in Hong Kong. He obtained his doctorate from Cambridge University where he specialized in Anglo-Saxon social history. He is editor of the *Journal of the Hong Kong Branch of the Royal Asiatic Society* and has published numerous articles on the New Territories of Hong Kong.

JAMES HAYES retired as Regional Secretary, New Territories, from the Hong Kong Civil Service in 1987. He was for many years President of the Hong Kong Branch of the Royal Asiatic Society. He has written extensively on the history and anthropology of the New Territories, and has recently completed his third book, on the history of Tsuen Wan District and its postwar development as a "New Town." He holds a Ph.D. from London University and was awarded an honorary Doctorate in Literature from the University of Hong Kong in 1992 in recognition of his services to culture in Hong Kong.

LIU ZHIWEI obtained the M.A. degree in history from Zhongshan University and is a professor at the Department of History, Zhongshan University, Guangzhou, People's Republic of China.

LUO YIXING has a Ph.D. degree in history from Xiamen University, was for many years Deputy Director, Institute of Ming-Qing History, at the Guangdong Academy of Social Sciences, and has published widely on the history of the Pearl River delta.

HELEN F. SIU holds a Ph.D. from Stanford University and is a professor at the Department of Anthropology, Yale University.

YE XIAN'EN graduated from Zhongshan University. He is a Senior Researcher at the Guangdong Academy of Social Sciences. He published a monograph on Huizhou lineages in Ming and Qing Anhui province, several papers on the social history of the Pearl River delta, and a monograph on Guangdong water transport.

DOWN TO EARTH

The Territorial Bond
in South China

Introduction

HELEN F. SIU

DAVID FAURE

THIS collection of essays brings together scholars in the People's Republic of China, Hong Kong, the United Kingdom, and the United States who are engaged in the reconstruction of the culture and history of the Pearl River delta. The authors share the starting position that a regional approach to the historical process in China is necessary. G. William Skinner makes this concern vigorously central to his work, which highlights the juxtaposition of the integrative functions of state and market with the country's regional variations. Summarizing his work of a few decades in his presidential address to the Association of Asian Studies, Skinner argued that however singular and unifying the chronology of dynastic fortunes might seem to have been, Chinese history has been patterned by unique structural transformations of regional systems.[1] This volume takes the issue further: Skinner's approach can be enriched if the region is seen as a conscious historical construct that may be captured in the cultural expressions of those involved in creating it. We suggest that marketing networks and administrative structures are not independent variables that shape cultural sentiments, but instead are intertwined with cultural meanings in the evolution of regional identities.

The Pearl River Delta

The evolution of regional identities in the Ming, the Qing, and the Republic had much to do with the growth of the market, with state building, and with the evolution of local society. All of these issues came together in the control of land. Contrary to common belief, land was not a static resource; for this reason, it is useful to remember that between 1500 and 1800, China's population quadrupled and both registered cultivated acreage and per acre grain yield doubled.[2] This achievement was brought about by large-scale land reclamation and changes in crops and farm technologies, aided enormously by an expansion in the national as well as the international market. It should only be expected that all this economic vitality was reflected in the growth of social institutions that might support commercial development, and it is not surprising that in the Pearl River delta at least, lineages came to be closely involved in commercial and land development.[3]

A close connection between the growth of the lineage and land development does not conflict with our current understanding of the lineage as a landholding corporation. However, an emphasis on a background of economic growth as a factor in the rise of the lineage adds a new dimension to its history. Until probably the sixteenth century, the worship of ancestors at ancestral halls and the compilation of written genealogies, essential characteristics of the Chinese lineage, were restricted to the aristocracy and to very senior officials. The connection that may be postulated between the lineage and land development suggests that the lineage institution was popularized as a new order unfolded in those areas of China where commercial agriculture took hold and, as in Europe, gave rise to varieties of land rights that complemented the growth of a market economy.

The Pearl is one of China's three major river systems. The Pearl River proper is the sunken valley through which the East River, the North River, and the West River are channeled into the South China Sea. Habitation in the area covered by these numerous waterways began early with the settlement of people long held to be of non–Han Chinese origin. It is only from the Song that families closely identified with the Han tradition can be firmly dated. Into the Ming, much of the hilly area surrounding the Pearl River delta was inhabited by aborigines whom the Han referred to as the Yao.[4] The shift of the imperial capital to Hangzhou in the Southern Song (twelfth century) made Fujian province a major source of food supply to the lower Yangzi, but as the local food supply failed to keep up with population growth, Guangzhou came to be an exporter of rice up the Fujian coast. The earliest record of such rice export, drawn from supplies that had come down the West River from Guangxi province, dates from this time.[5] Also from the twelfth century date the earliest extant records of river control and land reclamation projects in the vicinity of Guangzhou. Most major efforts of dike building during the Song were restricted to the West River; however, by the Ming and the Qing, practically all the major river channels on the delta were diked, and the reclamation of the *shatian* was taking place in earnest.[6]

Opportunities for land development had brought about the growth of population centers. In addition to Guangzhou and numerous historical administrative cities, there sprang up the industrial town of Foshan, now on a main river route leading from the North and West Rivers into Guangzhou, and the many towns on the border of what used to be the foreshore, beginning with Shawan in Panyu and proceeding westward to include Daliang, Rongqi, Guizhou, and Xiaolan. The principal motorway leading out from Guangzhou today reflects this historical development: north of the motor road is the land that had been exploited from the Song; south of it, land that was preserved as the *shatian*, the newly reclaimed land that came to be known as sandy land.[7]

By the late Ming, along with grain export, the delta area was caught up also with the development of handicraft. Long before the Opium War, the eighteenth- and nineteenth-century Pearl River delta exported silk, palm-leaf fans, pottery, oranges, cotton cloth, iron implements, incense, and sacrificial papers. However, to emphasize exports in the eighteenth and nineteenth centuries is to miss the point. The success of an exporting economy created a huge internal market for rural production; thus, although by the eighteenth century Guangzhou itself ceased to be self-sufficient in grain and imported from abroad, the thriving urban market set in motion in the mid-Ming continued to fuel agricultural developments in surrounding areas.

The diking of rivers to preserve existing agricultural land was an essentially different consideration from the bringing of unworked land under cultivation. Although all dikes were costly, those built to preserve existing productive land were usually communal undertakings, whereas the reclamation of the foreshore was regarded as capital-intensive, high-risk commercial development. As commercial ventures, these reclamation projects produced land to which a monetary value could be attached, that was bought and sold, rented, and exploited with hired labor. However, development also brought settlement, sometimes as the result of in-migration from outside the delta, but often by absorbing into the mainstream communities that had persisted on the border of what used to be marshes. The enforcement of communal rights, and the clash of interest between communities and individuals, came to be very much at the heart of social development in the delta.

When in the nineteenth century Westerners succeeded in demanding by right the trade that they had previously been granted as a privilege, the pattern of land development on the Pearl River delta had already been set. More trade led to more cash crops for export—until the 1920s, mainly silk—while more prosperity in Guangzhou and the silk-producing area created an even greater demand for rice. The shatian never lost its allure, holding out the hope of high return for large investment.

Alienable Rights and Land-Use Patterns

Land rights as they existed in the Pearl River delta and its vicinity have been the subject of considerable study. Much of the interest has concentrated on alienable rights. In this respect, the general rule is well known: land could be sold or rented; the owner who obtained his right through purchase was responsible for payment of tax and the renter, whether or not the arrangement conferred tenant status, was responsible for a rent. This grossly simplified statement of Chinese land law does not take account of the distinction between bottom soil and topsoil that was common throughout the Pearl River delta. The topsoil tenant for perpetuity was at times considered an owner of the topsoil in much the same way as the owner of the bottom soil was considered an owner. Particularly problematic in this regard is that such topsoil ownership might have been related to settlement status.[8] David Faure has documented the holding of "settlement rights," including the right to build houses and to exploit common land and other common resources, as the mark of distinction between villagers and outsiders. Whatever the terms of a deed of sale or tenancy, when with the lapse of time single tenancies had grown into entire villages, the fundamental relationships between landlords and tenants must have changed; and it is this sort of change for which a legal interpretation of land relationships would fail to account.[9]

Landholding patterns in the Pearl River delta may be viewed in terms of a continuum according to the intensity of land use. At one end were the heavily exploited Nanhai and Shunde silkworm-rearing districts; at the other, the highly productive but also very extensive shatian. The silkworm-rearing districts of Nanhai and Shunde specialized in the combination of silkworm rearing and fish farming, in which ponds were scooped out in between dikes so that mulberry might be grown on the dikes and fish raised in the ponds. This area had long been settled, since before the Ming. Land plots in the area had been fragmented through inheritance and sale, and were protected from flood by dikes on the principal waterways that were maintained through communal arrangements. This intensive land use was made possible by the use of short-term leases with fixed rents that had to be paid in cash. The produce of the land was readily sold for money at the market, with such crops as mulberry, silkworms, and silk cocoons being sold in specialized markets. Tenants came from outside the area as well as inside the villages, the outsiders living in huts that had been built near the land they farmed and not in the villages.[10] Until the 1930s, the living standard was high, and this was probably a rice-importing region.

Out on the shatian, land had been reclaimed in large tracts, which were then broken up into tenantable lots and then subleased. The frequent practice of subleasing resulted in layer upon layer of tenants. It is significant that Chen Han-seng, who wrote the first substantive report on tenancy in Guangdong in the 1930s that included tenancy on the shatian, abandoned the practice of describing social division in terms of landlord and tenant, instead adopting wealth categories that he termed "rich," "middle," and "poor" peasants. Ownership of land on the shatian was a manner of speaking: the owner would have been the party that registered the reclamation with the county government and was held responsible for tax—often, conveniently, an institution such as a charitable or ancestral trust. Actual land management might have fallen to the tenants and subtenants as much as to the institutions. The shatian was worth reclaiming because it could be put to paddy, sugarcane, or, in some places, palm, all of which could be sold at a profit. Paddy on the shatian was not grown as a subsistence crop, and landlords were able to control the shatian because, among other reasons, they controlled the towns on their borders in which the rice shops were located.

Between the ends of the land-use continuum was land such as that found in the New Territories, which yielded mostly the food that provided for local subsistence but also some surplus that could be sold. The process of land reclamation and frequent transfer left its mark in long or permanent leases and bottom-soil ownership, but the land was worked by settlers who resided in the vicinity in their own villages. Villagers gathered in markets that did not specialize. Most of the Pearl River delta would have fallen into this middle category of land use in which settlement rights and commercialized agriculture continued to be relevant to local life. We shall argue that the territorial bond, a cultural expression of this historical process, can be studied on its own terms.

Culture, Politics, and Land Control

The involvement of the lineage in landholding and territorial bonding is widely acknowledged. Chen Han-seng recognized the lineages as the dominant corporate landlords but saw in them little more than exploitation personified.[11] Maurice Freedman rephrased their functions: lineages were corporate groups characterized by their trust holdings, and even though the distribution of privilege within lineages would have been uneven, they formed the lowest unit into which south China society could be atomized.[12] While Faure, studying the New Territories, accepted many of Freedman's observations on the lineage, he varied one essential component of Freedman's construct. The binding principle of lineage membership could not have been founded on the alienable land that the lineage held in trust, but on the inalienable rights to settlement that would have been derived from common descent.[13] As Freedman would have accepted, there were different types of lineages, but according to Faure the difference depended not on lineage functions but on rights accrued to their members. All lineages granted rights of worship, some granted access to alienable property, and all local lineages granted the right to settlement.

On the role of lineage in property holding, Ye Xian'en and Tan Dihua have summarized materials from genealogies and miscellaneous sources, and their findings agree at least with Freedman's view of asymmetrical segmentation: the lineage did not as a single entity hold all properties; instead, properties were held separately by sublineage trusts founded in association with sacrifice to named ancestors. Within the same lineage, access to common properties that might be claimed by different branches and individuals might vary substantially.[14] Hugh Baker and Rubie Watson, in studying lineage villages in the New Territories of Hong Kong, have also documented this phenomenon.[15] What then holds the lineage together as a territorial entity in the face of internal class inequalities?

It is important to recognize that despite the similarity, the import of Ye and Tan's documentation varies from that of Freedman's. The intellectual stimulus for Ye and Tan was the work of Fu Yiling, in which, for some decades, an argument had been taking shape concerning the role of the lineage village (*xiangzu*) in land control that was meant to elucidate landlord-tenant relationships in feudal society. Fu Yiling stated the argument very clearly when he raised the issue in 1961:

China was a unified feudal country with extensive land and a large population. The landlord class governed the peasants not simply through a totalitarian regime or bureaucratic apparatus, but by adopting a more hidden method, that is, the employment of the influence of the village and the lineage (*xiangzu*), the remnant of the clan system, to stabilize the intensification of social class contradiction and conflict in order to achieve the actual results of ruling the peasants.[16]

This statement is reminiscent of Chen Han-seng in some respects, but, because the lineage system embraced more than the bare exercise of force, the argument opened the way to an analysis of the cultural milieu in which the lineage held land and commanded consent from its tenants.

The argument has been developed in considerable detail by Fu's associates at Xiamen University. Mori Masao,[17] summarizing the work of Fu and Yang Guozhen, Fu's successor at Xiamen, perceptively related the argument to descriptions of the *kyōdōtai* in Japanese scholarship. That, of course, was to turn at least one component of the class argument on its head: as much as one might expect the enforcement of class relationships within the lineage village, lineage villages were communities that were not themselves linked by class relationships. This argument came to be the center of the writings on the lineage by Fu's students Chen Zhiping and Zheng Zhenman.[18] Chen's book on the Fujian lineage, working primarily from genealogies, describes the rituals of the lineage, intralineage segmentation, and interlineage feuds as essential components of lineage-village society. Zheng takes the argument even further: lineages in Fujian were not necessarily the result of descent, for some lineages came into being through association and others through contractual arrangements, their origins ranging from common worship of deities to common interests in land reclamation.

The idea of the lineage village would agree well with research outside China that relates lineage competition to changes in lineage forms. The acceptability of the lineage as a mode of social organization may be related to Patricia Ebrey's discussion of the spread of Zhu Xi's family rituals from the Song.[19] The evolution of lineage forms was also touched on in papers presented at the conference on Family and Kinship in Chinese History in 1983.[20] The contest between lineages for land is a long-standing issue in the literature produced both in and outside China, with contributions in recent years from Lamley and Eng.[21] Faure's discussion of lineages and villages in the New Territories of Hong Kong may be characterized in the same vein; he argues that in the contest for land and influence physical power blended closely with the manipulation of cultural symbols, including origin myths in relation to settlement histories.

The contest for land went far beyond the distribution of wealth, but if the floodgate of a cultural element in the contest has been opened, there is no reason why it should be limited to a lineage culture and its language of power. As Helen Siu put it in her study of Xinhui county, "The concentration of wealth and power with which the gentry and merchant elites were able to impress the rural population was not based solely on the control of land, commodity markets, or even charity. Class and status surfaced in practical politicking, which took institutional form," in the case of Hui-cheng district in Xinhui, "in the county academies."[22]

The import of Siu's statement, captured succinctly in Prasenjit Duara's term "the cultural nexus of power," derives from a major revision China historians and anthropologists have made in the last decade to descriptions of Chinese society.[23] The point at issue is not that the naked hands of power were not at work in rural China in the form of the yamen and the landlord. Muramatsu Yūji's scholarly and well-documented descriptions of the rent-collection bursaries in Jiangnan should take care of that.[24] The point at issue is that even Muramatsu's descriptions had followed from the thinking of a previous generation, post–May Fourth, that had stripped Chinese society of religion, delegated culture to the realm of rustic idiosyncrasy, and divorced ideology from symbolic expression. Moreover, the professionalism of rent-collection bursaries, far from being a standard feature in landlord-tenant relationships, was the exception even in Jiangnan.[25]

Fei Hsiao-tung, writing in the 1940s, saw the fallacy of describing villagers in terms of landlords and tenants. Discussing tenancy practices in the village of Lucun in Yunnan province, where many tenants rented from their own ancestral trusts, he wrote:

It is evident that, though the changing of tenants is theoretically a prerogative of the landlord, the freedom of the representative of an owning group to evict members is definitely circumscribed and that, as a consequence, tenants of this class will, in general, enjoy permanent occupancy of their farms, often without payment for the privilege. On the other hand, the relations between the landlord and the tenant in cases where kinship ties are not involved are likely to be characterized by aggressive self-interest on the part of both participants in the transactions, though even here the scales are weighted somewhat in favor of the tenant.[26]

However, Fei's insights were not taken further in the literature of the 1950s and 1960s; instead, it was his argument on the Chinese gentry that gained ascendance. This was not the gentry as he might have described it from his ethnography, fallen upon sorry days after the abolition of the imperial examinations, but the gentry—as one might equally draw from his writings—that served as the middleman between state and society, the landlord and the holder of official recognition, often in the form of a degree. The anomaly in Fei is that while he defined the gentry in terms of awards gained from the examinations, he could have observed only the postimperial gentry who were not degree holders but holders of innumerable local positions that had appeared since the late-Qing government reforms. Fei's description, therefore, blurred the distinction between the status of the yamen's

appointee and that granted beyond the local yamen (such as degree holding), which was a central issue of dispute through the Qing.[27]

Fei argued that the gentryman, by virtue of his independent status vis-
à-vis the yamen, was able to reflect local opinions and, if necessary, to op-
pose governmental demands.[28] The choice of words is probably unfortu-
nate, for relating the degree-holding status of a gentryman to his expression of local opinions prejudges the case. Degree holders had their own
axes to grind, while opinions were obviously also expressed through other
channels—notably religious practices, the operas, legends, the marketing
networks, and the innumerable actions taken independently by villagers,
ranging from membership of societies that government officials regarded
as seditious to outright riots and rebellions. A rapidly growing literature
around the theme of a popular culture has in the past decade been discov-
ering the many such channels by which opinions might have been expressed. Why, then, in the midst of all this, should the schools be given a
position of preeminence? Were they visible arenas where the ambiguity of
being gentry could be creatively used to engage the state?

The existence of interlineage and intervillage networking via the schools
was very much a discovery, at least in the Western literature, of Wakeman.[29]
Looking at the three-day battle staged by twenty-five thousand people
against British troops that landed near Guangzhou during the Opium War,
Wakeman found that the intervillage organization that had summoned
them was the communal school, the focal point of gentry organization. The
word *gentry* in this context would have been used advisedly. The organizers of local militia in these Guangdong villages were degree holders or
people who had degree-holding pretensions. They were the same class of
persons discussed in Kuhn as militia organizers.[30] And, as Siu also discovered in Xinhui, the schools were institutions where local leaders operated
with the language of the literati.

In our view, as arenas where the cultural nexus of power was enacted,
lineages encompassed more than kinship and temples displayed more than
religious fervor. As for the schools, the one activity in which they did not
seem to be engaged was education. The schools met in buildings that were
often adjacent to the local temples. The schools owned land and held meetings and, in times of unrest, organized the local militia. But the schools did
not teach. They were schools not because schools as institutions of education might provide any facility for the other communal matters of importance, but because the school was the communal organization most acceptable to the state.

The community that was so adept at bending the common language of the state to its own communal ends was, without a doubt, participating in the wider state culture. The gentry was a well-defined concept within this culture, although as one would expect, in a local context, no single criterion, degree holding or other, would have been hard and fast. Through the 1950s and 1960s, students of Chinese society, followed the tradition of which Fei became the unwitting transmitter, speaking in the same breath of the degree-holding status of gentrymen and their ability to manage village affairs; it took James Hayes, with his administrative experience in the New Territories, to point out the obvious, that is, that rural leaders frequently were not degree holders and that few degree holders managed village affairs. Hayes has since reshaped his argument into one that dwells on village self-management, which pertains not only to lineage or defense but also to the many and varied facets of local life, including especially the very rich ritual life that has been noted in the Western literature from the time Westerners began to set foot in China.[31]

The manipulation of symbols, in which the control of land and influence would have been an objective, rested on a language of membership and exclusion adorned with an aura of orthodoxy. Helen Siu's study of the Chrysanthemum Festival in Xiaolan township (Zhongshan county) shows the extent to which culture might be manipulated toward these ends and yet be expressed as the community's own. Yet, the late Qing and the Republican era disrupted essential tenets on which this cultural heritage depended, with the abolition of the imperial examination, the conclusion of imperial rule, May Fourth iconoclasm, Party government, and then war. These events challenged no less than the legitimacy of the rural as well as the wider leadership, as Guy Alitto points out; and while it was clear enough who held power even in the absence of a commonly agreed upon standard of legitimacy, it was not always clear how the holders of power might be described.[32] The emergence of stark military power in Xinhui county, documented by Siu, and the inroads made by government into established village society in Hebei province, discovered by Duara, were expressions of the same phenomenon.

One would agree with Esherick and Rankin, therefore, that there might well have been great continuity among local leaders through the Qing and into the Republic, and even that there probably was considerable convergence between the local leadership and the holding of wealth. Yet one would hesitate to refer to the local leaders as members of an elite. The problem is that the word *elite* in English is ambiguous, referring sometimes to power and at other times to status.[33] Esherick and Rankin's concept of the local traditional elite, namely, the gentry, is riddled with this ambiguity.

Many who held power in the village in the Republic had descended from families that held power in the late Qing, but the legitimacy of the basis of their power was challenged in the Republic as it had never been challenged in the Qing. This is an argument well brought out in Rankin's earlier work on Zhejiang elites,[34] but hidden in the analytical language of the Esherick and Rankin volume. Taken to one extreme, their characterization of local patterns of dominance can be merely another way of resurrecting the theory of political control whose shortcomings are so obvious in Hsiao Kung-chuan (1960).[35] Those shortcomings arise from the characterization of the majority of the population as passive characters who were to be ruled, which ignores the intense competition for the power and influence that were so often culturally defined.

Ethnicity

Inhabitants of the Pearl River delta recognize by common agreement three ethnic divisions broadly placed within the category of Han people: the Punti (*bendi*), the Hakka (*kejia*), and the Dan (or *danjia*; popularly referred to in the English-language literature as the Tanka). Dialect and customary differences among the Punti are well recognized. The Xiguan and the Panyu accents provided the standards, and both were distinguishable from the thicker Nanhai, Shunde, and Siyi accents. The Hakka spoke a different dialect altogether, and although the Dan accent was close to the ordinary Punti accent, customs and status set the Dan apart. In the early Ming, there would also have been the Yao people to the east of Xinhui in the west. There were also pockets of dialectical variations, such as in the Longdu dialect areas in Zhongshan.

It is convenient to regard the Punti as indigenous, although many Punti surnames claim by their legends that they too had entered Guangdong from the north. Similar legends of common origin are recorded among the Hakka, and are given of the Dan by the Punti. The reliance on a common origin as much as on common speech as a criterion of demarcation suggests that native place holds a central position in their identity. In fact, native place identities have been used by merchants, laboring sojourners, and aspiring scholars to strategize and organize in order to capture scarce societal resources.[36] These self-ascribed identities must be contrasted with ethnic labels imposed by dominant groups to marginalize and exclude. Emily Honig examines the discriminatory attitudes of the Shanghai residents against those they named "Subei people." Although the label is prima facie geographical, she sees the issue as one of ethnicity. The places of origin of these people were in fact hard to pinpoint, but their lifestyle is considered so low as to be culturally marginal.[37]

We acknowledge that ethnic differentiation often occurs among those who consider themselves Han Chinese, as in the case of the Hakka and the Dan in the Pearl River delta, but we believe that the social processes underlying native place and ethnic categorization involve a crucial structural difference.[38] Native place identities differentiate populations who may have come from geographically distant places, who exhibit a clear division of labor in their trades within the community, who remain more or less social equals, and who actively use these affiliations to create a sense of solidarity; ethnic categories impose cultural distance and intensely unequal statuses among groups that lack clear physical and geographical lines along which to distinguish themselves and whose livelihoods are closely intertwined. These categories are not arbitrarily drawn. The criteria for defining high and low, Han and the ethnic other, were historically based on how the powerful improvised upon the "civilizing" enterprise of the imperial state to reinforce exploitive local relationships.

The myths and realities of migration and cultural diffusion in south China have always held a fascination for scholars with an interest in ethnic relations.[39] In the nineteenth century, few who lived in the prosperous towns and villages of the Pearl River delta would have questioned their identity as legitimate members of the Chinese empire. They might have acknowledged differences in dialect, living habits, and marriage customs among themselves, but all traced their origin from the central plains (*zhongyuan*). They said that their ancestors brought the institutions of family and lineage, Confucian education, literati connections, and shared religious beliefs. Their genealogies, displaying members as prominent scholar-officials since the Tang dynasty, insisted on elaborate myths of migration and settlement. The legend of the 92 households bearing 35 surnames that dispersed from Zhuji *xiang* of Nanxiong subprefecture during the Song is frequently cited. Higher-order lineages were often formed by groups claiming agnatic ties based on the legend.[40]

From the perspectives of these established lineages, the cultural and historical fringes of the middle kingdom were inhabited by the tribal Yao, She, and Zhuang in the hills of northern Guangdong. They were seen as descendants of the aboriginal populations of south China known as the Baiyue. Later migrants who occupied hilly land closer to the delta were considered the same cultural stock as those in the central plains, but were termed "Hakka."[41] Those who dwelt on their boats along the network of riverways were branded "Dan." These broadly differentiating labels appeared regularly in official and unofficial documents of the Ming and Qing and have long been assumed to be primordial in nature.[42]

A closer reading of the documentary and local ethnographic materials renders a more nuanced picture of the delta's cultural configuration. If there were indeed migrants from the central plains, they did not move into an unoccupied frontier. Local histories and traveling officials in the Qing expressed dismay at "dubious local customs" among agriculturalists whom they assumed to be Han.[43] Evidence of intense interaction makes it problematic to classify local populations discretely into Han, Yao, Zhuang, and Dan. In fact, marriage customs in certain prosperous Han communities appear too close to those of the Yao, Zhuang, and Li to deny affinity.[44] A similar observation applies to the folklore and to the pantheon of the gods (such as Tianhou, Hongsheng, Longmu) patronized by the landed communities and the "ethnics."[45] If there were indeed separate groups, as many historians have assumed, one must explore the reasons for the apparent mutual borrowing over a long historical period.

State policies and local reactions in the Ming and Qing further complicated the picture. Faure has pointed out that the difference between the Yao and the Han in the Pearl River delta in the Ming might reflect self-identification on the basis of qualification for corvée service.[46] S. T. Leong has drawn attention to a conscious movement conducted by the Hakka since the early nineteenth century to exert ethnic identity.[47] Local interpretations also created their own complex dynamics. The genealogy of a Gan lineage at the southern tip of Taishan county, for example, claimed that their ancestors came from the north centuries before. In the course of settlement, they somehow had acquired the ethnic status of Yao, and generations afterward, according to the genealogy, lineage members switched back to their "Han" identity because such status offered more protection against aggressive neighbors.[48]

The duplicity prompts several questions: first, could the migrants from the central plains have "gone native"? If they did, what were the circumstances of their sojourn? Second, could differentiation have occurred after these migrant groups adapted themselves to a varied environment? Third, is it possible that the migration from the north, however massive, did not account for the origin of the bulk of the population of the Pearl River delta but that, instead, the indigenous populations who became agriculturalist started from a different cultural baseline in a long process of assimilation and acquired Han cultural characteristics as they sought their respective places in the expanding Chinese polity? These questions reflect different scholarly assumptions about frontier, ethnicity, assimilation, and the gen-

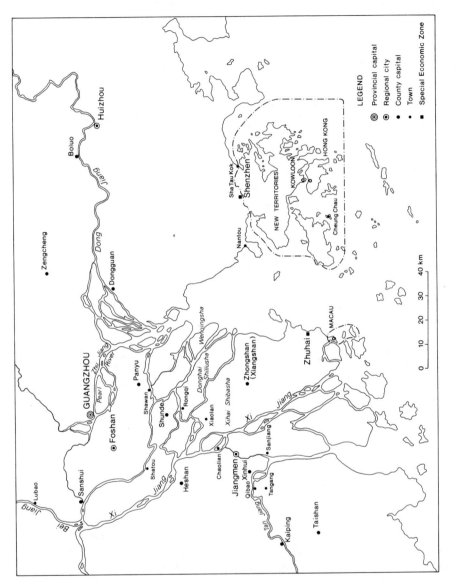

Map 1. The Pearl River delta

eral process of cultural construction. They also highlight the need to analyze the complex process of migration, mutual borrowing, and differentiation among the indigenous populations as well as the ways that incoming Han state culture, itself evolving, defined this process.[49]

We share the concerns of Morris Rossabi, Pamela Crossley, and Dru Gladney that representations of Chinese civilization by established historiography have been somewhat anachronistic.[50] Even if one acknowledges the enduring power of the "Chinese" tradition that acculturated indigenous populations at various historical times and places, one should also understand how the supposedly Han culture was reconstituted in the process.[51] A conscious cultural identity affiliated with the Chinese imperial order did emerge among the inhabitants of the expanding Pearl River delta in the course of the last five centuries.[52] The formation of an elaborate "lineage complex" and the associated literati pretensions after the Ming firmly positioned local populations in the Confucian schema. The schema promoted a hierarchical representation of expanding territory, with cultural authority radiating from the imperial political center. But despite this ideological stress on cultural identification with and political commitment to the larger polity, past and present, the delta continued to distinguish itself with a mosaic of linguistic enclaves, native place loyalties, and subcultures. It is an ideal site for exploring the fluidity of ethnic boundaries.

The Essays in This Book

Brief summary statements and the conclusions that may be drawn out of the essays included in this collection may be found in the conclusion chapter. It suffices in this introduction to state briefly the objectives of this collection and how the essays relate to the general issues that have been raised.

First, all the essays in this book are detailed ethnographic and historical accounts of the Pearl River delta and the Hong Kong region (see Maps 1 and 2). This collection provides a range of case studies for a growing community of scholars of traditional and contemporary China whose works focus on this geographic area but whose access to documentary and field resources has been limited. All the essays draw on field experience, and they do not attempt to simplify the complexities of local cultural life and the nuanced representations of these experiences in historical documents.

Second, the essays attempt to reconstruct the "civilizing process" in south China in the late imperial period in which the local inhabitants, both elites and commoners, used symbolic and instrumental means to become

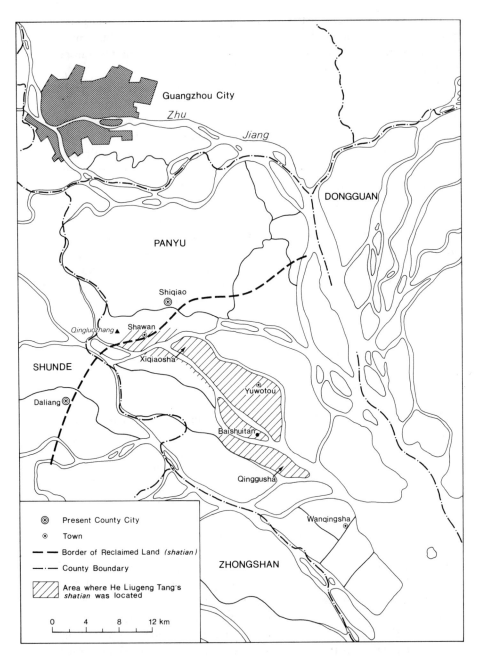

Guangzhou City

Zhu

Jiang

DONGGUAN

PANYU

Shiqiao

Qingluozhang▲ Shawan

Xiqiaosha

SHUNDE

Yuwotou

Daliang

Baishuitan

Qinggusha

Wanqingsha

◎ Present County City

⊙ Town

▬ ▬ Border of Reclaimed Land *(shatian)*

—·— County Boundary

▨ Area where He Liugeng Tang's
shatian was located

ZHONGSHAN

0   4   8   12 km

Map 2. Shawan and surroundings

part of Chinese culture and polity. They address a common question in history and anthropology, that is, how do we conceptualize the historical development of a state agrarian society with visible hierarchies of power and authority, attachment to which is unifying as well as diversifying? The process allowed the development of a region that was fiercely conscious of its regional culture yet bore the uniform imprint of the dynastic order.[53] Instead of posing the state mechanically against society, we see the state's concerns as intricately built into the very construction of community. Granted that the Chinese polity was made through the maneuvering of armies, the imposition of taxes, and the building of elaborate bureaucracies, it was nonetheless consolidated by the extension of the literati tradition to local society as a cultural system whose power lay in its naturalizing tendencies.

As Philip Corrigan and Derek Sayer argue for England, state making in China entailed cultural revolution.[54] But unlike what Etienne Balazs saw as a process weighed down by a "permanently bureaucratic" focus, the state bridged lively local cultures and a reified but malleable "Chinese" tradition to create a repertoire of values and symbolisms that contained multiple voices and agendas.[55] The construction of lineage, community, market networks, ethnic identity, and popular religion in south China were dialogues creating identities, setting boundaries, asserting entitlement, and enforcing exclusion. The processes were integral to the expansion of the late imperial state, which presented itself less as an administrative machinery than as a cultural idea.[56] As the former, the state was remote; as the latter, it was penetrating because its symbolic codes, however reconstituted and subverted by human agency, continued to shape perceptions of viable options. We use this conceptual framework to rethink certain paradigms in Chinese history and anthropology.

An awareness of the spatial distribution of the case studies is probably essential if the reader is to follow the argument that runs through them. The cases begin with Liu Zhiwei's study of Shawan, a township on the border of the shatian area, covering in the main the Ming and the Qing dynasties. This is followed by Luo Yixing's study of Lubao township in Sanshui county, on the North River, away from the shatian. These two essays describe the settlement typologies against which other essays in this book are compared: the Shawan model, dominated by a single surname with an intense interest in land reclamation, and the Lubao model, akin to what is still found in the New Territories of Hong Kong, where local lineages and villages congregated around the town, which itself was managed by its own committee.

Our scene shifts from there to a general description by Ye of the Dan, found commonly on the shatian, and then in essays by Chan, Choi, Hayes, and Hase, to the Hakka, the ethnic category set apart from the Punti and the Dan. Chan works his way from Hakka genealogies into religious practices that might at one time have been common among the indigenous populations of south China to argue that these genealogies were the products of a fundamental change in religion. Choi and Hayes describe the complexity of interethnic relations on Cheung Chau Island, at the mouth of the Pearl River within the New Territories of Hong Kong, on which was located a market of considerable scale through the nineteenth century. Through the study of an annual *jiao* festival, Choi examines the marking of territorial interests via the establishment of temples and shrines; Hayes provides the setting for this description in terms of voluntary organizations that on the island provided the territorial management structure. Both authors agree that the Dan, as boat people, were clearly set apart from the land people even as they were involved in the ritual life of the community. Hase's essay describes an intervillage alliance centered on the market town of Sha Tau Kok in the New Territories. Sha Tau Kok was at the southern tip of a network of markets controlled by the Hakka that stretched north and east up the East River. Together, these essays illustrate the dynamic reconfiguration of the local political economy and the mosaic of cultural identities.

Faure's essay then discusses a small village on the edge of the shatian in Xinhui, and Siu concludes with a study of the legitimacy of the local leadership in three communities on the shatian. Faure's essay draws on the minutes of a lineage association (*tongxianghui*) that met through the 1920s and 1930s in Hong Kong but that exercised control over its lineage village of Tangang in Xinhui county. Siu describes patterns of domination in several communities on the shatian in the 1940s, primarily from material gathered through fieldwork. Together, these two essays illustrate the transformation that overtook the lineage-village community as imperial legitimacy receded and a political void took over.

In terms of time span, the essays by Liu and Luo cover the Ming, the Qing, and the Republic. Ye's essay is primarily concerned with the Qing, as is Chan's. The essays by Choi, Hayes, and Hase encompass the nineteenth and twentieth centuries. Faure's essay covers the Republican era, as does Siu's, which focuses particularly on the 1930s and 1940s.

These essays, reflecting the cooperation of anthropologists and historians among a generation of scholars from China and the West, have been made possible by exchanges in the recent decade. Unlike many essay collections that are now produced, this volume is not the product of a conference, but rather the result of much continued discussion over a number of years through frequent contact among the authors. The essays may be uneven in their theoretical focus. Some of our anthropological concepts that require interpreting intangible cultural meanings might have been uncomfortable for historians who felt pressed for hard documentary evidence. They nonetheless have come to appreciate how ethnographic sensitivities can place written sources in context. Those of us who have been involved closely in cooperative research on the Pearl River delta are delighted that we have been able to learn from one another's orientations.

Lineage on the Sands:
The Case of Shawan

LIU ZHIWEI

THERE was a popular saying in the Pearl River delta: "The He surname of Shawan have no trouble finding wives for their sons." Underlying
this saying was the widespread belief that members of the He lineage were
so well provided for by their ancestral trusts that they could offer extravagant marital payments and wedding ceremonies with ease and that, for
this reason, families in the area were eager to have their daughters marry
into the He lineage. This popular view, no doubt, illustrates the impressive
wealth of the He lineage, but it also reflects the unprecedented flourishing
of ancestral estates in this area in the Ming and the Qing dynasties and
highlights the unique impact of such wealth on social life.

The He lineage settled on the edge of vast river marshes in the Pearl River
delta, and its fortunes rose with the reclamation of the sands (*sha*) and the
building of ancestral estates. In this historical process, lineage as a social
organization and a cultural symbol assumed unique meanings. In other
words, the development of the sands under lineage auspices had tremendous impact on the making of local society. It was a process of regional
economic development as much as a social and cultural construction.
These issues emerged in our discussions with the villagers as we conducted
historical and ethnographic research in Shawan primarily during the summer of 1989, and on subsequent visits in 1990 and 1991. This essay is a
preliminary result of our efforts.[1]

The Reclamation of the Sands

Present-day Shawan *zhen* is located three miles southwest of the municipal seat of Panyu county and eighteen miles south of Guangzhou, and

Translated by To Wing-kai and Paul Festa. The editors have done extensive editing.

is adjacent to Shunde county in the west. It has a population of 15,000 occupying an area of about a square mile and a half.[2] It was built along the eastern edge of a crescent-like ridge named Qingluo *zhang*. Until the tenth century, the ridge surrounding Shawan was an island in a shallow sea.[3] To its northwest, the North River flowed through a small waterway to join the Pearl River system. River marshes were formed from the tenth to the thirteenth century due to heavy sedimentation, linking the area to the older part of the delta.[4] Shunde Creek, a tributary of the North River, separated the river marshes from Shunde county and continued to flow toward the sea along the southern edge of the ridge. The eastern side of the crescent-shaped ridge became a bay that gradually silted up. "Shawan," meaning a bay filled with silt, attracted settlers.[5] It marked a natural starting point for the development of the sands in Panyu county in the Song and Yuan periods, and laid the foundation for further land reclamation. In time, Shawan's southwest became an extensive tract of reclaimed land. Known to geographers as the Panyu subdelta, it was second in size only to the sands in neighboring Xiangshan (Zhongshan) county.

Folklore dates the initial settlement of Shawan to the Song dynasty in the thirteenth century. The earliest inhabitants had surnames like Zhang, Lu, Cao, Kang, Mai, and Zhu.[6] Sites such as the Zhu Creek and the Mai River Landing are the only extant remains of these early inhabitants. Other surnames came later. Known eventually as the *wu daxing* (the five major surnames) in Shawan, they were the He, Li, Wang, Li (Lai), and Zhao. It is safe to assume that Shawan as a recognizable settlement could not have started before the thirteenth century. It developed into a sizable township on the sands of Panyu only from the Ming. By the late Qing and early Republican periods, people of the He surname had risen to become the most powerful lineage among the five surname groups in Shawan. Its unprecedented wealth and power rested on the control of extensive sands southeast of Shawan.

Founding ancestor He Renjian had settled at the foot of the Qingluo-zhang ridge. He started with 50 acres of land at the foot of the hillside and then extended his cultivation by 50 acres of alluvial fields in front of it. Thereafter, his descendants cultivated river marshes farther south. By the Jiajing reign of the Ming dynasty (1522–66), the He surname had expanded to Gouwei *sha* (near the present Yuwotou; see Map 2). The sequence from settling at the foot of the ridge to cultivating small patches of marshland and then to aggressively acquiring and reclaiming the sands for cultivation points to the step-by-step buildup of landed wealth that was integral to the development of the He lineage in the region. It came to be said that the people of the He surname had felt that purchasing land for cultivation was not as profitable as the reclamation of the sands, and that they therefore put their efforts into enlarging their holdings by land reclamation.[7] The lack of documentary evidence on this description makes one wonder about its validity. However, it fits the general development pattern in the delta.

River marshes had been formed by a natural process of sedimentation over the centuries, but the growth of the new sands in the delta in the last two to three centuries was "less a natural process than a result of considerable investment of labor and capital."[8] In other words, the building of dikes around these areas to convert the marshes into cultivable land accelerated the process of the sedimentation from the river.

The development of the sands followed a well-tried procedure that began probably in the Ming. Laborers were hired to drop stones from boats into the shallow seabed or to build stone walls outside the original polder. These stony skeletal structures (*shagu*) accelerated the silting process by slowing the flow of the water. As soon as the mudbanks emerged during low tide, dikes were built around them. The process was known locally as "constructing the polders" (*paiwei*). The He lineage as owners (*yezhu*) of the foreshore claimed ownership of the skeletal rights, and it was up to them to recruit contractors, known as *gengjia* (cultivator households), who put up the capital to build the polders at specified locations and were then leased the land reclaimed on a long-term basis. Construction was difficult and time consuming. The polder that surrounded the area being reclaimed rested on a foundation of bamboo poles that could be as wide as 60 feet and averaged 9 to 10 feet in height. Where the water currents were strong, rocks had to be added to the seaward side to protect it. On this foundation a middle layer of soil and bamboo was constructed that was often about 35 feet wide. Fruit trees were grown on this layer, but there could also be added an upper layer of soil that was about 5 feet thick. When soil in the polder had settled, contractor and owner together measured and parceled out the land.[9]

It is unclear when the members of the He lineage began to reclaim the sands. Shawan villagers firmly believe in the legends claiming that they had had control over the sands since the Song period, but the claim is dubious.[10] It is doubtful if much reclamation in the Pearl River delta was undertaken before the Ming, and almost certain that large-scale construction took place only after the mid-Qing.[11] Moreover, the record of the ancestral trust, the He Liugeng *tang*, clearly shows that the earliest land grants were received in the Ming dynasty and that most of its reclaimed land was registered with the government only after mid-Qing.[12] While it is true that registration did not necessarily coincide with reclamation—for the simple reason that the locally powerful would have managed to evade taxes by not registering—because conflicts over land rights were frequent it would also have been unwise for them to leave large areas totally unregistered. In these circumstances, landlords compromised: they invested in the building of large polders only after some land had been registered, although the amount of land reclaimed would not have tallied with the amount reported.[13]

The He lineage was affected by widespread tenant revolts during the late Ming and by forced resettlement inland in the early Qing. After the policy of forced resettlement was abandoned in the eighth year of Kangxi (1669), the He lineage recuperated and accelerated its reclamation efforts. A record in 1702 shows that it was building polders near Xichao.[14] In fact, from the end of the Ming to the early Qing, the He concentrated its efforts on the sands southeast of Shawan, near Dawu, Xiaowu, and Xichao. From mid-Qing on, the lineage expanded farther southeast to reach Baishuitan sha and Qinggu sha. Preserved today at the ancestral hall, the Liugeng tang, are two iron oxen measuring 30 inches long and 11 inches high and each weighing over 150 pounds. Engraved on them are the statements "Established by He Shixian and others in the 51st year of Qianlong" (1786) and "Established by He Kengtang and others in the 51st year of Qianlong," respectively. The iron oxen were sunk into the shallow seabed before the building of polders to mark boundaries in the sands, probably when Baishuitan sha and Qinggu sha were built. These reclamations comprised nearly half of the sands owned by the lineage. The date of construction indicates large-scale reclamation activities during the mid-Qing.

By the eighteenth century, the holdings of the Liugeng tang exceeded 1,600 acres. By the end of the Qing dynasty it controlled over 5,000 acres. Its landholdings in the sands doubled again in the Republican era, making it one of the delta's "super lineages" endowed with vast ancestral estates.[15]

Lineage Building

Lineage organizations commonly found in the Pearl River delta in the Qing dynasty were a cultural phenomenon that developed after the mid-Ming under particular social and economic circumstances.[16] The history of the formation of the He lineage through land reclamation was an integral part of this cultural process.

The Creation of Lineage History

The genealogical records of the He lineage claim their descent from a son of King Wu of the Zhou dynasty who was designated Lord of Han. After the Qin unification, like other aristocrats he adopted a surname—in this case, the surname He. The genealogies go on to record the literati achievements of the lineage over the centuries. Most of these claims were ostentatious exaggerations of which even genealogy compilers were skeptical.[17] In fact, it was not until the early Ming that the He lineage at Shawan began to keep written records. In 1371, He Zihai became a *jinshi* and recorded a genealogical chart. This is as early a record of the He lineage of Shawan as one can find.

In the preface of the genealogy, He Zihai wrote:

I have observed that all literati families have genealogies to pass down [to their descendants]. However, they either give up their own ancestors to venerate other people's ancestors, or search out reputable and virtuous people of past ages to serve as their ancestors. This is ridiculous. In our family, in the more than one hundred years of accumulated merits between the venerable Administrative Assistant (*fupan*) [He Renjian] and the middle generations, several tens of descendants have written poetry, practiced the rituals, and served as officials. Other lineages have not been able to surpass this record. The first and third segment (*fang*), in particular, have been particularly notable in their achievements. It is the effort of our Minister of the Court of Imperial Sacrifices (Taichang *qing*) that has led to the rise of our lineage, and is it not fitting that his sons and grandsons be plentiful? Now that the ancestral halls have been left broken, and ancestral sacrifice has been lacking, I wonder who it will be who will revive and expand our lineage. All of us descendants who see this genealogical chart should encourage one another toward this end.[18]

He Zihai lived in the late Yuan and early Ming and was in the fifth generation. Since he traced the lineage back only five generations to begin with He Renjian, and since he also criticized the production of fictive descent in literati families, it would appear that he had no knowledge of a genealogy of the He surname before Renjian's time.[19] However, Zihai's remarks about fictive descent also demonstrate that literati families had begun to objectify their lineage histories through the compilation of written genealogies. By the early Ming; his caution notwithstanding, a claim to official achievement was definitely made in that Renjian's son, said to have been a *jinshi*, was also noted as a Minister of the Court of Imperial Sacrifices.

Fictive descent must have been appealing, for sometime in the eighteenth century we witness an effort to pursue it by pushing back lineage ancestry. The beginning of an attempt to do so was recorded in the 1713 genealogy preface written by one He Guangzhen of the fifteenth generation:

In the early Ming, an ancestor who was known by his posthumous name as Zihai became a *jinshi* in *gengxu* year of the Hongwu reign and began to compile the family genealogy. Later, ancestor Zhiyi of the ninth generation, concerned with the genealogy, recorded the event of his uncle, Ziyi, visiting Maling to see the grave inscription of his ancestor Liguang. After that, he thought about going to Nanxiong to examine the gazetteer of Baochang county, but he was not successful in doing so. Later, ancestor Qiutian of the thirteenth generation, known by his posthumous name as Qiong, said that as he passed through Baochang on his way to the imperial examination, he met distant clan members in Nanxiong and inquired in detail about the origin [of the He lineage]. However, because he had to assume office, he did not have the time to compile the genealogy.[20]

Notably, this effort to extend the history of the lineage backward connected the lineage origin to Nanxiong prefecture in northern Guangdong. This connection with Nanxiong in many lineage genealogies in the Pearl River delta served as evidence of Han ethnic origins in the central plains.

The focus on Nanxiong brought about a decided shift in emphasis in the tracing of descent within the He lineage. In an article written in the early Ming, He Zihai had made no reference to any relationship between the He lineage and Nanxiong. Instead he had briefly referred to two ancestors, He Ze and his son He Ding, both of whom were *jinshi* in the Tang dynasty and were noted in the official histories as having originated from Panyu.[21] In the more elaborate lineage histories after the Ming, these two figures were deemphasized; instead, genealogy compilers described a certain He Chang as the first ancestor to have settled in Guangdong, and he was honored with ancestral sacrifices. It was recorded of He Chang:

Our founding ancestor from Nanxiong, the venerable Attendant Censor (*shiyu*), known by his posthumous name as Chang, originated from Xuzhou, Dongjing [the eastern capital, that is, Kaifeng]. He served in the court of Shi Jin [or Later Jin]. As a result of the invasion of the Khitans, he was assigned to a military post in Qinghai and eventually moved to Baochang of Nanxiong. In the Later Zhou, he was adviser to the military commander in Guangdong but died there serving the emperor. Local people were awed by the fact that his corpse flowed upstream for 30 *li*. Because of his virtue, people built a temple in Shashui Village to revere him.[22]

And:

He Chang was a native of Baochang, Nanxiong. He operated in the midst of mountain vapors and miasma. In the high mountains at the Mei *guan* Pass, sometimes there were ghostly sounds, sometimes ghostly voices, and sand would fly and stones could move. The local people were all struck by sickness. But every dawn and dusk, a gentleman in official attire appeared to save them. The evil spirits were eventually eradicated. Later, people came across a portrait of the venerable Chang, which resembled the gentleman who was seen. So people in Baochang gathered to build a temple for the respected Chang. The local temple started then.[23]

It would seem from this account that He Chang originated somewhat in the style of a local deity in Nanxiong, and was then appropriated by the He surname as their founding ancestor. As such, he became the key link between the He lineage and its Nanxiong origins.

It seems obvious that lineage legends were products of considerable borrowing, especially among groups of the same surname. The following account, ascribed to He Zhiyi, shows how the association with He Chang had come about:

Our founding ancestor, as previously recorded in the genealogy, was not given the details of name, birthdate, or title. In the early years of the Hongwu reign, I accompanied my uncle Ziyi to visit the temple in Nanxiong [meaning He Chang's]. I learned the details of his life. I thought often of researching further and recording the facts. Having heard that a lineage segment in Maling of Nanhai claimed similar ancestry, I went one day to Maling to meet with one of their descendants by the name of Fengjing. I was able to inspect the tombstone inscription of ancestor Guangli. I discovered that [He Chang] was originally from Xuzhou, Dongjing.[24]

Another account by He Zhiyi claimed to have found a record of the epitaph of He Renjian dated 1342 that begins with the following words: "A descendant of He the venerable Attendant Censor [He Chang] of Baochang, Nanxiong." The extant epitaph, significantly, had been recorded by He Zhiyi, who had discovered the connection with Nanxiong, and Zhiyi's account, now recorded in the genealogies, noted that the original inscriptions had been lost and that his information "was taken from old books." It is also significant that only after the early Ming did the He lineage in Shawan begin to make this association with He Chang. In fact, although both the preface of He Zihai's version of the genealogy and the early Ming epitaph of He Qilong, written by the Guangdong literati Sun Fen, contain passages praising the He lineage, neither mentions He Chang or the Hes' Nanxiong origin. It was only when the major lineages of the Pearl River delta had begun to trace their origins to Nanxiong that He Chang became the first ancestor of the He surname of Shawan to settle in Guangdong.[25]

Further discoveries were made in the 1713 genealogy compiled by He Guangzhen. He found "a genealogical chart of the He lineage from the Western Zhou to the Song together with an introductory essay to it that had been put together by ancestor Lijie of Baochang in Nanxiong."[26] These two documents became widely accepted in lineage genealogies compiled during the Qing as records of lineage history before the Song. It was said that the genealogical chart was compiled by He Jieli of Baochang in 1409, and that during the Jiajing reign (mid-sixteenth century), it had been recorded by the noted Cantonese scholar He Weibo, who, "returning to his native place for ritual observations and finding no genealogy he could refer to, had sent someone to Nanxiong to copy the chart." It was from the genealogy of the He lineage of Shajiao, Nanhai county, of which He Weibo was a member, that the He lineage of Shawan had copied the chart.[27]

In sum, lineage history was often constructed by merging legends, and inconsistencies were bound to result. Pushing lineage history beyond ancestor He Renjian (the focal ancestor at Shawan) to ancestor He Chang, and thus forging a connection with the migration from Nanxiong, the He surname created for itself an origin that was similar to that claimed by many nearby lineages. As a result, the genealogies led to a great deal of confusion about lineage history from the southern Song on. In 1771, a He Shirang, after reviewing the history for the first and second generations of the He lineage, complained "that the old prefaces copied were all muddled and unreliable."[28] He attempted to clarify the ancestral origins in the appendix of a written genealogy, but his claims are also problematic. Owing to space limitations, I am unable to present here a complete list of the contradictions in the He lineage genealogy. However, it is precisely these contradictions that reveal the great extent to which the compilation of the He lineage ancestral history was fabricated. By about the mid-Qing, the basic structure of the genealogy had already been assembled. Owing to obvious fabrications, different later editions of the genealogies contain varying interpretations and inconsistent accounts, particularly of the period before He Renjian and the migration from Nanxiong to the Pearl River delta. What is important, however, is not how much truth is in the narratives but that they provided important resources and meanings for the development of the He lineage.

The Construction of Ancestral Halls and Graves

Although the reconstruction of lineage history through written genealogies serves to legitimize a conscious claim of descent and identity, the institutional basis of a lineage organization lies also in other practices. In the process of building lineages in the Pearl River delta during the Qing, the construction of ancestral halls was one such means for perpetuating lineage solidarity. As the Guangdong scholar Qu Dajun of Panyu once said,

"Now the *zongzi* [principal descent line] system has not been restored, so there are only *zu* [clans] instead of *zong*. The decay of the *zong* led to an emphasis on the *zu*, whereas the discord of the *zu* led to an emphasis of *ci* [ancestral halls]. The *ci* links descendants together and unites families. *Ren* [humanity] and *xiao* [filial piety] can then be nurtured."[29]

From the vantage point of the He lineage of Shawan, the building of ancestral halls is particularly important for the maintenance of lineage solidarity. By the late Yuan and early Ming, five generations after He Renjian had settled in Shawan, the He lineage had grown considerably in number and in stature. Renjian's son, Qilong, was a *jinshi*, and many of his descendants became county magistrates and prefects. Most prominent was Zihai of the fifth generation, who became a *juren* in the Zhizheng period (1341–1368) in the Yuan, and a *jinshi* in the Hongwu period in the early Ming. This further enhanced the reputation of his lineage in the region. In the early Ming, the noted scholar Sun Fen wrote in the epitaph for He Qilong, saying, "For generations, the He lineage have lived in Shawan, Panyu, as a major lineage. . . . However, it was Zihai, by becoming *jinshi* in the Hongwu period, who brought fame to Guangdong."[30] Although these might be mere words of praise, they do indicate the beginning of a reputation for the He surname of Shawan.

Once a descent group had risen into prominence in the Ming, the establishment of a lineage institution came as a matter of course. In addition to compiling written genealogies, the He surname also renovated its ancestral halls and graves as a means of building the lineage. As an article in the genealogy entitled "Liugeng Tang *kao*" ("A study of the Liugeng tang") has recorded, "[The Liugeng tang,] first built in 1335, was managed by ancestor Zhennan and ancestor Zhuoyin. It was soon destroyed during warfare in the late Yuan. Descendants, therefore, sacrificed to their ancestors in private chambers. Not until 1393 did the venerable Heng and Zhengshi assemble lineage members to build a new ancestral hall. In 1440, the venerable Juyi and other lineage members planned to renovate and enlarge the ancestral hall again."[31]

The earliest record of the ancestral hall built in the late Yuan can be found in the writings of He Zhiyi, the genealogy compiler of the early Ming: "The epitaph of the venerable Assistant Judge [*qianpan*, reference to He Renjian] was destroyed during the wars toward the end of the Song. During the Yuan, his grandsons built an ancestral hall bearing the honorific board "The Liugeng tang" for sacrifice to him. In the Zhizheng period, they also repaired the grave and made an epitaph for it."[32] From the discussion of the demise of the ancestral halls and the graves in the preface of the genealogy compiled by He Zihai, it seems probable that an ancestral hall had already been built in the Yuan. Since the He lineage had produced degree holders by then, the building of a "family temple" (*jiamiao*) might also have been possible. That it was a descendant in the fifth generation who had achieved the official status to make sacrifice to Renjian possible, and that the ancestral hall should be revived by descendants of the ninth generation, tracing themselves again to Renjian, would also have accorded with neo-Confucian ritual principles. The holding of ancestral sacrifice within the household in the period between the two occasions perhaps indicates the fragmentation of the lineage at the end of the Yuan and in the early Ming.[33]

Moreover, the He lineage also repaired He Renjian's grave three times—during the early Hongwu (late fourteenth century), and in 1416 and 1466 respectively. In order to claim the burial site of a third-generation ancestor at the foot of Baiyun Mountain in Guangzhou, the He surname entered into litigations with other lineages. The rebuilding of ancestral halls and graves no doubt met the need for the worship of focal ancestors, but this increasingly institutionalized apparatus of worship also allowed the He lineage to become a visible social organization from early to mid-Ming.

The last years of the Ming and the early Qing were years of turmoil in Guangdong, from which Shawan was not spared. The "Liugeng Tang *kao*" has incorporated a description of the local situation:

In the winter of the *bingxu* year of Yongli [1646], the smell of blood began in the Nanling [the southern mountains], and disaster followed in our village. The bond-servants who had belonged to various surnames turned upon their masters and caused much disturbance. Fierce young men in seven villages followed them, set up camps and walled compounds, robbed, and could not be controlled. Under the name of the Guan'er *she*, they caused so much disturbance to us, the five surnames, that not even chickens and dogs were left in peace. Every family departed from the village to escape from their wrath.

The obvious targets of the revolts were the major surname groups like the He in Shawan. The account continues: "[They] plundered our houses, slew our kin, burned our ancestral halls and turned our pavilions into ashes. They were offensive and ungrateful to their masters."

The riots dealt a severe blow to the power of the He lineage in Shawan, but they were not the only catastrophe. After the turmoil subsided, the He lineage began to rebuild the Liugeng tang in 1663 and almost immediately were caught up with the coastal evacuation. They suffered severely: "People hastily scattered. Ancestral halls and villages were left in ruins. Ancestral chambers and temples were destroyed by soldiers and robbers. People in our local lineages all escaped separately with their families, and the spirit tablets of four generations in the principal descent lines were left to perish in the wild. . . . The five-hundred-year-old foundation of the Liu-geng tang was completely demolished."[34]

From these accounts, it would seem that the He lineage was on the verge of disintegration. It was not until 1669, when the Kangxi emperor re-scinded the coastal evacuation edict, that lineage members returned to Shawan. The initial step of rebuilding the lineage involved constructing a modest ancestral hall for the purpose of sacrificing to the venerable Attendant Censor. Fortunately, relatives in nearby Weiyong village to the northwest of Shawan who claimed to be a branch of the third segment of the He lineage in Shawan came forward with ancestral tablets that they had, defying danger, saved from the Liugeng tang and placed on their own ancestral altars. This small group of kinsmen were therefore looked upon as having done a great service to the lineage, and as a gesture of gratitude the lineage rewarded each of them with 8 mu (1.3 acres) of land.

In Kangxi 27 (1688), the He lineage could finally renovate the Liugeng tang. They first built a hall at which the apical ancestor was Renjian; its architectural features included a *houqin* (bedchamber at the back) and *toumen* (entrance hall), indicating that it was a *jiamiao* (family temple). Some members raised the issue that the rebuilding was straining lineage resources to the point that "although the area of the polders had increased, estate income continued to be depleted," and suggested that "the ancestral trust be audited and divided equally." However, lineage managers insisted on using the income from the estate to renovate the hall. Moreover, in 1700 they demolished this hall and during the next few decades built a five-compartment building occupying an area of almost an acre, including a *toumen* (entrance hall), *yimen* (ritual gate), *zhongzuo* (middle hall), *houqin* (back bedchamber), *dongxi liangwu* (side halls to the east and west), *zhonggu lou* (bell and drum tower), *dongxi cunci* (ancestral halls for villages of the east and west, possibly referring to side halls in which spirit tablets were also deposited), a kitchen, servants' quarters, and more. The project was finally completed in the Yongzheng reign. It was a grand effort.[35]

The new Liugeng tang became one of the most famous ancestral halls in the Pearl River delta during the Qing. Its completion signified the reconstitution of the He lineage in Shawan. For the next 200 years, it was an impressive symbol of solidarity and prestige for its members.

The Establishment of Lineage Common Property

Among the He lineage documents handed down, there is one, allegedly written by a famous Song official, Li Maoying, that talks about the time when He Renjian first settled in Shawan. "He Renjian paid a sum of money to the Provincial Administration Commissioner (*changping si*) and bought some uncultivated land, both hilly and flat, for his descendants to live on for generations so that there would be a place for the living to inhabit and the dead to be buried."[36] Local people in Shawan today believe that the emergence of common property began when the focal ancestor Renjian purchased the settlement rights in 1223. But in fact the accumulation of the estate was a continuous process that took place simultaneously with the compilation of written genealogies and the building of ancestral halls. It was part and parcel of the development of the He lineage during the late imperial period. By the late Song and early Yuan, certain members of the lineage had already started to expand their landed properties. For example, He Ruji of the third generation had "a prosperous family and bequeathed to his descendants land for ancestral worship."[37] However, it seems that this land belonged only to He Ruji's segment and had not become part of the estate of the entire Liugeng tang. It is not clear how much land belonged to the apical ancestral hall at that time. By the late Yuan and early Ming, when holdings by individual segments were expanding, collective property for the lineage also accumulated, but the amount might not have been substantial. In the early Ming, He Zihai contributed 15 mu (2.5 acres) of land to the lineage. The income from this land was to subsidize the educational expenses of descendants.[38] From this we may speculate that the amount of He lineage property was not extensive at that time. He Zhiming, of the first segment of the ninth generation, "through his management and organization skills, expanded the size of his holdings and accumulated a vast amount of wealth. He became the most affluent of all lineage members." Compared with He Zhiming's wealth, the He lineage estate was small. According to He Zhiming's tombstone inscription, "The He lineage was large and prosperous. They had an ancestral hall called the Liugeng tang. Because the income from the land could not provide for the maintenance of the Liugeng tang, [He Zhiming] often contributed money from his own pocket."[39] In addition, whereas necessities such as relief for a bad harvest were provided for from the lineage estate in later times, such funds still came from individual sources in the early Ming. Therefore, initially, Liugeng tang's estate could not have been sizable.

Not until the late Ming was there a substantial increase in the lineage estate. The preface to an account book on rental income of the Liugeng tang, written probably during the Kangxi reign, contains the following:

During the reign of Jiajing and Longqing [sixteenth century], the sands accumulated and so did the taxes. The reclamation of polder, along with the income from it, had increased severalfold. Each year, after allocating property to provide for the payment of state taxes and ancestral worship, income from the remaining property, designated as *jiatian* [*jia* fields], was given for the benefit of those descendants who had families. It seemed a fine idea. At first, the families were divided into ten *jia*. Every ten years, each jia received the income from the jiatian once. Later, they were combined into five jia, so that a full cycle was completed every five years. Thereafter, they were organized into three jia, and the cycle took only three years to complete.[40]

This record explains the method of rotation by which members of the lineage might partake in the income derived from lineage property. Married lineage members (possibly on the basis of their segment divisions) were divided into a number of jia that over a number of years took turns receiving lineage income. The decision to reduce a full payment cycle from ten years to three must have been due to the increase in lineage resources. If we take into consideration population increase over the years, the expansion of lineage property appears even more remarkable.

The common property of the He surname of Shawan was derived from five different sources. Inheritance from the ancestors has been discussed in the above section. The second source was donations from descendants. For example, in the Jiaqing reign of the Qing, He Huixiang of the second segment "gave his land to the lineage, and over time, more land grew out of it, like a mother giving birth to a son. Eventually, there was over ten thousand *qing*, and the income from the land topped the region."[41] The third source consisted of properties bought with donations collected from descendants. For example, the Shenxi tang of the first segment organized an association, the Sanyi *hui*, which collected the money used to purchase most of its property.[42] The fourth source was land confiscated from individual lineage members. For instance, He Duansou of the seventh generation of the fourth *fang* had "no learning, was idle and extravagant. His rancorous behavior was unbearable, so lineage members confiscated his share of lineage land for better management."[43] The final source was the reclamation of the sands organized by the lineage, which in fact constituted the major source of growth for the He lineage estate. In short, after the mid-Ming, the rapid growth and development of the He lineage and its property were based on two factors. The first was the accelerated reclamation of the sands; the second was related to the growing significance of the lineage among the He surname in a time of social and economic transformation.

The Meaning of Lineage

While interviewing in Shawan, I often asked the villagers why the people of the He surname were able to possess so much land. The response was almost always an unequivocal "Our ancestors bought it!" They seldom questioned the logic behind the statement. The assumption was that when ancestors purchased the sands from the government, they bestowed upon their descendants the right to ownership. In the He genealogy, it is emphasized that He Renjian purchased the uncultivated land so that his descendants in Shawan would have "irrigated land to farm, dry land for grazing, hills for gathering firewood, lakes and rivers for fishing," and, as mentioned, "a place for the living to settle and the dead to be buried."[44] As a result, the legend about He Renjian having bought from the Guangdong *changping si* large tracts of sands during the Song was the one that we heard most frequently during our field research.

Belonging to a lineage that had built an ancestral hall meant social status as well as the ability to assert rights to land. The five major surnames of Shawan were distinguished not by the size of their membership or property, but by the establishment of an ancestral hall and by historical accounts of pedigree and settlement backed up by written records. They enjoyed rights not available to the "miscellaneous surnames" (*zaxing*) or to "the people outside" (*kaimian ren*). We saw a stone tablet erected in the Fifth Month of 1885 in Shawan by the Renran *gongju* (the Renran Bureau, a local alliance formed by the four lineages, the Wang, He, Li [Lai], and Li) that read as follows:

In our town a clear distinction is maintained between master (*zhu*) and servant (*pu*). Those servants who are able to redeem themselves, by custom, should move far away. If they stay in the town, their descendants must continue to observe their status as servants in ceremonies of capping, marriage, funeral, and sacrifice, in the way they build their houses, and in their styles of clothing. They must never build an ancestral hall, large or small. No transgression shall be condoned or sheltered by the gentry (*shenshi*) of our town. People of our town are allowed to report [on such transgression], and if discovered, the culprits shall be immediately expelled by the town watchmen. This bureau will auction the houseplot [of the servant so expelled] and the price fetched shall be returned to him. In dealing with the case of Chen Yazhan, a servant of the Wang lineage, we promulgate the above regulation in public that will remain in force for the future.[45]

Oral tradition recalls that Chen Yazhan was originally a servant who took care of the ancestral hall of the Wang lineage in Shawan. After he had accumulated some wealth, he built a Chen family hall. The major surnames in town intervened and demolished the hall. At the same time, they erected a stone tablet promulgating the prohibitive regulation applicable to servants and former servants. This case clearly reflects that even if a servant had redeemed his freedom and had become wealthy, it was not possible for him to build an ancestral hall in the town. Building a hall would have signified the formation of a lineage, allowing its members to claim equal social status and the rights enjoyed by the major surnames. It is thus clear that lineage membership, ancestral halls, written genealogies, and foundation legends were important institutions for legitimizing status in the local community.

The relationship between the major lineages and the farmers of the sands was likewise unequal. The major lineages called themselves "the people inside" (*maimian ren*), and called the sands people "the people outside."[46] The difference between the inside and the outside was not only geographic but also social. The people who lived on the sands were also spoken of as *dan* (the Dan people), or "floating twigs" (*shuiliu chai*). The Dan were regarded as having neither culture nor historical roots. They did not have knowledge of their ancestral origins, lineage organizations, or ancestral halls. In our investigations, we discovered that people on the sands, unlike the major surnames of Shawan, were rarely able to tell us the names of their ancestors of four generations back. Although they had made their living on the sands for generations, they were denied the right to "settle" or to own any land. They lived in straw huts on the dikes and worked as tenants of the lineages.[47] Therefore these "floating twigs" had a very different livelihood from members of the major lineages in town. The latter manipulated cultural symbols associated with lineage formation on the edge of the sands. A regional political economy was thus formed so that over time the "people inside" dominated the "people outside" under the hegemonic ancestors' shadow.[48]

It is not difficult to discern the basis of the crucial cultural meaning of ancestral origins and settlement legends. By identifying with the literati cultural tradition, the lineage legitimized its social status and its rights. The historical legend of the He lineage, true or false, was an arena for articulating the collective memory of its members, and it was expressed in the community by the presence of ancestral halls, genealogies, ceremonies of sacrifice, and much more. The efforts to create lineage legacy were deliberate and conscious, as is concisely expressed in a couplet that hangs inside the He Liugeng tang to this day:

> From meritorious deeds planted by the ancestors,
> Have come fields in the heart to be farmed by their descendants.

We were told that this couplet was written by the famous Ming scholar Chen Xianzhang, specifically for the He Liugeng tang. One of the He lineage members explained the meaning of the couplet in this way: "Since our fourth-generation ancestor settled in Shawan, he cultivated the land industriously. He expanded his property, and his descendants have proliferated. The benevolence and prosperity of our ancestors have nourished those descendants who would take these virtues to heart."[49]

A clever play on words is embodied in the couplet. "Fields in the heart" (*xintian*) was spiritual legacy, but the reference to fields that might be farmed was an apt description of the popular belief in land inherited from ancestors. Ancestor worship and the literati ideal, therefore, intertwine with material circumstances to form the basis of a complex repertoire of lineage institutions. They are also an integral part of the percolation of state Confucian culture into rural society.

In other words, the material and the ideological bases of lineage formation are two aspects of one historical process. Traditional Chinese culture is characterized by a strong belief in the continual relationship between the living and the dead. Ancestors, not the individual or a legal entity, are symbolic representations of collective authority and rights. These rights do not come naturally but rather are created and maintained through manipulations of politico-economic interests on the ground. One such strategy is to reinforce the legacy of ancestors with a literati culture that is connected to the power of officialdom. In a time when struggle intensified among various local groups in the delta for the right to reclaim sands and to control territory, the full weight of such legitimized ancestral legacy was brought to bear.

In this process of lineage development, state ideology also assumes an important role. In the Ming and the Qing, the government employed the *tujia* (the *tu* units and the *jia* units) system for land registration and tax collection. The registration unit known as the *hu*, usually translated as the "household," was really a tax account unit. Legal ownership of land had to be registered clearly in the tax accounts, so that through these tax accounts the landowners might be taxed. Many tax accounts of the Pearl River delta, by the Qing, were held by lineages.[50] Thus the taxation system coincided with the cultural symbols of ancestral origins. Moreover, the men of power produced in the lineage, through their influence in the government, offered the lineage protection.

A clear case of such exertion of power occurred during the Guangxu period of the late Qing. When the provincial government of Guangdong attempted to assess the acreage of the sands in the delta, local bullies affiliated with yamen clerks and runners were said to have usurped about 650 acres of sands from Shawan. He Guilong, a member of the He lineage in Shawan who had become a *jinshi* in 1874 and served in the military, petitioned to the government for the land to be returned to the original owners. The land was returned.[51] Those local bullies were believed to have been Dan or "floating twigs" who became wealthy after the mid-Qing. In this case, it is clear that the government was inclined to defend the interests of the scholar-officials and the lineages who operated within the imperial paradigm. From this point of view the development of lineage organizations in the Ming and Qing can be seen as a cultural process that enjoyed considerable support from bureaucratic authority.

A Magnate Lineage

During the Qing, the He lineage of Shawan, with its control of large tracts of land, was a magnate lineage. Most lineages, it must be noted, were not landed magnates, and it is precisely their landed wealth that set the He lineage apart. In Shawan, although four other lineages settled at about the same time as the He surname, they remained smaller in size. The He lineage established at least 87 ancestral halls, while the Li had only 7, the Wang 12, the Li (Lai) 7, and the Zhao only 1.[52] These differences obviously were related to each lineage's own internal finances.

For an idea of the wealth of the He surname, we may assume a rent of 100 catties of grain from each mu of land held on the sands. In this case, by the mid-Qing, the annual rent intake of the Liugeng tang from the sands would have amounted to hundreds of thousands of piculs. This does not include the income from the property held privately within each segment or from individually held property. During our fieldwork, many He lineage members proudly asserted that "[before Liberation] we would not have starved even if we had kept our doors closed." What they meant was that even if members of the He surname never left their homes to work, they could live on rent derived from their estates on the sands. Some older people recalled how, every year, adult male lineage members were given as much as a hundred catties of pork and a sum of money ranging anywhere from 10 to 1,000 yuan. The expenses of births, weddings, funerals, education, and participation in the imperial examinations were subsidized by the ancestral trusts with income from the lineage estates. In the custom of distributing sacrificial pork to male descendants that was common in the delta before the Republican period—a practice elegantly referred to as *banzuo* (distributing the sacrifice), or more commonly *taigong fen zhurou* (ancestors distributing the pork)—the amount of pork distributed by most lineages to their members was usually meager. Its main significance was to symbolize the beneficence of the ancestors. By contrast, He lineage members were given enormous amounts in the ancestral hall several times a year. Because the meat could not be consumed in a short time, the ancestral halls distributed coupons instead so that members could obtain the meat from local butchers as they pleased. It is not hard to imagine, then, that this affluent *taigong* (focal ancestor) wielded great power of attention.

Before Liberation, the Liugeng tang, as the apical ancestral hall (*dazong ci*) of the lineage (*zu*), was the center of kinship rituals. Besides the Liugeng tang, the He lineage also established the Shuben tang, an administrative and judiciary apparatus for the internal affairs of the lineage. There was also the office of the principal-line ancestral hall (*dazong guan*), a financial apparatus for the management of lineage property, a team of local guards (*genglian*) to maintain public security in town, and a defense corps to patrol the sands. In the early decades of the twentieth century the He lineage set up not only academies and primary and middle schools in the township, but also a number of academies and martial arts schools in Guangzhou City. At the same time, it subsidized two middle schools in Guangzhou to provide for the education of He children. After the fall of the Qing, the lineage was active in organizing philanthropic institutions such as trade schools, hospitals, and orphanages. With these various social functions, the He lineage organization assumed almost the role of an autonomous local government.

Wealth from the sands enabled the He lineage to organize other large-scale public activities that displayed collective strength to themselves as well as to others. Besides the normal spring and autumn rites in the apical ancestral hall, the annual trip to the ancestral graves in Guangzhou was the most spectacular. There were two ancestral graves. One was in Woshan in a suburb to the northeast of Guangzhou where He Renjian, his second wife, and their two daughters-in-law were buried. The other was in Pujian Baiyunshan in a suburb of northern Guangzhou, where his first wife and younger sister were buried in the same grave, known as the Grave of the Sisters-in-Law (*gusao fen*). It is said that He Rejian's sister was so close to his wife that she never married just so they would not have to separate.

After they died they were buried in a single grave. It is worth noting, that although the Grave of the Sisters-in-Law is simply a grave in which two ordinary women were buried, and although the story seems neither stirring nor in accordance with cultural norms, the story of the grave was nonetheless a well-known lore in Guangzhou.

The lavish display of wealth and ceremonies by the He lineage at the grave sites might have contributed to the popularity of the story. According to the recollections of some older people, about fifteen days after the Qingming festival every year, lineage members would visit the graves in Guangzhou. After lineage heads decided on a date, they sent people to Guangzhou to hire a fleet of colorful boats (known as the boats from Zi-dong, a village in Nanhai county)[53] in which the literati types would sail to Guangzhou. The rest of the entourage would go in large ferries. Together they formed an elegant fleet, escorted by four armed boats equipped by the He lineage itself. They sailed to Guangzhou in this grand fashion and moored at a berth they had built for themselves. In the evening, they stayed at the four academies, the four martial arts schools, and the Chang'an Inn, all of which belonged to the He lineage; some people would stay at the homes of relatives or friends. They would also have bribed the city guards to open the Small Northern Gate in the city wall earlier than usual at the fifth watch (just before dawn) the next day. Almost all the sedan-chair bearers in the city flocked on the occasion to provide service and were paid by the lineage managers. The entire group paraded through the Small Northern Gate to the Grave of the Sisters-in-law to perform the grave rites. On the third day, they repeated the ceremonies at the graves of He Renjian and others. According to a 1911 record, the lineage spent more than 6,000 taels of silver for the grave visits that year.[54] These extravagant public displays became important rallying points for the collective identity of the lineage as well as for demonstrating to others its power and influence.

During the period of our research in Shawan in 1989, we also conducted a relatively brief investigation in Shatou *zhen*, Nanhai county. In Shatou, there is a Cui lineage, almost the same size as the He lineage of Shawan, whose branches are spread out in a number of villages. The Cui too had a magnificent ancestral hall much like the Liugeng tang, part of which had recently been repaired. However, there are obvious differences in the organizational structure between the He and Cui lineages. The rallying power, material or symbolic, of the apical ancestral hall of the Cui could not be compared with that of the Liugeng tang. A more detailed discussion of the Cui surname group is beyond the scope of this essay. However, there is one point worth noting: in a Pearl River delta lineage, whenever a lineage member had a male child, there was a *guahua* (hanging a flower, i.e., lantern) ceremony held in the ancestral hall, symbolizing that the new member had been formally admitted into the lineage. The He surname in Shawan held this ceremony in the Liugeng tang, whereas the Cui held theirs mainly in the segment halls. In other words, the Cui lineage was characterized by a process of segmentation and was not unlike what Maurice Freedman has called a higher-order lineage.[55] In contrast, the symbolic centrality of the apical ancestral hall of the He lineage in Shawan represented a process of fusion more characteristic of a "large local lineage" or even a "super local lineage." The He remained extremely localized, and segmentation failed to disperse its members. This is obviously linked to the historical circumstances under which the sands were reclaimed.

Its wealth and public presence also enabled the He lineage to dominate the local power structure in the town. In the late Qing and the early Republic, the administrative apparatus in Shawan was the Renrang Bureau, a political alliance of Shawan's five major lineages in which the He surname monopolized the leading positions such as ward head (*baozhang*) and township head (*xiangzhang*).

The dominant position of the He lineage in local affairs was further established in popular religious activity surrounding the worship of the Beidi (Northern Deity, known also as the Xuanwu or Zhenwu). The Beidi was one of the most popular deities worshiped among the village communities of the Pearl River delta, and it symbolizes the rule of the southern river-based frontier society by the state in the north.[56] Worshiping the Beidi entailed the symbolic acceptance of the orthodox Han state culture. Although people in Shawan worshiped a pantheon of deities, the Beidi remained the patron deity who occupied a central position over other cults. The cult provided an important cultural avenue for community integration in Shawan.

Folklore in Shawan attributed the image of the Beidi to the Yongle emperor in the Ming dynasty (late fourteenth–early fifteenth centuries), who had usurped the throne from his brother. This was probably related to the fact that the Yongle emperor paid particular attention to the worship of the deity. An old man in Shawan told us that the Beidi's image in Shawan was actually commissioned by the emperor himself. The legend maintained that after a battle in which the emperor's entire army was routed and only he and a general survived, the emperor told his followers that when he had been trapped, a sword-wielding, barefooted water deity had rescued him because he was the true emperor. This deity was the Beidi. So the emperor commissioned four images of the Beidi to be made in his own image. One was deposited in the imperial palace in Beijing, one was placed at Wudang mountain (a Daoist holy place), one was bestowed on the home of the general who had gone through the ordeal with him, and one was eventually lost. The general placed the image in his family temple. Its efficacy attracted believers from among his friends and relatives. During family division after the general had died, his two sons fought over the ownership of the image and were engaged in litigation for decades. It was only upon the mediation of their father's comrade, the Song minister Li Maoying, that they reached a settlement. The image was given to Li Maoying, who deposited it in the Qinglong temple outside Shawan. Later, people from Shuiteng of Shunde county stole it. It was retrieved only after the Beidi indicated in people's dreams its whereabouts. From then on, the image was put inside Shawan township. It was hosted by neighborhoods on a rotational basis for worship. The neighborhood hosting the Beidi was said to be in charge (*dangjia*).[57]

Although the legend is close to being absurd, it holds crucial clues to the history of Shawan. The unique way in which the Beidi was worshiped is an important element in the historical construction of Shawan's local culture and society. In the Republican era, the township of Shawan had seventeen neighborhoods (*fang, li*). The Beidi was hosted by one or two neighborhoods each year, and it took twelve years to complete a full cycle. The order of rotation was as follows: year 1, Tingchong li, Shishi li; year 2, Zhonxin li; year 3, Loshan li; year 4, Jingshu li; year 5, Dong'an li; year 6, Sanhuan li; year 7, Diyi li; year 8, Wenxi li; year 9, Shidong fang; year 10, Jingshu li; year 11, Azhong fang, Cuizhu ju; year 12, Sanhuai li. There were three other neighborhoods, the Chengfang li, the Guanxiang li, and the Xi'an li, that were not included in the rota. Among those that were, Sanhuai li was occupied by the Wang surname, Jingshu li by the Li (Lai), and Wenxi li by the Li surname. Households of the He surname were concentrated in the other neighborhoods, interspersed with several households of the Li and Zhao surnames.

According to a local 90-year-old villager of the Wang surname, the earliest rotation was based on surnames. Apart from the five major surnames, there was also the Zhu. In every twelve years, each surname hosted the Beidi for two. In time, the He grew numerous and powerful and the fortunes of the Li, Zhao, and Zhu surnames declined. Gradually, the rotation by neighborhoods replaced the original schedule.[58] What the man remembered merits further examination, but the fact that the Wang and the Li surnames, in Sanhuai li and Jingshu li respectively, organized the hosting twice every twelve years seems to indicate that the rotation might indeed have been based on surnames. Another person interviewed mentioned that the Li surname supposedly hosted the Beidi once every six years but the expenses became so large that they had to sell land to keep up the ceremonies. So in the end they hosted the deity once every twelve years.[59] If we examine the rotation schedule and the legend about the Beidi's origin in Shawan, it seems possible that the Beidi was first the patron deity of the Li surname. It later became the major deity for all the major lineages and finally its hosting was neighborhood-based.

The gradual transformation demonstrates that the He surname assumed an increasingly important role in the organization of community worship. This role in turn affirmed its pivotal position in Shawan. The worship of the Beidi involved theatrical performances, dragon dances, and colorful parades (*piaose*).[60] Moreover, on another occasion of popular worship surrounding the Bao'en *ci*, which commemorated a governor of Guangdong, Wang Lairen, who petitioned the court to withdraw the relocation order in the early Qing, the He lineage also enjoyed a privileged position in the ceremonies. These activities were perfect public arenas for the He lineage to display its power and wealth. They are also important lenses through which we may look into the social relationships and the configurations of power in Shawan.

Conclusion

Spread over a belt where the *mintian* (civilian land) used to merge with the *shatian* (sands) are numerous large towns. Besides Shawan, to name a few, they are Nancun and Shilou in Panyu county, Daliang in Shunde county, Xiaolan in Zhongshan county, and Waihai in Xinhui county. The lineages in these townships were large-scale operations controlling extensive tracts of sands on which they relied for income. Underlying the building of lineages on the sands of the Pearl River delta was a historical and cultural process. This process involved a shrewd interweaving of genealogical principles and literati culture to create, maintain, and transform local political and economic environments. The lineage phenomenon embodied many levels of meanings. It was a means to organize the development of the sands, a cultural strategy to obtain political recognition and authority within the imperial paradigm, and a method to stabilize the land tenure system in the sands and to create unique local configurations of power. Economic and social features certainly came into the development of the lineage, but it will not be enough to explain it in those terms. Instead, it has to be recognized that the historical process involved also an intense cultural discourse. To those who share these analytical interests, the formation of the He lineage of Shawan, a super lineage on the edge of the sands, offers a remarkable case for contemplation.

Territorial Community at the Town of Lubao, Sanshui County, from the Ming Dynasty

LUO YIXING

THE town (*zhen*) of Lubao is located on the northern edge of the Pearl River delta, 45 miles from Guangzhou. It stands on the bank of the North River. With its current population of 35,000 and cultivated acreage of 10,000 mu, it is the second-largest town in Sanshui county.

Lubao *zhen* originated as Xujiang Market (Xujiang *jie*). Historically, it was a focus of north-south traffic in Guangdong province. The North River traffic comes out of the hills to the north of the province and passes Lubao to enter the sedimentary lowland of the Pearl River delta. Where the river enters the plain, it divides into a number of distributaries, one of which is the Lubao Creek, at one time one of the most important channels leading to Guangzhou. This is why the main street of Xujiang, located at the mouth of Lubao Creek, became an important local market in this region as early as the mid-Ming dynasty. Aside from its central location, there was another reason for the fame of the town. Located there was the popular Xujiang Ancestral Temple (*zumiao*), which had a reputation that rivaled the ancestral temple of nearby Foshan. Since the Ming dynasty, it has been a center of worship and culture in the region. This essay, based on fieldwork conducted at Lubao from June to September 1989, attempts to reconstruct the development of the town and its relationships with surrounding villages from the Ming dynasty.

The Market

The earliest historical record of Xujiang dates from the Dali period of the Tang dynasty. In 767 the Tang military commissioner Si Gong stationed

Translated by David Faure

his troops at Xujiang when he moved against Ge Shuhang, who held Guangzhou. That incident gave rise to the place-name Xujiang Old Garrison (Xujiang *gutun*).[1] In the Song, Xujiang was still sparsely populated. The poet Yang Wanli wrote:

> At Qingtang [village near Lubao] there are no shops or people,
> Only the noise of green frogs and purple earthworms.[2]

From the end of the Song, attracted by newly exposed mudbanks, settlers arrived from Hunan and Hubei, Zhejiang, Fujian, and parts of Guangdong such as Panyu, Heshan, Gaoyao, and Nanhai.[3]

However, the prosperity of the town and its surroundings really dates from the early Ming dynasty. By the time the Ming encyclopedia, the *Yongle dadian*, was completed, Xujiang had become a market (*xushi*) or ferry crossing (*jindu*), and a police office (*xunjian*) was located there.[4] From approximately this time, Xujiang *du* was in charge of three *bao* (Letang, Qingtang, and Tutang). By the Jingtai period (1450–56), Han Yin, a native of Panyu, could write in his poem the following lines:

> Smoke rises like trees from ten thousand houses, hiding the clouds,
> As amidst peach leaves and peaceful waters I cross the river by night.[5]

The "ten thousand," of course, was used in a figurative sense, but, clearly, a settlement had grown at Xujiang.

For a description of the town in some detail, the earliest source available is the "Record of the Azure Clouds Bridge" (*Qingyun qiao ji*) by Lun Wenxu, possibly written in 1509. The essay records the building of the bridge across the Lubao Creek in front of the Huashan Monastery. The bridge held a central position in the town, for it was originally to be named after Wu Tingju, a military commander who had been commissioned to suppress bandits in the northern parts of Guangdong. Wu had come to Xujiang in 1505, "had established forts and garrisons, amalgamated markets, removed the dikes on the routes, and while staying at the space by the Huashan Monastery [in Lubao], ordered that it be transformed into a communal school (*shexue*)."[6] At the time, Xujiang was already a bustling town with "several ten thousand houses." However, Wu, the commander, refused to take personal credit for his campaign by lending his name to the bridge. Instead, he said:

The people of Xujiang are busy and distinguished. Yet they have been cast aside in the lines of military as well as literary honors. Scholars who deserve to ascend step by step into the azure clouds are still scattered unrecognized. Now, because your children go on the bridge in the morning to the community school, and again at sunset when they return home, the bridge should be named the "Azure Clouds." Those who go on it daily will become scholars of the azure clouds. This name will instill in them a spirit that they cannot hold in check.

It is not known if the school was ever built. That does not alter the fact that the building of the Azure Clouds Bridge was meant to integrate the people of Lubao into the elite society of the county. It was part of the gentrification process of the sixteenth century that was observable over much of the Pearl River delta.[7]

From our interviews, it would seem that in these early days, Xujiang Market was located at Peng Street (Peng *jie*) three miles to the north of the present market, occupied initially by people of the Peng surname. Peng Street was made up of an Upper, Middle, and Lower Street, along a symmetrical layout, stretching for a mile. In the market there were sellers of oxen, wine and rice, and paper.[8] One of the most famous shops of Lubao, "He Hongren's Shop for Eye Medicines," was located there. There were inns that, among other services, provided meals for travelers. There were also the "flower boats," said to be akin to brothels. In addition to the shops, at one time (probably in the eighteenth century) two periodic markets were held, known respectively as the Upper and Lower Markets, at Peng Street and at a location in front of the Beidi Temple that elderly people could still point out to us.[9] The Upper Market was a market for cattle, meeting on the fourth and ninth days of the ten-day cycle. The Lower Market was a "market of people" (*renxu*) meeting every second and seventh day, where laborers could be hired.[10] In addition, there was the "street-corner market" (*jietouxu*), which met on the third and eighth days. Peng Street was the only cattle market in the northern portion of Sanshui county, and it was attended by people from the counties of Qingyuan, Sihui, and Guangning. It is not clear how continuous progress was, but Lubao clearly developed into a busy commercial center.[11]

The Dikes

It was said that the geography of Lubao might be summed up in the animistic description, "The five horses gallop into Huashan Hill, and the dragon returns to the Wushi Cave."[12] The five horses refer to the five tributaries that converged into the Xujiang Creek, with their confluence at the Wushi Cave. It was said that they were a constant source of flooding, and that was why the dikes had to be built.

The records are silent on the building of the dikes. The 1819 edition of the Sanshui gazetteer refers to the collapse of the Changgang Dike (Changgang *ti*) at the end of the Ming dynasty, and in all likelihood it was built before then. By the Ming, the Dingfeng Embankment (Dingfeng *ji*), a portion of the Changgang Dike, was already one of the "eight scenic spots" of Xujiang.[13]

In our interviews, we were told that each village was in charge of its own dike. Thus, the Changgang Dike was managed by Changgang Village, the Upper Meibu Dike (Shang Meibu wei) by Dabu Village, the Lower Meibu Dike (Xia Meibu wei) by Lian'ao Village, the Changzhou *she* Dike (Changzhou she wei) by Wanggang and Lucun, the Qingtang Dike (Qingtang wei) by Liguochen Village and Upper and Lower Tang Village, and the Yongfeng Dike (Yongfeng wei) by Tanqi and Liuzhai. We suspect there must have been intervillage connections built on the basis of cooperative water control, but did not come across any evidence of it.[14]

The Temples

According to the 1819 Sanshui gazetteer, "The Zhenwu (i.e., Beidi) Temple on the slopes of Huashan Hill was first built in the Jiading years of the Song dynasty."[15] The claim is probably erroneous: it was the Huashan Monastery that was built in the Song.

The Huashan Monastery was built on the foundation of a Dizang chapel (*an*) that was first established in the Jiading period (1208–24) by the monk Fu'an and expanded in the Yuan (1264–94) by the monk Guqi.[16] In the Chenghua (1464–87) and Hongzhi (1488–1505) eras of the Ming, it was renamed the Huashan Monastery.[17] The monastery became quite well known to contemporary scholars and officials in Guangdong. In one of the rooms of the monastery was hung a commemorative plaque bearing the title "The scholar's chamber" (*xueshi xuan*) in memory of one Huang Jian, a Guangzhou *tongpan* who had slept in the room. When a local man, Fan Gui, added a "scripture house" (*jingshe*) to the monastery, the reputable neo-Confucian scholars Chen Xianzhang and Zhan Ruoshui both wrote poems to commemorate the event. The scenic complex of the surroundings of Xujiang consisted of the monastery, the Azure Clouds Bridge in front of it, and the Well for the Washing of the Begging Bowl (Xibo *jing*).[18] Until the sixteenth century, no reference was made in any of these records to the existence of the Beidi Temple.

· The Beidi Temple was probably established early in the sixteenth century. The Liu surname genealogy at Liuzhai Village notes that the seventh-generation ancestor, one Yipu (1465–1521), went on pilgrimage to the sacred Wudang *shan* Mountain and returned with an adopted son, given the name Xianglai, as well as various sacred flowers. It notes that for this reason the temple was built.[19] Moreover, the county gazetteer notes that in 1527 evil temples were destroyed and transformed into community schools.[20] According to a 1791 tablet inscription found at the Beidi Temple, it was at this time that the monastery lost its landholdings and its building became a community school.[21] In 1544, Sanshui county magistrate Zhu Duanming visited Xujiang and, at the request of local leaders Ouyang Sheng and Jiang Yong, wrote a commemorative essay for the temple, accepting the claim of the local leaders that the temple had been built in the Song. By then the temple had obviously taken the place of the monastery as the local religious center: its annual festival in the Third Month of the Year was attended by more than ten thousand people, while, as the magistrate noted, the monastery had become a school.[22]

The documentary records agree with the impression that is retained in the popular memory. In our interviews, we were told that "there was first the Huashan before there was the ancestral temple [that is, the Beidi Temple]." Local people still refer to the Huashan as Monastery Hill (*sishan*) and to the landholdings of the monastery as the "Monks' land" (*heshang tian*). Popular legend also reproduces the story of the Beidi in a form close to one version recorded in the *Beiyu ji*.[23] The Beidi was said to have been a cowherd working for the Jade Emperor who allowed himself to be killed and his body to be carved open to prove his innocence against the charge that he had eaten the cow he was tending. The association of the Jade Emperor with the landlord and of the local deity with the tenant is an obvious reflection of contemporary society.

Aside from the Beidi Temple, which served as a focus of worship for all settlers at the market of Xujiang, other temples with more local clientele were also maintained. The business center, Peng Street, was a multi-surname community, and separate temples were maintained in its various sections: the Upper Street had the Zhendu Temple, occupied by a Zhendu general; Middle Street had the Guanyin Temple; and Lower Street had the Tianhou Temple. The Liu surname at Liuzhai maintained the Houwang Temple in honor of Chen Ping of the Han dynasty; the Wang surname of Wang Bay (Wang *wan*) kept the Longmu Temple; the two unrelated Huang-surnamed groups and the Liu surname at Laogu Lane (Laogu *xiang*) maintained a Tianhou Temple; Haibian Street maintained a Guandi Temple; and the Ouyang surname at Ouyang Street, a Huaguang Temple. There was a common understanding, at least in the late Qing, that these eight temples made up the religious foci of all of Lubao. A broken tablet that we found at Ouyang Street, entitled "Tablet in Commemoration of the

Repair of the Wuxian Old Temple," recorded this line: "The eight temples of Xujiang abound in supernatural revelations. . . . One of these temples is the Huaguang Temple."[24] We also found the stone pillars that formerly supported the front portal of the Tianhou Temple at Laogu Lane, and they bore a couplet bearing Guangxu dates which read:

> Sacrifices [here] originated in the previous dynasty, the incense
>   fragrance of the eight temples is offered fervently in common,
> [The Tianhou's] mercy surrounds all land and seas, the merits
>   gathered by this corner are shared forever by all.

From the couplet, it would seem that while each of the eight temples represented the local interests of a recognized territory, together they also represented the collective presence of the market and its surroundings.

The Move to Lubao

Sometime in the mid-Qing, the market moved downriver from Xujiang Market to Lubao. In the Ming, Lubao had appeared as an island on the river. Continued silting had by the eighteenth century joined it to the riverbank.[25]

An indication of the shift of the market's center is the description of Xujiang in the 1819 edition of the Sanshui gazetteer, "Xujiang jie is located on the edge of Lubao."[26]

The move was probably affected by the configuration of the dikes along the river. When, as the gazetteer records, in 1799 the dikes at Upper Meibu and Qingtang collapsed in a flood, as did the dike of Yongfeng in 1813, Xujiang Market would have been submerged.[27] According to a tablet entitled "A Record of the Temple Festival of the First, Second, and Third Districts," in 1816 the He Hongren Eye Medicine Shop was still located at Peng Street, although, in our interviews, it was remembered as being located in the new Lubao Market. Lubao was remembered for holding four market days in every ten-day cycle. On the third and eighth days a cattle market met, and on the fifth and tenth a labor market.[28] Pigs were not sent to Lubao, for, as local people recalled, "pigs were not sent to the furnace [*lu*, homonym for Lu as in Lubao]," but were sold instead at Niulangang Market.[29] Lubao was also, in our interviews, referred to as a *wodixu* ("market in the bottom of the pan"), meaning that the market lasted into the early afternoon.[30]

Lubao was the dominant market of the region. Across the river from Lubao, Jiang'an Market, founded in the Kangxi years (1662–1722) and meeting also on every fifth and tenth, became a poor complement dealing in rice, grain, wine, and oil. Within a radius of six miles, a marketing network formed that provided a market meeting every day, for Datang Market met on every first and sixth, Niulangang Market every second and seventh, Street Corner Market every third and eighth, and Huangtang Market every fourth and ninth. We were told in interviews that on market day at Lubao, three market boats that could hold more than one hundred people each plied between Lubao and its surrounding markets. A division of functions also appeared, for while daily supplies might be obtained at the surrounding markets, it was only at the shops in Lubao that finer goods such as silk could be purchased.[31]

The Three Districts and Management via the Beidi Temple

Lubao and its surroundings were divided into three districts, or *pu*. The earliest reference to the use of the term appears in the tablet entitled "The renovation of the Huashan Monastery and the rebuilding of the Dizang Hall," dated 1791. The boundaries of the area known as the Three Districts have been established through interviews. Together they stretch four kilometers along the bank of the river, the First District incorporating Laogu Lane and the villages of Wangmu Bay (that is, Wangwan), Tiandi, and Liuzhai; the Second District, Mai Street (Mai jie), Fan Street (Fan jie), Ouyang Street (Ouyang jie), Haibian Street (Haibian jie), and the market of Lubao; and the Third District consisting only of Peng Street. Membership in the three districts was exclusive: neither the village of Tanji, located between Peng Street and Liuzhai, nor Xie Street, located within the vicinity of Lubao market, was a part of the three districts, because it was understood either that they had been settled later than other villages or that their inhabitants originally had been boat people.[32]

The territory covered by the Three Districts coincided with the territory demarcated by the "eight temples," and each settlement within the territory consisted of residents bound by territorial and lineage connections.

Peng Street was a multi-surname settlement, made up of more than twenty surnames.[33] None of the surnames possessed an ancestral hall, but collectively they maintained the Dengyi hall (*tang*), which was used for meetings on local affairs. The people there were known for being clever in business: as a common saying had it, "Peng Street people eat the head of the fish." We can document that some of them were merchants: the ancestors of the Peng surname owned the market at Niulangang Market, those of the He surname were butchers at Peng Street, and an ancestor of the Chen surname operated a pig market at Xi'nan. Many people were involved in handicraft industries, especially in producing ritual paper, which was sold in the markets.[34]

Like those in Peng Street, residents of Liuzhai, Laogu Lane, Wang Bay, Ouyang Street, Mai Street, and Fan Street were not farmers. Some of them owned substantial landholdings outside these villages, but little farmland was included within the confines of the villages themselves.[35] Residents of these places referred to themselves as the communities of the streets (*jie-fang*), as opposed to the people of the villages (*xiangmin*) in the farming communities. Length of settlement does not seem to be the criterion that governed the use of these terms. Instead, it seems that any settler on the "streets" (such as Peng Street) automatically became a member of the street communities. For instance, the Xie surname settled first at Dayigang[36] in the Ming dynasty, and the branch that moved into Peng Street in the third generation following the initial settlement became a part of the *jiefang* of the Three Districts, while those lineage members who remained at Dayigang were excluded from this description.[37] Similarly, a branch of the Deng surname moved into Peng Street in the second generation, settling at Baitu, and this branch was allowed to participate in the activities of Peng Street and the Three Districts whereas the lineage people who had remained at Baitu could not.[38] The Chen surname moved into Peng Street in the Kangxi period, and in one generation after settlement a member of the lineage became a headman (*shoushi*) of the Three Districts.[39]

The management of the Beidi Temple exemplifies the centrality of the Three Districts as a unit of organization in local affairs. At the simplest level, the districts took turns being responsible for organizing the celebrations held on the festivals of the Beidi and the Guanyin. However, donations to the temple were not restricted to the Three Districts. In the Three Districts, donations were collected on a per capita basis and recorded in the names of the districts, but up to the Jiaqing period (early nineteenth century) periodic donations were also made separately by more than three hundred surrounding villages.

Moreover, at various times voluntary associations were formed that gathered funds to support temple activities. In 1782 and 1789 respectively, two "money societies of the calendar cycle" (*huajia yinhui*) were formed for this purpose that together gathered more than 1,200 taels. The money was used to purchase property; the rent collected was spent on festival expenses. The two separate groups of managers recorded for these societies both consisted of persons from all three districts.[40] In 1812, yet another attempt to collect funds for the temple resulted in the formation of the "money society for the benefit of three parties" (*sanyi yinhui*). In this society, the three districts initially each donated 100 taels of silver, to which amount, in 1815, was added a further donation of 100 taels each that was to be collected by a per capita levy within each district. In addition, it was agreed that voluntary donations would be accepted and that the 760 voluntary donors would be allowed to participate in the communal feast that was held at the annual temple festival. Three individuals, one from each district, became the managers of the society.

In 1822, under a similar but not identical arrangement, yet another "money society" was launched. The "money society for the benefit of the one hundred" (*baiyi yinhui*) consisted of one hundred individual wealthy households (*fuhu*), each of which contributed 10 taels of silver. The 1,000 taels collected by the society was deposited with the managers of the temple for interest. Each month, the managers of the temple would credit the one hundred donors with 1.5 percent of the capital, which would be accumulated to provide for the feast to be partaken by members of the society at the annual temple festival. This arrangement was to last eighteen years, and at the end of the period, the managers of the temple were to return to the individual donors their capital with interest, keeping the balance on behalf of the temple for the purchase of land. An accompanying donation of 110 *shi* of grain ensured that the descendants of the donors would also be entitled to take part in the annual feast.[41]

Closely related to the various attempts to collect funds on behalf of the temple, it would seem, was the increasing formalization of the management of the temple and the amount of property that it controlled. These developments cannot be dated precisely, but it is clear that a "public bureau" (*gongsuo*) was built directly facing the temple that housed one chief manager (*zongli*) and six submanagers (*zhili*), two from each district. The temple also came to own one-third of the area of Lubao and collected rent (known as *disha*, literally "earth and sand") from shop owners who built their shops there. Aside from rent, the temple also derived an income from a shop selling sacrificial paper and candles and from an operation providing priestly services and fortune-telling.[42] It was the managers' duty to manage the properties of the temple as well as its religious affairs, which included hiring the theatrical company from Guangzhou and workmen to make the fireworks (*pao*) at the end of the calendar year, arranging for the procession of the Beidi on the occasion of his festival on the third day of the Third Month, and holding feasts for members of the Three Districts at the New Year, during the festival of the Beidi, and on the fourth day of the

Ninth Month. The couplet on the door of the "public office" reads: "Public discussions maintain the blessings of the deities, / a sense of humility and concession gives weight to his name in the neighborhood," well representing the purpose of the temple committee.[43]

The sense of community founded on religious practices is best seen in the arrangements made for the festivals. At the New Year, for five days from the last day of the year to the fourth of the First Month, the opera was performed by well-known companies at the temple. The opera was staged for the sake of the Beidi and the Guanyin, whose images were deposited on an altar facing the stage, but, of course, local people also came for the entertainment. They might for the price of a ticket sit at the "host's mat-shed" (*zhupeng*), or stand for free at the back. In front of the stage were placed twelve "flower fireworks" (*huapao*), which people from the entire *xiang* came to "fight over" (in a process known as *qiangpao*). They valued in particular the four fireworks given the names "The first firework of the first day of the New Year," "the new first firework," "the proper and complete firework," and "the complete firework for the leap year." Those who succeeded in laying claims to these fireworks were responsible not only for returning them in the next year, but also for paying for the floats (*piaose*) for the parade on the Beidi festival on the third of the Third Month.[44]

On the third day of the Third Month, the people of the Three Districts paraded the Beidi and the Guanyin in the streets. The parade consisted of three sections. The first included the deities Beidi and Guanyin, the second the gentry and elders of the Three Districts, properly dressed in ceremonial gowns,[45] and the third the floats, most of which were hired from Foshan. The object of the parade was to transport the two deities through the streets, to the ancestral halls, and even to the residences in the Three Districts, so that they might be worshiped by the local people. On this occasion, the local people set up "societies for welcoming the deities" (*yasheng hui*) to await their coming.

The parade lasted three days, and strict regulations governed the routes it took. On the first day of the Third Month, the parade would go to the First District, through Loagu Lane, Wang Bay, Tiandi and Liuzhai. On the second day, it would go to the Second District, through Mai Street, Fan Street, Ouyang Street, Lubao Market, and Haibian Street. On this route, it would pass by Xie Street but would not enter it. Even though every year the elders of Xie Street would set up a colorful altar in anticipation of the coming of the deities, the parade would go around the altar but would not stop. On the third day, the parade would go up to Peng Street, stopping at the He surname ancestral hall at the Upper Street, the Peng surname "big house" (*dawu*) at Middle Street, and the Tan surname "big hou::" ~t the Lower Street, so that offerings might be made to the deities. Again, although the route from the temple to Peng Street passed by Tanji, the parade would not enter that village. It would pass on the side of the village, and the elders of Tanji could only make offerings on the roadside.

After the parade, the "traveling hall" (*xinggong*) of the Beidi would be kept by the Three Districts on an annual rota, and it would be deposited in the villages within the district in the order they were entered for the parade. The deity would be placed in the ancestral hall or the "big house" in these villages, and village households would be responsible for lighting the lantern in front of it and supplying it with vegetarian food on a rota. The length of the period for which a household might have to be responsible for the deity varied, therefore, according to the number of households in the village. In Peng Street, for instance, each household was responsible for the deity for seven days.[46]

Three feasts were held at the temple annually, from the last day of the year to the fourth day of the New Year, from the first to the third of the Third Month for the temple festival, and on the ninth of the Ninth Month. These feasts were attended by elders from the Three Districts.[47]

In addition to these annual occasions, every sixty years a "great gathering" (*dahui*) and every thirty years a "small gathering" (*xiaohui*) were held. Funds were collected at the great gathering for rebuilding and major repairs (*chongxiu*), and at the small gathering for minor repairs (*chongxin*). Collection books (*yuanbu*) were issued by the temple on these occasions, and donations were solicited from those who were thought to belong to Lubao, even if they had moved abroad. The celebrations on these occasions were organized on a larger scale than were the annual ones. The last great gathering was held in 1888, when the present temple building was constructed. In 1918, a small gathering was held when the temple building was renewed. The celebration on that occasion lasted five days.[48]

A sense of identity among members of the Three Districts became apparent in the use of such terms as "street communities" and "sons and grandsons of the temple" (*miaozi miaosun*). People of the "street communities" saw themselves as being distinct from "people of the villages," the term that was used to designate people of nearby communities. Equally important, the periodic reenactment of the unity of the Three Districts in rituals affirmed the authority of their elders. It became the practice for officials from the police office of Xujiang to burn incense at the Beidi Temple on the first and fifteenth days of each month and, after that, to pay their visit to the elders of the Three Districts.[49] Official recognition added to the elders' local authority.

The centrality of temple rituals in territorial identity is reflected also in the internal organization of the Three Districts. By the Qing, each of the three districts focused its religious worship on a principal temple, most clearly exemplified by the Tianhou Temple of the Third District and the Wudi Temple of the Second District. The Tianhou Temple was built in the Ming dynasty, dedicated to the Wenchang, the Tianhou, and the Jinhua. It derived a regular income, known among the people of Peng Street as being managed under "the ancestral accounts" (*taigong shu*), from its ownership of two shops in Lubao and from payments made by priests and fortune-tellers. Two managers were elected each year, and on the Tianhou Festival on the third of the Third Month, villagers came to fight for the fireworks. A banquet was held every year, attended by males of the district who were aged sixteen and above. We were told that boys under sixteen years of age whose fathers had died might also attend, so it is possible that participation in the banquet signified some recognition for household, rather than individual, membership of the district.[50] Within the Third District, there were other temples, notably the Chendu Temple and the Guanyin Temple. Designation of the Tianhou Temple for the collective activities of the entire district certainly gave it a central position.

In the case of the Second District, it would seem that recognition for the centrality of the Wudi Temple entailed the construction of a new building. The Wudi Temple was one of two local temples in the Second District, the other being a Huaguang Temple, and a new temple building was constructed in the early years of Jiaqing.[51] The fragmentary remains of a tablet associated with the repair of the temple in the Guangxu years entitled "The repayment of accounts by the Wudi Temple to the Junyi *hui* (association for equal benefits)" show that members of the street communities of the Second District had formed the Junyi hui so that "when contributions had been fully paid they might collect two catties of sacrificial pork." Among the leaders of the hui were listed the ancestral halls of the Mai, Fan, and Ouyang surnames, and 30 shops in Lubao. Shops from Foshan also donated.[52]

Documentation on the central temple of the First District is less clear, and we were not able to identify it on the ground. We were told, however, that musicians were hired at the Tianhou Temple of Laogu Lane and that the fight for the fireworks was held there and was attended by villagers from Liuzhai, Tiandi, and Wangwan.[53] It is likely, therefore, that the Tianhou Temple was the central temple of this district.

Sacrifice to the Beidi and Its
Growing Importance in Lubao

A saying that we were told in and around Lubao had it that "Even if you are not afraid of the people of Xujiang, you have to be afraid of its deity."[54] The authority of the Beidi as reflected in this saying reached into the villages, and we believe religious ceremonies reported to us in interviews indicate the ascendance of the Beidi over the Hongsheng deity that in an earlier age had formed the focus of sacrifice.

The temple at the village of Dayigang, for instance, was known as Dawang *miao* (Great King Temple, popularly known as the "White Temple"). The temple belonged to the Li surname in the village, and in it, the Xie and Wang surnames of the same village held no part. On the third day of the Third Month (the Beidi Festival), the Li surname paraded the statues of the Beidi and the Dawang in the streets of the village. The parade was led by musicians, including a gong-beater, followed by the Beidi carried by two men, and the Dawang, carried by one man. They were in turn followed by the elders of the village (possibly only those of the Li surname) dressed in mock Qing dynasty official costumes. Carriers of the deities obtained their privileges by bidding at an auction for them. The parade went along a fixed route, first calling at the Yuanmou Ancestral Hall (the senior branch), and subsequently at the Rushan Ancestral Hall and the Xiumou Ancestral Hall. At each of the three ancestral halls, the statues of the deities would be sacrificed to by the local people.[55]

The Xie surname in the same village sacrificed to the Beidi in a different arrangement. Because the Xie surname occupied houses in three lanes (*xiang*) in the village, and each lane had its own ancestral hall, the practice was for the Beidi to be deposited in the three ancestral halls in turns. Each ancestral hall would keep the deity for one year, during which time a gourd-shaped board with the deity's name written on it would be circulated among member households. A *jiao* festival was also held in the Beidi's honor every three years, on which occasion the Beidi would be paraded in all three lanes.[56]

Another example may be found in the Hongsheng Temple in the village of Huanggang. The Hongsheng Temple, popularly known as the "temple of the three surnames" (*sanxing miao*) was owned by the three surnames Huang, Zeng, and Zhi. The temple had a regular income and was managed by managers elected from the "entire temple" (*tongmiao*, that is, the three surnames). The temple building consisted of three halls: the Beidi and the

Hongsheng occupied the central hall, the Guandi occupied that on the right, and spirit tablets of the surnames in the village that on the left. Any member of the three surnames of the village might deposit a spirit tablet in that hall upon the payment of five taels of silver. Adjacent to the three halls was a communal alliance (*xiangyue*) office where the elders met. On the third day of the Third Month, the statues of the deity were paraded in the streets. The parade was led by a team of lion dancers, who were followed by the statue of the Beidi carried by four persons, and then by the elders, dressed in red caps, shoes, and socks and their "longevity robes" and carrying white handkerchiefs. The parade went on a fixed route from the temple to the Huang surname in the south, then to the Huang surname in the east and to the Huang surname in the west, to the Zeng surname and then the Zhi surname, before returning to the temple. Villages on the route arranged for priests to be present to receive the parade. After the parade, the elders attended a banquet.[57]

In the Dawang Temple of Jiang'an the Beidi was also given central position. On his side sat the Hongsheng and the four protecting deities. The temple, known also as the "temple of the four surnames" (*sixing miao*), was owned by the Jiang surname of Jiang'an, the Li surname of Lijia, the Fan surname of Fanjia, and the Li surname of Liqu. It was the location where the four surnames met to deal with their communal affairs.[58]

Temples known as the Dawang *miao* would typically have been occupied by the Hongsheng. That the Beidi should hold such a prominent position in these temples indicates his usurpation of a previous deity. This exemplifies that even where, locally, village communities demonstrated allegiance to a host of deities, the appearance of a central temple in the market might nonetheless exert considerable unifying influence in matters of worship. The appearance of the deity of the central temple within local temples would have been one indication of such influence.

The Fight for Fireworks at New Year and the Wider Community

An indication of the influence of the Beidi beyond the town of Lubao itself was the celebration that was held at the temple at New Year. The celebrations from the last day of the previous year to the fourth day of the New Year were well attended not only by the people from the town, but also by people from a much wider area—from as far away as the counties of Qingyuan, Sihui, and Guangning. Many came to watch the operas that were held each night and to participate in the fight for the fireworks on the final day. Some, such as the Ouyang surname from Xiongqi, came to stay with their relatives of the same surname. The popular saying that described the occasion had it that "the rice vats would be empty but the latrines full."

On both sides of the stage constructed outside the Beidi Temple for the occasion there would be "seats for the hosts" (*zhupeng*), segregated for men and women. Tickets were sold for these seats. However, "standing room" (*qidi*) was provided and no tickets were required there. Every year, the shopkeepers of Lubao Market presented tickets to the gentry of Lubao so that they might attend the operas for free. The restaurants at the market would also post announcements advertising free refreshments for regular customers. Voluntary associations formed by people all around would have gathered money to provide sacrifice for the Beidi at his temple, and their members would combine worship at the temple with watching the operas and eating a good meal at Lubao. The ancestral halls would have provided for their elders to offer sacrifice. New Year was also the time when many Dan boats of the North and West Rivers would have gathered at Lubao. It must have been a spectacular sight to see thousands of boats clustered all the way from Peng Street to Lubao Market.

However, it was the fight for the fireworks that provided the climax for the festivities. On the fourth day of the New Year, teams of villagers would gather at the second ridge behind the Beidi Temple (known as the "place where the *pao* rockets would be fired"), watched by tens of thousands of spectators. It was customary for each large village, such as Dushugang, to produce a team, and for small villages to ally with other villages in their religious community, such as the six surnames of Dagangmiao, to produce teams in common. Dagangmiao, in fact, produced two teams: one shared by the Chen, Huang, and Deng surnames and another by the Xian, Ye, and Liang surnames. The theatrical companies and the Fuqing tang of the Dan also produced their own teams, and often succeeded in winning a token (known as the pao ring) for collecting the deity. People from as far away as Qingyuan, Hua *xian*, and Nanhai might also come for the fight for the fireworks.

Members of these teams would be clad only in a pair of trousers dyed in black false gambier (*shuliang*). Their naked upper torsos and the slippery nature of the dye ensured that they could not be readily grabbed by their competitors. Each team came with its own colorful banner bearing its name. The fireworks were launched by a man especially chosen for the occasion by the three districts. This would be a male aged over 40 years, who served on the occasion for only one year. On the 28th day of the previous year, he would have had obtained three successful trials at the fortune-telling blocks at the Beidi Temple, eaten only vegetarian food since, and kept himself ritually clean. He would have lived in the public bureau near the Beidi Temple for the previous few days and helped in preparing the fireworks. At midday on the fourth day of the New Year, he would appear in red for launching the fireworks. He would hold the tokens for the deities in his left hand and a large stick of incense in his right. An assistant would bring out the fireworks, that is, the rockets to which the officiator would attach the tokens. Twelve rockets were launched each year, the first four bringing the best fortune. The people who succeeded in catching a token could keep a statue of the Beidi for one year, but were obliged to return it the following year and to contribute to the procession of the Beidi on the occasion of his festival. It must have been an exciting occasion when the teams rushed in for the pao each time one was launched, in the midst of the cheering of crowds of spectators. The successful teams would take the tokens to the Beidi Temple to register their names, and then carry the statues of the Beidi back to their own villages. On the same night, at the celebration banquet in their own villages, they would auction the right of keeping the deity's statue to households within their villages.

It is clear that the community exemplified during New Year was not the same as that exemplified during the Beidi Festival. At the Beidi Festival, the three districts celebrated on their own. At New Year, the wider marketing community participated. Contributions to the processions of the Beidi Festival by successful contestants for the pao allowed the two communities to overlap, but at the Beidi Festival it was the Three Districts that provided the essential leadership.[59]

The Fuxu Community School and Community Control

The earliest reference to a community school in Lubao was the account of bandit suppression by Wu Tingju in 1505. The school probably did not survive for long, and the next attempt to found a community school came almost three hundred years later, in 1783, when Peng Jie of Peng Street obtained his *juren* degree. From 1783, the community school served not only as an institution that extolled learning, but also as one for resolving conflicts in the town and its neighborhood and as a place for collective worship.

The continuation of a scholarly tradition in Lubao was demonstrated both by the construction of buildings devoted to learning and by successes in the imperial examination. In 1803 the community school was rebuilt at a site by the river 500 meters from the Beidi Temple and given the name Fuxu Community School (Fuxu *shexue*). In 1808, an archway given the name Yumen ("Archway of the Emperor Yu") was built at the jetty near the community school. The structure embodied the propitious implication of the saying "the carp jumps over the dragon gate," signifying success in the examinations. In 1813, the Dakui *lou* ("building of great notables") was built on the slope of Huashan. Soon after that, a Wenchang Temple was built adjacent to the Beidi Temple. All these constructions demonstrated an interest in a literati appearance at Lubao.[60]

From the early nineteenth century, as more attention was given to education, Lubao families began to experience success in the examinations. In 1809, Huang Shanshu of Tiandi (First District) became a *gongsheng*. In the Tongzhi era, Huang Zhong'e of Laogu Lane and Wang Naitang of Wangmuwan (both of the First District) became *juren*.[61] In the Guangxu era, Huang Renxiang of Laoguxiang was a *juren*, Li Huanyao of Xintian was a Hanlin academician, and Xie Yixi of Dayigang was a *jinshi*.[62]

However, aside from its scholastic connections, the Fuxu Community school was also prominent as an institution for resolving conflicts. According to the "Tablet at the Longpo Community School [as the Fuxu was renamed in the Republican period] in commemoration of the spirit tablets from the villages," the "Longpo Community school was a place for lecturing, education, meetings and public affairs for the east and west sections [*dong-xi fang*] of Xujiang."[63] This description accords with what we were told in interviews. The *juren* Huang Zhong'e and Huang Renxiang of Laoguxiang both worked at the community school.[64] The *xiucai* Xie Jianpo from Dayigang also worked for the community school, and, moreover, he was a leader among the managers there, his word being taken very seriously by them all.[65] Cao Junting of Nan'an had also worked at the community school.[66]

The scholars were recalled as people with authority. One informant recalled that even the admiral of the Guangdong navy, Zheng Jin, paid his respect to Huang Zhong'e on one occasion.[67] In the Guangxu period, when the people of Peng Street were locked in dispute with the people of Caogang over some property, the Caogang people sought out a *xiucai* of Xiatang by the surname of Pan to represent them, while the Peng Street people enlisted a *juren* of Liaotanggang by the surname of Huang. Both parties went to the community school, and the scholars "sat in the bureau" (*zuoju*) to resolve that the property should be given to Caogang. From that time on, it was said, the land in question was known as Cao-Pan land (Cao-Pan *di*), and was farmed jointly by people of the Cao and Pan surnames.[68] In 1783, Peng Jie, the *juren*, was involved in rebuilding the Huashan Monastery and in negotiating with officials in the process.[69]

The Fuxu Community School also provided a depository for ancestral spirit tablets. Regulations for depositing these tablets were drawn up in 1803 when the school was built. The sum of twenty silver dollars was charged for each tablet deposited on the two sides of the Wendi and Wudi deities in the main hall, and ten dollars for each deposited in the side halls. A special staff, known as the *juding* (men of the bureau), were responsible for burning incense to them. From the genealogies and the names listed on the remaining fragments of the donation tablet, it appears that the spirit tablets deposited in the school fell into four categories: first, founding ancestors (such as Cao Liangbao of Nan'an, Cao Yanfan and Cao Yanqing of Nan'an, Cen Boyi of Cuntao, Hu Xingcun of Upper Letang [Shang Letang], Li Ren of Lizhou, Li Dehua of Liqu, and Liu Zhangshi of Liuzhai); second, degree holders (such as Hu Jinyuan of Lower Letang, that is, Xia Letang, who was an administrative clerk in the Bureau of Military Affairs in the Song; Cao Guang of Nan'an, who was a *juren* of the Wanli period; Li Kemian of Menkoubu, who was an assistant magistrate of Linchuan in the Ming; Luo Ruwei of Lian'ao, who was an instructor of Yangshan *xian* in the Qianlong period; and Li Huanyao of Xintian, who was a Hanlin academician of the Guanxu period); third, wealthy merchants (such as Li Zhanguang of Liqu); and fourth, reputable scholars (such as Li Bacai of Liqu, a guest of the *xiangyin* village drinking ceremony; Li Jubin, also of Liqu, noted in his genealogy for a style of writing that was close to the Tang poet Li Po's; Liu Beiyuan of Liuzhai, who was submanager of the Beidi Temple in the Qianlong period; and Liu Jing also of Liuzhai, who was decorated by the emperor upon his 96th birthday).[70]

Depositing the spirit tablets of exemplary persons at the community school worked in two ways: it added authority to the school and it gave recognition to the honors achieved by member lineages and villages. The combination of the authority to educate, to adjudicate, and to worship in one institution that was closely identified with the literati elite provided the semblance of a framework for literati governance, just as the combination of worship and territorial representation in the Beidi and other territorial temples in and around Lubao provided for communal expression.

Changes Toward the End
of the Qing Dynasty

Lubao was occupied for a year by the Red Turbans, led by Sanshui native Chen Jingang, in 1854. It became their stronghold from which they waged war against Lubao county city, and for that reason many nearby residents were drafted into the forces of the peasant armies. According to the genealogy of the Liu surname at Liuzhai, "At the time of the Taiping Heavenly Kingdom, many men of the sixteenth generation were drafted, and people whose names took the 'ru' character were greatly reduced."[71] Soon after that, the Qing armies, in their counterattack, killed many people in Lubao. Lubao was, therefore, much damaged during the Taiping wars.[72]

Our impression is that after the Taiping wars Lubao did not recover its former prosperity. The floods of 1877 and 1915 might have been partly responsible.[73] More decisive was the partial completion of the Guangzhou–Hankou Railway in 1916, which reduced Lubao's geographic importance by allowing much north-south traffic to bypass Lubao.[74] Without the substantial transshipment trade, Lubao became a center for local trade only. This happened as the lower reaches of the Pearl River delta saw a considerable increase in trade, and so push and pull factors combined to make it attractive for Lubao merchants to divert their business interests away from the town. At the end of the Qing and in the early Republican years, therefore, Lubao merchants traded in Guangzhou, Hong Kong, Foshan, and even Shanghai. All the male subjects that we interviewed who were over 70 years old had spent considerable time outside Lubao. In Liuzhai, only slightly over two hundred persons had remained in the village, whereas we were told there were over 300 persons from the village who had settled in Guangzhou, Xi'nan (Shanshui county city), or Foshan, and another 300 in Hong Kong, Macau, or overseas. Even the chief of the *lijin* (internal transit tariff) station, Liu Lichao, left with his capital in 1910 for Guangzhou and then Hong Kong, where he started the Yanfang Photographic Studio.[75] Many members of the Wang surname of Wangmuwan also went to Hong Kong, and there were only several families remaining in Lubao when we conducted our interviews.[76] In Peng Street, only one household each of the surnames Gong, He, and Peng remained.[77]

Emigration from Lubao of the most prominent merchants might have weakened the town's leadership while its local trade magnified the influence of surrounding villages. This change in political alignment might have contributed to the litigation between the Three Districts and the eastern and western sections on the control of Lubao in 1922. The term "eastern and western sections" was used to refer to the villages of Lubao, excluding specifically the Three Districts.[78] Among them was the village of Dushugang, the largest single-surname village in Sanshui county. In the early years of the Republican period, the Cai surname there consisted of a population of 7,000.[79] Cai Guannan was the local leader at Dushugang, and he was known as a bully who was well connected with officialdom. In the early years of the Republic, in a contest with the people of Xie Street for a plot of land, he sent people from his village to blockade a part of the dike so that no one might pass it. Then he himself erected a boundary stone at the Guanfang Pier, and on that basis took it over.[80] After that, he took over the Yuxiangkou Pier.[81]

It was Cai Guannan who raised the claim that because the Beidi Temple was known as the Xujiang Ancestral Temple (Xujiang *zumiao*), all residents of Xujiang, not only those of the Three Districts, were entitled to share in its property. He even claimed that because people of the Three Districts were transitory and rootless—referred to by the term *shuiliucai* (firewood floating on the water)—the property of the temple should not come under their control. In any case, he argued, the elders of the Three Districts had no claim to exclusive control over the income of the temple, which, including donations, was substantial.[82] For these reasons, he allied with Cuntao Village (single-surname, Cen) to make a bid for the control of the temple properties. At one stage, the villagers, under Cai's leadership, broke down the gate of the public bureau near the temple.

Litigation followed, and the county government initially ruled that the eastern and western sections had the better case. A year after the ruling, the village elders of the sections held a feast at the temple. However, the former *lijin* chief, Liu Lizhao, who was also leader of the Three Districts militia and had already moved to Guangzhou or Hong Kong, contested the decision. He provided the initial capital of five hundred dollars and collected contributions from members of the Three Districts for further litigation. Through the help of Zou Lu (Guomindang member and principal of Guangdong University), the case was brought to the high court in Guangzhou, which ruled that the temple should belong to the Three Districts. The court provided an official announcement on the ruling to be posted at the temple. The people of the Three Districts formed the Sanhe (Alliance of Three) Company to manage the temple, and the Liu surname of Liuzhai, from that time on, became the company director.

Success in litigation did not bring about prosperity in Lubao, nor did it break the power of the Cai surname. There apparently were casualties among the merchants: the largest store for dried seafood, Li Xiang Fa, was picketed by people of the eastern and western sections for contributing several hundred dollars to the litigation, and it had to close for lack of business. The year after the litigation, Dushugang demonstrated its strength at the "fight for the fireworks." The village fielded a fireworks team of over a thousand men, who came under the insignia of a green leafy vegetable (homonym for Cai, the surname). They even set up machine guns on the dike, and demanded that the fireworks launcher launch the fireworks in their midst. Social harmony, by then, was clearly broken.[83]

After these events, power in Lubao shifted from the gentry of the Three Districts to local bosses (*datian'er*), who rose and fell one after the other. Cai Guannan was murdered in Guanyao (in Nanhai country), and was succeeded by Tan Xin. After Tan Xin, there was Ou Fang. This situation remained essentially unchanged until the Liberation in 1949.[84]

Ordination Names in Hakka Genealogies: A Religious Practice and Its Decline

CHAN WING-HOI

MANY Hakka genealogies contain names for ancestors described as *langming*, *faming*, or *duming*. The three terms are used interchangeably.[1] These names are of two forms. The first has the character *fa* as the first of two characters. The other consists of a nonnumeric character followed by a numeral and then the character *lang*, the nonnumeric character sometimes indicating the generation to which the ancestor is ascribed and sometimes being taken from one of the characters in the individual's other names. In the genealogies, a variant of the *lang* form found in earlier generations consists of only a numeral followed by the character *lang*. In the case of women, similar names are given in the form of either a numeric character followed by the character *niang* or a two-character given name beginning with the character *miao*.

Especially in early generations, an entry in a genealogy may consist of only a name written in one of these forms. In later generations the entry often includes a name written in this form together with names in which the numeric element does not appear. Later still, typically in recording the generations that lived during the seventeenth century and later, names in these forms disappear altogether. Sometimes the list of numeral-cum-character *lang* names in a genealogy can be quite lengthy. Even if one allows for some fiction in the practice, the case remains that *faming*, *langming*, or *duming* appears in an early section of the Hakka genealogy, and not in later generations. What can this transformation in genealogical naming practice represent?

The Nature of Ordination Names

The use of *langming* in Hakka genealogies invites comparison with Yao or She traditions involving the ordination of males as an initiation into adulthood. Other circumstantial evidence also suggests considerable affinity between Yao (Iu Mien) or She and Hakka religious practices: ritual manuals used by Cantonese and Hakka village priests, like those of the Yao, identify the priestly tradition as being closely tied to Daoism but are written in a literary style that is markedly different from that of manuals found in the Daoist canon.[2] They also share a peculiar group of deities that are not found in the canonical tradition but which appear sometimes in the Lüshan tradition, which also uses *langming* for some of its deities.

Information on the Yao people of Thailand and Laos suggests that the Hakka *langming*, *faming*, and *duming* were ordination names.[3] According to Jacques Lemoine,

[A] Yao man is introduced to the Taoist Pantheon through the *kwa tang* "hanging the lantern" ceremony. Its main purpose is to entitle him to perform some rituals, and to confer on him a first "official" degree in the celestial hierarchy. As a result he will be granted a religious *fa bua* [*faming*] when he will drop his middle generation name and replace it by the word *fa*, "the Law (of Tao)." For example, somebody whose adult name reads *Tang* (family) *Fu* (generation) *On* (personal) will then be called *Tang Fa On*, that is "the faithful On of the Tang family," in all religious documents and ceremonies, including his own funeral.

At the next level in the hierarchy he proceeds to mastership (*tousai* [*dushi*]) [through] a still more important ceremony. . . . but this already high position can still be further improved, to two higher levels with more important qualifications of varying degrees. . . . Henceforth, they will use, in similar religious contexts, what one may call a "knightly" or "gentlemanly" name. For instance, a man who has already been granted a *fa bua*, as in the example "Tang Fa On" given above, will now change it to "Tang On *yet-long*" if he is first-born, meaning, "On, the First Squire of the Tang Family." If he is second or third son, this will also be stated in a similar way.[4]

Lemoine also notes that the deity Zhang Zhao Erlang is noted as the patriarch of the Yao religion. Zhang Zhao Erlang, as we shall see, was known as a disciple of Lüshan Jiulang, the patriarch of the Lüshan tradition of esoteric practices. It would seem, therefore, that the use of ordination was combined with the continuation of the Lüshan tradition.

Among the She people, an initiation ceremony was conducted for young men of sixteen years or older. That ceremony was known as the *jiaoming* (possibly corrupted from *zouming*, that is, submitting a name in a petition), *dushen* (ordination), or *rulu* (entering the [Daoist?] register), and often also described as *jizu* (sacrifice to the ancestors). Descriptions of She practices available to me suggest that the ceremony legitimizes the use of ordination names in much the same way as that cited above for the Yao. It is reported that persons initiated through the ceremony adopt *faming*. Esoteric continuity is also implied in the claim that the She initiation ceremony may be traced to the practices of Lüshan and Maoshan, from where the first She ancestor acquired his magical powers.[5] Reports that give examples of such names show that they all have the *fa* prefix. Also found among the She are names in the *lang* format, which is often referred to as rank sequence (*paixing*). According to a report on She villages in Guangdong province, custom dictates that only those ordained through the *jiaoming* ceremony may have names in the *lang* format and be recorded in genealogies. There are variations in the way *lang*-style names among the She relate to ordination. According to reports from some other areas, almost everyone is given *lang*-style names automatically.[6]

The connection between the ordination ceremony and ancestral worship, already alluded to in the case of the She, is quite explicit for both the Yao and the She. In the case of the Yao, a study of the Bapai in Liannan in Guangdong province notes:

When [a person] dies, his religious name is written on a piece of white paper pasted on his head so that he can join his kin group. If he has not been initiated to this higher degree, the ancestors [*zugong*] will not know that he is one of their own and will not admit him into the walled city of mutual aid, wealth, and peace. He will, instead, be shut out, to wander outside the walled city in poverty.[7]

It is also acknowledged in this source that among the five benefits of ordination the most important is that, after death, the ordained person will have his name recorded in the genealogy and be held in respect and sacrificed to as an innocent or pure (*qingbai*) member of the lineage (*jiazu*).[8] Another study describes the case of a Yao man who shifted his clan affiliation. It is noteworthy that this happened in a *kua tang* initiation that confirmed his membership in the new clan.[9] Among the She, it has been reported that the strips of red cloth hanging from the "dragon-head cane," the symbol of lineage authority, bore the names of those for whom the "sacrifice to the ancestors" had been performed. Evidently these names would have been the names of persons who had gone through the initiation ceremony.[10]

Comments preserved in Hakka genealogies suggest that a very similar process was at work in the use of *langming*, *faming*, or *duming*, and that these names were ordination names. Such comments often explain that these names were given to the initiated by religious masters, the latter often referred to as Daoists (*Daojiao*). The genealogy of the Liu surname of Chaozhou and Mei *xian*, revised probably in 1920, argues:

> In the previous compilation [of the genealogy], the ancestors from the Song to the Yuan dynasties had names incorporating the *fa* and *lang* characters, and numerals involving ten, hundred, thousand, or ten thousand. The sequence of the numerals does not tally with seniority among brothers. This was because the custom of those times gave Daoists (*Daojiao*) considerable power, to the extent that they could provide these names [for the ancestors].[11]

Similarly, a genealogy of the Lin surname of Hang Ha Po Village in the New Territories of Hong Kong explains:[12] "During the time [it is not clear when] it was a popular custom for people to be ordained by Heavenly Master Zhang. Those who were so ordained were called by the *faming* and *langhao*, which were passed down to future generations and never forgotten." A variation of the same theme may be found in cases where the ancestors given ordination names were regarded as persons possessing extraordinary powers. The He surname of Sixing county believe that the eleven sons and one daughter of an ancestor Weitai were referred to by their *langming* because they had become immortals.[13]

The test of the general acceptance of a religious origin of *langming* may also be found in its occasional denial. The Luo surname genealogy of Luobei in Xingning contains a scholarly attempt to refute the popular belief that the *langming* names were ordination names. The genealogist argues that the *langming* names were results of *lijia* registration rather than initiation by sorcerers (*shiwu*).[14]

The best evidence of the practice of initiation among the Hakka, however, is the Xingning county gazetteer of 1552, which has a rather detailed account of the custom of ordination:

> The ceremony takes place on a chosen auspicious day in the wilderness. A tall temporary altar is built, on which sits a sorcerer (*wushi*), and below which the candidate kneels and bends down. All relatives and friends of the candidate come to witness the rite. [At the end] they stick in his hair flower (*huahong*) ornaments and congratulate him for having received the "mandate for official status" (*guangao*). The sorcerer gives him a *faming* ordination name, a certificate, a seal, a cow's horn, and a ritual knife, collectively known as "implements of magic" (*fazhang*). The candidate bows to receive them and takes them home accompanied by wind and percussion music, where they are installed in his bedchamber. The ceremony is known as *shoufa* (receiving the *fa*) or *dushui*.[15] It is repeated once every year for the same person. The candidate is initially granted the grade of Surveyor of Merit (*dugong*)

and of the Auspicious Alliance (*mengwei*). He is promoted after each subsequent celebration to a higher rank. After several years he will reach the rank of "minister of the first [i.e., highest] grade" (*yipin dafu*), and is qualified for a red garment with which he will be buried upon his death. Those who are eager for quick promotions have the rite performed three or four times a year, getting a higher rank each time. One or two members of the literati (*shiren*) are known to have shamelessly knelt below such altars and received ordination in this manner.[16]

The ranks are noticeable borrowings from canonical Daoism.[17] But the "implements of magic" involved are the hallmarks of the sorcerers of the popular tradition.

Corroborative evidence can be found in the early Qing collection of miscellany on Guangdong province, the *Guangdong xinyu*. Under an entry on the sorcerers of Yong'an county (present-day Zijin, inhabited by Hakka) is a description of distinct practices still found today in the Hakka priestly (*sang*) tradition.[18] Included among such practices were the singing of the "chicken song," associated with ceremonies of exorcism, and the dance between two priests, one of whom dressed up as a woman. The entry refers to the ordination ceremony for males in unequivocal terms: "The men build an altar to perform the *dushui* ceremony of ordination in which white [ordination] certificates and yellow [celestial] mandates are received." Presumably names would have been stated in the ordination certificates. It is clear, therefore, not only that the Hakka conducted ceremonies for their males in which, like the Yao and the She, they were initiated into priestly traditions, but also that names used for the process of ordination were given and recorded.

Fengchao: A Hakka Religious Ritual and Ordained Ancestors

The description of the initiation ceremony in Xingning and Yong'an counties quoted above may be supplemented by an account given in the 1822 edition of the *Yong'an Gazetteer*, which repeats essentially the same information as in the *Guangdong xinyu* but adds that on the same occasion it was necessary to "slaughter an animal for sacrifice at the *fengchao* ritual."[19] The *fengchao* ritual was until 1985 still practiced in some Hakka villages in the New Territories of Hong Kong, and features of it may also be found in the *Zhonghua jiu lisu* (Old customs of China), a manuscript on beliefs and rituals from Mei *xian* and Xinning county in the 1930s.[20] Toward the end of the Guangxu era (1875–1908), an initiate of Zijin county who reportedly held an imperial degree composed secular songs for performance after the ceremony known as the *huazhao* opera, which became an independent genre around 1950.[21]

Fengchao rituals are performed by Hakka priests known as the *sang*. They claim to be Daoist, but their practices are clearly more akin to what is commonly referred to in the Qing Guangdong sources as Maoshan magic than to canonical Daoism. They are distinct from other ritual specialists who may be found in Hakka villages, the male and female spirit mediums (*sienpo* and *gongtung*) and the laymen practicing "Buddhist" rites (*wosong* or *nammo*). The rituals of the *sang* include the unique feature of the dance between the master and his assistant, a man who is dressed as a woman. They use ordination names consisting of the prefix *fa* character in their ritual documents and in chanting. This is true at least of Mr. Miao, the only surviving *sang* priest in Hong Kong in 1981. His family practiced the profession for four generations, all using the *fa* character prefix in their ritual names. On one occasion he claimed thirteen generations of descent, probably including nine earlier ordained ancestors whose names in the *lang* format he recited in some sessions of the fengchao ritual. A Hakka "Buddhist" specialist whom I interviewed on the subject informed me that he had never heard about the use of *langming* or *duming*.

In the Hakka villages of the New Territories, the fengchao was performed for the groom before his wedding to ensure that his children would be born without defects. Villagers I spoke to seemed to believe that otherwise defects were quite likely. In the village of Cheng Tau, where I witnessed the celebration of a fengchao in 1981, there was a deformed son in the family, and in a joke during the ceremony the priest's assistant told this child that when it was his turn to marry, the priest could be willing to perform the ceremony for him for free. At the village of Ping Yeung, I was told that if the ceremony was not performed, the slaughtering of pigs for the wedding would have to take place in a "faraway" place, suggesting that if the ceremony had been omitted, other precautions against polluting influences would have had to be taken. The Ping Yeung villager added that when there were two or more sons in the family, the ceremony would be performed for at least one of them.

According to the priest who was hired to perform the fengchao at Cheng Tau, although the ceremony was not performed in all Hakka villages, it was, nevertheless, quite common. He cited as examples of villages in which the ceremony used to be performed So Lo Pun, Kat O, Hung Ling, Ping Yeung (for the Chen surname), Cheng Tau (for the Peng surname), Ha Hang (for the Li surname), Shan Tau Kok (for the Zeng surname), and Lin

Au (for the Zheng surname). By the time of my interview with the priest in 1981, most of these villages had already ceased to hold the ceremony. He believed that the practice declined from the time of the Second World War when it became difficult to find the priests who knew how to execute the rituals. He also supplied the information that the same rituals were held in nearby Yantian in Bao'an county, and in Shiqi in Zhongshan county.

According to the standard memorial used for the fengchao that I obtained from the priest who officiated at Cheng Tau, it is clear that sacrifice was directed to the deities as well as to the ancestors. The ceremony was referred to as the *zuchao* (ancestral *chao*), and the spirits sacrificed to were the *shangzu* (early ancestors). References were made in the memorial to an "immortal army" that was under the control of the ancestors. When the priest read the memorial aloud at the ceremony, and again when he read it out for me at the interview, he added the term *zugong* (ancestors) before the term *bingma* (soldiers and horses) written in the document, indicating that he thought of the army as belonging to the ancestors. In the interview, he explained that the army was like the police, for it guarded the village from outsiders. The memorial says that the ceremony was needed to make up for losses of soldiers and horses that had occurred due to the shortage of provisions, for the possible losses suffered by the banners (*wuhua qihao*, i.e., banners of the five patterns) for the command of the troops, and for losses that had occurred to their military camps (*yingsuo*). A particular feature of the memorial was that it was primarily a request to the Jade Emperor and his subordinates for the issuance of an authority to recruit soldiers (referred to as the *zhaobing pai*). As such, the fengchao ceremony is based on the premise that the ordained is granted a spiritual troop under his command, an element that was essential to the initiation ceremonies of the Yao and the She.[22]

The fengchao ceremony that I witnessed was performed inside the ancestral hall with the exception of a session "to pacify the kitchen deity," which was held at the kitchen stove in the bridegroom's house. At the ancestral altar of the hall, the priest hung a picture showing the Three Pure Ones and deities peculiar to the popular tradition, including the Three Ladies. Three temporary spirit tablets were set up on a table before this picture. The one in the middle was for the Taishang Laojun (styled Taishang *hunyuan jiaozhu daode tianjun*), and, without personal names, the masters of the priest. The one on the right-hand side was for the ancestors of the groom, and styled "Founding ancestors, great-grandfather, grandfather, and their wives," and the one on the left was for the deities of the four domains—Heaven, Earth, Water, and Yang. Offerings on the table included plates of homemade red-colored buns, presented, I was told, by every household in the village.

The ceremony started at 6:45 in the evening and continued until 4:00 the next morning. It began with an invitation sent to the deities. I noted in my notebook that in the final section of this ritual, the priest turned toward the ancestral altar and addressed the ancestors, emphasizing those who had *langming* and those who had *gongming* (titles awarded in the imperial examinations). The ceremony included dances in which the priest's assistant, dressed as a woman, joined the priest. The ceremonies made frequent use of the horn, the divination block, and mudra formations. A musician at the percussion instruments provided all the music there was. The deities were seen off at the end of the ceremonies. For reasons that are as yet unclear to me, the assistant dressed as a woman did not take part in the invitation of the deities or in seeing them off, while the priest took no part in the rituals at the kitchen stove. I did not hear any performance of the "chicken song," but the villagers present expected it at the session known as the *jianchao* (witnessing the *chao*), when a raw pig was offered to the deities. I was told that the song had been omitted because the priest and the assistant were suffering from sore throats that they had contracted while performing at another ceremony at Cheng Lan Shue Village several days earlier. I noted that there were various sessions in the ceremony related to the ancestors' armies: one session dealt with the "issuing of the token of authority for the recruitment of soldiers" (*fa zhaobing pai*), another with the "recruitment of soldiers" (*zhaobing*), and the third with the "distribution of army provisions" (*san maliang*). I was present also at the earlier ceremony at Cheng Lan Shue, which was an *anlong* ceremony, and I noticed that these three rituals had also been performed at that ceremony.[23]

My subsequent attempts to arrange for making copies of the priest's books were futile, but what I saw at this ceremony, along with my brief interview with the priest and the one memorial I was able to collect, together convince me that the ancestors did have an important role in the fengchao. The priest did quickly show me a document in his books that he referred to as a *chaodie* (certificate for the *chao*), which would suggest that records of ordination names were essential to the ritual. Corroboration of this conclusion may be found in references made to the fengchao in Hakka genealogies in the New Territories.

The genealogy of the Chen surname at She Shan Village, for instance, notes specifically that ordination names (*langming*) are to be remembered for the purpose of preparing documents for use in the fengchao, and it provides a list of such ordination names. The list begins with names of ancestors who cannot be found in any of the four sections in the genealogy. One of the sections begins with ancestor Pujiao, who is on the list and whose name, although not of the *lang* format, was religious in nature and therefore looked upon as an ordination name.[24]

A clearer example in terms of how the name lists relate to the genealogy is the Huang surname genealogy from So Lo Pun Village, which has been noted as a village where the fengchao ceremony was at one time performed. Here, again, there is a list of ordination names, apparently provided for the ceremony. This list begins with the names of an ancestor in the 144th generation and his brother, and they are followed by the names of ancestors from the 145th to the 148th generation, and then an ancestor from the 151st generation and his brother. It is significant that it was the ancestor from the 156th generation, enumerated on the same line, who was, at the time this present genealogy was compiled in 1876, considered the "first ancestor of the Qing dynasty" and from whom a separate enumeration system began, and that it was someone in the 10th generation down the line who was responsible for the compilation. The ancestors named on the fengchao list, therefore, were ancestors from before the present settlement at So Lo Pun. Since the family had moved to this village from Yong'an county, precisely where the *Guangdong xinyu* had noted rituals similar to what I observed in the fengchao, and given the time span occupied by ten generations—say, three hundred years—the ordination name list must have been compiled almost precisely at the time when the *Guangdong xinyu* was written. Significantly, the genealogy also contains a spirit tablet relating to the Lüshan tradition and the Three Ladies (of which more will be said), a passage of invocation, and two talismans.[25]

In the New Territories, the correlation between the use of ordination names in the genealogies and the known occurrence of the fengchao is not restricted to Hakka villages. The first ancestor of the Hou surname of Punti descent was one Hou Wulang, and one segment of the lineage, at Kam Tsin Village, has continued to this day to celebrate the *hongchao* in the New Year. The ancestor of the Peng surname at Fan Ling Village was one Peng Faguang, and Fan Ling is the only other village that still holds the *hongchao*. Observations made at the *hongchao* show that there are many points of similarity between this celebration and the fengchao. The celebration was conducted by priests who claimed affiliation with the Zhengyi tradition, but the officiating priest for the *hongchao* discarded Zhengyi robes and donned a red headdress for this particular ceremony.[26]

The Decline of Magic and
the Rise of Literati Orthodoxy

I have made several references to the Lüshan tradition in relation both to the use of ordination names and to the celebration of the fengchao. Before more is said about the subject, it should be pointed out that, as a result of the extensive diffusion of ritual practices and texts, Daoist traditions in the village context are never found in any pure form, and reference to descent from any Daoist master does not preclude the adoption of practices from rival schools or even a claim of descent from them. In fact, terms that designate traditions of ritual skills and knowledge can come to be so loosely used as to lose any such exclusive association; the evolution of the term *Maoshan* is a well-known example of this process. In the case of the Lüshan tradition, however, although the evidence is admittedly thin, I think the argument may be advanced that its continuation from the thirteenth century or so to the nineteenth had much bearing on the use of ordination names among the Hakka and on the continuation of such practices as the fengchao.

Certainly both the use of numerals in names and the use of the character *lang* in names was, at one time, a fairly common practice and not restricted to ordination names. It is evident in the list of *jinshi* degree winners of the year 1256 that there was in wide use in areas of southern China a system of *di* seniority that assigned to an individual a numeral, often prefixed by a nonnumeric character shared by his brothers.[27] Attention has also been drawn by a Qing scholar to the implication of a passage in the *Yijian zhi*, the well-known Song dynasty miscellany, that to find a person one needs to know the surname and *di* seniority, rather than the surname and given name (*ming*).[28]

The Qing scholar Zhao Yi noted that the character *lang* was used as a title for the sons of officials during the Han dynasty.[29] In the Tang, the same usage is apparent in Han Yu's well-known essay in memory of his brother, styled the Shi'er *lang*. In a short article on commoners' names in the Song and Yuan dynasties, the historian Wu Han cites numerous instances to illustrate the use of numerals in names. In particular, he notes that, from the Song to the Ming, the two characters *xiu* and *lang* were commonly used in names of people of different social background, the character *xiu* being used by the prominent and the character *lang* by people of no consequence.[30] While the general argument that such characters carried social meanings agrees with examples that I have seen, it is possible to show that

Wu Han's argument on the implication of the character *lang*, at least, is probably overdrawn. One need go no further than the *Zhonghua dazidian* to see that the character *lang* was a common term of address with a very wide range of uses, generally indicating some degree of respect toward the person for whom the character was used. One may argue that the implication of the term derived from its meaning in the Han, that is, that as a term of address, it accorded the person on whom it was used the respect fitting for the sons of officials. In this sense, one can understand the following example in the *Yijian zhi*:

> In the southern section of Huzhou city, there was one Xu Liu [Xu No. Six] who sold biscuits and sweetmeats for a living. People called him Xu the Sweet Biscuit. He had some to spare from his daily earnings and so lent money to people in the neighborhood who were in need. As he collected more interest than other people, his family gradually became wealthy. So, he came to be called Xu Liulang.[31]

The argument from Zhao Yi and Wu Han, therefore, is an example of the explanation of social practice by relating it to secular changes. While the argument is plausible as far as their evidence goes, the appearance of these names in Hakka genealogies shows that there could also have been a strong religious element in the proliferation of the practice. For three reasons, an argument based upon secular change alone does not adequately explain the Hakka situation. First, *lang*-style names do not appear with comparable frequency in Cantonese genealogies. Second, there are many examples of *lang*-style names in Hakka genealogies that include a nonnumeric prefix that is identical with the second character of another name of the same person, showing greater affinity with the rules of the Yao than with rules identifiable in Han sources. Third, the use of names in the *fa* style, apparently of the same nature as those of the *lang* style, remains unexplained. In the case of the Hakka, therefore, an argument that links the Hakka practice to the evolution of religious rituals seems particularly plausible.

The earliest record of Hakka ordination in sources other than genealogies already cited here derives from the Ming dynasty. In view of the foregoing, further study is required to see if names in the *lang* format from earlier times represent different usages. However, *lang* is known as a title of sorcerers according to the Tang dynasty compilation *Daodian lun* in the Daoist canon, which quotes *Mingzhen ke*, an earlier work. The information is found in a passage that denounces ritual experts of popular "excessive cults," who called themselves *gu* (for female) and *lang* (for male).[32] Similarly, the use of the character *fa* in a name commonly signified initiation into specialized religious practices. It is in this connection that the particular practices of Lüshan exorcism, whose later patriarchs use names of the *lang* form, seem to relate to the adoption of ordination names.

Probably the earliest mention of the Lüshan Jiulang tradition is a passage about the method of exorcism practiced by sorcerers (*wuzhe*) in the *Sayings of Bai Yuchan*, the famous Daoist who was active in Guangdong, Jiangxi, Zhejiang, and Fujian around 1220.[33] The passage refers to various shamanistic traditions that, even at the time, were considered to have been existing "from the past." The account begins, curiously, with King Suotan, which can be interpreted as a sinicization of Satan. The magic that originated with King Suotan, however, was passed on to King Pangu, who in turn, passed it on to King Asura, then to King Weituoshi, King (of?) Changsha, King Toutuo, Lüshan Jiulang, Mengshan Qilang, Hengshan Shilang, Zhao Hou Sanlang, Zhang Zhao Erlang, and then "countless others." Of the names on this most interesting list, only Lüshan Jiulang, Zhao Hou Sanlang, and Zhang Zhao Erlang appear in the Cantonese and Hakka priestly manuals. The same may be said for the Yao ritual manuals found in Qujiang county in Guangdong province and in Guangxi, but the Yao manual from Liannan does refer to King Asura, King Toutuo, and King Changsha as well.[34]

Strickmann has suggested that the appearance of the name Suotan on the list attests to the influence of Manichaeism in southeastern China.[35] It should be noted, however, that a separate passage is included in the *Sayings* on Manichaeism (referred to as *chicai shimo*) that does not make any mention of the magic practiced by the "sorcerers."[36] Pangu was, obviously, known as a southern deity and ancestral figure. King Asura's presence, no doubt, represents a Persian influence via Buddhist connections. It would seem, then, that Bai's list begins with names that appear foreign and continues with those that seemed closer to home. King (or Kings) Changsha (or the King of Changsha) would have referred to historical characters from Han times, the first King of Changsha being Wu Rui. The King of Weituoshi, interpreted by Strickmann as the Buddhist deity Wei Tuo (Skanda), could just as well have been Wei Tuo, better known as Zhao Tuo, a contemporary of Wu Rui and the troop commander who conquered Guangdong on behalf of the Qin dynasty.

For our purposes what is significant is that the pattern of the names on the list changes after King Toutuo, whom we cannot identify. The names are of two sorts. The first sort incorporates what appears to be the name of a mountain, a numeral, and then the character *lang*. The other sort begins with two surname characters, a numeral, and then the character *lang*. It is this last pattern that resembles the names that appear in Hakka genealogies. Bai has left no clue as to how he came across the list. However, if it can be assumed that what he described was fairly close to the local traditions with which he came into contact, the naming would reflect, first, a clear awareness of the tracing of a line of descent in religious powers from Lüshan Jiulang to his eventual disciples Zhao Hou Sanlang and Zhang Zhao Erlang, and second, the prevalence of the use of the -*lang* suffix appended to a numeral character in names among the masters of this particular line of descent. It is this numeral-cum-*lang* suffix that appears again in the Hakka genealogies, possibly from the time when, as far as we can document, the fengchao became a common ceremony.

The appeal to Lüshan Jiulang or his disciples Zhang Hou Sanlang and Zhang Zhao Erlang is quite common in ritual texts that have been found among the Yao, the Hakka, and also the Punti—this last in the New Territories of Hong Kong. The claim of descent from Lüshan Jiulang also appears sometimes in association with the cult of the Linshui *furen*, known otherwise as Chen Jinggu, one of the Three Ladies. In the Ming work the *Sanjiao yuanliu soushen daquan*, the compendium to popular deities believed to have circulated in Fujian, Chen Jinggu is noted as having learned her skills from Lüshan, and the accompanying illustration to her biographical entry shows a man in Daoist costume holding a horn standing in front of her, which is characteristic of the vernacular "Daoist" traditions.[37] Material from Taiwan and from the Yao also links Lüshan Jiulang to Xu Xun, of the Jin dynasty (third century). It is significant that these names appear as a recognizable conglomerate, even when the texts in which they appear would seem to have evolved substantially over the years and to have blended thoroughly numerous ritual traditions.

Appeal to these deities (Lüshan Jiulang and Chen Jinggu), among others, is closely related to a tradition of religious rituals that have variously been identified as the Redhead or the vernacular. At least in the New Territories of Hong Kong, enough has been said to indicate that the continuity of such a tradition within the village community might have been maintained in two separate ways, that is, through communal observance at festivals and through the continued invocation of ordained ancestors in rituals. Insofar as we can document it—in the New Territories, at least—it seems that where the tradition was continued, the fengchao was periodically held in the village and ordained specialists were found for the celebration. Ordination names are not commonly found in the genealogies of Punti villages in which the *nammo* priests were hired. The few cases where the *hongchao* may be documented, and where ordination names were found, probably represent the blurring of ethnic boundaries.

Until much more is known about the evolution of priestly practice within the Hakka traditions, the argument must remain tentative. But Lüshan Jiulang and his disciples do occupy important roles as patriarchs of the priestly traditions of the Hakka and the Punti.

In the fengchao memorial, the Hakka *sang* ritual expert calls himself a follower of the doctrine of the Three Pure Ones, who are known to us as the highest deities of Daoism since the Song dynasty. He appeals first to the Jade Emperor and the Taishang Laojun, and subsequently to a list of other deities, starting with Wangmu and Lüshan Jiulang and with Ladies Chen, Lin, and Li in the fifth position. It is clear that Wangmu and Lüshan Jiulang are two major sources of power in the *sang* tradition, because in response to my questions about them, the *sang* priest responded with the following parallelism:

> Wangmu catches ghosts [*shougui*],
> Lüshan expels evil influences [*zhixie*].

Moreover, in the ritual manual for Issuing the Token for Recruitment of Soldiers, the recruitment officer, whose name, Chen Lianglang, is similar in form to the Hakka ordination names, is addressed as a "disciple of Lüshan" (Lüshan *menxia*). The only evidence that can be found to support a *sang* specialist's claim of being Daoist, at least in the case of Mr. Miao, is the inclusion of Daoist deities in the list of deities to invite and the chanting of three volumes of the *Sanyuan Repentance Scripture* during the *anlong* ceremony. The rest of his ritual repertoire is mostly in the colloquial style, except for some Buddhist hymns converted not very thoroughly by substituting some Buddhist terms with Daoist ones.

More is known of the Punti *nammo* priests of the New Territories of Hong Kong. In their case, canonical Daoism has deeper influence, especially in their ritual performances in *jiao* festivals and funeral services. Exorcism and curing services, in which appeals to Lüshan, Wangtaimu, and the Three Ladies are made, have almost disappeared amid the cultural changes of the last few decades. But these elements were clearly important in the tradition of the Punti *nammo* priests. It appears that the deity Wangmu in the Hakka tradition is the same as Wangtaimu and different from the better-known Daoist deity Wangmu. The Wangtaimu is known to have subdued the ghosts or evil spirits of "six caves," both in the Punti tradition and in a magic spell recorded in the mountainous southwestern parts of Zhejiang province.[38]

One of the Punti priests, Mr. Lam Pui, whom I interviewed several times, remembered certain ritual elements that suggested close resemblance to the Hakka *sang*. He could not help laughing when telling me that in the *hongchao* ritual as it was performed at one Punti village, one of the priests had to dress himself as a woman and offer tea to the villagers representing the community. Some of the deities invited to the *hongchao* ceremony, he admitted, did not belong to the Daoist orthodoxy (*zhengdao*). In connection with these heterodox elements he mentioned the feat of climbing sword ladders, and said that it was part of a practice known to him as *soey*. I do not know how the character for this term is written, but in Punti it is a homophone of *shui* (water), of the expression *dushui* in the records of Hakka ordination cited above, and it appears that in the Hakka case too, the use of *shui* (water) was only an attempt to record the pronunciation.

According to Lam Pui, his great-great-grandfather (or great-grandfather?), who had been to Daoist Heavenly Master's headquarters at Lunghu Shan, took a vow against the *soey* practice. Since then, Lam said, his family had practiced orthodox Daoism (*zhengdao*) only. What I observed of what he performed did not quite live up to the claim, and on other occasions he admitted and indeed attempted to justify certain departures from orthodoxy. The claim is probably more significant for its implication that his family was not as discriminating before. On another occasion he provided the following justification for inviting the heterodox deities in the ceremonies: the orthodox deities were too preoccupied with the pursuit of the Dao and immortality and did not concern themselves with the pragmatic well-being of the community, therefore the deities of Maoshan and Lüshan were to be invited to drive away evil spirits from the village, while the orthodox deities who were invited in the first rite in the series kept an eye on the eccentrically inclined heterodox deities lest they bring harm.

Similar attempts at integrating conceptually canonical Daoism with a ritual tradition that appeals to Lüshan and Maoshan deities can be found in a manuscript handbook entitled the *Daojiao yuanliu*. Punti priests, including Lam Pui, often referred to the manual in response to my questions, saying that the answer was in the manual. The manual provides more evidence of the importance of Wangmu and Lüshan in the Punti priests' tradition.[39] The handbook deserves translation in full, but for the purposes of this essay, a summary will have to suffice. Briefly, it gives an account of the sources of the priests' authority, including short statements on the attributes of their masters, the deities, and the ritual objects that had to be used in ceremonies—all presented as part of a coherent theology.

In a section that explains "the use, name, and meaning of Daoist ritual implements," the handbook divides the repertoire of "Daoist" rituals into three categories: the *zhengyi jiao* rituals, the *lingbao* funeral services, and the *hunyuan* for exorcism and appeal for blessings. It is in the description of the ritual implements of the latter category, such as the ritual knife, the red headdress, and the straw mat, that claims of connection with Wangmu and the Lüshan deities are made.

The most significant section of the book for our purposes is an essay entitled "Daotong yongchuan," which gives an account of practices descended from different masters. According to the "Daotong yongchuan," there were four different schools of practices that might bring fortune or avert misfortune. The first kind, referred to as *shi* (gentlemen) wearing yellow headdress and feather garments, consisted of followers of a tradition starting from the Yellow Emperor and derived its authority from the Heavenly Emperor. These *shi* "of the yellow headdress and feather garments" were responsible for holding the *jiao*. The other three varieties of religious specialists are all referred to as *wu* (sorcerers).

Of the three kinds of wu, there seems to be a less than subtle grading, the first two being *daowu* (sorcerers of the Dao), and the last simply wu. The first kind of wu prayed for fortune by practices that involved the celestial constellations, while the second kind practiced *fa* (magic), making use of *fu* (talismans) and *zhou* (chants). The skills of the *daowu*, like those of the *shi*, were ultimately derived from ceremonies that had been used by the Yellow Emperor and the Jade Emperor themselves (both being included among the Five Emperors). The last variety of wu, however, were persons who were involved in rites of exorcism. These wu were originally summoned by the grandson of the Yellow Emperor (himself a member of the Five Emperors by one reckoning) to drive away the ghosts that had been spreading disease and harming his son. Practices learned from these wu, therefore, unlike the other practices, were not fitting for the Five Emperors themselves and, by implication, were practices of a lower order.

The typology of religious powers in the "Daotong yongchuan" is followed by an account of the history of these practices. The history consists of the identification of the masters whose practices contributed to the repertoire of later practitioners and a loose grouping of those masters into various lines of descent. Laozi, it is acknowledged, is the founding master (*daozu*) of all, but following him were the Perfected (Zhenren) Hongfan, who produced the *Daode jing*; Yinshan (whose contribution is not specified); Kangfou, who controlled epidemics; the master (*fashi*) Yunshan, described elsewhere in the book as master of Maoshan, who "by a shout could turn reeds into swords and broken blades of grass into soldiers"; and so on. These were all "masters" (*zushi*) of the Daoist tradition.

If the inclusion of the Maoshan magicians among the antecedents of the Daoist tradition is unexpected, the distinction between heterodoxy and orthodoxy is further blurred in the subsequent section, which continues with powers emanating from Wang Taimu and from Lüshan Jiulang, whose practice was said to be akin to Maoshan and Xueshan. The list continues with the Three Ladies (the *sannai* or *sanwei furen*), Chen, Lin, and Li, who are said to have learned their skills from Wang Taimu. They are followed by Tianhou, Guanyin, and (only after all these) a Daoist called "The Grand Master of the Great Mystery" (Xuanzhong dafashi), now said to have led Emperor Xuanzong of the Tang dynasty on his visit up to the heavens.[40] The section then continues with Zhang Zhao Sanlang and Zhang Zhao Wulang, disciples of Lüshan Jiulang.

The conclusion of the passage, however, does not accept the incorporation of all these sources into one tradition. It states:

Thereafter, knowledge of the *Dao* [*daoxue*] divides and sorcerers [*shiwu*] proliferate. The teachings of the Yellow Emperor and Laozi continue together, and the methods [*fa*] of the *nainiang* also emerge. What is followed is evil teachings [*xiejiao*], and rarely is the correct *dao* [*zhengdao*] practiced. For this reason, later people blindly worship [*mifeng*] the bureau of exorcism [*quxie zhi yuan*], and this is the source of dances to drive out ghosts [*tiaogui*] at night.

To emphasize the point, the passage continues with the statement that at the time of Laozi, the many sorts of wayward sorcerers (*yaowu*) were not needed for ceremonies of disaster aversion (*rangzai*), praying to the bushel (*gaodou*), requesting good fortune (*qingfu*), or acting out the canon (*yanjing*); this statement is followed by another list of deities from whom protection might be sought, some of whom do not appear more orthodox than Lüshan Jiulang or the Three Ladies.

Nainiang probably refers to the Three Ladies, who are known alternatively as Chen Lin Li *nai*. The full name of the Bureau of Exorcism, supplied elsewhere in the handbook, is Pole Star (Beiji) Bureau of Exorcism, whose members include Xuantian shangdi, the Three Ladies (*sanwei furen*), and, finally, the four generals/marshals named in canonical sources as members of the Pole Star Bureau of Exorcism. Rather than as a rejection of "heterodox" elements in general, I see the foregoing as the rejection of the Three Ladies and the associated Bureau of Exorcism alone. Various facts suggest that the Lüshan and Wang Taimu tradition was well established before the cult of the Three Ladies came to this part of south China.

The *nammo* priests recognize a small difference in style (tune and words) between *hongchao* rites and *tiaogui* exorcism. There are some curious ritual implements that are found only in the rite of *hongchao*. And in the set of *hongchao* manuals collected from the New Territories, appeal is made to a Zhang Sanlang—probably a shortened form of Zhang Zhao Sanlang of Huainan, that is, one of the two masters referred to commonly as Zhang Zhao Erlang—and to Wang Taimu, but there is no explicit mention of the Three Ladies.

The inclusion of the fengchao celebration among the Punti would have been acceptable to their Daoist priests, as part of one of the many traditions well established in their practices. Nevertheless, the influence of ordination on naming is seen in the genealogies within Hakka communities but not in those of the Punti communities. How to explain the difference is a question whose answer must be sought partly in the reception, by successive generations, of rituals and religious texts that might have been associated with ceremonies such as the fengchao, and partly in the particular manner, or timing, in which written genealogies were compiled. It would seem necessary to assume that ordination names would have been entered in the written genealogies only if they had already been preserved in written records, such as ordination certificates, before the compiling of genealogies became the dominant practice in lineage building. The gradual decline of ordination would not, therefore, have implied discontinuation of the tradition as religious practice within the lineage, but rather that the practice was considered to be outside the proper lineage rituals. What we observe, therefore, was not the decline of magic as such but the redefinition and restriction of one set of rituals, so that room might be found for another.

If the argument here is correct, the use of *langming*, *faming*, and *duming* in Hakka genealogies represents the retention of practices that were not only common but, because of the connection with the ancestors that was set up via the fengchao, were elements of the lineage before the written genealogy became popular. The abandonment of these names in the written genealogies in favor of names more common in the literati style represented the acknowledgment of the supremacy of a new tradition. This tradition did not create the Hakka lineage, but showed it in a light that made the Hakka more akin to the orthodox literati tradition and that much closer to what was becoming a uniform society.

A turret at Chong Kou, a village in the sands south of Shawan, built during the Republican period (1989)

Village in the sands south of Shawan. Straw huts are still used as dwellings (1991).

Old woman wearing typical style of dress found in the sands, Shawan, Panyu (1991)

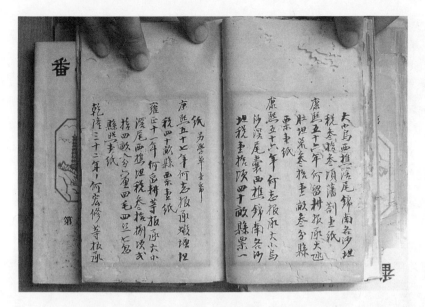

Document entitled "Liugeng ge shatian zhi" recording acquisitions of river marshes by the He lineage during the Qing (photographed 1989)

A typical landscape (Chaolian xiang near Tianma, Xinhui) showing layers of settlement as the sands were reclaimed. Note the large cluster of older houses with their backs to a hill, and the layer of more recent houses built along the dikes. Fields and fish ponds are closer to the river (1991).

A social club of local powerholders during the Republican period, Shawan, Panyu (1991)

Notes on the Territorial
Connections of the Dan

YE XIAN'EN

THE historical evidence on the Dan boat people clearly shows that they were closely connected to territorial administration from at least the Ming dynasty. According to the description of the Dan in the 1561 *Records of Guangdong Province*, which is repeated in numerous later records,

From the early Hongwu, [the Dan] were registered in households under the *lizhang*. They paid the fish tax [*yuke*] annually to the river-mooring stations [*hebosuo*]. However, [the Dan] people are peculiar in that people of the same surname intermarry, in that they do not wear hats or shoes, and are foolish, illiterate, and ignorant of their ages. Many of these people are found particularly in Dongguan, Zengcheng, Xinhui, Xiangshan, and even Huizhou and Chaozhou. They are less numerous in Leizhou and Qiongzhou. In recent years, those who live in the center of Guangdong are beginning to learn to read. [Some] have moved ashore and, having attached themselves to registered households, are themselves registered in the same way as commoners. There are even some who have succeeded in the examinations. However, most of the places where they have set up stilt nets [*zengmen*] have been taken over by force by powerful families, and many Dan people are also robbers.[1]

Derogatory comments aside, this passage records three observations on the Dan: first, that they were registered in the *lijia*, but under their special demeaned status; second, that although the Dan people were known to be boat-dwellers, they were affected by claims to land rights extended to the foreshores where they operated; and third, that over the years some Dan people did integrate into land communities.

Supplementary notes attached to the passage, citing the *Local History of Huizhou Prefecture*, spell out how the Dan were registered in Huizhou prefecture and in Xingning county. In both cases, headmen were appointed

Translated by David Faure

and registered. In Huizhou they were known as *danjia lizhang*, and in Xingning, as *jiashou* (head of the *jia*). Within Huizhou, in Guishan county, the Dan lived and dressed like other natives and intermarried with people from subservient households (*xiahu*), but were registered at the river-mooring stations. In Xingning, they were registered within one district (*du*) under their own registered headmen (*jiashou*), but their taxes were registered at the river-mooring station.

These passages are reproduced almost in their entirety in the entry on Guangdong province in Gu Yanwu's *Tianxia junguo libingshu* (The strengths and ills of all regions in the realm). In addition, he notes under the entry on Huizhou that there were two kinds of Dan people in this prefecture, bamboo-basket weavers and fishing households, and that the weavers were registered for tax in Dongguan county and the fishing households, in Guishan.[2]

Corroboration for these observations may be found in Ming and Qing records. Qu Dajun recorded in the *Guangdong xinyu* (New items relating to Guangdong) numerous passages on the livelihood of the Dan. Under the entry on "Dan boats," he noted:

The Guangzhou river-mooring stations include a quota for Dan households. They are registered in nineteen categories, incorporating the big *zeng*-stakes, the small *zeng*-stakes, the hand *zeng*-stakes, the *zeng*-stake inlet, bamboo *bo*-stakes, bamboo-basket *bo*-stakes, open *bo*-stakes, big *bo*-stakes, small *bo*-stakes, big river *bo*-stakes, small river *bo*-stakes, the *bo*-stake with its back to the wind, the square net, the centrifugal net, the circular net, the bamboo *duo* [boat?], the cloth *duo*, the fish basket, the crab basket, the big *gu* net, and the bamboo *gang* net. Every year, each household is enumerated and each boat reckoned so that it may be assessed the fish tax. They [the Dan households] are therefore regarded as commoners. The Dan are also gradually learning to read, and some have lived ashore in villages. To the west of Guangzhou, Zhoudun and Lindun are such villages. However, good families do not intermarry with them, because they are fierce and are prone to become robbers, often forming a menace in places near the rivers.[3]

Because the precise fishing methods of the Dan are not known, it is difficult to render with precision the nineteen categories that were established for the purpose of registering them. However, it is significant that with hardly any exception, they were not descriptions of boats but of fishing methods—in some cases, obviously, methods that required setting up stake-nets on the shoreline. In a separate passage on the planting of the *bo*-stakes to the west of Guangdong, Qu records that unless the Dan people possessed their own boats as they planted these stakes, it would have been unprofitable for the stakes to be maintained, implying, it would seem, that the

Dan boats would have harvested from stake-nets planted in different places. The same passage confirms that the stakes were taxed.

The published literature of the Qing on the geography and customs of Guangdong after the *Guangdong xinyu* adds little to the passages cited. However, descriptions of the Dan can be found in various legal documents that have been preserved for reference as legal precedents in Guangdong. The most important legal document on the Dan is certainly the Yongzheng emperor's edict of 1729. The edict summarizes the cohabitation of Dan and commoners in coastal areas, acknowledges the discrimination against the Dan, and guarantees their right to live on shore. It reads:

In Guangdong, aside from the four people [*simin*], there is a kind of people known as the Dan household. They are similar to the Yao and the Man. They make their homes on boats, and earn their livelihood from fishing. Dan boats are found in all the waterways of the province, and the population is so large that it cannot be enumerated. The people of Guangdong regard the Dan as people of the mean sort and forbid them from living on shore. The Dan people are also afraid of holding out against the commoners, and in fear of their strength, they [the Dan] bear [their dominance] in silence. They squat in their boats, and for their entire lives fail to gain the happiness that derives from peaceful settlement. This is pitiable. The Dan are originally commoners of good standing, and there is no reason to despise them. Moreover, they pay the fish tax and are of one body with other people. How can they be made to wander without peace as a result of local customary practices? The governor-general [of Guangdong] is hereby ordered to instruct his officials to post notices throughout that Dan households that are incapable [of moving ashore] may at their convenience continue to live on their boats and are not forced to move ashore, but that those capable of building houses and sheds are allowed to live in villages near the water and may be included in the household registers along with ordinary people. Powerful families and local agitators may not upon any excuse bully them or drive them away. Officials are to be instructed to persuade the Dan people to develop wasteland, to cultivate, and to become the fundamental support of society that farmers are [*wuben zhi ren*]. In this way, they will fit in with my intention to treat all my people equally.[4]

Various legal documents may be found in a manuscript collection now held at the University of British Columbia. Essentially, with one exception, these documents deal with the rights of Dan people in exploiting coastal inlets in the early Qianlong period (mid-eighteenth century). The general principle is stated in a report made by the Guangdong provincial treasurer in 1737:

It is recommended that . . . all stations [*bu*] on the coast be investigated in detail. In those cases where the persons in charge [*guan*] possess as evidence stamped deeds of sale and receipts for tax payment, the control [of the inlets] should be retained by them. Those [inlets] the control of which is not demonstrated by evidence are to be noted and put under the charge of Dan people of the area. If there are no Dan people, then they should be placed under the collective charge of nearby villagers.[5]

Whether or not the ruling was put into practice, it demonstrates that there was much dispute over territorial rights between established families and the Dan people—in this case, in relation to the places where stake-nets might be set up.

The one document in this collection that does not relate to land rights on the foreshore discusses the status of the Dan. This ruling by the Guangdong legal commissioner in 1746 is given the title "Dan people who put themselves under the protection of powerful households in the Ming are to be permitted to assume the status of commoners in good standing and not to be addressed as bonded servants [shipu] and continued to be dealt with as mean people." In this document, the commissioner noted:

Dan households were originally fishermen. In the Ming dynasty, many sought to preserve their lives by putting themselves under the protection of powerful people. For many years, because it has been difficult for them to make a living, many have continued to allow these powerful people to seize them and order them around. It is necessary to issue the instruction that all counties post the notice to the effect that [Dan people] who many years ago had put themselves under protection [of the powerful], who are not fed by the households of their masters, and who for a long time have lived outside and made their own living, be allowed to become persons of good standing and not to be addressed as bonded servants.[6]

It is significant that the instruction, coming shortly after the 1729 edict, was worded not to include all Dan people who held bondservant status, but only those whose status might, with the passage of time, have lapsed. It is implicit in the document that not only were many Dan subservient by virtue of their being Dan, but that by putting themselves under protection, they were also under obligation to designated masters or master households. The Dan people were not less subservient after the 1729 edict, as is well known from documentation on them into the Republican period. What the edict was intended to achieve was the integration of those Dan people of better means who had moved ashore.

An instance of social integration that might have been covered by the edict may be found in a legal precedent of 1825 included in the *Yuedong chengan chubian* (First edition of legal precedents in Guangdong). The legal principle illustrated by the case is indicated in the title that it is given: "Descendants of Dan households who three generations after they have given up their former practices have acquired the licentiate status [*qian-sheng*] by donation, whose sisters nevertheless are married into Dan house-holds, are to be expelled and caned." The details of the case are as follows:

Liang Jinrong is a *danhu* [Dan householder] of Xinhui county. The household has since Qianlong year 20 [1755], when his ancestor went with his family there, lived as outsiders [*jiju*] in Dianbai county. No report has been made to officials con-cerning any change of occupation. His sisters are both married to danhu, Zhou Shihuan and Zhou Yajiu, who still pursue the polluted occupation. In the Fourth Month of Jiaqing year 21 [1816], because he has left his original registration for a long time, and because he seeks honor and glory, Liang Jinrong changed his name to Liang Duokui, and following established regulations, donated the funds needed at the provincial treasury for the title of a licentiate. He was given a certificate for this title. Subsequently, the provincial governor discovered upon investigation that Liang Jinrong, knowing that he himself was a danhu, and having found no one to enter collective surety on his behalf, had furnished the information that he had come from a commoner's family in good standing [*shenjia qingbai*] and for names of persons offering collective surety provided the names of nonexistent persons, Liang Wenxiong and Huang Ying, as neighbors and lineage members. This case was on record at the county. Subsequent to that, student Chen Shanben and others learned that Liang Jinrong was a danhu and had against regulations made false claims for the purpose of his donation, and brought charges against him at the county. Liang Jinrong was placed under arrest, and the plaintiffs had been sum-moned to testify. They testified and it was found that Liang Jinrong had changed his name to Liang Duokui for the purpose of making a donation toward his title. The regulations were clear and demanded his expulsion and trial. According to the details furnished by the county in this trial of him as a criminal, Liang Jinrong was personally a danhu, who since Qianlong year 20 when his ancestor moved with his family to Dianbai, had lived ashore as an outsider. As a third-generation descen-dant, who has not reported any change of occupation to the officials, whose sisters are both married to danhu such as Zhou Shihuan who are still pursuing the pol-luted occupation, that Liang Jinrong should dare by false pretense to donate for the licentiate title is against the regulations. Liang Jinrong is, in accordance with the regulations governing false pretenses by descendants of prostitutes and actors who change their names for the purpose of obtaining a title, to have his title re-moved and, in accordance with the punishment by the law of being beaten one hundred strokes by the pole, be given the remitted sentence of forty strokes.[7]

What is significant in this judgment is that the sentence was not based on the fraudulent claims alone but also on the fact that, three generations after the family had moved on shore, the change of occupation had not been reported to the officials. That and the fact that the sisters were married to Dan people were reasons enough for the culprit to be treated as another Dan. It is true that the Dan held land, but it must also be true that unless his status was recognized by both his neighbors and the state, his integration into commoner society remained precarious.

It would seem from these documents that the claims that Dan people might make to territorial rights—to places where they planted stake-nets, moored, or perhaps even moved ashore for settlement—must be treated separately from the acceptance of the Dan people in land communities.[8] This distinction is apparent in Chen Xujing's study of the Dan people's dwellings in the early 1930s. Chen found that these dwellings might be classified as brick houses, wooden houses on stakes, wooden houses on rafts, and boats. Those Dan people who lived in brick houses were de facto land residents. However, all continued to maintain boats, and some might even have regarded the houses as secondary residences.[9] As one would expect, there was no sharp divide between living on land and living on water; there was, rather, a continuum, and at no stage would territoriality have been completely irrelevant.

Notes and Impressions of the Cheung Chau Community

JAMES HAYES

WHEN serving as district officer, South/Islands in Hong Kong's New Territories between 1957 and 1962, I usually spent the lunar New Year period at the District Office bungalow on the island with my family. During the festival, all members of the Cheung Chau Rural Committee used to come in a body to the house to pay a courtesy call and to express their best wishes for the coming year. It was a large committee, on which the leaders of the various resident landsmen's groups were well represented, and practically anyone who was anybody on the island was a member or had been co-opted as an adviser. That is, save for the boat people in the anchorage. In management matters, they did not count, as I shall explain.

Through contacts made at that time, I was able to learn about Cheung Chau's diversified community and its organizations, along with their origins and history. The Rural Committee itself, although a newly established organization, had venerable antecedents. It was the direct lineal successor to the former Cheung Chau Kaifong (*jiefang*, street association), a managerial body for the community at large whose continuous history can be traced back at least to the middle of the nineteenth century. During the three-and-a-half-year wartime occupation by the Japanese (1941–45), under changes made by the military government in the captured territory, the Kaifong had seemingly been displaced by another body, styled the Cheung Chau Residents Association. However, this was merely the old Kaifong under a new name; it appears to have operated under the same leadership and to have remained the owner and manager of all the property accumulated by the Kaifong in the past to defray the various expenses incurred in carrying out its various duties in the public interest.

The Rural Committee had been established in 1960. Indeed, as district officer of the day I had had a lot to do with its formation, through canvassing and negotiating support for the establishment of the new body. Only after considerable effort, and with some compromise over the committee's composition, had it been possible to hold elections in accordance with an officially imposed but locally accepted constitution. These elections had ended the five-year hiatus due to the withdrawal of official recognition from the Cheung Chau Residents Association in 1954. Recognition had been withdrawn in response to unauthorized preelection changes to the constitution by the association's officeholders in a bid for electoral advantage at a time of continuing rivalry within the leadership.[1] In the interim, the Cheung Chau Chamber of Commerce had carried out the managerial duties of the Residents Association with the recognition and support of the New Territories District Administration.

Despite the general support for our efforts to replace the Residents Association with the Rural Committee, I was unable to arrange for the transfer of funds and property from the older management body to the new, owing to the unwillingness of the association's leaders to allow the transfer and the lack of legal powers to require it. Recognized or not, the Residents Association had clung to life, able to perform some of its former functions—such as management of the Fong Pin (*fangbian*) hospital and dying house—by refusing to turn over the public property to the Rural Committee.[2] On the other hand, management of the boat shed used to store the three dragon boats raced by the local boat population each year, hitherto in the hands of the Residents Association, had been transferred to the fishermen's representative on the new committee.

The partisan behavior inside the Residents Association that had led to the withdrawal of official recognition highlights the factional and personal feuding to which the island community was at all times subject. Besides the animosities and rivalries between individual leaders that affected their public and working relationships,[3] the mixed composition of the land population and the continuance of old antipathies between its various groups complicated the work and functioning of the Kaifong and its managers; even so, the very difficulties of the situation seem to have been a challenge and an inspiration for some of their number over the years.

A Diverse Population on Land and Sea

On land, nineteenth- and early twentieth-century Cheung Chau was noteworthy for the variety of settlement among a population that by 1911 numbered no more than a few thousand.[4] The most numerous as well as probably the earliest among its settlers over the previous few centuries were Hoklos (Fujianese, *fulao*) from northeast Guangdong. Coming first into local waters as seasonal fishermen, they came by degrees to settle on the island. Although living on land, they maintained their connection with the sea, which, after generations of settlement there, still provided their principal livelihood even into the 1950s. Some among them also worked as marine hawkers in the anchorage, selling vegetables and other commodities to the Tanka (*danjia*) families living on their fishing boats. Others became shopkeepers and businessmen on the island, catering to their own people, to the local boat population, and to visiting craft from the wider area, and setting up businesses as varied as shrimp paste manufacturing and ropewalks. Their leaders established the Beidi Temple (1783) and built a clubhouse that also served as a school.

However, sustained population growth continuing throughout the nineteenth century brought linguistic diversity and some cultural differences to the island community. The 1911 census shows that Punti (Cantonese, *bendi*) speakers outnumbered the Hoklo residents by more than two to one.[5] By then, the land population included many people from other parts of Guangdong province, from equally long-settled groups that were different in language and customs from the Hoklo residents. These were especially to be found among the local shopkeepers and businesspeople who, unlike the Hoklos, had mostly been attracted to Cheung Chau by its favorable location on the trade routes and the many opportunities available in all lines of retail and wholesale business connected with the boat people and the fishing industry.

Inquiries among old persons indicate that in a place like Cheung Chau, with a lot of coming and going in the region, there was a degree of assimilation in individual cases. One of the Hoklo elders (born in 1885) was by descent a Punti from Dapeng City, in eastern Xin'an; but, living among Hoklos and sharing the same occupation (a sea fisherman), and with a Hoklo mother and wife, he, the first settler's grandson, had become one with them, regarding the Hoklo dialect as his natural speech.

By the early twentieth century, the Tanka boat population outnumbered the land residents. People in this major group lived their lives entirely on water; only in death did they move ashore. Whole families lived on board their craft, which varied from the largest seagoing trawlers to the sampans that fished only in local waters.[6] A leading shopkeeper and old Kaifong told me that the four types of fishing craft using the Cheung Chau anchorage before the Pacific War (1941–45) had between twenty to forty or fifty persons of all ages on board, the number depending on size. Whole families lived on their boats, including old people, many children—since very few went to school—and a few hired hands.

At the 1911 colony census, the floating population of the Cheung Chau census district was stated to be 4,442, and at the next decennial count it was 3,550.[7] The census officer for the latter census said that the count in the New Territories was not as satisfactory as that for the urban boat population, "as it must be remembered that at Tai O and Cheung-chow a large proportion of the fishing fleet is at sea at any given time."[8] At other times, the number would have been swelled by boats from other districts, come to off-load fish and take on supplies.[9] There was much coming and going among the fishing craft, and indeed generally.[10] After the British takeover, the Hong Kong harbor master's new out-station on the island recorded the number of arrivals and clearances in the anchorage and the number of licenses and permits issued, and some figures are provided in official reports.[11]

A good description of the Tanka boat people is given in the Hong Kong Annual Report for 1938, by which time little had changed:

To these [junks] they have confined their entire lives for generations, regarding them not only as their sole means of support but also as their only home. The fact that there are some 100,000 persons living in 5,500 boats, the largest of which does not exceed 85 feet in length, and the majority of which are less than 60 feet long shows the extent of the overcrowding to which their traditional occupation subjects them. A boat of 70 feet in length provides space for the accommodation of 40 to 45 persons of all ages, besides space for fish, salt, gear, food and miscellaneous cargo. The average earning capacity of a single able-bodied fisherman is $70 per annum. This general low standard of living combined with the hidebound allegiance to a centuries-old tradition has prevented the infiltration of modern methods and the adoption of modern appliances.[12]

However, as in other places, the interdependence of the land and sea populations and their daily intercourse in business matters did not lead to social fusion. The two communities kept to themselves.[13] This even applied to the long-established land-based Hoklo fishermen's families and marine hawkers. From my interviews with their old people, it was obvious that Hoklo of this group regarded themselves as totally distinct from the Tanka fishermen. The difference lay in the fact that, though the sea provided a lifelong occupation, the Hoklos were essentially landsmen, mostly congregated at Pak She near their own Beidi Temple. The style of fishing was also different. The Hoklo boats ("over a hundred when I was young," said a man born in 1894) went out for only a few hours at a time, and, significantly, "no rice was [cooked and] eaten on board" (according to a man born in 1885).

In the Hong Kong region, the existence of groups of sea fishermen other than Tanka was quite common. I encountered a degree of occupational blurring in my widespread inquiries. On nearby Peng Chau, both Cantonese and Hakka villagers undertook sea fishing from boats, as did many of the families in some of the Hakka coastal villages of Tsuen Wan. However, in all such cases, it is important to note that occupational blurring did not mean social intercourse or intermarriage between these land-based fishermen, who clung to their own kind, and the Tanka.[14]

With the rest of the land population, the land-sea dichotomy must have been even more marked. Any melding was the result of a one-way traffic open to very few. The only means open to Tanka to rise to social and political influence on land was by engaging in business and becoming wealthy, as some among them were reported to have done in the lifetime of my elderly informants.[15] Then, and then only, could they attain membership of the Kaifong committee, which in local landsmen's eyes was surely the supreme manifestation of success.

Perhaps as a result of this long-established social divide, the Tanka boat people of Cheung Chau were excluded from participation in the organization and ritualistic elements of the *jiao* festival. They were also excluded from any say in the political arena, that is, in the management of the island's affairs.[16] In keeping with what was clearly old practice, this will to exclude the Tanka came to the fore during the discussions with local leaders that led up to the formation of the new Rural Committee in 1960. The floating population, indigenous or not, was not included in the islandwide electoral roll. And while the constitution approved by the New Territories District Administration provided for two representatives from among the boat people to be appointed by the district officer to the General Assembly of 39 members and one to the 17-man Executive Committee, these men could not vote on matters not pertaining to the boat people that might come up for discussion in either body. They were basically observers.[17]

At the same time, we must take into account several factors that made such practices rather different from mere discrimination. The boat people lived in a completely different environment, as reflected in their occupations, customs, and lifestyle. Moreover, their numbers were at all times subject to fluctuation, according to the seasons and the fortunes of the catch. Even as late as 1960, it would not have been realistic to include them in an organization that was mainly concerned with the management of a land-based community. At the same time, it is wrong to think of them as universally poor and downtrodden. Some Tanka trawler owners were comparatively rich, and a run of good catches could put a good deal of money in their crewmen's hands.[18]

Separate Loyalties, Intergroup Rivalries, and Ill Feeling

The resident land population of nineteenth-century Cheung Chau was particularly noteworthy for its highly segmented organizational development. By 1898, there were established communities of Cantonese speakers from the nearby counties of Xin'an and Dongguan and others from the more distant Siyi complex in the southwest part of the province.[19] Each of these groups provided its own mutual help association and clubhouse; and, as in the case of the older Hoklo population, their separate identities had been preserved and perpetuated by their having named each of the district societies for its own area.[20]

The premises of the district associations were to be found in the streets from which they drew their membership. This was no coincidence, since the different sections of the population had tended to settle in separate parts of the residential and business areas of the growing township.[21] In time, as the numbers in each locality increased, this would lead to the establishment of street offices and associations.[22]

Offsetting the undoubted assistance and mutual support that the district associations provided to fellow countrymen, their existence as important elements in the organizational structure of the community must also have served to accentuate and solidify linguistic and cultural differences among the mixed population. They did nothing to discourage divisive and separate loyalties, since each of the groups remained distinct and self-directing. Socially and politically speaking, their members had very little in common. Other than a self-interested need for cooperation in the maintenance of law and order to sustain stability and prosperity, the only shared concern among shopkeepers of different origin was the pursuit of gain. However, that was, presumably, for the most part an individual matter.

Separate identities had much to do with the underlying general antagonisms and suspicions between members of the Cantonese and Hoklo groups. Documented in the records of Christian missionary work on the island, these antipathies had not originated with the two groups' shared residence there, but had been nurtured by centuries of mutual antagonism in and away from their home areas. However, the excitements and rivalries that characterized the jiao festival and other celebrations connected with the local temples were undoubtedly an aggravating factor in their perpetuation. During the processions and congregations that characterized such events, there were often minor scuffles and larger-scale fights between teams from the different groups, especially when they competed for prized or lucky objects; and besides the deeper causes of strife, the heat of the moment so readily generated on these occasions heightened the old antipathies and helped to perpetuate ill feeling.[23]

The general roughness of the population owed something to the turbulence and uncertainties of the times. As a flourishing coastal market center, known to people all over the outer parts of the Guangzhou delta, Cheung Chau was to attract the attention of robbers and pirates into the period of British rule.[24] In earlier days, with or without the consent of the local people, it had itself been a base for pirate bands.[25] It is also quite likely that some of the island's shopkeepers had dealt regularly in stolen cargoes and had assisted in the reprovisioning and fitting out of fishermen-turned-pirates.[26] Whenever the opportunity presented itself, any kind of smuggling was also a welcome source of gain and excitement.[27]

Temples and Shrines

Any curious visitor to the island in the late nineteenth century would have noticed its many temples. Dedicated to a variety of Daoist deities, they were prominent features in their several localities. By 1898 there were seven of them. In step with population growth, this was more than at the beginning of the century. In the interim, the three oldest had been rebuilt or extended.[28] Besides the Beidi Temple already mentioned, there were two other eighteenth-century temples, both of them dedicated to Tianhou the Empress of Heaven. However, only the Beidi Temple had an overall, island-wide importance, serving as the principal venue for the important yearly jiao rituals performed to protect the land population from epidemics and supernatural harm, and for the associated and other opera performances.

Although both land and boat people patronized all the temples, there was one that was particularly linked with the floating population. This was the Tianhou Temple at Sai Wan, which, from the perspective of one walking from the town (but not of one approaching from the sea), was located in an outlying part of the island. Here, the firing of lucky rockets (*qiangpao*) was still taking place annually in the second lunar month when I was district officer, as I knew from invitations to attend the event and set off the principal rocket.

In the course of my inquiries, it became apparent that each of these temples had its own geographical boundaries. The people living within them were aware of the limits and would normally seek advice and protection from their local temple's deities. At the same time, the temples' clientele was probably varied: in addition to people from the locality seeking help from the temple gods, other worshipers might come from any of the resident ethnic landsmen's groups or from the fishing fleets. In keeping with the "shop-around" attitudes common to this type of worship, the efficacy of the god in meeting requirements and performing miracles were the primary considerations in the supplicants' minds. Only in the case of the island's earth-god shrines did a more specific territorial jurisdiction apply: because each shrine was associated with a particular street or locality, the devotees were usually confined to the families in residence there.

The Kaifong and Local Self-Management

Despite their importance as places of religious resort by the people, and notwithstanding the considerable sums of money raised to build, extend, and restore them periodically, neither the temples nor their managers were part of the infrastructure for managing the island community's affairs. This important role was played by the district associations and the Cheung Chau Kaifong.

It has already been noted that, in imperial times, local communities were expected to make their own arrangements for management. In neither town nor countryside were government officers charged with such duties, or even with coordinating management among villages or groups of townsmen. Although there had been a customs post on Cheung Chau from 1868, and for much longer a small body of island-based soldiery whose surveillance was supplemented by occasional visits by patrolling naval vessels, none of their personnel participated in local management. Yet in places like Cheung Chau, where, in addition to the mixed population, there were many visiting outsiders to give rise to or complicate problems, some kind of commonly accepted authority was clearly needed across the board to help keep order and sustain progress. There, as in other towns and cities large and small, the responsibilities of local management were shouldered by a Kaifong committee.

In accordance with the usual practice, the local Kaifong committee was drawn from the ranks of the shopkeepers and businessmen in the various speech groups. Each leader commanded the respect and obedience of his own people and worked with others of his kind to provide local management. The Kaifong committee's duties ranged over a wide field. They comprised the provision of watch and ward in the business streets (which, as was customary in the region, were barred off and patrolled at night); the operation of a hospital cum dying-house; the supply of free medicines and coffins; and the maintenance of a communal grave for the indigent dead without relatives.

The Kaifong also made some provision for education, though this responsibility was undertaken mainly by the district associations. The water supply and local public works were among its other concerns, according to need. The head of the Kaifong also represented the community to the outside world, especially to the imperial officials. Less enviably, its leading members bore the brunt of any unpleasantness to be encountered in emergencies, ranging from attacks by pirates to the onslaught of contagious disease. The performance of these miscellaneous but important duties can be detected from various sources, and especially from the information provided by old or retired Kaifong members and other elderly residents. However, although the Kaifong's position and contribution to good government were crucial, it did not possess authority, only influence. It relied upon the district associations, lineage elders, and family heads for cooperation and support in all its actions, and could not act responsibly nor guarantee the continuation of local order without this sustained backing.

In such a structured and generally ordered community, the presence of the government was in normal times practically superfluous. The district magistrate's principal responsibility, for the maintenance of law and order and the avoidance of major popular unrest and disturbance, was being carried out in practice by other hands through the good work being done day in day out by the Kaifong leadership. His other main duty, the collection of the land tax, was also made lighter by the fact that the Wong Wai Tsak Tong (Huang Weize *tang*) of Nantou (Xin'an, the district city), was the subsoil owner of much of Cheung Chau, including its principal sand beaches. As such, the Tong was responsible for making the regular land tax payments for its holdings, and thus relieved the magistrate from the necessity of chasing after a mass of individual owners.[29]

Though largely left to their own devices, the merchant Kaifongs of Cheung Chau could not avoid dealing with the local authorities from time to time. Besides the officers of the military and customs posts located on the island, occasional visits could be expected from other officials in the course of their duties. From time to time, as the need arose, representations would have to be made to them on behalf of the local people. By the later nineteenth century, such liaison was facilitated by the ease with which ranks and degrees could be purchased from the government. The information provided on the still surviving commemorative tablet for the establishment of a defense office in 1870 shows that, in line with the general practice of the time, some of the Cheung Chau leaders had taken this step, improving their social status and gaining better access to officials.[30]

The largely obligatory liaison with officials continued into British times. A former district officer, Austin Coates, states it very well, though in exaggerated form to give effect and make a point.

For example, it may happen that the District Officer visits Cheung Chau on Monday, the Divisional Superintendent, Marine Police on Tuesday, the Assistant Director of Education on Wednesday, the Chief Engineer, Port Works, on Thursday and the Medical Officer of Health on Friday. If prior notification is given, as it sometimes has to be, to enable local discussions to be held, this means, by local etiquette, a substantial restaurant lunch every day of the week, which for the Chairman is a very considerable outlay.[31]

The frequent repair or extension of the island's temples, and of public buildings like the Defense Office (1860s–1870s) and the Fong Pin Hospital (1877 and 1908), provided a convenient means for local leaders to forge and maintain those informal connections with officialdom which, in a traditional Chinese social and cultural milieu, were so important to individuals and communities alike. Either upon request or on their own initiative, some officials were donors to these projects, and their titles or appointments appear on the commemorative tablets set up to mark such events. Others presented honorific boards or couplets for the buildings, or themselves wrote the characters for them.[32] These valued indications of interest and respect would be pointed out to their successors in office, and no doubt would help to smooth relationships with minor officials and thus promote the public business of the place.

Though widely operative, the Kaifong per se had no part to play in the organization of the opera performances and the performance of the protective rituals in the jiao festival and on other periodic or irregular occasions. Such duties were left to individual leaders in the ethnic and street groupings, although these men were more than likely also to be leading members of the Kaifong. Herein lay both the strengths and the weaknesses of the traditional Kaifong organizations of the day.

Men Rather Than Institutions

In any discourse upon the nature of local authority on the island as it was in the nineteenth century, or indeed as I found it in the late 1950s, it would be misleading to give any account of the Kaifong and other principal institutions that purported to show a ranking between and among them. As already mentioned, it was individual men who mattered, and they often carried more weight than the institutions to which they belonged and which they led. Their influence and activities were widely distributed. It was quite usual for the top Kaifongs to hold posts in the district associations, street bodies, annual temple committees, and any ad hoc working groups that might be formed to meet the needs of a particular occasion or purpose. Since it was also the leaders who made the many financial contributions required to keep the Kaifong committee and the district associations in existence and able to carry out their various projects and responsibilities, the financing of many activities assumed a semiprivate nature. This gave rise to a good many problems, especially upon the death of a leader. The resulting melding of public and private affairs could also lead to misappropriation and malversation.[33]

This confused dichotomy in financial matters is significant because it emphasizes the importance of the merchants and men of business in local management. Their financial contributions and personal effort were crucial to its operation and continuance, as carried out through the Kaifong and the four district bodies. Each and every local association had to rely on donations from the wealthier merchants and businessmen for their very existence. Often this took the form of purchase and presentation of property that provided a regular basic revenue. At other times donations would be made toward running expenses or special projects. As a rule, public subscription was required only for major repairs to buildings and reconstructions. Even then, any shortfall had to made up by the leadership.

The Sinews Provided by Business

It follows that the leaders' continued success in business underpinned the whole system of local management on Cheung Chau. It is therefore worthwhile to indicate the ultimate sources of the island's prosperity, which provided the funding for public and community purposes.

First and foremost must come Cheung Chau's popularity with the boat population and the fishing fleets of the region. This stemmed from its favorable location for business. By the mid-nineteenth century, the island was well positioned in the trading triangle formed by Guangzhou, the ports of the Pearl River delta, Macau, and the flourishing new entrepôt of British Hong Kong. Merchants were quick to seize on its potential for trading in fish and other marine products with these places, as well as for catering to the various needs of the fishing fleets themselves. Among their number were representatives of the big Hong Kong firms dealing wholesale in marine products. The junk masters, too, must have recognized the advantages of a place that so conveniently met all their requirements, for the fleets that used the island anchorage to sell their catches also needed to reprovision their stores of salt and victuals as well as to repair and refit their craft. Thus, in business matters, the relationship between the land and sea communities was (and had to be) strikingly close and symbiotic.

The Cheung Chau boatyards flourished accordingly, as did those shop-keepers who supplied ship chandlery services and salt to the boatmen and their families and who dealt in the basic staples of daily life (rice, salt, soy, firewood, and oil, which were needed by all, whether afloat or ashore). They also dealt in the large volume of fish landed by the fishing fleets, send-ing it fresh or mostly salted to markets in Hong Kong and the large towns of the Pearl River delta. These prospering concerns were carried out in roomy premises, often with internal courtyards.

I was fortunate to be able to see some of these old shop premises during my visits to the island in the 1950s and 1960s. Constructed with imported blue-grey bricks, they were functional rather than elegant. Typically narrow-fronted, they were long in depth with one or two internal yards. By the time I saw them for the first time, most had been partitioned into front and rear parts and were being used for other purposes. Long dilap-idated or in ruins, some had been partly rebuilt as temporary structures.

Cheung Chau's business net was cast wide. The principal shopkeepers were not content to sit in their shops waiting to deal with the catches that the fishing fleets brought to their doorsteps. Widespread inquiries reveal that the ties of business stretched all around, from the village settlements on nearby Lantau and adjacent islands to the much wider area to the south and west among the outer island port villages of the Ladrones. Besides deal-ing in the catches landed on Cheung Chau itself, shopkeepers also collected fish from the many village fishermen operating stake-nets throughout the whole area. The larger retailers also supplied goods to the smaller shops in the islands; but because of the mark-ups there and the greater variety of items on sale in the Cheung Chau shops, the boat and land people preferred to shop in Cheung Chau whenever they had the opportunity. The island's principal shopkeepers also made loans to villagers and boat people, with land or catches pledged against failure to repay.

It was these various lines of business that enabled the leading men of the place to participate effectively in local affairs, to pay a considerable part of the routine public expenses, and to make major donations to worthy causes; but ultimately, of course, it was the presence of the boat people, local and visiting alike, that was the basis for good business prospects on the island. Thus any increased prosperity ashore must ordinarily have been a reflection of greater prosperity afloat, given the constant and close connection between these two main sectors of the local economy.

Another aspect of their contribution to the local scene was that during their periodic stays in port the visiting fishing fleets added to the community's already diverse social mix. Swelling the already considerable number of locally based boat people, their crews and family members came ashore at the main festivals. At such times, they must have landed by the thousands to enjoy the color and excitement of opera performances and take in the competing attractions of eating, gambling, and opium smoking, together with the other diversions provided by the land population and other persons drawn in season by the rich pickings to be found there.

Dynamics in the Leadership Group

Given the growth in the island's population and the steady increase in its business over the years, it is hardly surprising to find that these changes were eventually reflected in the power structure at the center, that is, among the Kaifong leadership that performed managerial duties on behalf of the community as a whole.

A significant change took place in the early twentieth century, when the leadership of the Kaifong shifted away from the Hoklo, who had predominated up to that time. This change was ascribable to the growing number of prosperous merchants in the Cantonese-speaking groups, to their undoubted financial clout, and probably to a less than altruistic desire to take their fair share of local management in order to further their own interests. Curiously enough—and perhaps more significantly—the leadership struggle took place outside the Kaifong, though the results were soon reflected in its composition. It came about in connection with the Beidi Temple.

Despite competition from other old temples, the Hoklo community's Beidi Temple had always been regarded as the main one on the island. Established by them in 1783, it had remained largely if not solely under their management for the whole of the next century. The nineteenth-century Kaifong is reported to have held its meetings on the premises. This circumstance would be a sure sign of the Hoklo inhabitants' political predominance in that period, and it is corroborated by the fact that for long Hoklos had formed the majority of the Kaifong committeemen. However, upon the occasion of the temple's repair and enlargement in 1908, the commemorative tablet erected to mark the event shows that, for the first time, the list of organizers included people from the Guangzhou prefecture.

Whether the Cantonese element had insisted on having a say and paid their dues, or whether their financial assistance had been requested, is not now known. Another record that relates to the time states that the Hoklo managers approached the Guangzhou leaders in order, together, to raise sufficient funds to maintain the temple fabric. Either way, help with the cost of enlargement and maintenance of this important building was very likely given in exchange for certain agreed-upon changes in the Kaifong's management. Thereafter, the leadership is reported to have been broadened by the inclusion of non-Hoklo persons, and the head post to have become subject to rotation among the principal men of the main speech groups. These managerial adjustments reflected the new balance of power within the business community, thereby achieving a more realistic balance between the various speech groups in regard to the management of communal affairs.

The dramatic change at the top probably made little difference to the "rank-and-file" leadership in the other managerial bodies within the community. The leadership group as a whole had ever been subject to slow but constant change. Any vacancies of a routine kind in any of the managerial bodies were filled by co-opting deserving assistants, of whom there were always a number learning the ropes by carrying out routine work for their bosses. This applied to the Kaifong as well as to the committees of the various speech group associations. The ad hoc committees that managed the temple festivals and activities connected with the street shrines were also manned and renewed in this way.

Concluding Remarks

The longtime vitality of the island community, intensified as it was by the continuous presence of the boat people, offshore and occasionally on land, is evident both from historical sources and from the reminiscences and information provided by local residents. Yet there was always a sharp division between its principal components on land and sea, and a partisan approach to affairs among its residents owing to their diverse origins and divided, self-contained loyalties.

In recent decades, the land community has greatly increased in numbers and diversity, while the number of casual visitors to the island seeking good food and recreation has also risen significantly. In sharp contrast, the fishing fleet has greatly diminished and many boat people have come to live ashore. Within today's much wider community, the lines of ethnic division have become blurred. However, as Choi Chi-cheung's essay in this book shows, the jiao festival, still so popular with old and new residents alike, yet retains its traditional organization, reflecting the divisions and prejudices of an earlier age.

Reinforcing Ethnicity: The Jiao Festival in Cheung Chau

CHOI CHI-CHEUNG

HERE is a story about a Tanka (*danjia*) man who put on the clothes of the land people and slipped into a gambling house on land in the 1940s:[1] "Most of the gamblers were so engrossed in their game that they did not notice his darker skin color and distinctive features. But then he got involved in an argument while gambling. The moment he spoke his distinctive accent gave him away. And they all burst into loud laughter when they saw that he had no shoes on. The man quickly fled."

This story was told me many times in the last thirty years by my uncle, a longtime resident of Cheung Chau. Even today, elderly people on the island still remember that boat people ("Tanka" in colloquial Cantonese) were not allowed to come up to land or wear shoes on shore.[2]

Discrimination toward the Tanka may seem to have disappeared as many of them have moved ashore, especially after the 1962 typhoon, when they were relocated to houses. However, only land people qualify as eligible voters for the Cheung Chau Rural Committee, the island's representative body recognized by the Hong Kong government. As recently as December 1990, ethnic differentiation could still be observed on the island. A notice inviting the locals to the polls in December 1990 specifically stated that an eligible voter was one who was a *lushang jumin* (land resident) who had lived on land for ten or more years. This regulation indicated that people who lived on boats moored at the island did not have the rights enjoyed by people who lived on the land. Thus, the islanders are clearly classified into two distinct groups: the "land people" (*lushang ren*) and the "water people" (*shuishang ren*), and ethnic identity changes with the acquisition of settlement rights on land.[3]

Many boat people on Cheung Chau, according to a bank manager I spoke to on the island, are not poor at all. Many own houses on shore, and they are major customers at local goldsmiths and restaurants.[4] The growing economic power of the boat people can also be seen in their political achievements, for, many, having moved ashore, are entitled to the vote in local elections. In 1980, the first boat person was elected into the rural committee and the district board.[5] In 1991, a second representative of "boat people" origin was elected into the rural committee. Still, they continued to be discriminated against. In 1988, I picked up through the Cheung Chau grapevine the story of a Chaozhou family who objected strongly to marriage talks between their youngest son and a girl of "boat people" origin.[6] So although different ethnic groups live harmoniously together on Cheung Chau, original ethnic identities still survive. Such identities can easily be observed in religious activities.

Cheung Chau as a Market Town

Cheung Chau is an island of about one square mile located at the southeastern exit of the Pearl River, approximately ten miles southwest of Hong Kong Island. It is part of the New Territories of Hong Kong, an area leased to the British government by the Qing dynasty in 1898. The island, shaped like a dumbbell, is made up of the northern and southern hills, each approximately three hundred feet high, joined by a narrow strip of low land. In the southern valleys are scattered some vegetable farms. The island has never been agriculturally productive. It was recorded in 1779 in an official land license that the island was so infertile that only supplementary crops (that is, any crop other than rice) could be grown there.[7] Many of the early farmers also fished in order to make a living.[8] In fact, the island was, and still is, mainly a fishing or fishing-related economy. The earliest temples established on the island are dedicated to Hongsheng and Tianhou, both deities of the sea. The majority of the population, at least until the beginning of the twentieth century, were boat people.[9] Industries on the island in the early twentieth century were related to fishing.[10] Processed fish products such as salted fish and shrimp paste are still two of the most famous local products. The seafood (*haixian*, fresh seafood) restaurants on the island attract thousands of vacationers from Hong Kong every weekend.

There is little documentation on the history of the island before the eighteenth century. Like most coastal areas in south China, stories of piracy abound; the pirate Zhang Bao's cave is still a noted tourist spot. In the eighteenth century, a Huang surname, originally from the Xin'an county city of Nantou, claimed ownership of the island and became its subsoil owner.[11] The island was also recorded as a *xu*, or market, in an inscription

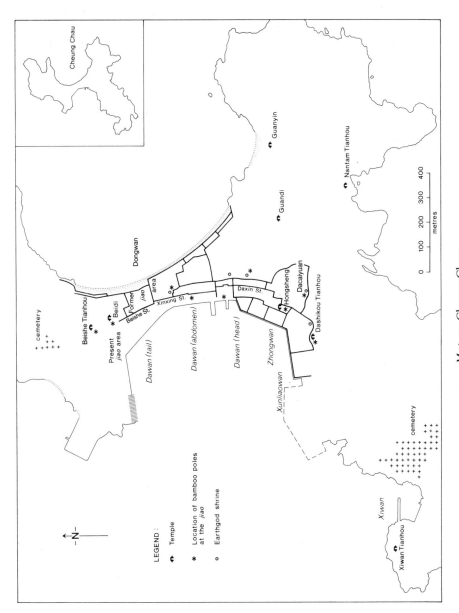

Map 3. Cheung Chau

of 1785 recorded on an incense burner at the Tianhou temple at Pak She (Beishe) on the island.[12] The island flourished after the Qing government successfully took control over the South China Sea by defeating pirate leaders Zhang Bao and Zheng Shishi in 1810.[13] In the 1820 Xin'an gazetteer it was officially recorded as a "newly added market."[14]

As the island grew in prosperity, more people moved in. According to Mr. Zhu Beisheng, with whom I spoke, the Huang, Lu, Zhu, and Luo surnames were at one time the four most influential surnames on Cheung Chau. The early ancestors of the Zhu and the Luo surnames moved to Cheung Chau in the mid-nineteenth century, the founding ancestor of the Zhu lineage having come from Haifeng during the Taiping Rebellion[15] and the first Luo-surnamed settler, whose great grandson Tian'en died in early 1992 at the age of more than 80 years, came to the island at about the same time. According to their genealogy, the Luo surname originally came from Haifeng county but had lived in Dongguan county for about fifteen generations. Tian'en's great grandfather Shun-shan migrated to Cheung Chau and settled in Pak She Street.[16]

Most of the historical documentation relating to the island comes from the second half of the nineteenth century and after. The large number of immigrants during and after the Taiping Rebellion period probably contributed to the island's rapid growth. According to one inscription, there were as many as two hundred shops in 1907.[17] A self-defense organization was established in 1863 and a public hospital was built in 1872.[18] The presence of one of the few customs substations in the Hong Kong area on the island also attests to its importance as a commercial center.[19] The island was so prosperous that it continued to be attacked frequently by pirates. In 1912, for instance, three police constables were killed during an attack. However, although Cheung Chau was "beset in turn by plague and by pirates," G. R. Sayer, assistant district officer, Southern District, commented in 1913, "Cheung Chau however has sufficient enterprise to rise superior to bad fortune. It has added two storeys to the ill fated pawn shop. It has overcome considerable opposition to its new market run strictly on municipal lines. And it has established its own electric light plant and supplies light at a cheaper rate than Hong Kong can do."[20]

Territories, Deities, and Ethnic Groups

There were originally five residential districts on the island: Tai Wan (Dawan), Chung Wan (Zhongwan), Shun Liao Wan (Xunliaowan), Sai Wan (Xiwan), and Tai Tso Yuen (Dacaiyuan); see Map 3. The rest of the island, such as the northern and southern hills, began to be inhabited only from the 1950s.[21] Tai Wan was subdivided into a "head," an "abdomen," and a "tail." The town area including Tai Wan, Chung Wan, and Tai Tso Yuen, marked by the two oldest Tianhou temples, was occupied predominantly by land people. The Tanka boat people were, and still are, concentrated near the third-oldest Tianhou temple on the island in Sai Wan.

As late as the 1960s, the different ethnic groups that settled on Cheung Chau maintained traceable territories.[22] The "tail" of Tai Wan, including San Hing (Xinxing) Street and Pak She Street, was predominantly occupied by immigrants from Huizhou (especially from Haifeng and Lufeng counties) and Chaozhou.[23] Both of the two earliest Huizhou families, the Zhu and the Luo surnames, built their ancestral halls in this area, the Zhus' being in San Hing Back Street and the Luos' in Pak She Street. Only one other ancestral hall exists on the island, and that belongs to the subsoil owners, the Huang surname of Nantou, who were Cantonese. It is located at Tai San (Daxin) Street.

The "abdomen" and the "head" of Tai Wan are occupied by Cantonese people from Guangzhou prefecture. This area, including Tai San, Chung Hing, and Hing Lung Streets, was the old Cheung Chau market, and even today it remains the business center of the island where most of the goldsmiths, teahouses (*chalou*),[24] markets, and banks are situated. During the annual Lantern Festival on the fifteenth day of the First Month, a temporary mat-shed temple is erected at the back street behind Tai San Street.[25] This mat-shed is popularly referred to by the locals as *lao dengpeng* (the old lantern mat-shed) to distinguish it from the new one at the San Hing Street. According to the mat-shed keeper, it is so named because it is built by the descendants of the earliest inhabitants living in the area. By "the earliest inhabitants," he refers to the Cantonese-speaking people.[26]

Each street of this town area is protected by an earth god, located at his shrine, the *shetan*. The shrines remind people of their nearest protectors. For instance, a person who lives in San Hing Street would sacrifice to and be protected by the earth god of that street. Cross-street sacrifice, though not prohibited, is not consciously practiced by anyone. Besides the earth god, there are also temple deities. However, worship of temple deities follows a different custom: a resident may worship the deity of any temple if he or she feels that the deities could bring him or her good luck.

There are eight temples on Cheung Chau. Of the eight, four are dedicated to the Tianhou, the deity who is believed to protect those at sea and bring good catches of fish. Of the four Tianhou temples, the Pak She Tianhou Temple is the oldest on the island, followed by the Tai Shek Hau Tianhou (Dashikou Tianhou) Temple. These two temples are located at the two ends of the old Cheung Chau market. The third Tianhou Temple, the Sai Wan Tianhou (Xiwan Tianhou) Temple, is located on the southwestern coast where most of the boat people now reside. It is believed that all residents in Cheung Chau, be they fishermen or fish dealers, producers or distributors, need the protection of Tianhou, but the existence of the Tai Shek Hau Tianhou Temple marks the boundary of the market town and symbolically excludes the boat people from the area where the land people live.

Despite the number of Tianhou temples, it is the Beidi (northern deity, also known as *xuantian shangdi*, the high deity of the dark heaven) who is now generally accepted by the islanders on Cheung Chau as their patron deity. However, until the end of the nineteenth century the Beidi Temple was solely owned and managed by Huizhou people.

Beidi was invited to Cheung Chau in 1777 by Huizhou merchants who brought along to the island the incense ashes (*xianghuo*) from the Beidi Temple in Xuanwu Mountain in Huizhou. No temple was built until six years later when Lin Yuwu, a native of Guishan county in Huizhou, took the responsibility. The temple was renovated three times. The leaders in charge were always descendants of Lin Yuwu. Other members of the temple committee were always Huizhou and Chaozhou people. In other words, the temple had always been managed by Huizhou and Chaozhou people, centering around the Lin family. However, as donations from the Cantonese-speaking people increased after the mid-nineteenth century,[27] disputes occurred frequently between the Huizhou and Chaozhou people and the Cantonese over the control of the temple. In 1903, the Huizhou and Chaozhou people sought economic support from the Cantonese to expand the temple. Since then, all three ethnic groups, Huizhou, Chaozhou, and Cantonese, have agreed that the temple be equally divided among them. The three operas dedicated to Beidi (*shengong xi*) each year are presented one each by the three groups.[28] Beidi thus became not only the patron deity of the Huizhou and Chaozhou people, but also that of the Cantonese people.[29] Serving as the patron deity of the island, Beidi is celebrated in the annual *jiao* festival on the island, and his temple is visited by and his festivals celebrated by all the local people. No one, except perhaps the boat people, would argue about Beidi's position as Cheung Chau's patron deity.

The Jiao Festival and the Hailufeng Group

The jiao festival on Cheung Chau is celebrated every year in the first half of the Fourth Month and lasts for three days. The exact date of the festival is decided by divination on the sixteenth of the First Month each year.

Many stories are told by people of Cheung Chau relating to the origin of the jiao festival on the island. Many relate it to the misfortune brought by disease and pirates during the Qing dynasty.[30] However, Messrs. Zhu Beisheng and Luo Tian'en, two elders of Huizhou origin, both over 70 years old in 1990, relate a different story.[31] According to them, the Cheung Chau jiao festival had its beginning in the Taipingshan District on Hong Kong Island. Many people died in this overcrowded district when it was hit by bubonic plague.[32] A Hailufeng resident took the Beidi out from his own domestic altar, put the deity on the street, and asked that the pestilence be stopped. Other residents offered incense and prayers. After some time, the disease subsided.

Thereafter, people continued to celebrate the occasion. A festival centering on Beidi to pacify the spirits of the dead and other forces that might bring misfortune was held once every year at Taipingshan. However, with tightened measures to ensure fire safety in the city, the festival was prohibited at that place. During that time many Hailufeng people lived on the Pak She Street of Cheung Chau, so the festival was transferred to Pak She and held once a year there. Thus, according to the two elders, the festival began in Cheung Chau as a festival of the Hailufeng people, and all devotees to the Beidi at that time had come from Hailufeng, that is, the two counties of Haifeng and Lufeng on the border of Chaozhou that in the Qing dynasty came within the administrative jurisdiction of Huizhou prefecture. People from other parts of Huizhou or Chaozhou began to contribute to the festival only after 1945.

It is said that at one time, like the Tanka, the Hailufeng people on the island also lived on boats. However, the Hailufeng people are now thought of as land residents. We can assume that when the jiao festival was introduced into Cheung Chau, it was looked upon as a land people's occasion.

The two elders' account of the origin of the festival on Cheung Chau may be corroborated by an arrangement that is made for the *chuhui* (procession) at the festival: the procession is always led by the sacred sedan carrying the Beidi of the Taipingshan Hailufeng group, followed by another sedan chair carrying the Beidi of Pak She.

The important role of the Hailufeng ethnic group in the festival can also be seen from its rituals. The rituals and the priests who conduct them— which have been described by Tanaka Issei as "purely Hailufeng style" —and the three-day Huizhou opera performance following the end of the festival are some of the more obvious features that indicate the Hailufeng origin of the festival.[33] Moreover, by tradition, the Daoist priests (*nammo* in Cantonese) hired to officiate the ceremonies at the festival, who served as middlemen between the sacred and the secular worlds, come from the Hailufeng group.

A story circulates among the islanders of how the incompetence of Daoist priests from other ethnic groups led to the disastrous typhoon Wanda in 1962. According to the islanders, the chairman of the 1962 jiao organizing committee was an ethnic Chaozhou. Going against tradition, he invited a team of Chaozhou Daoist priests to perform the rituals. At the opening-of-the-eyes (*kaiguang*) ritual, where the eyes of the ten-foot-high effigies—the Ghost King, the Mountain God, and the Earth God—were symbolically opened, the Chaozhou Daoist priests, instead of taking a mirror from the feet of the figures and dotting the eyes with red ink by looking at their reflections in it, climbed on a ladder to reach the eyes of the three deities so that they might look at them directly. This action angered the deities, and that year, in June, the typhoon swept through the island, killing many people. The residents blamed this bad omen on the chairman and made him repent by kneeling three times and praying nine times all the way to the Beidi Temple from the foot of the hill at the eastern seashore. Since the incident, it is said, no chairman of the jiao organizing committee, be he Hailufeng or Chaozhou, would employ Daoist priests from any ethnic group other than the Hailufeng.[34]

Moreover, at least until the death in 1984 of effigy maker Mr. Li Hangxiang (1923–1984), alias *dashigong* (master of the ghost king), effigies, including images of the deities and spirits and other sacrifices made of paper, were made by Hailufeng people. According to the late Mr. Li, a native of Haifeng who in 1951 succeeded his paternal uncle to become a master in the making of effigies for the festival, the ghost king for the Hailufeng people was different from those made for other ethnic groups. The Cantonese-style ghost king was always seated, and that for the Chaozhou people stood on both feet, but the Hailufeng one stood on his right foot with his left foot lifted in the air. This posture had at least two functions: first, when one went round under his foot, it was believed that one would be protected by the ghost king from evil spirits. Second, the paper forming the sole of the raised left foot had protective qualities. Believers might tear off the portions they needed to take home, burn them to ashes, mix the ash with tea, and drink the tea. In this way, they would receive the protection of the ghost king.[35]

The functions of the ghost king described by Mr. Li are accepted also by ethnic groups other than the Hailufeng people. After Mr. Li's death, his wife, a Thai woman, succeeded him for two years. After that, a group of Haifeng youth in Peng Chau, an island nearby, who claimed to be disciples of Mr. Li, took over the job and have continued making Hailufeng-style effigies.[36]

Another indication of the Hailufeng connection to the festival is that, until 1965, it was celebrated in the area where most of the Hailufeng people lived. Today, although the ritual area has been moved to the playground in front of the Beidi Temple, on the night the "great offering" ritual is performed a "small offering" ritual is still held at a place near the location where it was originally held.[37]

The Cheung Chau jiao festival is signified by three bamboo towers, approximately forty feet high and each loaded with buns neatly arranged from top to bottom. Until 1978, all three towers were donated by three Hailufeng groups who, according to local gossip and a police report, had close connections with Triad societies of the same ethnic group in Hong Kong. According to the report, these Hailufeng ethnic groups played a major role in the festival until 1978 by being "heavily involved in the festival's organizing committee," "financing the three bun towers [baoshan] (some HK $25,000 each)" and "providing approximately one third of all the participants in the main procession, including the more militant elements, namely the lion dancers, flag-carriers, marshals and procession escorts."[38] Since 1979, the Hailufeng people have continued to participate actively in the festival under the names of Cheung Chau Hui-Hai-Lu (that is, Huizhou and Hailufeng) Chinese Opera Committee and Cheung Chau Hui-Hai-Lu Regional Company Ltd. They are, besides the Cheung Chau Chaozhou Regional Association, the only regional associations that participate in the festival.[39]

The organization that administers the festival is the Cheung Chau Huizhou and Chaozhou Prefectures Association.[40] The chairmen and vice chairmen of the festival organizing committee are selected from among the members of the association. The organizing committee, which in 1991 comprised 99 members, including 3 chairmen and 7 vice chairmen, was, according to the two elders, strictly limited to members of the Prefectures Association before 1960s, although it included a small number of Cantonese in 1991.[41] The chairmen, as religious representatives, are chosen in front of the Beidi on the sixteenth of the First Month by the casting of two kidney-shaped divination blocks. The ones chosen have to keep to a vegetarian diet from that day until the last day of the festival.[42] They begin festival preparations as soon as they have been selected, and one of their first duties is to collect donations from people who reside in the town area of Cheung Chau as well as from members of the Huizhou or Chaozhou communities, including those who do not live on the island. Any shortage will be covered by the chairmen's own donations. In 1992, each committee member donated a minimum of 600 Hong Kong dollars, the single chairman donated 5,000, and the two vice chairmen, 2,500 each.[43]

As we have seen, the Hailufeng people provide the most important religious, financial, managerial, and recreational support for the festival. Their role in the festival is not limited to Cheung Chau, for their connections extend to other Hailufeng communities outside Cheung Chau and as far as their hometown in China. In 1991 and 1992, for instance, the Hailufeng opera troupe invited to perform at the festival was hired from Huizhou.

Other ethnic groups' participation in the jiao is limited in different degrees. The Chaozhou now play a role second only to the Hailufeng group. They are the only ethnic group other than the Hailufeng that are eligible for membership on the organizing committee and to be elected as chairpersons of the festival. In fact, the chairmen of three of the recent five years (1988–92) were ethnic Chaozhou. As noted above, they financed the festival through their own contributions and from donations collected from their acquaintances. The Chaozhou Regional Association has since 1978 been the only ethnic association that presents small bun towers, 36 in all, placed on the side of the 3 large bun towers in the jiao area.[44] Besides the Huizhou people, it is the only ethnic group that participates in the procession. Moreover, since 1990 when the government withdrew from sponsoring the bun towers, a Chaozhou person has been in charge of seeking financial support for the three large bun towers. The wealth of many Chaozhou merchants and their business connections play an essential role in the survival of the festival since the government's ban on Triad involvement. Yet, the rule remains that Chaozhou Daoist priests are not to be employed.

Besides the Huizhou and Chaozhou groups, a small number of Cantonese-speaking local leaders are also members of the organizing committee of the festival. However, they are not eligible to serve as chairmen of the festival. In Cheung Chau, there are eight regional associations, only two of which are associations of the Huizhou and Chaozhou people (the Huizhou and Chaozhou Prefectures Association and the Chaozhou Regional Association), the others being associations of Cantonese-speaking groups. Leaders of Cantonese-speaking groups, such as the Zhongshan and Wuyi people, have never served on the organizing committee, while the Shunde group has had representatives only since 1988. In other words, leaders of only three out of six Cantonese groups, that is, the Dongguan, Bao'an, and Siyi groups, have traditionally had representatives on the committee. In fact, members of the rural committee are almost always drawn from these three Cantonese groups and the Huizhou and Chaozhou groups. Moreover, the Cantonese associations have never participated in the festival as a united body, nor do they support the festival financially. Though the town area is protected and blessed by the deities, the Cantonese people participate in the festival only on an individual basis.

Another ethnic group on the island is the Tanka boat people, whose participation in the festival is limited. Administratively, the two boat-people leaders who are members of the rural committee have not served on the organizing committees of the festival. Economically, their residences fall beyond the boundaries of the area visited by committee members to collect donations, for which reason they are neither purified nor blessed by the activities of the festival. Although the Sai Wan Tianhou, patronized by the boat people at Sai Wan, is invited to the jiao area, she, unlike other deities, is not invited there in full recognition by the jiao organizers with a troupe composing of a priest, a *suona* (narrow trumpet) player, and four workers employed by the organizing committee. Instead, she is brought along by members of the association organizing the Sai Wan Tianhou festival. According to Mr. Zhang Ya, vice president of the association and a boat person, they would leave the deity with the jiao organizing committee until the day of the procession, when they returned to carry the deity's sedan chair themselves.[45]

Moreover, the Hongsheng, who is believed to be another boat people's patron deity, does not participate in the festival in the same way as other deities.[46] Until at least 1981, in a ritual known as the *zou* Hongsheng (the running of Hongsheng), practiced on the day of the procession (usually a day before the deities are sent back to their temples), the Hongsheng deity, carried in his sedan chair, "stealthily" sneaked back to his temple as the parade approached it. Thus, unlike all other invited deities, Hongsheng did not participate in the festival to its very end. The lack of ceremony attending the invitation of the Sai Wan Tianhou, and the stealthy escape of Hongsheng, indicate that the Tanka boat people participate not by right but by sufferance.

The participation of the boat people themselves is also restricted. Instead of participating in the jiao festival, they hold a three-day sacrifice in the Seventh Month with the help of local Daoist priests. This sacrifice, known as the *shuishang yulan*, serves similar functions as the jiao, such as pacifying the souls of the drowned and feeding wandering spirits in the sea.

Ethnicity, therefore, does not necessarily coincide with territorial boundary, but, as in the jiao festival, supersedes territorial coherence.[47] The following section illustrates how such ethnic relations are displayed in the festival.

Territorial Boundaries of the Jiao Festival

In the New Territories of Hong Kong the territorial boundary of a community can be observed overtly during its jiao festival. Resident members of the community enjoy their right of participation at the jiao in full without question. Nonresident members and nonmember residents are themselves aware of their limited rightful shares. To participants of the jiao, the demarcation of territorial boundary indicates who has a share (*youfen*) and who does not.[48]

During the jiao, the right of participation is translated into ritual practices: some such practices are marked by clear indications on the ground, others are articulated, and many are observable but never discussed. Having a share means being entitled on the one hand to religious cleansing and protection, and on the other, to the practical acknowledgment of the right to settle in the community. The Cheung Chau festival, overall, is well regarded as belonging to all islanders, but some portions of the festival are restricted to only a portion of the Cheung Chau population.

The Daoist altar (*nammo peng*) is the location where the Daoist priests perform all but four of their rituals. The altar is the most sacred place in the festival area. The Daoist priests should not be disturbed, since it falls to them to plead with the highest deities to pardon the islanders' sins for the past year and to grant them good fortune in the coming year. The area is protected by the Daoist Pure Ones, and the five cardinal points at the altar are purified and guarded through the magic of Daoist talismans. The Daoist altar is Daoist territory proper.

Besides the Daoist altar, the jiao shed (*jiaopeng*) includes a deities' altar (*shenpeng*) for the deities of the whole island; a "three deities' shed" (*sanwang peng*) where three large paper effigies are located; a stage (*xipeng*) where the opera and some Daoist rituals are performed; the bun towers; and a temporary office (*zhili peng*) for the committee members, the police, the first-aid team, and other personnel.[49] Although the location of the jiao shed was moved in the 1960s from the beach on the east of the island to the open ground in front of the Beidi Temple, the basic structure of the area has always been the same. Spirits entering this area are watched by the ghost kings and his colleagues at the "three deities' shed." In the same manner, people entering the area are under the protection of the committees and the police. It is an area where both the spirits and the living come to enjoy the rituals and the opera and to interact with friends and relatives. The four Daoist rituals performed outside the Daoist altar are nonetheless

performed within the confines of the jiao shed. These are the rituals performed by the Daoist priests that concern directly the welfare of the islanders.

The Huizhou-Chaozhou territory at the jiao includes Pak She and San
Hing Streets, where the ancestors of the Huizhou people first settled. These
two streets, including San Hing Back Street, are actually and symbolically
washed before the festival is inaugurated. In 1981, at about three in the
afternoon on the eve of the festival, residents of this area washed and
cleaned the streets. Then, in a ritual known appropriately as "washing the
streets" (xijie), the area was cleansed by three Daoist priests, who walked
through the area dressed in black robes and black hats, carrying black umbrellas.[50] After the streets had been cleansed, three deities—the Pak She
Tianhou, the Taipingshan Xuantian Shangdi, and the Pak She Beidi, in that
order—were paraded through it. After the parade, the three deities were
deposited on the deities' altar. No other deities could be placed on the altar
before their arrival. The very symbolic parade is indicative of the Huizhou
and Chaozhou origin of the festival.

The festival area of the island is marked by nine long bamboo poles
(fan), erected a day before the festival is officially inaugurated. To ensure
cleanliness of the festival area, the streets are ritually cleansed again at
about eight in the evening in a ritual known as "purifying with incense"
(jingxiang). During it, five Daoist priests, accompanied by the child disciples of the Daoist priests for the occasion (baiguan) and members of the
organizing committee, invite all the earth gods of this area to the jiao area.[51]
This is done by the committee members placing lighted incense sticks along
the streets, especially at crossroads, and also distributing them to residents.
The residents place the incense sticks in front of their doors to keep evil
out. After the festival has started, the bamboo poles are visited by the
Daoist priests with their child disciples three times a day. This is also the
area within which the procession takes place.

The festival area that is cleansed and blessed does not include the whole
island. It covers the area of the old Cheung Chau market, but not the Sai
Wan area where the Tanka boat people are concentrated, the southern hill
with the Chinese cemetery, the churches, the foreigners' residences, or the
northern hill with the Christian cemetery and a new settlement of boat
people's houses. However, from the "purifying with incense" ritual in
1992, one could observe how the blessed territory of the land people had
expanded.

On their way around the festival area, the small group accompanying
the Daoist priests in the distribution of incense sticks argued among them-

selves as to whether they should walk through the new housing estates adjacent to the boundary of the traditional territory marked by the Tai Shek Hau Tianhou Temple and distribute incense sticks to residents there. Present on this occasion, I heard one member of the committee say, "Since we have collected money from these people, we should distribute the incense sticks to them." By the same argument, they also went into a seaside reclamation on Tung Tai Road where most of the holiday houses were located, ignoring the complaints of the Daoist priests. Even then, the group did not go beyond the traditional town area, up to the southern and northern peaks, or into Sai Wan, the residential area of the Tanka. Thus, the festival remained exclusive to the land people on the island.

Exclusion of the boat people was more marked in 1992 because of the relative openness of the jiao to participation from land people other than longtime Cheung Chau residents. First, through donation, Huizhou and Chaozhou people who were not living on the island received the deities' blessing and protection by having their names written on the name list (*bang*).[52] Second, the festival has in recent years become a tourist attraction. Crowds flock to Cheung Chau from the rest of Hong Kong to watch the procession, and the Hong Kong Tourist Association organizes "Bun Festival tours" for foreign tourists. That the boat people should still be excluded from the festival in the face of the popularity of the festival in the whole of Hong Kong represents the obstinacy of the continuation of a long-lasting custom.

The Rituals of the Jiao Festival

The Cheung Chau jiao festival is a three-day event.[53] Although preparation of the festival starts at the beginning of the lunar year, the festival is always held during the first half of the lunar Fourth Month. During the three main days of the festival (known as the jiao proper, or *zhengjiao*), all islanders are requested to refrain from eating meat, and no meat is sold on the island. On the day before the main festival days, nine bamboo poles are posted into the ground at various points around the festival area. The deities are then invited to the deities' altar and the streets are washed, physically and symbolically.

In the evening, a ritual known as "cleaning the altar" (*zhengtan*) or "setting the altar" (*putan*) is performed to remove all the unclean and evil influences from the Daoist altar. After the jiao area is cleansed, the "opening eyes" ritual is performed on all deities, including the three large effigies, in a process that is also thought of as the invitation of the presence of the deities. Before midnight, a ritual to formally open the festival is performed in front of the Daoist altar. In this ritual, a paper horse-and-messenger is sent to the three spheres, heaven, earth, and waters, carrying notices and invitations to named deities. The deities having been invited, after midnight the festival is officially inaugurated. The same evening, the Cantonese operas begin, to last three days and four nights.

During the three main days, the Daoist priests, on behalf of the islanders, offer vegetarian sacrifices to all the deities invited to the festival. A regular daily rhythm is set by the rituals known as "three offerings and three repentances" (sanchao sanchan)—held in the morning, at noon, and in the evening—which are the offering of vegetarian sacrifices to the deities and supplication for forgiveness. However, in Cheung Chau the rhythm is interrupted by two special ceremonies performed by the local people rather than by the Daoist priests.

On the first day after the morning offering and repentance, the register of donors for the year (renyuan bang) and a record of daily rituals (huangbang) are taken from the Daoist altar by the Daoist priests and given to the chairman of the organizing committee. The chairman, assisted by his family members, takes these registers to the center of the market where they are pasted on a temporary notice board.[54] At night, in a ritual known as "evening prayer" (wancan), the Daoist priests, on behalf of the islanders, pray and offer sacrifice to deities of the three spheres. The Daoist priests then perform a "summoning the general" ritual (zhaojiang) to recruit a military deity to protect the cleanliness of the Daoist altar. At noon on the second day, instead of the regular "offering and repentance," a "running the afternoon offerings" (zou wuchao) ritual is performed in front of the opera stage. Five tables, each representing one of the five cardinal points, are arranged. Vegetarian offerings from the jiao committee and the islanders are put on the tables. Five Daoist priests, each with a basket of offerings, go round each of these tables. This ritual signifies offerings of food and clothes to the deities of the five directions.

At night, one Daoist priest, dressed all in black, sails on a fishing boat to and fro on the sea outside Tai Wan to feed the hungry spirits of people who have died at sea. The ritual is called "feeding the water ghosts" (ji shuiyou). As the Daoist priest chants, helpers from the jiao committee throw offerings into the sea, thus feeding and placating the dead. At the same time as the ritual is being conducted, the Daoist priests at the Daoist altar perform the "welcoming the sacred ones" (yingsheng) ritual. The presence of the Jade Emperor is invited, and he descends via a bridge represented by white cloth at the altar. Ten types of offerings are offered to the Jade Emperor, the highest deity of the three spheres.

On the third day, the last of the main days, a ritual called "thanking the pole gods" (*xiefan*) is performed. The lanterns that have been hung on the bamboo poles are removed, and the paper shrine at the foot of each is burned. At about ten o'clock in the morning, a "sending off the flower boat" (*qianchuan*) ritual is performed on the opera stage. The ritual begins with the exchange of jokes, and at times threats, between a Daoist priest and the paper messenger of the flower boat held by another Daoist priest not wearing his Daoist attire. After that, the Daoist orders the messenger to throw away the flower boat, which is loaded with things that represent impurity, including a duck (*uup* in vernacular Cantonese, and *ahh* in Hailufeng, which is phonetically close to "danger" or "bad" luck).

A helper then runs with the boat to the sea at the western boundary of the festival area near the Tai Shek Hou Tianhou Temple. He sends the boat and the duck in the direction of the Tanka boat people's area, while the impurities are thrown away from the festival area. Immediately after that, the Daoist priest "distributes talismans" (*banfu*), primarily to Huizhou and Chaozhou people.[55] He cuts the comb of a cock and lets the blood drip onto the talismans. The blessed, the Huizhou and Chaozhou people, will paste the talismans on the main door and kitchen of their homes or carry them on their bodies for protection. The cock represents the spirit of life (*yang*), and therefore, to throw the duck away and to receive the blood of the cock is to throw the bad luck away and to receive good luck.[56]

In the afternoon on the third day is the procession, in which, behind the Beidi, the deities are paraded around the festival area of the island so that evil spirits will be placated and diseases prevented. At the head of the procession is the sedan chair with the Beidi of Taipingshan. It is followed by the deities of the eight temples of the island. Next come the Daoist priests, followed by the representatives of various district associations within the bounded festival area, of the Huizhou and Chaozhou associations, and of other voluntary associations such as martial arts clubs and schools.

The parade is a spectacular sight. Made up of deities in their sedan chairs, flags, unicorn dancers, and floats, the whole procession begins at the Beidi Temple and passes through the entire festival area (see Map 3).[57] When approaching the Hongsheng Temple in Tai San Street, the Tanka carriers hurry to carry the Hongsheng in his sedan chair back to his temple.[58] When the procession reaches the Tai Shek Hau Tianhou Temple, the Daoist priests set free some birds and turtles.⁵⁹ After that, the participating groups go back to their respective offices along the returning route, but the carriers of the sedan chairs hurry their steps and race toward the deities' altar in the jiao area. The islanders believe that the temple and religious group associated with the first sedan chair to reach the altar can expect a good year ahead. In past years, the fierce competition for first place often resulted in violence.⁶⁰

Although the jiao is not over, when the procession is finished meat will again be sold. At night, the "great offering" (*ji dayou*) to the wandering spirits is held. The Ghost King is brought out to an open space where an altar is set up facing it. Between the Ghost King and this altar are placed 36 sets of vegetarian offerings. In this ritual, the Daoist priests, on behalf of the islanders, offer sacrifice to the wandering spirits, and, with the power of the Dicang (king of the underworld, known to Buddhist scholars as Ksitigarbha)⁶¹ symbolized in the headdress worn by the chief Daoist priest for the ritual, salvage the wandering spirits from the underworld. At the end of the ritual, the spirits, believed to be responsible for misfortunes and disasters, will leave the island, and the Ghost King will be sent off (by the burning of his effigy). While the great offering is carried out, a small offering is made on the eastern beach where the jiao was held in the past, presumably so that no wandering spirit will be left out.

At about eleven o'clock, the climax of the festival begins. In past years, considerable violence erupted as participants scrambled up the bun towers to grab their shares of the buns. In 1978, after one of the bun towers collapsed, injuring many people, the scramble up the bun tower was banned by the Hong Kong government; today, the buns are distributed quietly the next morning. The Cantonese opera ends on the same night. At midnight, all paper effigies are burned. The islanders bring along sacrifices to the deities' altar to pray for a good year.

In the afternoon of the next day, a second procession is held, in which the Daoist priests do not participate. The route of the procession is similar to the first one, but this one includes all the temples (with the exception of the Hongsheng's, up to 1981), the streets, and the Huizhou and Chaozhou associations. The deities are returned to their respective temples during the procession. Starting from this night, the Hailufeng opera is performed for three consecutive nights. With the end of the opera, the jiao officially ends.

The rituals described above can be divided into two groups. The first group consists of rituals that require a minimum of local participation. They include daily offerings and repentances, cleansing the Daoist altar and the festival area, inviting the Daoist deities to attend and to supervise the festival, commanding the messenger to throw away dirt and evil, distributing talismans, and carrying out charitable acts such as setting free captured birds and turtles and feeding the hungry wandering spirits. These rituals are performed by the Daoist priests on behalf of the islanders. Although the islanders may not necessarily be aware of the significance of the coherence of the rituals, to the Daoist priests they are a process of renewal by which pollution is removed through purification and repentance, and as a result of which good fortune will be bestowed on the community. The rituals are symbolic, and the process and substance of the rituals cannot be changed by the local people.

Another group of rituals, however, is closely related to the identity and rights of those people who have a share in the festival. In these rituals, great emphasis is placed on local participation, and the Daoist priests act only as middlemen between the people and the deities. The motif of each ritual—such as the incense sticks used at "purifying with incense," the presentation of the register of donors for the year, the boat and the duck at "sending off the flower boat," and the distribution of talismans—is that blessing is passed from the deities, through the Daoist priests, to the members of the jiao committee. Only people who have a right to participate, and the territories that they inhabit, can receive the good fortune that results from these rituals. Therefore, if the shareholding participants and their territories change, the rituals encompassing them will change as well. Who has the right and who does not is an issue decided by the land residents on the island.

Yichu xiangcun yichu li (each village has its own custom) is always the reply given by villagers and Daoist priests when asked the reason for the different practices of jiao rituals in different places. As Tanaka Issei has pointed out, the Daoist portions of the rituals of the jiao festival are always similar. The differences lie in those rituals that "belong" to the community.[62] It is only at these rituals that we see the boundaries of social groups in the community.

Cheung Chau nowadays is in many ways an integrated economic and political unity. With the growth of economic influence, leaders of the Tanka boat people who have settled onshore are joining the local leadership, which formerly consisted only of the land people. Even so, a noticeable social boundary seems to have remained between the two social categories, the land people and the boat people. The historical process indicates that to move from one category to another requires the acquisition of settlement rights on land. Those Tanka boat people who, like their Hailufeng boat-people predecessors, have successfully moved ashore are regarded as land people. Regardless of their ethnic origins they are eligible to participate in local political affairs. However, such openness of social boundary is not without limits. Local ethnic associations continue to enhance identities through the welfare and religious activities they organize.

The jiao festival in Cheung Chau illustrates how this social boundary is at the same time inclusive and exclusive. The jiao festival in Cheung Chau began as a single ethnic group's activity and grew, in time, into an event of the whole island. It changed gradually from a pure Hailufeng festival to include other Huizhou and Chaozhou groups. The festival further developed to include the Cantonese and then all those who lived on land. Thus, over the years, the social boundary of the land people, as highlighted by the festival, has expanded.

However, from different aspects of the jiao festival we can see also the exclusiveness of this social boundary. First, although people who do not live on the island are not excluded from celebrating the festival, among nonresidents only Huizhou and Chaozhou people can receive the blessing of the deities. Second, although some of them live on the island and many of them mingle with the land people, the Tanka boat people and their original residential areas are excluded. They are not allowed to participate in the organizing committee, and their original residential area is the place where the symbols of misfortune are discarded. Third, although the Cantonese are blessed and purified by the deities, they are excluded from the organizational and the religious arena of the festival on ethnic grounds. Only members of the Huizhou and Chaozhou Prefectures Association can be elected as chairmen and vice chairmen of the festival, and only their associations participate in the procession. Finally, the symbolic core of the festival remains firmly Hailufeng.

"To describe a social boundary is not only to describe a group which this encloses but to imply that there is at least one other which it excludes."[63] The social boundary indicated by the jiao festival in Cheung Chau is, using Marshall Sahlins's term, a "complementary opposition" in which different ethnic groups unite and at the same time deny the others.[64] The Hailufeng people and the Tanka boat people are at the two extremes of this centrifugal ethnic continuum, while the Cantonese have been brought gradually into the ritual continuity in a centripetal process. While economic and political development strengthens the forces of ethnic unity, religious activities enhance the counterforces of ethnic boundaries.

The Alliance of Ten:
Settlement and Politics in
the Sha Tau Kok Area

PATRICK HASE

The Settlement of the Hakka
and the Growth of Population

Mirs Bay is a forbidding place. Its coast is almost uniformly mountainous. There is very little flat land: only patches here and there where one of the mountain streams reaches the sea (see Map 4). It is likely that, following the recision of the Coastal Evacuation Order in 1668, the whole of the northern half of Mirs Bay was abandoned and empty of people, waste and silent. Certainly, all the families who live in the area now—all of them Hakka, by definition latecomers to the area—claim to have first moved there only after the recision of the Coastal Evacuation Order in 1668.

The northwestern quadrant of the bay, from Tolo Harbor to Mui Sha (Meisha), is the area whose residents traditionally marketed in Sha Tau Kok (Shatoujiao).[1] Within this area there were, in 1900, about 60 or 65 villages, about three-quarters of which were in the New Territories of Hong Kong. Only about 15 had been founded (or, probably, in many cases, re-founded on the sites of abandoned Ming villages) within the first 50 years after 1668, according to the family traditions of the present villagers. A dozen or so were not founded until after 1800.

These villages were not established by large numbers of newcomers. Most were settled by a single "founding ancestor" and his nuclear family. Wo Hang is a case in point. This village originally had four indigenous resident families. The Lee family arrived in 1688. They probably bought the land from the Cheung family of Wong Pui Ling (Huangbeiling).[2] The settlement group consisted of Lee Tak-wah, his wife, and their only son, Lee Kuen-lam. Lee Kuen-lam had been born in 1644. He was probably not married in 1688, since none of his three sons seems to have died before 1759—they were probably all born in the period from 1690 to 1710. The Lee family believe the other three families had settled at Wo Hang before

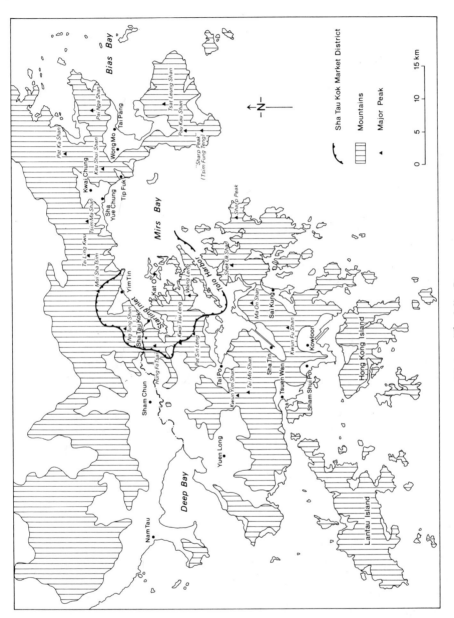

Map 4. The Mirs Bay area

the arrival of Lee Tak-wah, but none of the three arrived with more people than the Lees did. In 1700, Wo Hang cannot have had a total population of more than about 15 adults and a handful of children.

It is unlikely that the other villages in this area in 1700 were larger than Wo Hang. Many must have been smaller, especially those founded by only a single family. The population of the whole area may not have exceeded 450 in total in 1710.

However, with plenty of abandoned land wanting only labor to become fruitful, the population increased rapidly. The Lee clan had only one male in its first and second generations, but three in the third, thirteen in the fourth, and thirty-nine in the fifth who survived to produce children. The fifth generation of the Lees was the generation dominating the village about 1800. In a hundred years the family had expanded forty-fold. Not all families were as successful as the Lees, but very rapid expansion of the population seems to have been general in the area in the eighteenth century. In addition, immigration into the area did not stop so long as cultivable but empty land remained available: new villages continued to be founded throughout the eighteenth century.

It seems likely that, in the period from 1800 to 1825, the population of the Sha Tau Kok area had reached about 7,000. By 1825, most of the cultivable land had been taken up, and most of the lowland villages founded. This period, from 1668 to about 1825, can be called the "period of village foundation" in the population history of the area. From early in the nineteenth century, however, signs of pressure on the land begin to appear: villages began to be founded on clearly secondary mountainside sites, and reclamation projects were undertaken, aimed at increasing the area of arable land by draining the inshore seabed. Reclamation, beginning about 1800 and ending about 1890, by extending the cultivable area, probably allowed the population to continue to expand until about 1875.[3] By then, Sha Tau Kok probably had a total population of about 11,000 or 12,000.[4] This period, from about 1825 to about 1875, can be called the period of reclamation.

A population of this size, however, was as much as could be supported. Thereafter, the population could only remain static—any increase had to be offset by an equivalent emigration away from the area. Shortage of land and subsistence problems in bad years are stressed in a description of the area in 1853, in the middle of the reclamation period.[5] Emigration is attested from the 1850s and was clearly a major social factor from the 1880s.[6] In 1896, the villagers of the Sha Tau Kok area rebuilt their main temple, the Kwan Tai (Guandi) Temple at Shan Tsui. They decided to seek donations for the rebuilding from villagers living abroad. Over a thousand young men from all the villages of the area responded. These young men were then living in Australia and New Zealand, Peru, California, British Columbia, Hawaii, and many other places.[7] Since the total young adult male population of the area is unlikely to have exceeded 3,500 at the end of the nineteenth century, the evidence of this temple rebuilding suggests that a third of the young men of the area were living away from home by then.[8] The period from 1875 onward can only be called the period of emigration.

The 1911 census figures show a population for the Sha Tau Kok area of 8,570 resident within Hong Kong, suggesting a total resident population for the whole marketing district of about 12,000, and a total population, including emigrants, of over 13,000.[9] Thus it appears that from well below 1,000 in the early eighteenth century, the population rose very fast to about 7,000 or 8,000 in the early nineteenth century, to about 9,000 or 10,000 at midcentury, and to about 11,000 or 12,000 from about 1875. In this pattern the population expanded to exploit all the available fertile land, and there followed a period when the resident population was static and the excess males had to emigrate to make ends meet.

A factor in the settlement of the area is the settlement of the boat people. The land inhabitants of the area regarded the Tanka (*danjia*) as second-class people and denied them most civil rights. The Tanka could settle only on isolated islands. If they did not, they risked being ill treated by the land people.

As a result, the Tanka tended to settle on islands at some distance from the primary market. They used the same market as the land people, for that was the only place where their essential buying and selling and exchanging could be done. But they generally did not live there. Thus, most of the boat people of the northwest quadrant of Mirs Bay settled on or in the anchorage at Kat O Island, four and a half miles from Sha Tau Kok, although they traded at Sha Tau Kok. From the seventeenth century onward, the settlement pattern of the Sha Tau Kok area is, therefore, one of fast-growing Hakka dominance of the land, coexisting somewhat uneasily with a Tanka community essentially offshore.

Reclamation Behind the Sha Tau (Shatou): Sha Tau Kok in the 1820s

When the Hakka people first came to Sha Tau Kok, the immediate Sha Tau Kok area was a shallow bay, with creeks stretching inland where streams reached the sea. On the eastern edge of the bay is the mouth of the Sha Tau Kok River. This river carried a large burden of gravel and sand torn out from the mountainside ravines by its tumultuous passage through them. This burden was dropped as the river reached the sea. As a result, the immediate mouth of the river was a cluster of sandbanks and bars, swept aside with each rainstorm. Further away, however, the sand formed a line of dunes that was more permanent, and which became stabilized by grasses and small trees.

This line of sand dunes curved away from the river mouth to the west for about half a mile, as a row of islets about three hundred yards off the original shoreline. Near the river mouth the dunes formed islands some ten feet high and up to a hundred feet broad; farther away they were smaller and narrower, ending up in tiny hummocks of sand only a foot or two above high water, and less than ten feet broad. These sand dunes were called Sha Tau (*shatou*, sand bar), or Sha Lan (*shalan*, sand barrier).

These sand-dune islets had the effect of protecting the strip of water between them and the shore. This strip was shallow and crisscrossed with drainage channels between mudbanks and mangroves.

The original shoreline, behind these mangrove swamps, consisted of a narrow strip of fertile land, almost immediately giving way to the steep slopes of the mountains behind. The fertile land was mostly mixed silt and clay, with some boulders, formed by washdown from the mountains behind. All the old villages of the area were established on the upper edge of this fertile strip. These were Shan Tsui, Tam Shui Hang, and Tong To.[10] These villages formed the Sam Heung (*sanxiang*, three villages) village alliance.

The normal way villagers reclaimed land for arable use was to mark out a line close to lowest water with bamboos rammed into the mud, in an area with plenty of mangrove. Against the bamboos a stout bund of turf and mud would be built to keep out the sea. The mangrove, once dead, would be burned off. The whole area would be flooded with fresh water to leach out the salt from the soil. After some years of use as a fishpond, the water would be drained out, sluices put in the bund, and fields marked out. The sluices would regulate the water levels: fresh water would be allowed to collect behind the bund at high tide, to be released at low tide. Streams too large to allow this to be done safely had to be trained along the edges of the area, between parallel bunds, and drained to the sea away from the reclaimed area.

This process was highly expensive and required a good deal of cash up front: income from the new fields would appear only after perhaps ten or

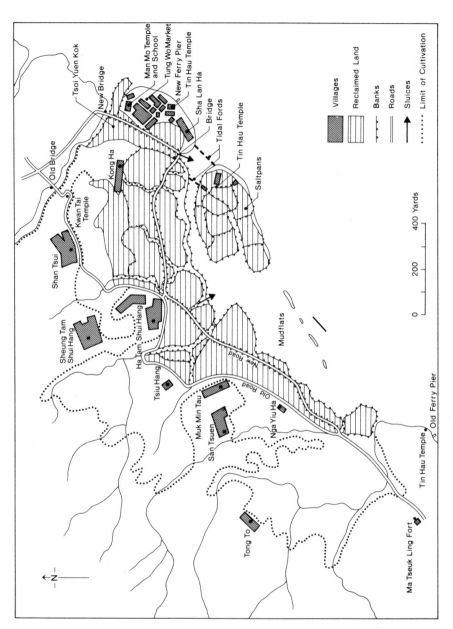

Map 5. The Sha Tau Kok reclamation, 1825

Villages
Reclaimed Land
Banks
Roads
Sluices
Limit of Cultivation

Tsoi Yuen Kok
New Bridge
Man Mo Temple and School
Tung Wo Market
New Ferry Pier
Tin Hau Temple
Sha Lan Ha
Bridge
Tidal Fords
Tin Hau Temple
Old Bridge
Kong Ha
Saltpans
Kwan Tai Temple
Shan Tsui
Sheung Tam Shui Hang
Ha Tam Shui Hang
Tsiu Hang
Muk Min Tau
San Tsuen
Nga Yiu Ha
Mudflats
New Road
Old Road
Tong To
Tin Hau Temple
Old Ferry Pier
Ma Tseuk Ling Fort

0   200   400 Yards

even twenty years. Usually, shares in reclamation projects were sold to villagers: they received a pro rata allotment of the eventual fields when formed. Occasionally, villagers providing labor without pay would also get an allotment in due course.

At Sha Tau Kok, the villagers decided to plan a major reclamation of the heavy mangrove formation in the shallow waters behind the line of sand dunes (see Map 5). To the east, where the sand dunes were broadest and highest, the villagers reclaimed an area inside the dunes, converting them from a low crescent-shaped island into a rough rectangle of land.[11] Further west, where the dunes were lower, and regarded as an insufficient barrier to storm, an artificial bund was constructed shoreward of them, running roughly parallel to the original shoreline from the mouth of the San Tsuen stream to a point close to the eastern reclamation. From here, the artificial bund ran northeast back to the original shoreline on the western mouth of the Sha Tau Kok River. Thus, two areas of reclamation were formed, one an island behind the easternmost dunes, the other a strip along the original shore.[12] The two areas of reclamation were separated by only fifteen feet at the closest point. At three or four places, the new bund crossed significant streams—in each case, the villagers protected the reclamation by constructing bunds running back from the new shoreline along both banks of the stream.

There has always been a road of significance in the area, running from the county city of Nam Tau (Nantou) to the deputy county magistrate's city at Tai Pang (Dapeng). This road, indeed, must have continued in use, and been policed, even in the period immediately after the recision of the Coastal Evacuation Order, when the area was otherwise unoccupied. The road can be traced on the old maps. It ran immediately above the old shoreline, in a sinuous curve around each creek and bay, and immediately in front of Ha Tam Shui Hang and Shan Tsui villages. Leaving Shan Tsui, the road passed around the Kwan Tai Temple and crossed the Sha Tau Kok River by a bridge in front of the temple. After the bund across the bay was built, this road was replaced by a new, straight road along the top of the bund. Where the road reached the eastern corner of the reclamation a bridge was built across the fifteen-foot gap to the island reclamation, and the new road then ran across the island reclamation until the banks of the Sha Tau Kok River were reached, and then crossed that river by a new, large, three-span bridge (see Fig. 1).

This major reclamation project was not the last reclamation in this area. Further reclamations were carried out seaward of the main bund. These may have been envisaged from the first—they permitted the main streams

Fig. 1. Sha Tau Kok from the west. The town can be seen in the distance, across the salt pans, with the C19 reclamation and railway in the foreground (Cho Shin-wing collection, early 1920s; photograph courtesy Hong Kong University).

crossing the reclamation to be gathered into one, with the combined out-flow controlled by a substantial sluice system—and, even if not part of the original plan, were probably undertaken not long after it. Still further piecemeal reclamations were carried out in the beds of the streams, by nar-rowing the areas left for their flood channels. Rather later—probably a generation after the other reclamations—the triangle of land left between the island reclamation and the main reclamation was closed off to form the area known as Tsoi Yuen Kok (Vegetable Gardens Corner). Taken together, all the various arable reclamations totaled a little under 69 acres. Most of the land, once it became productive, was of high quality and was registered as Class 1 agricultural land at the time of the Block Crown Lease, although some of the land within the river channel and next to the most seaward bund, and all the land at Tsoi Yuen Kok, was poorer.

Shan Tsui, Tam Shui Hang, Wo Hang, Nam Chung, Luk Keng, and Kong Ha owned between them seven-eighths of the total arable land on the reclamation (see Table 1). The remaining eighth was owned, in 1905, by nine other villages, plus Sha Tau Kok Market. All were from the immediate area except for Yim Tin, Shuen Wan, and Loi Tung. Several villages im-

TABLE I
Landholding on Sha Tau Kok Reclamation by Villages

Village	Area not including salt pans (acres)	Area including salt pans (acres)
Shan Tsui	5.02	5.02
Tam Shui Hang	13.58	29.07
Kong Ha	23.14	23.14
Wo Hang	7.83	9.22
Yung Shue O	0.62	0.62
Sha Tau Kok	1.93	2.86
Yim Tim	1.09	1.09
San Tsuen	0.87	0.87
Nam Chung	4.68	4.68
Tsiu Hang	0.37	0.37
Luk Keng	5.87	5.87
Loi Tung	0.80	0.80
Shuen Wan	1.55	1.55
Tai Kau	1.04	1.04
Fung Hang	0.29	0.29
Tong To	0.28	0.28
TOTAL	68.96	86.77

SOURCE: Block Crown Lease, Hong Kong

mediately adjacent to the reclamation owned nothing, or very little, on it—Tong To, for instance, San Tsuen, and Sha Tseng Tau (Shajingtou).

In addition to these reclamations for arable land, an area was reclaimed behind the central section of sand dunes. These lower dunes were considered too risky as a protection for farmland, but acceptable as the outer limit for an area of salt pans. This salt-pan reclamation totaled about 21 acres.[13] The salt-pan reclamation formed another island of reclaimed land that was connected with the mainland by fords usable at low tide. The fords joined the salt-pan island with the bridge at the western end of Tsoi Yuen Kok and with the area of reclamation to the east. The salt pans had their salt stores on the mainland next to the western ford—this area was consequently known as Yim Liu Ha ("At the Salt Huts").

The westernmost section of sand dunes was considered too low for any use to be made of it; this section of dune islands still survives as the last relic of the original Sha Tau.

In most cases, the villages owning land on the reclamation did not do so as units. It was only parts of the villages that owned land—typically, just one or two communal trusts or individuals of the village in question invested, while others in the village did not.

Thus, of the land held by Wo Hang in 1905, 4.47 acres was held by the

Kwok Kei Tso (*tso* is the equivalent of *zu*, ancestral trust), 1.91 acres by the Kwok Yam Tso, and 0.69 acres by the Kwok Yau Tso. A further 0.43 acres was held by the Pak Hap Tso, and 0.33 by the Kam Hoi Tso. The Kwok Kei, Kwok Yam, and Kwok Yau Tso were Tso of the sixth generation in Wo Hang—there were at least ten trusts based on ancestors in this generation in that village in 1905. The Kam Hoi Tso was a trust of the eighth generation. The Pak Hap Tso was a trust in which a number of descent lines from the fourth generation shared.

None of the major ancestral trusts, centered on first- or third-generation ancestors, nor any of the major trusts centered on fourth-generation ancestors, were represented. However, the Wo Hang holdings of land on the salt-pan reclamation were all held by the Sam Yue Tong, the trust centered on the main ancestor of the Third Fong of the clan—one of the most important of the ancestral trusts. Much the same is true of the Nam Chung holdings, almost all of which were held by the Tsing Kwun Tso, and of the Luk Keng holdings, which were held by the Wong Tsok Hing Tso, the Chan Yam Kwan Tso, and the Chan Yam Wo Tso—in neither case were more than a small proportion of the village trusts and a very few individual villagers represented as landholders on the reclamation.

The sixth-generation ancestors, whose trusts owned most of the land held by Wo Hang on the reclamation, would have been in the prime of their life in the 1820s. Since that is the most likely date for this reclamation project, it seems probable that when the money was invested into the reclamation project by the Lees, it was individually held cash, rather than communal income, that was in question, and that the holdings were turned into a trust only after the death of the original investors. The investment in the salt-pan reclamation, however, must have been made by an already existing communal trust: the Sam Yue Tong was centered on ancestors who had died a full hundred years before the salt-pan reclamation took place.

The implications of the few villages owning land on the reclamation, and the partial pattern of landholding even within the villages that were represented, make it indisputable that this reclamation was not a communal effort involving the district as a whole, but a commercial development in which individuals or trusts invested cash as they had the opportunity and interest.[14]

Only Kong Ha does not follow this pattern. Effectively all the land of this village lay on the reclamation—the few tiny plots owned away from the reclamation were almost certainly late purchases. The village of Kong Ha itself is built immediately on the edge of the reclamation, and, indeed,

Harvesting. Sha–tau–kok. New Territory

Fig. 2. The Sha Tau Kok reclamation. Harvesting on the early C19 reclamation in front of Kong Ha Village (postcard, 1920s; photograph courtesy Hong Kong University).

some of the buildings on the periphery of the village were actually built on reclaimed land (see Fig. 2).

Kong Ha was founded by members of the Tang clan who had previously lived at Wo Hang. Of the four original founding families of Wo Hang, the strongest were the Lees. The Tsangs and Hos declined, and the last remnants of these families left the village in the later nineteenth century. The Tangs were stronger than the Tsangs and Hos. The Lees believe that the removal of the Tangs from the village, and their resettlement at Kong Ha, was amicable, and the Tangs are still regarded as part of Wo Hang for certain purposes.[15]

Recently, a collection of land deeds was discovered at Wo Hang; these are the deeds of the ancestral and communal trusts of the Third Fong of the Lees, the richest and most powerful group within the clan.[16] The Third Fong bought land in or near the village from the Tangs at a number of dates: 50 taels worth in 1762–65; 189 taels worth in 1769–76; 206 taels worth in 1778–85; 176 taels worth in 1795; 175.2 taels worth in 1815–17; 407.4 taels worth in 1823–28; and 64 taels worth in 1837. It is difficult not to believe that the 974.6 taels worth of land sold by the Tangs to the Lee Third Fong ancestral trusts in the 50 years from 1778 to 1828 represents the period when the Tangs moved out to Kong Ha, and, by extension, the date when the reclamation was undertaken. I assume, on the basis of this information, that reclamation in the Sha Tau Kok Bay began in the last decades of the eighteenth century or early in the nineteenth century, and was completed and productive by the mid-1820s. The huge sales by the Tangs to the Lees in 1823–28 must represent the period during which the Tangs definitively moved to Kong Ha and gave up their older home.

It is difficult to date the reclamation of the salt-pan area, or of Tsoi Yuen Kok. The Basel missionaries, in their full description of the area in 1853, mention rice cultivating, fishing, selling fuel, and operating shops or workshops in the market as ways local villagers made a living. It is, perhaps, unlikely that they would have kept silent about so significant a local industry as 21 acres of salt pans. It is possible, therefore, that this reclamation was undertaken after 1853. Sha Tau Kok was temporarily almost deserted in the face of the close approach of the Taiping rebels in 1854, and the salt-pan reclamation might have been undertaken in the period following the reestablishment of the market in the late 1850s. The salt pans may well have been moved to Sha Tau Kok from an earlier site near Wu Shek Kok, where the name of the tiny village of Yim Tso Ha (At the saltworks) suggests that there must once have been salt fields. The Yim Tso Ha area was reclaimed for arable use in the second half of the nineteenth century.[17] As for Tsoi Yuen Kok, this was probably undertaken last of all, perhaps not until the 1880s.[18]

The Foundation of the Market at Sha Tau Kok

In 1911, the populations of the various primary marketing districts within the northern New Territories ranged from about 7,000 to about 24,000. It seems likely, therefore, that a dependent population of 7,000 was about the minimum necessary in this area for the successful establishment of a market.[19] Successful establishment of a market in this area seems to have required also a clearly differentiated dependent area, separated off from other market districts by a mountain range or some other significant physical barrier.[20] This physical separation was necessary because establishment of a new market invariably led to realignments of local political and social structures to the detriment of those groups that had previously dominated the older markets. Successful establishment of new markets seems to have required the confidence engendered by a clear district identity, to say nothing of the physical protection of a defensible boundary line.

In the Ming and early Qing period the Sha Tau Kok area was within the Sham Chun (Shenzhen) marketing district. The Sha Tau Kok area is physically separated from the Sham Chun area by the Hung Fa Tsai range, which is crossed by only one easily usable pass, at Miu Keng. This suggests that the marketing district of the old Sham Chun Market could have been split, with a new market established on the Sha Tau Kok side of the pass once the Sha Tau Kok population and its self-confidence had risen to the necessary levels. As we have seen, the population of the Sha Tau Kok area had probably reached about 7,000 by about 1800, and 8,000 by about 1825. It had, therefore, reached the point where it could support a market by the early nineteenth century.

By the early nineteenth century the district not only had the necessary population but had also developed to the point where its inhabitants had started to look to an end to dependence on wealthy outsider families. Even before 1825, local self-confidence in at least the wealthier parts of the district had led to the establishment of intervillage alliances.[21] By about 1825 the district started to have enough gentry leaders for it to have had some access to the magistrate, which would have facilitated any moves to throw off dependence on outsiders.[22] Finally, by the early nineteenth century, at least some of the villages had enough wealth to act as leaders.

The wealthy villages were those from which the men who had invested in the Sha Tau Kok reclamation had come (Wo Hang, Nam Chung, Luk Keng, Tam Shui Hang, and Shan Tsui) plus Lin Ma Hang and Yim Tin (Yantian). These villages seem to have produced all the early leaders of the area. It is likely that, after the reclamation had proved to be a success, the leaders of these five villages got together to found a market and an alliance of the local villagers to support it, so that they could enjoy a life free of external interference. The alliance they formed to support the market, and in whose name the market was owned, was later called the Shap Yeuk (*shiyue*, "Alliance of Ten") from the ten or eleven intervillage alliances that united to form it. The Shap Yeuk, its organization, and its political management of the town and district are discussed in greater detail in what follows.

There is no direct evidence of the date of foundation of the market and the Shap Yeuk, but it must have been between 1825 and 1840, most probably between 1830 and 1835. The market must have been founded after the major reclamation of the bay, since part of the market stands on reclaimed land on the eastern island of reclamation, and access to it would have been difficult, if not impossible, until the reclamation had progressed to the point where the bridge could be built across to the new market site.

It is possible that the existence of a large island formed from sandbanks recently thrown up by the sea may have helped in giving the villagers confidence in their fight for independence—perhaps the older clans were felt to have less claim on this "new land" than on the villages and fields on the shore, which had been theirs since time immemorial, and such a site was therefore felt to be particularly suitable for the founding of a new market to symbolize the independence of the district. The market at Yim Tin was founded on exactly the same sort of site—an island of sandbanks some distance offshore—which suggests that a site of this sort had some advantages.

As we have noted, the history of the Tang landholdings of Kong Ha strongly suggests that the reclamation was completed only in about 1823–28. It is, therefore, most likely that the market was founded after that; probably quite soon after that. Two references to the foundation of the market occur in genealogies in the area. Both suggest a foundation date of about 1835.[23] The latest possible date for the foundation is about 1840. By 1848 the Basel missionaries found the new market to be in a flourishing condition. In that year, they said of it that although it was "newly built," it was nonetheless developed enough to be called "a substantial market bustling with business"; a town with its own formal name (Tung Wo Hui, Donghexu, "Eastern Peace Market"), market elder, and town watch, and 72 substantial shop units, surrounded by a wall with four gates.[24]

The Shap Yeuk built their towns with walls, and defense of the town against attack from outside was clearly a factor in district thinking. At some date after 1854 the Shap Yeuk added two tall gun towers to the town, one on either side of the main gate facing the bridge. Guns were kept there by the Shap Yeuk. At the same time, defenses were never a dominant feature of the town—the Shap Yeuk did not preserve the integrity of the walls, which were breached by doors and windows even before 1850. It is doubtful if the town could ever have been defended against determined attack.

Sha Tau Kok was not the only market in the northwest of Mirs Bay. As mentioned already, there was also a market at Yim Tin, built on sandbanks some distance offshore. This market is mentioned in the 1688 county gazetteer, which probably means that there was a market there before 1661.[25] It must, however, have ceased to operate when the district became depopulated as a result of the Coastal Evacuation. A market here is also mentioned in the 1819 county gazetteer.[26] A market must have been refounded here perhaps a generation before Sha Tau Kok. This market, however, was small (only a handful of shops), badly sited (it was on an offshore sandbank island; the only access was by a ferry from the shore), and poorly located (it was at the far eastern edge of the district, and had nothing to its east but several miles of almost uninhabited country). The Ho (He) family of Yim Tin was one of the richest families in the area in the early nineteenth century. The market on the sandbanks at Yim Tin was probably refounded as an expression of Ho family pride about 1800. It was never very successful, serving only the single valley of Yim Tin with its half-dozen villages.[27] When the Shap Yeuk was established, the Yim Tin people joined in, and they invested considerably in the new market—as soon as the new, better located market was founded, the older market at Yim Tin became a subordinate, satellite market to it.

Sha Tau Kok stood at a nodal point in the local road and ferry system. In the 1688 gazetteer several of the ferries and roads are mentioned.[28] Of the ferries mentioned there, the most significant is the "Ma Tseuk Ling Ferry," which "ran along the coast" to Sha Yue Chung (Shayuyong).

Unfortunately, neither the 1688 nor the 1819 gazetteer states who owned the ferry to Sha Yue Chung before the market was founded. But it is likely that the first thing the Shap Yeuk did when the new market was established was to move the ferry pier from Wu Shek Kok near Ma Tseuk Ling into the new market and take over its ownership and operation. By 1848, when the first description of the route to Sha Tau Kok was written by a Basel missionary, the ferry pier was securely established at Sha Tau Kok; by the early twentieth century, the ferry was certainly owned and operated by local villagers and had probably been so since the market was founded.[29]

Sha Tau Kok's position in the road system of the area gave it one major economic advantage: its geographical location in relation to Sham Chun. Sham Chun was at the head of navigation on the Sham Chun River, and was a busy port for the junks that came up the river from Deep Bay. But Sham Chun had no water route to the east, to Mirs Bay. Sha Tau Kok was, in effect, the port of Sham Chun to the east.

The trade in the rice, salt, and fish of Mirs Bay carried by coolies to the bigger market seven miles away was what made Sha Tau Kok prosperous. It was surprisingly large—according to surveys conducted by the Hong Kong government between 1904 and 1910, some 20,000 travelers were carrying about 200–250 tons a month, rising to 400 tons in peak periods, from Sha Tau Kok to Sham Chun in the early twentieth century, while total

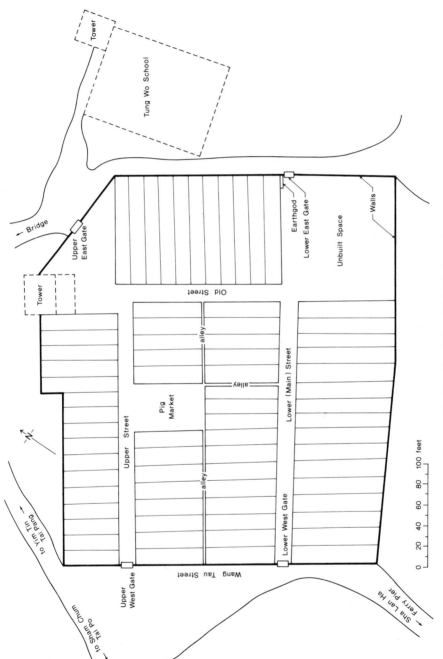

Map 6. Sha Tau Kok (Tung Wo) Market, 1853

Tower

Tung Wo School

Tower

← Bridge

Upper East Gate

Old Street

Earthgod

Lower East Gate

Walls

Unbuilt Space

alley

Pig Market

alley

alley

Upper Street

Lower (Main) Street

to Yim Tin
to Tai Pang

to Sham Chun
to Tai Po

Upper West Gate

Wang Tau Street

Lower West Gate

Sha Lan Ha
Ferry Pier

0   20   40   60   80   100 feet

traffic on all the roads out of Sha Tau Kok to the west averaged 75,000 travelers and 900 tons of goods a month, and perhaps double that at peak periods.[30]

Undoubtedly, traffic on these roads was far less in 1830, when local populations were so much smaller. Nonetheless, these early twentieth century statistics suggest what the founders of the market, the early leaders of the Shap Yeuk, were trying to capture for themselves, and what a substantial prize was available to the "small families" if they were able to free themselves from dependence on the great clans and their markets.[31]

The Market at Sha Tau Kok in the Nineteenth Century

What we know of the market at Sha Tau Kok before 1899 comes entirely from the descriptions and maps produced by the Basel missionaries. They describe the town in these words:

Tungfo[32] is a substantial market, given over to trade. It is newly built, and bustles with business. . . . Living there is to be in the midst of a teeming crowd of Chinese.

In the village of Tungfo, "Eastern Peace," there are no family houses because this place is a market. All the buildings are used as shops and workshops. Amongst them are six pharmacies. In total there are fifty such shops, large and small, which are all built closely together, and form two east-west streets running parallel to each other. The whole place would look like a square if the second street were as completely built up as the first. Such a shop is narrow and dark. During the day it is aired through the open door, which is as wide and high as the shop itself. In front of the door is a row of round posts which are let into the beams of the roof, and, at the bottom, into a stone footing. During the day, the middle posts are removed in order to allow entrance to the shop. Just behind the row of posts is the door, which consists of movable wooden planks, which fit into a slot. At dusk the posts are put back, and the planks moved forward into place, and barred from the inside with a cross-bar. Inside the shop the goods are piled up on shelves on one or both sides of the shop, just as in European shops. Across the middle stands a long counter used as a till, on which goods are weighed and measured. From the roof of the shop some paper lanterns hang down which light up the shop during the night. Most of the shops are general goods stores. Most do retail business. Only a few of them have significant trade. The owners of these shops, both large and small, do not live in the town, but in the neighbouring villages, and only come here for business and trade, or have it conducted by a substitute/manager.[33]

This description is clarified and amplified by the map produced by the missionaries, probably in 1853 (see Map 6). This shows that the town formed a rough square, about 350 feet by 300 feet. There were three streets—two main streets running northeast-southwest, joined by a street running at right angles to them toward the east of the town. In the 1920s these streets were respectively known as Upper Street; Lower, or Main Street; and Old Street. At least the first two names were probably used from the first foundation. The streets were narrow (about fifteen feet wide) and lined with terraces of shops. The map shows 72 shop units in place in 1853, 29 in Upper Street, 32 in Lower Street, and 11 in Old Street. There were three open spaces—a triangular space behind the Upper East Gate, a three-shop-unit space in the middle of Upper Street used as a pig market, and a seven-shop-unit space inside the Lower East Gate. The last of these was not planned; it was just an area of building plots not yet taken up at that date.

The Shap Yeuk, clearly, had laid out the market by first building the walls, gates, and roads, and then offering plots for development. Those plots backing onto the walls required developers to build back from the prebuilt wall to the street. This is clear since the unbuilt space inside the Lower East Gate had the walls already in place, although the plots had not yet been built on. Once the shops were all built, the walls became the continuous back wall of the shops. The Shap Yeuk did not keep control over the integrity of the walls after the shops were built, allowing windows and doors to be inserted through them. The Basel missionaries rented the five houses immediately inside the Upper West Gate, the fourth and fifth in 1848, and the others in 1852. A door through the wall had already been inserted in the first house, and a window in house three, before the missionaries rented them; the missionaries inserted a door in house four, and a further window in one of the houses.

It is not clear if at Sha Tau Kok development plots were distributed to the founding villages, because little evidence survives of landownership within the market. It is probable that there was some kind of distribution of at least some of the lots, but once the central part of the town was laid out, the remaining lots may have been sold. It is known that the five houses rented by the Basel missionaries immediately inside the Upper West Gate were owned by three landlords, and that houses four and five were owned by a gentry elder of Yim Tin. The pawnshop on Old Street was also owned by Yim Tin people in the 1920s. Other shops on Lower Street in the 1920s were operated, and probably owned, by Wo Hang (including the largest shop in the town), Tong To (Sam Heung), Tsat Muk Kiu and Nam Chung (Tai Tan Yeuk), Au Tau (Luk Heung), and Tai Long (Wo Hang Yeuk). Of the shops on Upper Street whose ownership in the 1920s is remembered, one was owned by Sha Tseng Tau (Luk Heung) and one by Yim Tin. This range of ownership suggests that each Yeuk owned at least some shops in the old market, and that there had been, therefore, some distribution of plots. It is a pity that no better evidence of this important feature of the town survives.[34]

Since Lower Street was also called Main Street, it is probable that most of the significant shops were there in the early days. By the 1920s, most of the shops had moved to Wang Tau Street, the street outside the western wall of the 1830–35 market, but the largest shop was still in Lower Street, probably because it had been founded several decades before and was committed to the premises that had been rebuilt for its occupation then. The pawnshop, too, was away from Wang Tau Street—it stood at the junction of Old Street and Upper Street, occupying the lower floors of the gun tower built next to the Upper East Gate, as well as the adjacent lots. This location probably also reflects heavy investment in the specialized premises needed for a pawnshop—it could not move easily when the other shops started migrating to Wang Tau Street.

The design of the town seems to suggest that it was expected that the bulk of the traffic through it would enter through the Upper East Gate and leave through the west gates, either to the ferry pier through the Lower West Gate, or toward Shek Chung Au through the Upper West Gate. It is possible that the road running past the town directly from bridge to bridge was not open at this early date, which would certainly have meant that the traffic was forced through the town. The main gate was, clearly, the Upper East Gate, which was built in a section of wall angled to face the bridge squarely.

The shop units formed single- and double-unit shops. Many of the shops were built in pairs, with the wall between the shop sections made of planks. This plank wall could be removed. Such pairs of shops could either function as two single shops or as one double shop. The Basel missionaries seem to have rented two pairs of shops and one single shop. It is because of this feature that the 72 shop units present in the town represented only about 50 shops—there must have been some 20 large shops occupying two units and some 30 smaller shops each occupying just one.

The shops were built as single-storied structures, comprising a front shop or workshop room and a rear residential or storeroom, separated by a *tin-tseng* (*tianjing*, airwell), which doubled as a kitchen (see Figures 3 and 4). The rear rooms each had a cockloft. The front rooms had a small cockloft immediately inside the door, for storage or to provide sleeping accommodation for hired staff. Most of these front rooms also had an open cockloft above the rear part of the shop. Most of the shop units were about 65 feet long and 15 feet or a little less broad, although some of the premises

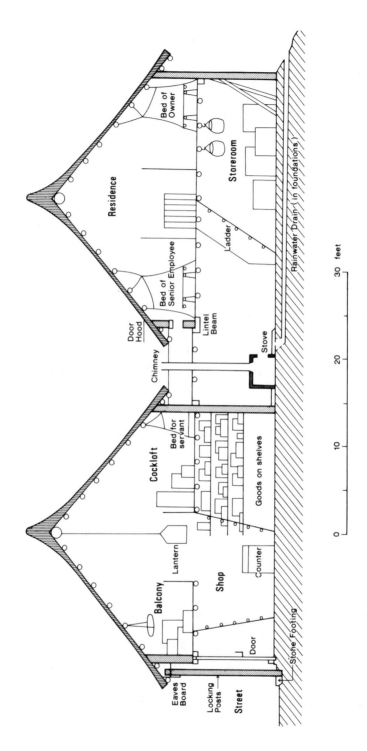

Fig. 3. Shops in Sha Tau Kok (section)

on Old Street and toward the eastern end of Lower Street were bigger, about 120 feet long—these had particularly large storerooms and may have had two *tin-tseng*, or open storage areas, at the rear. The shops were built of brick, with tiled roofs resting directly on beams supported by the side walls, although the Basel missionaries mention mat-sheds in the area as well.

The missionaries' account of the market excerpted above makes it clear that although most of the shops were retail establishments, some were wholesale, and that although most were small scale, some were more significant. Most were general stores, but more than one in ten were pharmacies. The wholesale establishments, it can confidently be assumed, would have been, as later, mostly in the fish business. The Basel missionaries imply that fuel hawkers were active in the town—probably, as later, in that part of Wang Tau Street outside the Lower West Gate. Other hawkers there must have been as well, although the only one specifically referred to by the missionaries is an itinerant barber who traveled with his tools and a portable charcoal stove (to heat shaving water) in two small cabinets carried on a shoulder pole. This probably indicates that there was no barber's shop in the town then, as there would be later.

The existence of a specific pig market area implies that villagers brought animals to sell and that someone in the market wished to buy. In the 1920s at least two shops in the market operated as pig slaughterers, and we can safely infer that at least one did so in 1853. There was also in the 1850s at least one carpenter in the town, and at least one "totally comfortless" guesthouse. Some of the merchants in the town were regularly trading by sea with Hong Kong and elsewhere, and were employed by the Basel missionaries to bring money from the mission's agents in Hong Kong. This suggests a substantial line of business for such merchants.[35]

The accounts from 1853 do not mention any restaurants in the town, but a later report, from 1882, speaks of a man selling noodles from a wooden hut "at the entrance to the market" (probably in Wang Tau Street) while his family lived in their village house. So, if there were no such establishments in the town in the 1850s, there were by a generation later.[36]

It has been suggested that the early commercial development of the town was due to outsiders—Hoklos from the east and Punti people from Guangzhou.[37] This is clearly not the case. The early development of the town was indigenous, with shopkeepers from the Hakka villages of the immediate neighborhood. The early political and economic development of the town were both entirely local in character. Punti and Hoklo merchants

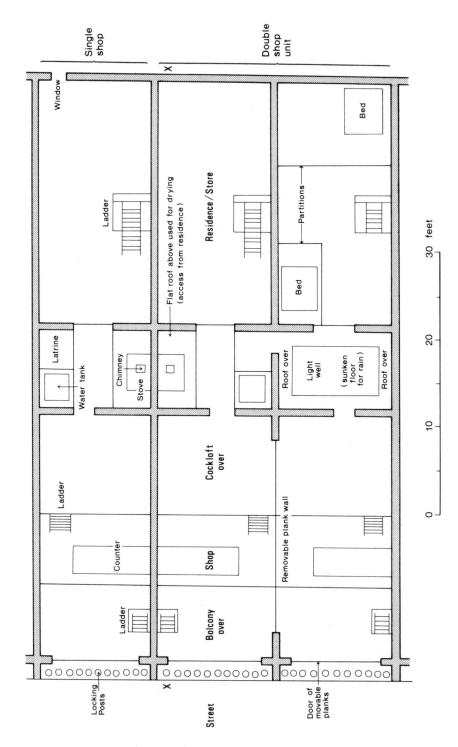

Fig. 4. Shops in Sha Tau Kok (floor plan)

came only later, after the town was well established, and they never dominated the town, either politically or economically.

There was no temple in the town in 1853—only an earth-god shrine inside the Lower East Gate—and no school. (The missionaries considered that a school would be the evangelistic medium most likely to succeed in Sha Tau Kok, and even though their school existed for only a few months, it soon had 25 students.)[38]

Another thing missing in 1853 was a system of realistic defenses. The town walls were breached by doors and windows very early, as we have noted, and the town would not have been defensible against any real attack. At some date between 1853 and 1915, the Shap Yeuk added two significant gun towers to either side of the Upper East Gate. Both were tall—four or five stories. The date (or dates) when these towers were built is not known, but it must have been at a period when attack was feared from the east, over the bridge. This is the direction from which the Taiping rebels had come, and at least one of the towers might well have been built as a response to this threat. The western tower was the older—it was much more weathered than the eastern one in the youth of the present-day elders, although both were already there by 1915. It is unlikely that they were both a response to the chaos of the early Republican period, although the eastern one may have been.

There is no reference to a custom-built pawnshop in the town in 1853, and it is unlikely that there was one—such premises had to be specially built, with a strong tower surrounded by courtyards and storage rooms, and could not be fitted into a standard 15-foot-wide shop unit. No site suitable for a pawnshop can be seen on the map included among the Basel Mission's records. However, a pawnshop must have been established shortly afterward. A Sha Tau Kok pawnshop donated to the 1896 rebuilding of the Shan Tsui Temple, and, although this pawnshop had a different name from the Sha Tau Kok pawnshop in the 1920s, it is likely that the 1896 pawnshop occupied the same site as the 1920s one—that is, the lower floors of the western gun tower along with the adjacent shop units.[39] Hence it is very likely that at least this tower dates from the nineteenth century—if so, it was very probably built in the period of the Taiping, since later decades were peaceful.

The Basel missionaries were finally forced out of Sha Tau Kok in 1854, because of its lawlessness and the large number of undesirables always congregating there.[40] Although the implications of this are not clear, such conditions probably reflected the busy traffic of travelers passing through the town and over the ferries, with the attendant instability and insecurity. The situation that led to the missionaries' departure is probably to be read as evidence of the town's prosperity and vigorous life.

Thus, the documents from the Basel Mission Archives give us a clear picture of life in mid-nineteenth-century Sha Tau Kok—a unique picture, indeed, for a market town in this area. They show a vigorous—perhaps too vigorous—town, full of shops and traders, already firmly set into the pattern that would become more clear in the 1920s. Above all, they show us the clear interrelationship that existed between the town and the nearby villages that provided its shopkeepers and clients. They show us what a genuinely *local* market was like in this area—one devoid of external control and having its life within the local community.

Temples and Religious Ties in the Sha Tau Kok Area

There were six temples that had a relationship with the market. These were "the four Tin Haus (Tianhou) of Sha Tau Kok," the Kwan Tai Temple at Shan Tsui, and the Man Mo Temple within the market.

The four Tin Haus were those of the temples at Am King (Anjing); Sha Lan Ha (Shalanxia), just outside the market; Yim Liu Ha; and Wu Shek Kok. Before 1949, the Sha Lan Ha Temple was the most revered, being worshiped by the fishermen, the Sam Heung villagers, the villagers of the wider Shap Yeuk area, and the townspeople. This temple was probably founded during the second quarter of the nineteenth century, about the same time as the most likely date of the foundation of the market. The leading figure in the foundation of this temple was probably a self-made villager of Shan Tsui. This can be taken to imply that the temple was, from the beginning, owned by the Sam Heung group of villages. Until the 1940s, these villages celebrated the Ta Tsiu (*dajiao*) Festival in front of the temple.[41]

Ritual practice at the Ta Tsiu Festival at Lai Chi Wo makes it clear that the Am King Temple was quite old. The villagers at Lai Chi Wo often cross over to Kat O to worship Tin Hau in her temple there, and they therefore include the Kat O Tin Hau in their Ta Tsiu, as well as the Kwan Tai from their own temple at Lai Chi Wo. However, they also worship the Tin Hau from Am King at the Ta Tsiu. The villagers' legends on this (which say that the Kat O Tin Hau floated from Am King over the water to Kat O via Lai Chi Wo) imply that the Kat O Tin Hau was a daughter temple of Am King.[42] The Kat O Tin Hau Temple dates at the latest from 1763, when the villagers of the "Kat O Heung" dedicated a bell "to stand forever before the altar of the Lady Tin Hau."[43] The Am King Temple, therefore, dates at least from the early Qing. This temple was owned by the Luk Heung, and they used to celebrate the Ta Tsiu Festival there once every ten years.

Another probably old Tin Hau Temple in the area is the one at Wu Shek Kok. This temple stands immediately adjacent to the likely site of the pre-1835 Ma Tseuk Ling ferry pier, and is now extremely remote and little frequented. The oldest piece of temple furniture at present is the bell, cast in 1922, but the temple is at least pre-British, since it appears in the Block Crown Lease Survey. It almost certainly dates from the period when the ferry left from alongside it, that is, from before 1835. The Ma Tseuk Ling Yeuk owns this temple.

The fourth temple, at Yim Liu Ha, in the middle of the salt pans, must be the youngest of the four. It could not have been founded before the salt-pan reclamation, so probably dates from after 1854. Tin Hau protects those in danger from the waves. The salt-pan workers, protected only by the flimsy shelter of their inadequate bunds, were definitely at risk during storms, and a Tin Hau Temple was, therefore, suitable for them. The temple here was frequented only by the salt workers. It was owned by Tam Shui Hang village, which was the majority owner of the salt pans. Thus these four Tin Hau temples were owned by four separate villages or groups of villages. None were owned by the Shap Yeuk as a whole.

The other significant and early temple was the Kwan Tai Temple at Shan Tsui. This temple is intimately connected with the old, pre-reclamation road, which runs, in fact, around three sides of it: the temple was, according to Shan Tsui village elders, built across the original line of the road to deflect a dangerous Fung Shui (*fengshui*) influence. This temple must date from before the new road was opened in about 1835, although the oldest datable items in the present temple are the tablet and altar furniture recording the 1896 rebuilding. This temple was owned by Shan Tsui village.

It will be seen that the Shap Yeuk originally lacked opportunity for any ritual expression of its existence as the representative of the unity of the whole district. The major temples were in existence before it was established, and were owned by individual villages or groups of villages. In 1853, there was no temple or ritual center owned by the Shap Yeuk as a whole.

However, at some point after 1854—probably quite soon after—the Shap Yeuk took steps to remedy this lack. The alliance founded, just outside the walled market, a large school, the Tung Wo (Donghe) School. This comprised three courtyards, one behind the other. The front two were the school. The back court, however, was a temple owned by the Shap Yeuk, dedicated to the gods of the civil and military virtues (Man Mo Yi Tai,

Wenwu *erdi*). Next to the Man Mo altar, the Shap Yeuk established a "Hero Shrine" on the one side and a meeting hall for the alliance on the other. The Hero Shrine seems not to have been, as is usual with shrines of this title, dedicated to those who had died in intervillage wars; rather, it was a general shrine to the unremembered dead, the unrequited and hungry ghosts. The Shap Yeuk collected uncared-for bones and buried them in a communal grave. The elders worshiped annually at the grave and at the spirit tablet to these dead in the Hero Shrine.[44] The Hero Shrine and the Man Mo Temple gave the Shap Yeuk a ritual focus and allowed for the annual religious acts that most local associations found essential to keep their members together. It is possible that it was the dislocation of the life of the market caused by the near approach of the Taiping rebels that caused the Shap Yeuk elders to make these changes.

The Shap Yeuk, as well as owning the Man Mo Temple and the Hero Shrine, also seems to have developed a relationship with the Sha Lan Ha and Shan Tsui temples. The present-day elders cannot remember in detail what communal worship the Shap Yeuk elders used to conduct. They believe, however, that they worshiped annually in the Man Mo Temple and the Hero Shrine, and very possibly at Sha Lan Ha as well. The Shan Tsui elders are positive that the Shap Yeuk also worshiped regularly at the temple there. Nonetheless, even though the Shap Yeuk owned one temple, seem to have worshiped regularly at two others, and had some sort of vague relationship with yet three more, it seems likely that the ritual underpinning of the alliance was not as powerful in the case of the Shap Yeuk as in some others. There was, for instance, no Shap Yeuk Ta Tsiu, and the Shap Yeuk Temple does not seem to have been particularly revered. The wider Shap Yeuk interest in the Shan Tsui Temple can be seen from the contributions to the 1896 rebuilding, which, as noted above, came from young emigrants from all the villages of the area, and not just from Shan Tsui.

The Shap Yeuk and the Political Structure of the Town and District

The Sha Tau Kok villages were established in the market district of Sham Chun. Sham Chun was dominated by a group of extremely rich and powerful Punti clans. These rich clans, despite the enmity that often existed between them, united to keep the "small families" subordinate. At some date probably in the late eighteenth or early nineteenth century they founded the Community School in Sham Chun. This was not only a school but also a forum where the clan elders and degree holders of the great families could meet and adjudicate disputes arising in the district. This meeting was recognized by the magistrate as representing the Eastern Division of the county. The degree holders called their meeting the Tung Ping Kuk (Dongping *ju*, "Council for Peace in the East"). The Tung Ping Kuk must have become particularly powerful in the 1850s, when the onset of the Taiping rebels reduced the effectiveness of the magistrate to a low level.[45]

The power of the great clans was resented by the "small families." Much of the history of the Hong Kong region in the nineteenth century is of the struggles of the "small families" to free themselves from the domination of the great clans and to become political forces themselves. The "small families" could achieve this by uniting into mutual defense associations, or Yeuk (*yue*). While an individual "small family" was no match for a great clan, the united forces of a whole district of "small families" was normally greater than that of any one great clan on its own.[46] The "small families," in their struggles with the great clans, attempted, first, to free their districts from the dominance of the great clans; second, to free themselves from having to do their marketing in the markets owned or dominated by the great clans; third, to take over control of the nodal points—bridges and ferries, especially—of the local road systems; and fourth, to free themselves from having their contacts with the magistrate mediated through some organization of great-clan gentry. The Hakka villages of the Sha Tau Kok area achieved all four of these aims during the second quarter of the nineteenth century.

In the early twentieth century, the villages of the Sha Tau Kok area were arranged in eleven Yeuk alliances, and the district as a whole was usually called the Shap Yeuk ("Alliance of Ten") in consequence.[47] The Shap Yeuk covered most of the Sha Tau Kok marketing district, but not all of it: in particular the boat people at Kat O remained aloof (see Map 7). At this date the market at Sha Tau Kok was owned by the Shap Yeuk, which also controlled all the ferries in the area. The village elders and degree holders of the Shap Yeuk also had a gentry meeting in Sha Tau Kok, which the magistrate recognized—the gentry called this the Tung Wo Kuk (Donghe *ju*, "Council for Peace in the East") in clear emulation of the Punti council in Sham Chun. Clearly, the establishment of the Yeuk, and the Shap Yeuk Alliance, in the Sha Tau Kok area was a crucially important political milestone in the history of the area.

The establishment of the Shap Yeuk was accomplished by the second quarter of the nineteenth century. The Basel missionaries said in 1853:

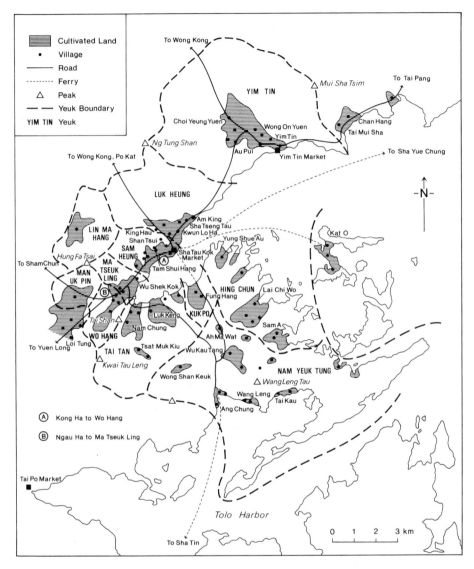

Map 7. The Shap Yeuk (Alliance of Ten)

All who take part in this market [Sha Tau Kok] have united into an association, which is called the "Market Association." This consists of eleven small associations to which belong 45 smaller and larger villages. The owners of the shops in the market come from these villages. Of course, not everyone who belongs to the "Market Association" has a share in a shop, but they all have an interest in the market, and therefore have been accepted as members of the Association.[48]

This description makes it clear that the Shap Yeuk was in full operation in 1853 and that, as later, it was an alliance of eleven Yeuk groups of villages. Perhaps of even greater interest is that this description makes it clear that the Shap Yeuk was closely linked with the market. The description strongly suggests that the Shap Yeuk was established in order to facilitate the foundation of the market, and in the same period, that is, about 1835.

It seems likely that the area was, in the eighteenth century, dominated by the Cheung clan of Wong Pui Ling near Sham Chun and the Tang clan of Lung Yeuk Tau. Of the great Punti clans of the Sham Chun area, the Cheungs, based to the east of the town, tended to dominate all those "small families" living yet farther east in Ta Kwu Ling and Sha Tau Kok, whose route to the market lay through Wong Pui Ling and via the ferries owned by the Cheungs. Similarly, the Tangs, the oldest and one of the greatest of the clans of the area south of Sham Chun, lay astride another of the major routes of the area—the road from Sha Tau Kok to Yuen Long.[49] The overlapping areas of influence and the mutual enmities of these two great clans may have helped the "small families" in the Sha Tau Kok area set up their Yeuk alliance system so early.

In many cases, alliances of "small families" succeeded in wresting independence from domination by the great clans only following open warfare or long litigation and dispute. However, at Sha Tau Kok there is no memory of any fighting or litigation.

The Shap Yeuk district had a political structure not dissimilar to that of other districts in the region. Each of the eleven Yeuk areas had a committee of elders, which made decisions for the community of the Yeuk as a whole and which dealt with the magistrate where necessary. These committees consisted of the prominent elders of the villages of the Yeuk and the degree holders of the Yeuk (if any). We have little evidence of how these Yeuk-level committees functioned. The best evidence is in the four petitions translated, and the further three petitions referred to, in the documents submitted to the Colonial Secretary by the various Yeuk of the Sha Tau Kok area during the process of taking over the New Territories in 1899.[50]

The Wo Hang petition was signed by five "elders and gentry," all of Wo Hang. Two or three of the signatures were holders of *xiucai* degrees; one other was the most senior of the clan, the last surviving member of the sixth generation (he was not a *xiucai*); and one or two of the remainder were also non-degree-holding elders. The Luk Keng petition was signed by two men—one certainly a *xiucai*, and the other probably a non-degree-holding elder—both of Luk Keng.

The Nam Yeuk Tung petition was signed by three men. The names are probably corrupt in the text, but all three were probably non-degree-holding elders of Wu Kau Tang. The names of the persons signing for the Sam Heung (there called the Ha Po subdistrict) are unfortunately not included in the translation. The Kuk Po petition was signed by a non-degree-holding elder, as was the Hing Chun petition (there were no degree holders in these Yeuk). The Lin Ma Hang petition was signed by a *xiucai* of that village.

These petitions make it clear, first, that the Yeuk leadership was shared by degree holders and non–degree holders. In Wo Hang and Luk Keng, both degree holders and non–degree holders signed, and in both there were important degree holders who did not sign. In Wu Kau Tang, no degree holders seem to have signed, although there were degree holders in that village. In each case, however, the terms of the petition make it clear that the petitions were communal in character, having been issued on behalf of the community and after agreement by all the elders.[51]

Second, the petitions make it clear that individual Yeuk were dominated by single powerful villages. The Wo Hang petition was signed for both the Wo Hang and the Ma Tseuk Ling Yeuk, but only Wo Hang people signed. Only Luk Keng people signed for their Yeuk, with no one from the Nam Chung half of the Yeuk appearing. In Hing Chun Yeuk and Nam Yeuk Tung Yeuk, only the dominant villages of Lai Chi Wo and Wu Kau Tang signed. The villagers believe that all the villages of the Yeuk had a right to have their elders present at Yeuk meetings; but, clearly, in practice, the major villages dominated.

The elders of the eleven Yeuk in turn formed the committee of the Shap Yeuk. Each of the Yeuk had the right to take part in the deliberations of the Shap Yeuk—or so the villagers believe—but, in practice, the villages that dominated the individual Yeuk tended to dominate the Shap Yeuk committee as well. The Shap Yeuk committee was known as the Tung Wo Kuk, as noted above. It was essentially a gentry committee, and when it wrote to the magistrate, only the degree-holding elders of the committee signed. Only one list of persons representing the Tung Wo Kuk has survived, in the translation of a petition submitted by the Shap Yeuk to the magistrate of San On in 1899.[52] The names are corrupt in the surviving text, but degree holders from Wo Hang, Luk Keng, Wu Kau Tang, Lin Ma Hang, and Yim Tin can be identified. It is unlikely that there were no representatives of important Yeuk like Hing Chun or Kuk Po on the committee, but, although they were probably generally regarded as leaders of society, they did not sign the petition to the magistrate. It seems very likely that the Tung Wo Kuk was a flexible body, sometimes deciding matters with a small group of very influential elders, sometimes calling a meeting of a broader group of elders.

The Shap Yeuk met formally in the meeting house of the Shap Yeuk, which was the side hall of the Man Mo (Wenwu) Temple, next to the main altar. It is mentioned in the 1899 petition, in terms that make it clear that the ten or so gentry who signed that petition did so after a very full meeting of the Shap Yeuk, involving the elders of all the villages of the district: "Several hundreds of the gentry of over eighty villages from the neighbourhood assembled in the Meeting House, and complained that the territory had been leased with the object of improving the defences of Hong Kong. . . . Your petitioners therefore consider it their duty to represent the case in detail to Your Honour, in addition to petitioning the higher authorities at Canton."

The gentry—certainly the degree holders, but probably the senior non-degree-holding elders as well—sat in the meeting house in rotation on market days to adjudicate disputes and arbitrate quarrels. Not much is remembered of these duties of the elders, because they tended to be interfered with after the town became the site of so much government interest after the establishment of the Hong Kong boundary immediately outside the town in 1898, and especially after the Guomindang takeover of 1925. Particularly full meetings of the elders were held before the communal annual worship by the elders at the Shan Tsui Temple and the Man Mo Temple. There was a small office next to the meeting house, in which the Tung Wo Kuk kept its papers.

The meeting hall of the Tung Wo Kuk was in the rear courtyard of the Tung Wo School. That school, as noted above, had been founded shortly after 1854; probably quite soon after. Although the Tung Wo Kuk reserved for their own use the rear courtyard with its meeting house, office, temple, and shrine, the area left for the school was very large. With its two courtyards and side halls, it was as big as, or bigger than, any of the schools in the New Territories. The building was by far the largest in the whole Shap Yeuk area, even after 1898, when the imposing new customs station was built on the waterfront.

The elders of the Shap Yeuk were determined to ensure that the people of their district had access to the very best education. Their school was always of a high level: in the 1920s the standard was far higher than the average village school, with five teachers, two being graduates from Canton, one a *xiucai*, and one a "returned student" from America. The school at that date prided itself on its up-to-date teaching, which included English, physical education, and the "New Books," as well as the classics. Boys from all the Shap Yeuk villages came here for education, usually after some years of preliminary schooling in the individual village schools. Those from too far away to walk daily slept in the school cocklofts. There can be little doubt that the elders' concern that their school be a model was equally prominent in the later nineteenth century.

It is the political, administrative, and ritual duties of the Tung Wo Kuk that stand out in the surviving documents, but it should be remembered that the elders probably spent as much time on the school as on all these other duties combined. Making sure that good teachers were hired, that the fabric of the school was kept in good condition, that its finances were sound, and that enough boys from the villages came in to receive education to keep so large an institution viable must have taken a great deal of time. It should be noted that these educational duties were, it would seem, not conducted for the Tung Wo Kuk by the district headman, who acted for the elders in most other matters. It is no coincidence that the Tung Wo Kuk met in the school: they were justifiably proud of it, and the imposing school buildings, dominating the main approach to the town from over the bridge, were a permanent memorial to their self-confidence and to the coherence and unity of the district.

The elders of the Shap Yeuk had an unofficial meeting place as well as their formal hall in the Man Mo Temple. There was a three-storied house in the market owned by the Sam Heung (or possibly by Tam Shui Hang Village). The upper two floors were used as a residence, and the ground floor as a club for the elders. Here the elders met to chat, drink tea, and play cards or mah-jongg. A good deal of district business was conducted there, which could thus avoid a formal airing at the meeting house.

In their mid-nineteenth-century descriptions of the town, the Basel missionaries mention the "village elders" and stress their social importance within the town—for example, it was a critical step in the establishment of the mission that "the old teacher Yip led the elders of the villages into [the mission house], and they listened to the preaching."[53] These village elders must have been the elders of the Shap Yeuk, and they retained much of their influence down to 1941.

The missionaries also mention the "market elder" and a "Council" in which formal decisions were taken by that elder. In an analysis of the market elder's position and influence, the missionaries noted that "the elder takes his name from the 'Neighbourhood' which the people have set up, and this allows him to require [wrong-doers] to behave properly." In 1853 the Basel missionaries fell into a dispute with a carpenter in the town over the death of a dog. Because of the strength of antiforeign sentiment in the town, the case could not be settled until the "elder personally, in the Council, handed over the compensation [offered by the missionaries] to the carpenter."⁵⁴ This "Council" must have been the Tung Wo Kuk in action, the Council of the Shap Yeuk. The "elder," however, is clearly the market elder, and must be the same as the official known in the twentieth century as the "district headman" and discussed below.

The way the Shap Yeuk managed the market was rather unusual. The Shap Yeuk owned a common fund (it was called the Shap Yeuk Fan, "The [funds] divided between the Ten Yeuk"). This probably consisted, at first, of the invested remainder of the money originally collected to build the market, and, later, of the money collected to build the Tung Wo School and the Man Mo Temple. According to the memories of the present-day village elders, the Shap Yeuk managed this fund through a manager, appointed by the Tung Wo Kuk as a whole. The manager was called Heung Cheung (*xiangzhang*), "district headman." Despite this title, however, this man was not the leader or chairman of the Tung Wo Kuk, but its employee. His duties were to manage the common fund, keep the temple and the meeting house, manage the town scale, and manage the market. He had to be a Shap Yeuk villager who operated a shop in the market and who lived there most of the time. Once appointed, the district headman remained in the post as long as he wished to and as long as the Tung Wo Kuk was satisfied with his performance. During most of the 1920s and 1930s the post was held by Tsang Ah-ching, a villager of Kwu Tau Tong (Gutoutang) in the Luk Heung who operated a shop selling paper offerings in the market. The district headman had to give an annual account of his management of the funds to the Tung Wo Kuk as a whole.

The district headman's most onerous duties were to arrange for the town watch and the coolies who kept the streets clean. Every shop unit in the town had to pay an annual sum to the headman toward the costs of these services—this payment was two dollars per unit in the 1920s. In addition, the rent proffered for the use of the town scale went toward these costs as well. This rent was not very high—the scale was used mostly by the people trading in the grain market, who paid a few cents each time it was used. One of the Shap Yeuk grain merchants would proffer a rent to the headman for control of the scale for a year and collect the fees for the year.[55] The headman also let the keepership of the Man Mo Temple and received an annual sum from the keeper. The keeper had to keep the temple and the meeting house clean and provide services to worshipers. In the 1920s, the keeper was Lee Kam-shing of Wo Hang, who doubled as the town letter writer.

The headman, therefore, had a number of sources of income—interest on money loaned out from the common fund, the two-dollar "rate" charged, the rent from the temple keeper and the town scale, and probably some others as well, such as payments from ferry operators, which were also subject to letting by the Shap Yeuk. He employed a cleansing coolie who kept the streets clean. This coolie was not paid very much, it being assumed that he would make much of his income from the sale as fertilizer of the rubbish he collected. This post was let by the headman, probably annually, to whoever was willing to do the job for the least pay. The town watch was recruited from the young men of the town and surrounding villages, and their job was to protect the townsmen from theft and banditry, by day and night. The job was, again, probably let by the headman to whomever was willing to do it cheaply. The members of the watch, however, had to be trained in martial arts, and, while they doubtless "squeezed" extra payments from shop owners, they could not be allowed to become too outrageous in this respect—so the watch was probably paid reasonably well. Despite all these expenses, however, the headman usually made a profit, some of which he kept.

The Basel missionaries make it clear that the market elder, that is, the headman, had considerable police powers: "The beginnings of the Mission [in Sha Tau Kok] were good. Friendly visitors came to see them: when a drunkard waving a big knife burst into the house, the Elder personally gave him a public thrashing with a cane, saying that [the Missionary] was a good man, with good intentions."[56] The Basel missionaries mention the town watch, too: "The tribulations of life under the Chinese, outside British rule, were substantial. In [Sha Tau Kok] they suffered attacks from robbers, until they bought immunity by a payment of cash to the Town Watch."[57]

At least in the 1850s, the Shap Yeuk and the town watch were not very effective in keeping the peace. The Basel missionaries were constantly anxious about robbers and pirates frequenting the town, and it was the town's lawlessness that eventually drove them out.[58] Problems with pirates in the town lasted to the early twentieth century.

It can be assumed that this structure, with the town dominated by a district headman appointed by the committee of elders of the surrounding villages, had been in place from the foundation of the market—it was clearly in place both in the 1850s and in the 1920s.

None of the political arrangements instituted by the Shap Yeuk within the villages of the Sha Tau Kok area are particularly unusual. Mixed groups of degree holders and non-degree-holding elders, in which the major non-degree-holding elders are given prominence and the degree holders dominate only when representing the district before the magistrate, are commonly found in the region.[59] A hierarchy of local subdistrict Yeuk areas and a higher-level inter-Yeuk alliance district is very common. The dominance of district politics by a few very influential villages is also common. The presence of both formal and informal meeting places and of both formal and informal arbitration opportunities is not rare. Communal worship by the elders is almost universal. Clubs of influential elders are known in many places in the region.[60]

The arrangements for the management of the town were unusual, however, insofar as they did not include a Kaifong (*jiefang*). A Kaifong—a committee of shop owners who ran their own affairs—was to be found in almost all the local towns.[61] The town at Sha Tau Kok was, clearly, very firmly controlled by the surrounding villages that had founded it, and these villages were, it would seem, unwilling to allow their town any real independence. It seems likely that this close control by the Shap Yeuk was feasible because of the strongly indigenous nature of the shops in the town. Given that almost all the shops, and all the major ones, were owned by Shap Yeuk people, control by the Shap Yeuk must have been more acceptable than might have been the case had a large percentage of the shops been owned by outsiders. The richer shop owners do not seem to have exercised much direct political influence, except perhaps within their native Yeuk. However, the informal meeting house in Old Street, where the elders played mah-jongg, probably provided a forum where the influential shop owners could meet and influence the elders.

The post of district headman, with its very real influence and pivotal position within the Shap Yeuk (the post could be held only by a Shap Yeuk shop owner) also provided a means by which the views of shop owners could influence the Shap Yeuk. Nonetheless, it was unusual to have a single district headman undertaking what in other towns was done by committees of shop owners. Also unusual was the lack of any clear distinction between the duties and funds of the district and those of the town, exemplified by the district headman's being responsible, under the Tung Wo Kuk, for both.

Between 1853 and 1898, therefore, the elders of the Shap Yeuk had been able to secure the effective freedom of their district from the interference of the great clans in the area around Sham Chun. They had managed to establish their own system of local administration, functioning within an efficient two-tier structure. They had secured control of the local ferry system. They had founded their own market, providing it with an administrative and police system and basic defenses, and had had the satisfaction of seeing it become prosperous and bustling. The villages of the Shap Yeuk had come to form, therefore, a coherent and self-confident district, vigorously self-run by a homogenous group of indigenous elders.

However, it has to be said that this was achieved, to a large extent, because no one except the local villagers cared very much about what happened in this remote and mountainous area. The local proverb has it that "The mountain is high and the emperor is far away," and in truth few parts of the empire were, in practice, as remote from the apparatus of imperial control as was Mirs Bay. In the 1830s the villagers around Sham Chun may well have been exercised when their former clients around Sha Tau Kok broke away and achieved independence, but the magistrate was not greatly concerned, either then or later.

The lease of the New Territories was, therefore, a very traumatic event for the Shap Yeuk and its market. The line originally proposed for the frontier would have run along the Sha Tau Kok River from source to sea. This would have put the Luk Heung and Yim Tin into China, the market and the other Yeuk into the New Territories. This was unacceptable to the Chinese authorities, who were unwilling to allow so significant a place as Sha Tau Kok to become part of the area administered by Britain. Eventually it was agreed that the frontier should run along the Sha Tau Kok River from the source to the Sha Tau Kok bridge, and then be diverted from the bridge down the center of the road to the sluice at Yim Liu Ha, then run in a straight line to the sea, and thence east along the high-water mark to the mouth of Mirs Bay. This boundary, therefore, ran immediately along two sides of the market. By 1910 a Chinese Imperial Maritime Customs staff of seventy to a hundred men headed by an expatriate assistant superintendent of customs, twenty or so Chinese soldiers, and about the same number of Hong Kong police were posted in or immediately outside Sha Tau Kok to patrol the new frontier; the waters of Mirs Bay, hitherto quite uncontrolled, were the patrol zones of a couple of gunboats. Sha Tau Kok, from being remote and of no real account to any government, had suddenly become of immediate and pressing interest to the bureaucrats of two great powers.

The Shap Yeuk continued to function throughout the period between the lease of the New Territories in 1898 and the coming of the Japanese in 1941 and of the Communists in 1949, but less effectively than before. The strong military presence in the town, the close government interest in it, and the elders' inability to control the Customs, greatly weakened it as the effective local administration. The guns that had been placed by the Shap Yeuk in its gun towers were confiscated very soon after the 1911 revolution, and the eastern gun tower, at the front of the Tung Wo School, was taken over as the military barracks (on the lower floors) at about the same time. The imperial (1898–1911), warlord (1911–25), and Guomindang (1925 and later) administrations were usually unwilling to discuss problems with the local elders—noticeably less so than was the district officer within the New Territories—and so the Shap Yeuk elders and their committee declined until they effectively had responsibility only for the school and those things the officials could not be bothered to interfere with, especially the running of the market night-watch and cleansing services.

By 1910, the elders were already talking of moving the market over the frontier into the New Territories, with its better security, better relations between villagers and administration, and absence of problems with the Customs.[62] Nothing, however, was done until 1925, when the chaos of the anti-British boycott started to push the market across the frontier. Shops began to be built on the New Territories side of the border street in 1925, and this process continued until 1935, by which date only a few shops were left functioning in the old market—mostly those (like the pawnshop and the boatyard) that could not move because of physical restraints. A terrible typhoon on September 2, 1937, destroyed most of what was left of the old market; it never recovered.[63]

The main effect on the market at Sha Tau Kok of its exclusion from the New Territories in 1899, therefore, was a relocation of the market into the New Territories a generation later. The events of 1898, 1925–35, 1941, and 1949 all conspired to weaken the self-confident and vigorous leadership of the Shap Yeuk. After 1898, the heavy government presence in the town crushed any effective local self-rule, leaving the Shap Yeuk only its routine town-management, school-management, and ritual duties. Between 1925 and 1935 the market was forced to move across the frontier because the villagers who shopped in the market were no longer willing to put up with the difficulties implied by leaving it on the China side of the frontier. But, on the Hong Kong side, the government provided many of the basic services that the Shap Yeuk had provided on the other side, and this further reduced the Shap Yeuk's responsibilities, limiting them for the most part to ritual and educational duties. The district officer's need to consult with local leaders on all matters of significance in the district, however, gave the New Territories elders of the Shap Yeuk a new role of some significance.

Under the Japanese, this incipient division between the Hong Kong and China parts of the Shap Yeuk intensified, because for some part of the Japanese occupation, travel and contact between the two parts of the district were forbidden. The ban was enforced by the erection, for the first time, of a high barbed-wire fence along the frontier in the Sha Tau Kok area.

With the coming of the Communists in 1949, the Shap Yeuk area was finally and decisively split into a "Sha Tau Kok Rural Committee" area (essentially the New Territories part of the old Shap Yeuk district), and a "Sha Tau Kok District" (essentially the part of the Shap Yeuk remaining in China). Contacts between the two areas, while they were never broken off entirely, in practice became difficult and infrequent. The ancient temple at Am King and the greatly revered temple at Sha Lan Ha were destroyed, together with the Shap Yeuk temple within the old market, essentially ending the elders' ritual role. The Tung Wo school was taken over by the new government, similarly ending the elders' educational role.

Since 1949, therefore, the Sha Tau Kok village elders from the New Territories, in their new Rural Committee, have functioned as the district officer's advisors on affairs in their part of the old Shap Yeuk district, just like other Rural Committees elsewhere in the New Territories. The Rural Committee can thus be seen as a pale reflection of the old Tung Wo Kuk, with some status and influence, if little power. In the China part of the old district, however, nothing can be seen that can be claimed as a descendant of the old system: anti-landlord campaigns, the introduction of communes, campaigns to destroy the "Four Olds" (especially the destruction of temples, lineage institutions, and communal trusts), the Cultural Revolution, and the total dominance of local life by Party officials have led to what seems to be a total break with the history and traditions of the district since 1835.

Front entrance of He Liugeng tang, Shawan, Panyu (1991)

A smaller ancestral hall of the He lineage, which has been transformed into a ware-
house, Shawan, Panyu (1989)

Cheung Chau in the 1950s (photograph courtesy Public Records Office, Hong Kong; photo collection 901/1)

A dragon dance group paying respects to the Huizhou-Hailufeng Native Place Association during the Bun Festival at Cheung Chau (1993)

Preparing the Bun Mountains, Cheung Chau (1993)

Main street near the ferry pier in Cheung Chau, with Dan women and men soliciting business in front of their boats (1989)

Worshipers before the Beidi Temple, Cheung Chau (1993)

Making the buns, Cheung Chau (1993)

A boatload of worshipers attending the birthday celebrations of Tianhou at Xiwan (1993)

Marching into the Tianhou Temple at Xiwan (1993)

Lineage Socialism and Community Control: Tangang Xiang in the 1920s and 1930s

DAVID FAURE

IN 1919, the Ruan surname at Tangang xiang, Xinhui county, Guangdong province, under the auspices of its xiang association, raised funds in the form of a loan to rebuild its village, which had been destroyed in intervillage warfare. A particular feature of this effort was communal control of land. Regulations were drawn up that required that all ancestral estates be placed under the management of the xiang association for indefinite periods of time, and all personal properties for fixed periods of approximately ten years. The income derived was spent on repaying the initial loan for the rebuilding of the village as well as on village welfare. Because the directors of the association met regularly in Hong Kong, management of village affairs was left in the hands of a hired manager, who kept the directors informed of events in the village by correspondence. The reports of the manager were then recorded, in full or in summary, together with the responses of the board of directors, in the minutes of the board's meetings.

This essay is based primarily on those minutes.[1] It can be readily appreciated that a continuous run of these records from 1919 to 1948, with the omission of only the war years from 1941 to 1945, provides a rare account of 30 years of village life and of a peculiar arrangement whereby the village manager was supervised from a distance by an urban xiang association. Those 30 years represent almost the entire Republican period, and they encompassed early attempts to impose some order into village government, the rise of party affiliations in the 1920s, years of economic hardship in the 1930s, war, and, to some extent, restoration. The imposition of external control on the village, furthermore, reflects the increasing influence in the village of the tiny core of villagers who had succeeded in the modern world, in this case, primarily as merchants in the cities.[2] Hence, as may be expected, one finds in Tangang the mingling of new ideas in village management that emerged in the Republican period with long-established village practices and ideals. Tangang should be a case study of social and political change in the Republican period, but perhaps change was much less dramatic than should be expected.

Organizational Structure

The decision to rebuild the village was formally taken at a meeting of the Tangang Lineage Restoration Savings Association in Hong Kong on September 22, 1916. The meeting was attended by representatives of communities of Tangang villagers living outside the village in Indochina, the British colony of Hong Kong, the Portuguese colony of Macau, Guangzhou, Foshan, the town of Yanbu outside Guangzhou, the treaty port of Jiangmen, and Xinhui county city.[3] The decision was taken at the meeting that funds would be raised from these communities for the rebuilding of the village, but it was not until March 1919 that an organizational meeting was held, also in Hong Kong and only by representatives of Tangang expatriate communities, to launch the Tangang xiang Association that was to have authority over village affairs, including its rebuilding.[4]

It was stipulated at the first meeting of the Lineage Restoration Savings Association that the funds raised for lineage rebuilding were of the nature of a loan that must be repaid, and for this reason it is possible to understand why the directors of the savings association continued to be involved in village affairs. Nevertheless, it is far from clear what legal authority, if any, they might have had to set up the xiang association, whose board of directors appointed and supervised the village manager and drew up regulations for village affairs and which, as will be seen, dealt not only with financial matters but also with punitive measures for criminal activities. The Tangang xiang Association, in a strict sense, had been set up without consultation with resident members of Tangang xiang. However, in view of the fact that the village manager employed by the xiang association was accepted as such by the Xinhui county magistrate (this will be discussed further), and that the manager had to report to and take into consideration the decisions of the xiang association's board of directors, one cannot doubt that the regulations, whatever their legal status, were enforceable.

At its foundation, the board of directors of the xiang association consisted precisely of the same persons as the Lineage Restoration Savings Association. The two associations differed in that the chairman of the xiang association was not identical to the director-in-chief of the Lineage Restoration Savings Association, at least up to 1921. We know very little about the backgrounds of the people who served as xiang association chairmen, savings association directors-in-chief, or directors of both associations, except for what can be worked out from the attendance records. These records show that over the years, 44 persons served on the board of directors, of whom several seem to have provided continuity. Instrumental in raising funds for the savings association, however, was one Biaoji, normally resident in Indochina, who was apparently ousted as director-in-chief of the savings association in 1921.[5] His post was filled by Yeying, son of a Hong Kong merchant and chairman of the xiang association from 1919 to 1936.[6] One Shide, the chairman of the board, served for nineteen years, and became xiang association chairman in 1937. Neither Yeying nor Shide seems to have been unduly dominating in the management of the day-to-day affairs of the xiang, which were left very much to the appointed manager, Jiji, who remained in this position from 1919 to 1935.

The manager in the village was known variously as "manager and treasurer" (*sili jian siku*) or "director of the village office" (*banshisuo zhuren*). Including the manager, the village office consisted of a paid staff of about eight persons. In addition, the village also provided for its own guard force, consisting initially of a captain, his deputy, twenty long-term workers, and thirty night workers, all of whom were paid. In addition, on the village payroll were the school headmaster, a teacher, and a doctor. The impression emerges quite clearly from the minutes of the xiang association's board of director meetings that close supervision of the village office was necessary to ensure that the board's decisions were carried out. Such supervision included the regular correspondence between the village manager and the board of directors, of course, but apart from this, it also involved the dispatching of specially appointed representatives from the board to the xiang, principally to oversee the monetary accounts.

It must be recognized from the start that the relationship between the board of directors and the appointed manager was anything but a straightforward employer-employee contract. Given the peculiar political situation of the xiang association being located outside the county, through the 1920s and 1930s numerous opportunities arose whereby the appointed manager could seek direct legitimation of his position from the Xinhui county government. On the whole, the board of directors recognized that any direct appointment from the county would have weakened its control

TABLE 2

Budgeted Incomes and Expenditures, 1920–1931

| | Incomes | | |
	Rent from farmland	Misc. fees and rents	Total
1921	17,500	1,700	18,500
1922	24,746	2,204	28,000
1923	24,820	2,890	27,860
1924	24,650	3,296	28,540
1925	32,391	3,676	35,000
1926	32,375	3,714	36,000
1927		No record available	
1928	31,183	7,759	38,864
1929	30,829	4,396	36,266
1930	30,331	5,189	36,562
1931	31,014	5,913	37,169

| | Expenditures | | | | | | |
	Office	Guards	School	Rent	Loans	Improvements	Total
1920	1,464	6,000	552			4,000	17,100
1921	1,950	6,650	500	600		3,000	16,500
1922	2,895	6,000	550	2,300	8,000	3,000	26,635
1923	2,970	6,000	850	2,300	4,000	3,000	24,000
1924	3,710	7,000	1,000	2,533	2,000	4,000	26,000
1925	3,536	6,000	1,500	2,660	2,000	7,000	32,000
1926	3,668	6,000	1,500	7,300	2,000	14,000	39,000
1927			No record available				
1928	4,257	7,200	1,000	9,700	2,000	2,600	35,500
1929	4,458	7,200	1,800	9,500	2,000	3,300	35,000
1930	4,176	6,600	2,200	9,500	2,000	3,300	39,500
1931	4,219	7,000	2,000	8,034	2,000	3,300	36,000

NOTE: Rent = rent disbursements; loans = loan repayment; improvement = building construction and purchase of equipment including armaments. All values in dollars as reckoned in twenty-cent coins.

of the village office, and it took great care to ensure that the village manager remained subordinate.

A ready rendering of the ability of the board of directors to supervise, and of the village office to govern, may be found in the annual budgets available for the first eleven years of the records (see Table 2).[7] The main body of the income of the village office, it is apparent, was derived from land rent, while a minor but not inconsequential portion came from the renting out of fishponds, the granting of fishing and duck-raising rights, and a crop-watching fee levied on land being harvested. It is also apparent in the records that overall income built up quickly from 1921 to 1925 and stabilized from then on.

A substantial portion of this income, say a quarter, was paid to individual landowners whose land was being managed by the xiang association.

The balance from this paid for the expenses of the village office, the guard force, the village school, the local clinic, the rebuilding of the village, purchases of necessary equipment, the meetings of the board of directors, and redemption of loans advanced by the Lineage Restoration Savings Association. Even though the expenditures of the village office tripled from 1920 to 1930, the meetings of the board of directors continued to be provided for, substantial increases were made in the disbursements for the landowners, a total of $26,000 was repaid to the lenders, and $38,000 went into village construction.[8] Annual payments made to the guard force did not increase out of direct village funds, although, as will be shown, the guard did receive larger incomes over the years from other sources. Indeed, the budget figures cannot reveal irregularities in expenditures, which must be expected, but the point has to be made that whatever irregularities there might have been in the first ten years of its establishment, the village office quite successfully fulfilled its essential financial duties.

The regulations adopted by the xiang association in the first two years of its foundation for the management of village affairs were extremely comprehensive, dealing with matters that varied from taxation to land management to the operation of the village school, the adoption of a village song, and rewards and punishments. Some of the measures, such as the village flag and the village song, reflect new practices of the Republican period, but many, for instance, the auctioning of the duck-raising rights, were carried over from traditional village practice.[9] The minutes of the board of directors of the xiang association give the impression that the written regulations played a substantial role in enforcing conformity from the village manager, but the view also comes across strongly that any compliance was not automatic and that it was subjected to the interplay of power, both between the board of directors and the village manager and between the manager and the villagers.

The Business of Village Government

In the first two years of the reestablishment of the village, the immediate business of village government was to build sheds for members of the village to live in, to distribute farmland for cultivation, to ensure a sufficient food supply, and to set up the basic amenities of village life. By the third year, a rhythm had set in and the pattern of village affairs as it might reflect the social and political milieu of the Republican period had emerged.

By the third year, a typical meeting of the board consisted of reading the motions adopted in the previous meeting, reading the accounts of the previous month, discussing matters raised in correspondence received, and adopting resolutions on these and other matters. In the 26th meeting of the board held on March 13, 1921, for instance, the three letters from the village manager that were read reported on the costs of various construction projects in the village and on various incidents, such as a villager stealing garlic in another villager's fields and members of his lineage segment creating a commotion at the village office; another villager building an earthen wall without permission from the village office; and neighboring Liangjia Village, Luojia Village, and Tianhu Village contesting for village ferry rights. Also reported in the letter were a request from a villager of nearby Qibao xiang to resolve a dispute in which a member of Tangang continued to collect rent on a plot of land in a disputed area that had been mortgaged to him; and, finally, someone in one of the camps set up in the village having asked a fellow villager to start a school there; the village manager wanted to know if that should be allowed.[10]

In discussing these and certainly other issues raised at the meeting, the board ruled that the earthen wall in question should be dismantled; that the village should stand firm on the question of the ferry rights; that the land disputed by Qibao should be rented out by the village office while the loan due to the Qibao man should be repaid by the villager who had contracted it; and that the teacher should find his own premises for teaching, for, the board noted, only those teachers who taught in a fashion acceptable to the board might teach on public premises. No reference was made to the village construction suggested or to the incident of the garlic thief. However, seven other cases were dealt with that involved petty theft.

In addition, the board made numerous decisions, including not allowing rent reduction for the coming harvest; approving confiscation of grain exported from the village without license, various appointments and salaries, and minor construction (such as a gate separating the Ruans' section of Tangang and adjacent houses owned by the Huang surname); and ruling that only those doctors permitted by the board might practice in the village. As the record of this particular meeting shows, the business of a village government was necessarily fragmentary. The government adjudicated disputes, managed the resources of the village, provided the paramilitary force, and interceded in intervillage relations. In many ways, it acted as a state within the state.

None of this should be very surprising to students of Chinese rural society. In the Qing, village and lineage elders, meeting in the village office (*gongsuo*) or the ancestral hall, would have had to deal with similar issues. All that really needs elaborating is how the exercise of power, now vested in the Republic, blended with the reification of traditional ideals, and, in this particular instance, why supervisory authority exercised at a distance might still carry weight.

Adjudication: The Village over the Individual

A useful starting point is probably the involvement of the xiang association and its hired manager in the adjudication of disputes. A substantial number of the cases that were adjudicated, admittedly, dealt with disputes over land, a subject that has to be examined in conjunction with concepts of land law in the village; however, insofar as authority over land was exercised as a part of overall law enforcement, the authority to adjudicate and to enforce a judgment was, in many ways, fundamental to the functioning of the village government.

The following account, taken from among the seven cases considered by the xiang association in the 26th meeting of the board, illustrates very well the involvement of the various parties in the judicial process:

Yaguan, styled Shiguan, originally resident of Shimen li, in Republic Year 8 summer had a plot of land that was adjacent to the land farmed by Yatang, styled Shangnong, of Longhang li. After the second harvest of the year, Yaguan sold the straw on his plot to a person from Wu Village in a neighboring xiang, and that was the plot that was adjacent to Yatang's land. After the price was agreed upon and money was paid, the Wu surname man returned to his village. A few days later, he came in his boat to cut the straw. However, he made a mistake and went into Yatang's land to cut the straw. At the time, Yatang passed by his land and saw what the man was doing. He asked the man cutting straw why he was cutting it there and from whom he had bought the straw. The buyer said he had bought it from Yaguan. Upon hearing that, Yatang went to Yaguan and reasoned with him. Yaguan said, "The straw I sold was mine and not yours, and it is the buyer who has made the mistake." Yatang said, "This is your taking advantage of the situation on purpose." The two could not agree and went to the village office. At the time, the village manager was away and so the captain of the village guard force Liang Fusheng said to Yaguan, "You are under suspicion. How is it possible that the buyer can come to take his straw without notifying you, and why did you not take him to your own plot? Even if you weren't trying to take advantage of the situation, you were certainly too careless. Now, never mind how the mistake was made, you are to pay a penalty of five dollars to make up for Yatang's loss." Yaguan said nothing and so the decision was reached. However, Yatang was never paid and so the case has remained unresolved to this day and cannot be closed. Although the rights and wrongs of this issue are still unclear, former captain Liang has made a ruling on it and it was not disputed. The ruling should be upheld and Shiguan should be told that he should pay Yatang five dollars to settle this incident.[11]

It may be noted that a year had lapsed between the occurrence of the incident and a judgment being reached on it by the xiang association. The village office, and then the xiang association, had been drawn in, not out of contingency but in the due process of law.

Several points may be made on the basis of the case. First, the matter was brought into the judicial process by the parties involved in the dispute. Second, initial judgment on the issue was made after summary hearing by the captain of the guard force, no distinction having been drawn, in time-honored custom, between the enforcer of the law and the judiciary. Third, the board of directors of the xiang served as a court of appeal and expected its decisions, within the context of the xiang, to be final. Finally, its ruling extended only to members of the lineage: the buyer of the straw from the next village was not involved in the litigation, either as witness or as culprit.

The Tangang records bring out constantly that the authority of the village office was limited to members of the lineage. To appreciate the import of this limitation, it is necessary to look briefly at the geography of the village. Tangang xiang was a cluster of eight villages, with a total population of probably 2,000 or so, that were located on the sediments collected to the south of the Tanjiang River (see Map 1).[12] To its northwest, along one of the inlets of the river, were located Luokeng and Chenchong, settlements that outmatched Tangang and dominated local politics, particularly in matters related to market and ferry rights. Further afield were Qibao to the north and Sanjiang to the far south, which were heavyweights not only locally but also in the county and whose landholdings were extensive. Qibao and Sanjiang had obvious interest in the farmland within the reach of Tangang. The relationships that Tangang formed with these settlements would fall by necessity into inter-village diplomacy.

Nearer home, the Ruans had to contend with the Huang surname of Shuibian, whose territory lay immediately to the north of the villages of Tangang, and the Lin surname of Lingbei to the immediate west. The Lingbei Lins owned a pond within Tangang itself, and the Shuibian Huangs built a wall to separate their houses from the Ruans'. One of the decisions that the board of directors of the xiang association made in its 26th meeting was, as noted, to build a wooden gate to separate the Huangs' houses from the Ruans', and the reason given was indicative of the jurisdictional limitation that the board had to recognize: the gate was to be closed at night, so that "people of this xiang might not go between [the two lots of houses] throughout the night in case of unexpected incidents." The Tangang xiang association had no authority over the Huangs or the Lins, let alone the county dominants. The rules of Tangang, therefore, tended to be restrictive of what the Ruan surname villagers might be involved in, for instance, by imposing a fine should they rent the land owned by people from outside the village, rather than directly circumscribing what outside villagers might do within the xiang (see Map 8).

The authority of the xiang association was occasionally also extended to Tangang Ruan surname villagers who were temporarily resident outside the xiang. In one case in 1927, the xiang association adjudicated a dispute in which one party sought to collect a debt on the basis of a loan contract that was discovered in the possession of a Ruan surname villager who had died in Hong Kong. The village manager had ruled in favor of the plaintiff, but the decision was overthrown by the xiang association's board of directors. This particular case was handled with more legal pomp than most disputes that the board adjudicated, possibly because the defendant obtained legal representation, presumably in Hong Kong. In this case, that the loan was made outside the village did not seem to have restricted the board's authority to adjudicate, and a case can possibly be made that this was because in question was the ownership of a village house that was quoted as collateral in the loan contract.[13]

However, in another case in 1923, the two parties locked in dispute over the accounts of a shop located in a place known as Qibang had come to the xiang association for a judgment on no other grounds than that they were villagers of Tangang, and accepting the judgment of the board, they signed a collective agreement based on the board's decision.[14] The point that is made here is not that the xiang association frequently extended itself to affairs beyond the xiang, but that the implicit definition of its authority over its own lineage members meant that it could.

The summary manner by which the village manager might pass judgment on disputes, however, spoke of a close connection between law enforcement and routine village management, a situation that would have closely resembled Qing dynasty administrative practices.[15] A particular feature in this connection is a subtle difference that may be detected between the exertion of authority by the village government on members of the village, and reciprocal privileges that the village administration might demand from them on the provision of service, frequently defined in relation to territorial rights. A case in point would be the ability of the village guard force to raise a direct income from its law enforcement activities as a supplement to its regular income derived from the village budget. At issue

西 (West)

(slope)

(Shuibian Huang surname village)

(Road to Lengbei, etc.)

姓 (Ruan surname)

阮步石里

边水黄姓村

阮姓交界黄闸

阮姓橋龍躍 (bridge)

姓阮塘 (pond)

姓阮川

阮姓圍塘

塘阮 (pond)

塘阮 (Huang gate)

黄闸

阮姓步里滩村

阮石姓步下村

(river)

姓阮滄咀坦

田

坦胖拘 田

田 边水闸

田 田

田 田 (fields)

田 (road)

上祭 (ancestral grave)

阮姓 (Ruan surname)

黄姓 (Huang surname)

(road)

南 (South)

(North) 北

(river)

新深冲圍

蓝深冲圍

吉慶圍

(river)

LEGEND

例圖

路界 road border

水海界 river border

水 river

路 road

Diagram of natural boundary between Ruan and Huang surname "duck ports"

阮兩黄姓鴨埠天然界限圖

Map 8. Sketch map of Tangang-Shuibian border

is the collection of a crop-watching fee (*hegeng*), levied over land held within what the village considered its territory, on landowners of the Ruan surname as well as other surnames.

One must guard against a romantic view of village crop-watching. The crop-watching fee, however efficiently the guard force might keep watch at harvest time, was levied as a tax. It was levied on the cultivator, not the owner, of the land that fell within what the village office considered its territorial boundaries. Upon payment of the fee, the cultivator was given a receipt, and not until he was in possession of this receipt was he allowed to harvest his crop. There seems to be no basis for the village to collect such a fee other than custom. In litigation at the Xinhui county government, or even at the provincial governor's office, it was sufficient to prove that the practice had been previously established to demonstrate the right to collect the fee. Documents produced in litigation at the Xinhui county government by contestants with the Ruans show that in the Guangxu era 70 cash was charged for a mu; the Ruans themselves reported that in 1921 the fee was 30 cents for each mu.[16]

The fee was not collected from all land held within Ruan territory. It would seem that the general rule was that it was charged on reclaimed land that was diked, and in one particular locality that the Ruans were concerned about, a guard shed was built in the diked area so that a guard might stay on daily duty to issue the harvesting receipts. Because for most of the Republican period all land at Tangang was managed by the village government, the rule was made that these receipts might be issued only to people who had paid their rent. The point that has to be noted here, however, is not that the guard force operated under regulation from the village office, but that a portion of the payments received was allotted directly to the force's income. The guards' income was of two sorts. In the first place, they received half of all fees derived from the harvesting receipts. Second, in the event that a thief was caught, the guards who were responsible for the capture received a fixed bounty ($5, in one recorded case).[17]

Although the total receipt due the village government every year in the 1920s amounted to no more than $1,000 (rising to $1,600 in the mid-1930s), the income must have been considered worthwhile, because the crop-watching boundaries were the focus of much intervillage dispute. One must envisage in this sort of arrangement the guards taking the law into their own hands, even though no specific report in the Tangang records directly bears this out.[18]

The xiang government, therefore, was in a position to make two kinds of law. It made law that was binding on the village membership and imposed territorial boundaries that it was itself committed to defend.[19] However, because the village was not a self-contained unit, the law that it could impose on its members was necessarily insufficient for the defense of its self-imposed boundaries. The xiang government had constantly to negotiate with persons outside its jurisdiction the rights it held to the exploitation of resources (principally land). In such negotiations, as can be seen in the case of crop-watching, it would represent its vested interests as service provided in return for reciprocal obligations. Because the persons with whom negotiation was carried out were similarly placed under their village or lineage laws, common lineage, village, and land practices provided ground for negotiation. Consequently, while power mattered, the exercise of it in the village setting did not have to be arbitrary.

The Management of Land

That the village government should enjoy some right of adjudication was a fairly common feature in southern Guangdong. That it should set itself the task of renting out *all* of the privately owned land in the village and collecting rent on it, however, was probably peculiar to Tangang. The idea, nonetheless, was not original. Collective management of lineage resources was an aspiration that can be documented in the lineage literature, even though it was seldom put into practice.[20] Moreover, in Tangang, the need to repay the initial loan for rebuilding the village might have prompted it.

The general principles for the village government's control of land were written into the regulations of the Tangang Lineage Restoration Savings Association that were drawn up in 1916 in preparation for the rebuilding of the village. As stated in these regulations, income from the village government and for the repayment of the initial loan for village rebuilding was to be derived from levies imposed on wage labor, trade, and rent. The principle was already established at that time that the village government should have permanent control of all public properties and also should control the management of private properties for a fixed number of years. It was to be responsible for renting out all the land owned by villagers of the Ruan surname at Tangang; while the saving association's loan was being repaid, the village government would keep all the rent received from lineage holdings, and a fixed portion of the rent received from privately owned properties—30 percent as planned in 1916 and 20 percent when the regulations were put into practice—was to be returned to the owners. In practice, little income was derived from the wage or business levies. The major portion of the village government's income derived from rent receipts.

One might think that, given the imposition by the village government, there would have been considerable incentive for private landowners to hide their holdings from its knowledge, and also the possibility that they might wish to shelter formal ownership under the names of persons other than members of the Ruan lineage while retaining indirect control. The records note some such practices but do not indicate that they were common. The concern of the village government was essentially to maintain Tangang's territorial integrity by encouraging members of the Ruan lineage to work on their own land rather than land owned by other surnames.

The principle seems to have been established early that a distinction was to be made between the renting out of developed farmland and other land rights, such as the rights to raise ducks or to set up fishing stake-nets at particular locations on the rivers. Although the rule was on the books that all such rights should be auctioned to the highest bidder, when the farmland was ready to be distributed the village manager reported that much objection was encountered from members of the lineage because the auction prices were far too high, and the solution he accepted and put into practice, without previous consultation with the xiang association's board of directors, was to distribute the land so that each member of the lineage received two mu of good farmland on which a fixed rent of four dollars was charged.[21] The distribution was not questioned, or ever reopened. The records refer to private purchase and selling, sometimes without a report made to the village government, but no farmland that was continuously under use was ever auctioned.

The right of exploiting land other than farmland was, indeed, regularly let to the highest bidder, with the exception of the collection of the crop-watching fee, which was reserved as a regular income for the guard force. Land that was let in this manner included duck-raising "ports" (*yabu*), stake-net sites, and the village fishponds. Also included in the same category would be the right to run the village ferry, which, although not itself a land right, was closely related because it was explicit in the auction that the successful bidder would have exclusive use of various ferry points owned by the lineage, including the pier at the nearby market where the Ruans had considerable interest. Except in the case of the bidding for the ferry, successful bidders did not have to be members of the Ruan surname, and in some instances it is clear that they were not.

In its management of land, the village government seems to have had to balance the maintenance of a realistic income with its regard for village welfare. The preference that was placed on renting land to its own lineage members is understandable, for the village office would have been able to exercise greater judicial authority when its tenants were also members of the lineage. Nevertheless, it was in the nature of land operation in the village that there was considerable coming and going among members of neighboring villages, and so, especially in areas where common land rights among several communities overlapped, such as in the enforcement of the crop-watching fee, it was not possible to keep land management distinct from intervillage politics.

It should be expected, therefore, that much of the village government's concern was to develop potential sources of income. Such effort included to a limited extent a concern for increased production; but more commonly, the government sought new opportunities for extending its taxation rights. Some occasional opposition to such attempts is evident in the records, and one can detect in the village government's response a stubborn reliance on its ability to legislate. For instance, from as early as 1922, the village had recognized that it held the right to auction the collection of pig dung in the village—a common village right on a regular source of manure—but was frustrated in its auctioning of the right when no one bid for it. Undaunted, the office proposed to the xiang association to make it a punishable offense to pick up pig dung without prior official approval.[22] No further reference was made to the rule after the three meetings in which it was raised, and although the ruling was made it is unlikely that it could have been enforceable in the village setting, but it illustrates just how petty the exertion of government power could be in the village.

The advantage that a government within the village enjoyed in enforcing rent and tax payments, of course, was close knowledge of terrain and personalities.[23] In the case of Tangang, this advantage was coupled with some attempt at record keeping, the ability to legislate, the presence of a paramilitary force, and the design of various measures to ensure payment. The stated policy of the village government makes very clear what these measures might be:

Ten days after the harvesting tickets have been issued, in order to collect the grain, the manager of the village office with his staff will lead members of the guard force to approach the door of those members of the lineage who owe their rent and have yet not paid. . . . If a boat should arrive in the village to collect grain [for the market], the village office will dispatch a member of its staff and one or two of seven [representatives of the xiang association's board of directors] who with the assistance of one or two guards will stand by the boat and register whoever dispatches grain and whatever amounts.[24]

A similar regulation less the control on the sale of grain applied to renters of fishponds.[25] Moreover, if the wording leaves in doubt what the village manager might do in the event that a tenant in arrears was someone from outside Tangang xiang, the following incident should make clear that basically the same principle prevailed:

In the listing of farmland submitted by a member of our lineage, Zuochong, a year ago, there is a plot of land known by its local name as Bridge of Pig and Deer, consisting of 1.6 mu, that has not yet been registered. This is because when he submitted the information, he did not state who the tenant was. Afterward, Zuochong died, but his younger brother did not know who the tenant was either. It is only now that it has been found out that the plot of land is located immediately adjacent to plots owned by the Liang surname, and that it was formerly rented to someone of Liang Family Village. Rent has been owed on it for a long time. Elder [of our village] Yaoquan said it was farmed by Liang Yayao. So Yaoquan was asked to go with Elder Chaofu to that village to ask for the rent. However, Liang You [another name for Liang Yayao] refused to see them. Their people even refused to point out where his door was. Yaoquan said that he knew where the plot of land was, and on a future day he would take the guard force with him to cut the grain. Because he was afraid there might be dispute when the grain was being cut, he wrote in to ask that a meeting be held and a judgment made.[26]

In the next meeting of the board, the village manager reported: "Concerning Zuochong's land, I sent the guard force there yesterday to protect the people who cut the grain. The tenant dared not raise a question."[27] As always, in the circumstances of the village, rent payment was contingent upon the support of naked force and diplomacy.

The capability of the village government to collect rent was an incentive for at least some managers of ancestral trusts who owned land in areas that were dominated by villages other than Tangang to offer their holdings to their village office. In at least two instances, an ancestral trust drew up a contract with the village office providing it with information on its holdings in return for a share of the rent collected.[28] It would seem from these instances that members of the village who complied with the regulations of the xiang association, especially the larger landholders, did not do so without some room to maneuver.

Yet, most Tangang villagers were not substantial landowners. The record of landholding in Tangang shows that in 1919, of 222 registered owners of land, 124 (56 percent) held less than 4 mu and only 40 (18 percent) more than 8 mu, with the largest owners holding only 38 mu.[29] Obviously, it was not in the interest of a smallholder to place his property under corporate management, especially when a fee amounting to 60 percent of the rent would be charged. Moreover, because much of the farmland would have been let at fixed rent, increasing prices in the 1920s and early 1930s would have put pressure on landholders to shift their holdings outside collective management. Therefore, it is probably an anomaly that the records do not contain more references to opposition to the rental arrangement imposed.

Some indication of an undercurrent of discontent surfaced in 1939 and 1940, after the retirement of both Yeying and Jiji, who respectively served as president of the Lineage Restoration Savings Association and village manager from the time the lineage rebuilding efforts began until the late 1930s. In 1939, at the instigation of the larger ancestral trusts, a public meeting was held in which objection was raised to leaving privately owned land in the management of the village office. The issue was sufficiently serious for the county government to send a representative to be present at the meeting, and the result was that the xiang association agreed to return management rights to all owners except for those who voluntarily submitted their land to it. In place of the deduction charged out of rent received, a fee of 30 percent from individual holdings and 40 percent from ancestral holdings was imposed. The status of the xiang association was questioned in the meeting, but the motion was carried that it should be retained.[30]

Opposition to the xiang association did not stop there, however. In 1940, a vehement protest against the xiang association and the village office was submitted by a group of villagers to the county magistrate during the rare occasion of his giving a talk at Tangang. Dissatisfaction began with Yeying's rule. It was charged that the annual accounts of the village had not been published as originally promised and that the board of directors had not been elected according to the constitution. Worse, since the new village manager had taken over, extra dues had been demanded while incomes had not been correctly recorded. Those villagers who had dared to object were arrested and placed in a private prison. Privately held farmland had been placed under the management of the village for twenty years, and the village government had proposed even then that the arrangement be continued for seven more years. Possibly, thanks to the decision taken the year before, the magistrate could declare that he did not find the xiang association's authority *ultra vires*, but the open challenge would seem to indicate that the time when the association might rule with a strong hand was over.[31]

The removal of collective management from the village office relegated it back to its more traditional role as law-and-order enforcer, adjudicator, and welfare provider. It was probably the harsh reality that in 1940, a fee of 30 to 40 percent of rental receipts was needed to maintain these services in the village. That, however, may now be beside the point. If the village office no longer acted as village land manager, would it be possible for it to charge its members such a high fee?

Intervillage Relations

Enough has been said to demonstrate that in Tangang and its vicinity the village was conceived of as a viable political unit. A substantial portion of the minutes of the board of directors of the Tangang xiang Association, therefore, reads like diplomatic history, recording office bearers in the village making representation to and signing agreements with officeholders of other villages. This is the impression of the village conveyed when, for instance, description is given of the armed feuds that led to the burning of Tangang in 1913, of the contest for control of the local market or of newly reclaimed land (*shatian*), of the settlement of disputes with adjacent neighbors on fishing, duck-raising, and crop-watching rights, or simply of the association's right to collect rent on behalf of its village members. This is the image of the village enmeshed in a web of intervillage alliances that together made up a territorial power configuration.

An excerpt from the minutes of the board describing the events of 1913 is illustrative:

On April 30, the second year of the Republic, because the Lin surname of Luokeng had devastated the Ye surname of Shatang, an armed feud had developed, and the county magistrate, Shen Bingyan, came to the xiang with the gentry and elders to make peace. At the time, the Lin and the Ruan surnames of Lingbei and Tangang were also at loggerheads, and so the magistrate gathered the gentry and elders of these two xiang and bade them hold their young people in check and not resort to violence. [He said] the xiang that started the violence would be held responsible, and [thereupon] the gentry and elders of both xiang drew up a peaceful agreement, a copy of which was deposited at the county government. However, although the agreement was made on the night of the seventh of the Fifth Month, the next morning, of the eighth, the Lin surname of Lingbei burned down Pingbu li, which was the northern part of the Ruan surname's Tangang, and kidnapped and killed some people. All the neighbors know about this.[32]

As we know from another account, the Lin surname of Lingbei had been allied with the Lin surname of Luokeng, and Tangang's involvement in the event was interpreted as an extension of Luokeng's long-standing feud with another neighboring village.[33]

This relationship between the neighboring villages as corporate structures says little, however, about personal connections that had been built
up, for instance through landholding or marriage. The following from a
case that the xiang association's board of directors had to adjudicate illustrates some of the complexities:

Your supplicant Ruan Yepei states the following. In the Qing dynasty I rented a
plot of land at Longkengkou, tax acreage 0.8 mu, from Lin Xiangqiu, descendant
of Lin Tongzhong, for cultivation. In the early years of Guangxu, Lin Xiangqiu
mortgaged this land to a corporate trust of the Ruan surname in Tangang. Thereafter, he mortgaged it again for over twenty taels of silver [presumably to the same
trust]. *This was because at the time they were relatives and had much coming and
going* [italics added]. Therefore, for many years, rent was collected on that plot
of land by people of the Ruan surname, and while people of the Lin surname saw
that a tax was levied under the head "ancestor Tongzhong," they did not see that
any rent was received. A relative of Lin Xiangqiu, Lin Hao, made special inquiries
into this situation. There was Uncle Lin Shaoxia of that xiang who for many years
was responsible for tax collection [*liangzhang*] and knew about it, and so he told
Lin Hao the story, and they wanted to know how the land was sold, how it might
be redeemed, and how the tax heading might be removed. Now my son and I in
these years had bought several mu of land belonging to people of our xiang. So
when Lin Shaoxia found out that for many years the land had been rented to me,
he wanted me to tell him where it was. As I was his tenant, it seemed reasonable
that I should tell him. No cunning scheme was involved in that. To my surprise,
Lin Shaoxia and Lin Hao wanted me to buy the land for both my convenience
and theirs. I said I must do this according to proper procedure. I must first post
a notice for several months, and only when the situation was clear would I dare
buy from them. This was in case there were things unexpected. When the notice
was posted for more than ten days, and no claim of a mortgage appeared, I still
did not dare close the deal and posted a second notice. I stated in public that I
would accept the deed only when everything was settled. After the second notice
was posted, the manager of the village office told me that I must not buy this land
from the Lin surname. At the time I replied that I had not yet paid for it, and if
there was any dispute involved, I certainly would not buy it so as not to be impli-
cated. This being the case, the entire event was only empty talk. How can I have
broken the law?[34]

The offense he was charged with having committed was offering to buy
this land from the Lin surname, and the xiang association's board of directors persisted in its judgment that he was guilty despite this protest.

   In the charge against the defendant in this case, the village manager
claimed that the mortgage deeds produced in evidence were faked. The
point at issue there, it seems, was that the documents gave the purchaser,
Yepei, a role in the original mortgage. Nevertheless, the argument pre-

sented is plausible. A person of the Lin surname had mortgaged land to a trust in the Ruan surname for land that was rented to a man of the Ruan surname not connected with the trust. The connection between mortgagor and mortgagee was marriage, and that between landowner and cultivator was landlord-tenant. However, since the land had been mortgaged, the landlord had lost effective control even though he had retained the tax responsibility. One can understand, in these circumstances, the involvement of the village manager in this attempt to dislodge the mortgagee. On the one hand, he might be interested in protecting the mortgagee, and on the other hand, he could be concerned with the transfer of the tax to a Tangang villager.

The extension or contraction of village territory through purchase or sale made by members of the village must have been a common phenomenon. This would be one reason for the xiang association's ruling against members of the village selling land to people outside the village, while encouraging them to purchase land from outsiders.[35] One can also see how the collusion of a person within a village might help to dislodge land held in that village by an outsider landowner. In one case, a member of the Ruan village attempted to take over a plot of land at Tangang that the village manager had recognized as being owned by the Ye surname of Shatang by claiming he had rented it from the Chen surname.[36] In this case, the main consideration of the village manager seems to have been upholding the right of the first tenant rather than serving the interests of the owner. Obviously, amicable relations between village governments would have mattered in such cases of disputed ownership.

Precisely how the county government could be involved in intervillage relations is a crucial question in the definition of the powers of the state, and in an assessment of this involvement a distinction must be made between the ability of the county government to employ force in terms of money or military strength and its role as a source of legitimacy for actions taken among the villages. The 1920s and 1930s were years of considerable disorder in Tangang and its surroundings, as in most of China. Tangang was confronted through these years with several cases of kidnapping, and as late as 1924, rumor of impending intervillage feud was sufficient to make the villagers of Lingbei move out of their village.[37] Back in 1919, it was the presence of the county military that imposed some order and allowed the restoration of villages in this area.[38]

Insofar as the county's forces had to be paid for, the Tangang village government realized that their involvement in village affairs must be minimized. Taxes should be collected and delivered by the village, for exam-

ple—and if necessary, the village office would advance any payment due—
because the presence of the county troops in the village to enforce payment
would cost the village (in 1924, for instance) $60 per day.[39] However, in
1937, when the village disputed the rights to certain newly reclaimed land
with the Zhao surname of Sanjiang, a powerful lineage in Xinhui, it turned
to the county government for military support at the time of harvest. The
county's resources were limited: it could dispatch no more than ten soldiers, a demonstration that put down the threat of the Zhao surname immediately but did not prevent the eventual loss of the territory by the Ruan
surname.[40]

The direct involvement of the county government through the dispatching of troops to the village was a rare occurrence. The county simply did
not have the resources. What is revealed in the Tangang records is the continuation of the power politics of the late Qing, wherein the county served
as a center of litigation, and, in times of tension, as the focus of mobilization. Three examples in the records demonstrate at some length how litigation was conducted at the county: the Ruan surname fought the Lin
surname of Lingbei for certain rights of crop-watching in an area where
their territorial boundaries overlapped, their immediate neighbors the
Huang surname of Shuibian over duck-raising rights, and the Zhao surname of Sanjiang over the newly reclaimed land.[41] The Ruans won in the
first two suits and were advised by the magistrate to compromise in the last.
For the pursuit of such cases, the Tangang village government maintained
an office at the county city and retained formal legal counsel.[42]

Yet the outcomes of the legal decisions probably did not justify the emphasis given them by the Ruans. The Huangs of Shuibian were relatively
weak and had to acquiesce in the legal decision. The Lins took to arms
almost immediately after the legal decisions were reached, and collected
their crop-watching fees until events took a turn when a change of leadership occurred and a formal contract on crop-watching was proposed by
the Ruans in 1937.[43] The Zhao surname did not buy the reclamation from
the Ruans, but sought to cultivate well inside Ruan territory, and as a result
of this action the Ruans had to seek military support from the county.

Politics and Legitimacy

Where the state seems to have been able to penetrate village politics, its
authority did not come from the direct exertion of force but from the more
subtle process of cultural change. It had to do with the evolution of the state
structure in the Republican period and the consequences it might have for

the legitimation of village leadership. Up to 1940, the state had little impact on the power configuration among the villages in the vicinity of Tangang, but the political language did change, and that may have paved the way for a new definition of the role of the state.

Tangang was probably never a very powerful village or one dominated by official degree holders.[44] A new definition of politics was imposed on the village from the time it was rebuilt in 1919, possibly giving it more clout within the vicinity. Certainly, the principles of the lineage were maintained, but the xiang association did not set itself up as another lineage trust. On the contrary, along with banning gambling and opium smoking in the village,[45] it sought to divorce itself from numerous traditional practices that it saw as decadent. In the initial regulations drawn up for the village, "except for a temple dedicated to Confucius, no temple was to be erected in the village."[46] The rule did not exclude the building of an ancestral hall, but a regulation did state that "after [our] return to the village, only the ancestral hall dedicated to the apical ancestor, and no private ancestral halls, were to be built."[47] The board of directors of the xiang association continued in this vein for at least the next ten years, for in 1929 it decreed that certain practices related to the teasing of the bride that were part of the village nuptial ceremony were to be abolished.[48]

None of these rulings probably had much effect. There were temples in the village in the 1930s. The village did not hold a jiao festival on its own, but villagers petitioned the board for permission to receive the deity from a neighboring jiao procession on the pretext that this might help to maintain neighborly relations.[49] As late as 1938, the village manager was fighting the practice of maintaining territorial linkage through the earth gods. In a report to the board of directors of the xiang association, he said,

There is this evil practice in the village that if someone moves his residence from A Lane to B Lane he must become a member of the *she*. If he does not [become a member], the newcomer may not give birth or die in the lane. However, to join the *she*, it is necessary to pay an unspecified amount of money. How much is required depends on the love and hatred in the lane. Such evil practice is not of convenience to our people, and may, because it imposes limits on the open sale of house plots, also adversely affect house plots owned by the xiang. It is necessary to abolish such an evil practice. I should be grateful for instructions.[50]

The change in culture in the village did not lie in what the village government could abolish, but with what it was able to impose.

As opposed to village religious practices, the village government was in favor of an annual xiang celebration that remembered the rebuilding of the village in 1919. The published program of the annual celebration for 1935, for instance, specified that participants would gather at 4:50 in the after-noon, sit at table at 5:00, raise their glasses and drink at 5:15, and rise at 5:20 to sing the "Our love for the xiang" song, at which time firecrackers would be let off.[51] The minutes of the xiang association noted that the celebration always took place on the 21st day of the third lunar month; that it involved worship at the ancestral graves in the morning as well as the distribution of sacrificial pork; and that after the singing of the xiang song, the board of directors of the xiang association, followed by the staff of the village government, the school headmaster and his students, the paramilitary forces, and then representatives of villagers at Tangang as well as villagers resident outside the village, in this order, paid respect to the ancestral shrines.[52] Modernity, Republican-style, blended with ancestral rites on the day of the xiang celebration.

Beneath the veneer of solidarity as expressed in the xiang song and celebration came the jostling for position and personality conflicts that characterize every political situation. Early in the history of the xiang association, the president of the Lineage Restoration Savings Association had been dislodged. That he sought to retire in 1921 with the publication of a pamphlet detailing the loans he had raised for the association and where he had deposited the funds suggests that he had reason to want to leave a clear record, and discussion in the board meetings of the xiang association immediately upon his departure confirms that feelings had been ruptured.[53] The ascendance of Yeying as president of the savings association brought some stability, but a rift began to appear between the village government and sections of the village.

The first outburst came in 1926, with the organization of a farmers' association (nonghui) in Tangang. The farmers' associations were first reported in a letter by the village manager in that year. He stated: "Recently, in many xiang the farmers' association has been formed, and once it is formed it comes into conflict with the militia [mintuan]."[54] In his letter tabled at the next meeting of the board of the xiang association, he reported that the farmers' association of Shatang xiang had posted a notice in Tangang market telling all tenants of the Ye surname [of Shatang] to pay their rent directly to the association. In the same letter, the manager also speculated that involved in these associations were the writers of a letter representing a Ruan ancestral trust demanding that the xiang association return the management of the trust to individual members of the lineage segment.[55]

The next reference to the farmers' associations came in 1927 when the village manager reported that members of the lineage had disrupted the village government's efforts to start a branch of the Guomindang in the village. The disruption involved a sizable portion of the village population, for the manager drew up a list of 156 names as the associates of the "reactionaries" of the xiang. One of the objects of starting a party branch in the village, he stated in his report, was to organize another farmers' association, and when the ringleader was arrested, he was sent for trial first at the "joint office" (*lianhe banshichu*) of the xiang level farmers' association of the county.[56] Such a power struggle would seem to be in accord with what is now known of the progress of the farmers' associations in Guangdong, that is, that from approximately 1927 extremist elements were being eliminated from them. That the village government could succeed in putting down the commotion so readily testifies to its strength within the village.[57]

It is apparent that by 1928 the county government was in a position to streamline government at the xiang level.[58] Much of the effort was directed at realigning intervillage organization and at transforming the village guard force into a militia, although other measures, such as the abolition of traditional-style village schools (*sishu*), were also promulgated.[59] New-style education was readily acceptable; in fact, Tangang could claim that it had been on the track from the time the village was rebuilt. However, county-level demands did not make any progress toward changing the xiang-level power alignments at Tangang.

In terms of its organization, the county demanded in 1930 that Tangang be grouped with the six clusters of villages known as the Lubao into the sixth district (*qu*) of Xinhui. By virtue of its sheer size, Tangang would have carried some weight in the self-government association (*zizhihui*), and it sought to put its influence to work immediately in its disputes with Shuibian. It also found very soon—in 1931—that while it could exert pressure on Shuibian within the self-government association, "the district association was only an arbitrator, and had no power to enforce [its decisions]."[60] Tangang probably still found its involvement in self-government convenient, for the village office continued to liaise with the county government on its dispute with Lingbei. The chairman of the provisional committee of the xiang self-government association was a member of the xiang association's board of directors.[61]

However, unity within the self-government association did not last another year, for by 1932 it was clear that someone from one of the Lubao villages, who had been liaising with the county government for the appointment of officers to the self-government association, had appropriated for himself the chairmanship, much to the dismay of the Tangang village manager. To make matters more complicated, the vehemence with which the Tangang manager took the defeat apparently suited the purpose of the xiang association, which did not in any case wish to see the bond between the manager and the county government strengthened. The Tangang village manager, consequently, refused to serve as the association's deputy president, and the xiang association applied to the county to withdraw totally from the Lubao alliance. The application was approved, and once again it was clear that Tangang did not share its sovereignty with any other village and that the final right of adjudication rested not with the village manager, but with the board of directors of the xiang association.[62]

If the county could not penetrate xiang politics on the strength of its prestige as the legitimate government, it had even less chance to do so by drawing on its meager resources. To begin with, the finances of the self-government association relied on contributions from its member villagers, and it was probably an indication of Tangang's strength that it was responsible for half the total outlay. A justification that the village manager could offer the xiang association's board of directors for withdrawing from the Lubao self-government association was, therefore, the financial one of being able to cut costs. Nowhere does it seem that the county was in a position to offer financial assistance. The matter of financing self-government was, in fact, raised in a communication with the county government in 1936, and the county could only respond by demanding that the *xiangzhang* (village head), its term for the chief executive of the xiang, adhere to his approved budget and seek new sources of income from a general meeting of members of the village.[63]

The several years from 1932 to 1936 saw some developments in the village that had far-reaching consequences. One of these was the first appearance of the telephone, which was useful for transmitting messages between the county government and the village.[64] Another development that promoted common purpose not only in Tangang but also in nearby villages was the building of the Xinhui-Taishan motor road, which gave the Tangang village government the right to impose a poll tax on its villagers.[65]

However, these years were also years of considerable economic distress and currency confusion, and the Tangang records show that the village government succumbed to much financial hardship as a result. Several reports refer to tenants giving up their plots and to the need to raise more funds, not only for the village government itself but also to meet demands from the county government in the name of defense.[66] All the while, Tangang maintained its own tax records, and so, despite meetings held at the county city to coordinate xiang-level administration, and common exercises for the xiang militia, Tangang's autonomy was never really compromised. When the president of the savings association, Yeying, retired in 1937, he probably did so of his own volition and in honor. The next year, he installed his father's portrait in the ancestral hall during the xiang celebration.[67] The xiang government maintained its prestige throughout Yeying's tenure of office.

It is hard to judge on the basis of the records whether personalities alone might account for the fate of the village government from 1937, or to explain how the county magistrate might or might not have had a role in the village government's returning to individual owners the right to manage their own land. What one does see very clearly in these records is the resilience of the power relationships in the village and between the village and the state, even as the language of political discourse evolved in the Republican period.

Postwar Finale

The essay on the village feuds that preceded the rebuilding of Tangang xiang concluded on the following note:

The committees set up by many surnames [after the feuds] included many people who genuinely worked for their own home villages. However, some people worked for their own private interests under the mask of the public good, and using the pretext of providing relief for the village, set up companies in Macau to contract [*baolan*] ancestral land which they then rented out, and caused much dispute. This is a heartbreaking development from the feuds.[68]

It would seem from this description that the collective management of land in the rebuilding of the villages in the Tangang vicinity was not unique to Tangang, and that, as one would expect, the claim of collective management was not beyond dispute. Yet, to argue that public and private interests must necessarily be separate, as is implicit in this line of reasoning, is to miss the point.

A useful contrast that can bring out what had happened in the two decades of the Republican period in Tangang politics is the structure the xiang association's meetings took as reflected in the minutes, which resume after 1945. The minutes begin by recording the general meeting that was held in Tangang in 1945. The meeting was held in three separate sessions. The first session was attended by the elders, defined as men over 60 *sui*; the second was attended by the *baozhang*, *jiazhang*, and able-bodied men, possibly a reference to members of the guard force; and the third by the young men. The xiang association continued to play a part in the village, and Shide remained the chairman of its board of directors, which continued to meet in Hong Kong. However, three members of the board of directors were to be stationed in Tangang.

Both the general meeting itself and the appointment of Tangang residents to the board of directors would seem to indicate that the expatriate communities no longer had total authority in designing how village affairs were to be managed. Nevertheless, it is the financial arrangement that departed most significantly from decisions made at the first meeting in 1919.

Deprived now of the collective management of private landholdings, the xiang association had within its control only public holdings in the village. These it divided into two groups. Most farmland, the market, and some donations were placed within an ancestral trust in the name of a common ancestor, while the remainder was kept in a separate trust. No decision was taken on how funds derived from the ancestral trust were to be spent, but it is stated in the minutes that income from the other trust would pay for the expenses of the village office. A line that provided for assessments not accrued to the ancestral trust being classed as income for the village office leaves open the possibility that a levy might still be charged on private land, but the lack of discussion on the subject suggests that most such levies had disappeared. The holdings of the xiang association now took on the appearance of an ancestral trust, and the role of the village office must have been considerably reduced.[69] Centralized administration of resources had not worked well, and the traditional diffused pattern of property management was resuming its past dominance.

Conclusion: Lineage Socialism, Control, and Cultural Change

The experience of Tangang was a strange story for which a parallel will be hard to find. Yet, the currents that took Tangang created ripples not only in this one village. The idea of centralized land management (if not ownership), the involvement of overseas members of the village in village politics, the split in ideology between persons who wanted radical reform for whatever purpose and a leadership holding onto national guidelines issued by governments whose legitimacy varied from decade to decade, the village song and flag, and a rigid timetable for village celebrations—all seem so familiar in Republican society. As in other villages, these currents of change seem, temporarily, to break down the bastions of traditional order, only to subside in time. At the end of the day, the ideals give way to the reality of personal ownership of land and a collective authority heatedly contested for by factions within the village. The language of the contest is the language of national politics; its substance remains land, status, and power in the local context.

The appearance that the state might have made some particular incursion into village society, in these circumstances, is probably an illusion. The recognition that the diffusion of economic control must go hand in hand with the broadening of representation of opinion was the result of the momentary expression of the shift in power between the xiang association and the village office. History does repeat itself: the adoption of a political language sanctioned by the state without the abandonment of the power relations of the village had happened before. One might characterize the rise of the lineage in the sixteenth century or the rise of territorial alliances in the eighteenth and nineteenth in these terms. Boards of directors, managers, minutes, and general meetings were creations of the Republic, but the village could absorb them as readily as it had absorbed ancestral halls, *gongsuo*, communal schools, and degree holders.

Subverting Lineage Power:
Local Bosses and Territorial
Control in the 1940s

HELEN F. SIU

IF LOCAL power in south China rested on lineages endowed with vast estates and the ability to flaunt literati pretensions, how did the lineage institution change after the fall of the Qing dynasty?[1] At the turn of the century, the He lineage in Shawan of Panyu county, as described in Liu Zhiwei's essay in this volume, appeared in full command of its resources. With an imposing solidarity, the lineage members expected deference from other inhabitants of the sands who were considered Dan and were excluded from community activities. But the bond of kinship and territorial power was at least malleable if not ephemeral. Less than a decade after the Qing dynasty fell, overseas merchants who had occupied peripheral social positions made a serious attempt to rebuild a lineage community in Xinhui county strictly according to the books. Their difficulties, David Faure argues, arose from the fact that the reality of community control, locally improvised, was in conflict with the language of lineage solidarity.[2]

What, then, was the fate of the lineages when China plunged further into crisis in the 1930s and 1940s? In the Pearl River delta, a more unorthodox generation of local strongmen rose rapidly to fill the power vacuum. They were tax farmers for regional warlords who maintained an uneasy truce with the Japanese army. They took over ancestral estates, created new networks of territorial control, and prospered through extortion and smuggling. Assuming that earlier social bonds continued to be reconstituted through time, I examine the power play revolving around the lineage institution in three closely situated communities in this period. What did lineage and territory mean in these areas, and how were the meanings transformed in a period when war and disorder entered into the daily experience of the villagers?

The local bosses were formidable challengers to the literati tradition. But they underwent a rapid demise at the time of the land reform of 1950 conducted by the newly established Communists. Judging from the relatively lenient treatment of the nonmilitaristic elites at the hands of the peasants, one may suggest that traditional authority based on lineage and community had remained significant in the popular mind. Going after the bosses might have been the peasants' way of attacking the excesses of the earlier system. However, even if traditional institutions persisted after the Communist revolution in 1949 in some forms, could the meanings behind lineage and community have changed in a number of ways over the preceding decades?

In Xinhui county, the lineages at and near the county capital (Huicheng) collected cash rents from their estates and invested them in commerce. The Japanese occupation, which lasted from 1938 to 1945, devastated them. Militaristic strongmen at Tianma, a township at the edge of the sands south of the county capital, took over many town-based estates and effectively collected rent and taxes from the farmers.[3] With these resources, they built their own ancestral halls. Although despised by the town population as inferior elements living close to the sands, the Chen of Tianma enjoyed an unprecedented prosperity and cultural awakening based on traditional notions of lineage power.[4]

The market town of Xiaolan was situated in Xiangshan county to the east of Xinhui. In the nineteenth century, it perched majestically on well-cultivated lands of the delta. Its numerous ancestral halls, merchant houses, and well-patronized temples bore witness to the residents' domination over the sands. Its elites controlled land reclamation, collected rent, and prospered on the trading of grain, mulberry leaves, silk cocoons, pigs, and wine. But the decades of warlord politics and the Japanese occupation eroded the economic bases of the three major surnames, He, Li, and Mai. Local strongmen of a variety of surnames took over the landed estates.[5] They moved into the town from the sands, became active in its administration, in local temples, and in neighborhood associations. Over a hundred smaller ancestral halls were dismantled. The focal ancestral halls were "hollowed out" and left to their demise.[6] The power of the militarists made a visible impact on the town's social life. Old party cadres I interviewed in 1986 recalled that the campaigns launched by the Communists against the lineage complex in 1950 were merely beating a dead horse. The lineages had collapsed long ago.

The township of Shawan in Panyu county, neighboring Xiangshan, was situated at the edge of the most recently formed sands. It was dominated by a He lineage, although other surnames, the Wang, Li, and Li (Lai), also had ancestral halls. Many local bosses from the sands moved into town in the 1940s, allied themselves with members of the major surnames, and fought fiercely for the right to collect grain from estates owned by ancestral trusts.[7] During this period, the estates remained important objects of contention and the halls remained centers of activity. Only a few of the 116 halls were dismantled.[8] Residents of Shawan today clearly identify themselves with specific lineage segments under the focal ancestral hall.[9]

The differing fortunes of the ancestral complex in Tianma, Xiaolan, and Shawan raise the question of how the lineage was tied to the development of these communities that had been enriched by the reclamation of the sands in the delta, how the volatile politics of the Republican era transformed these relationships, and to what extent local populations adopted the emerging political vocabulary to create enduring identities as they acquired new perceptions of power and authority.

Tianma Xiang, Xinhui County

In the first quarter of the twentieth century, Tianma xiang of Xinhui county was a large township with over two thousand inhabitants, all surnamed Chen. It had a daily market and was connected to Sanjiang (inhabited by the Zhao lineage) and Shuangshui (inhabited by the Chen, Tan, and Lin lineages), both sizable market towns south of the county capital. The Chen of Tianma maintained only a few ancestral halls, built early in the course of settlement, which functioned as tenant contractors. The focal ancestral hall, Wuben tang, owned fewer than 100 mu of land.[10] The managers paid cash rents to ancestral trusts of the He and the Mo lineages in the county capital six kilometers away, and parceled the land out to their kin to farm. Rent was collected in kind to maintain lineage rituals. Wuben tang also served as the community office.[11] Lineage elders and managers collected rent, paid taxes, repaired dikes, mediated disputes, and kept public order. Local residents paid nominal fees to the hall in order to grow fruit trees on the dikes, to fish in the numerous waterways, and to use the river landings and market.

The claim of genealogical ties to Wuben tang was vital to the Chen residents. Those ties guaranteed the right of settlement in the village, of contracting for farmland, and of obtaining a livelihood by other means. On the southern edge of Tianma a poor hamlet was inhabited by "people of mixed surnames," including outcasts from the Chen lineage. They were referred to as the "mean households" (*xiahu*) and "sands people" (*shamin*) who farmed the marshes beyond the diked village fields. Few were allowed to build permanent dwellings. Most lived on boats or in straw huts along the dikes.[12] "People of mixed surnames" could be numerous. They might have lived in the area for generations. However, the term was a metaphor for disenfranchised elements in the community, people who had never demonstrated a genealogical link to an ancestral hall.

It is also clear that being a member of the Chen lineage entailed two different predicaments, social and economic. Although the Chen looked down upon those living farther out in the river marshes, established communities closer to the county capital gave the Chen little social recognition. In their eyes, the Chen were "Dan." As described in Ye Xian'en's essay in this book, the Dan were officially categorized as one of the "mean peoples" and barred from taking the civil service examinations until the reigns of Yongcheng and Qianlong in the eighteenth century relaxed the discriminations.[13] The Chen whom I met over the years never acknowledged this social characterization, although their own written genealogy contains revealing evidence of starting out as a boat-dwelling, migratory people. Instead, they dissociated themselves from what they named as *shamin* living out in the sands.[14]

The fact that such labeling created a complex social hierarchy demonstrates that the claim of settlement rights based upon genealogical ties, fictive or real, constituted a shrewd expression of political and economic interest and was a significant element in the history of community building in and around Tianma.[15]

The commercialized ancestral trusts in Huicheng succumbed to the chaos of warlord politics and of the Japanese occupation in the late 1930s. The rise of local bosses in Tianma accelerated their demise. The bosses encroached upon the land of these town-based trusts in order to build their own. They took over the thriving grain trade and diverted it to market towns farther south. They were also engaged in smuggling opium, liquor, and other heavily taxed goods to various warlord regimes. When war broke out in the late 1930s, they supplied goods both to the Nationalist government and to the Japanese military by rerouting the marketing networks. Together with Sanjiang and Shuangshui, major market towns to which the Nationalists had retreated, Tianma formed an important part of a regional nexus, earning the name of Little Macau. Through shrewd maneuvers, the local strongmen kept both the Japanese military (who occupied Huicheng, the county capital) and the Nationalists (who regrouped in the market town of Shuangshui) at a distance. While these local bosses did not favor their kin, the township under their control experienced a certain boom because wealth and cultural resources were diverted from the county capital.

On the eve of the Communist takeover, Tianma had 35 ancestral halls. Over a dozen of the halls, which villagers called "private," had been erected in the twentieth century. During a visit I made to Tianma in 1987, villagers eagerly showed me a modern-style ancestral hall built by the powerful local boss, Chen Shufen, in the early 1940s. Chen's ties to the literati were tenuous. He claimed that his grandfather had once acquired a low-level degree. He himself had advanced through connections with the military. When his mansion was built, he held a banquet. To show his influence, he invited local bosses from the area together with representatives from the Japanese army and the Nationalist government, who arrived with their respective entourages of body guards and machine guns. Villagers identified the mansion as a *sheng citang*, meaning a memorial hall belonging to an extended family. It was a three-story house without the conventional wide entrance and curved roof that signified literati status, but it supported the village school that was physically attached to it.

Neither did the numerous small halls have the conventional wide, tall entrances. Together with Wuben tang, which had amassed a formidable arsenal for community self-defense in wartime, the new ancestral establishments worked to strengthen kin relations, affirming both genealogical ties to the focal ancestor and asymmetrical segmentation through the establishment of independent estates. It is ironic that for the Chen of Tianma, the fuller cultural meanings of a lineage complex, denied by the exclusiveness of the town-based lineages in Huicheng for centuries, became a reality in the unsettling decades of the Republican era.

Xiaolan Zhen, Xiangshan County

Xiaolan, a market town midway between the county capitals of Xiangshan (Shiqi) and Shunde (Daliang), had become a center of commercial wealth, literati accomplishments, and lineage power in the nineteenth century. The three major surnames were He, Li, and Mai, each tracing genealogical ties to a focal ancestor who supposedly settled in the area centuries earlier. The He had two lineages. Based on the popular settlement myth espoused by lineages in the delta, they claimed that their focal ancestors were brothers who had fled from the Nanxiong subprefecture during the Song dynasty. The branch that traced descent from the tenth brother (Xihuan tang) was superior in wealth and numbers to the one that traced de-

scent from the ninth brother (Liuqing tang). Both built elaborate focal ancestral halls, and in 1873 some members bought shares with the aim of
establishing a hall for a minister in the Song court who was regarded as
the grandfather of the two brothers. As in Tianma xiang, links to focal
ancestors provided the Xiaolan residents with claims to settlement rights
in the area.[16]

This functioning genealogy was buttressed by three new developments.
In Guangdong during the late Ming and early Qing period, ornate ances-
tral halls tied to leading scholar-officials became the dominant mode of
lineage building and aggrandizement. Prominent Ming officials who had
tremendous impact on the shaping of literati and popular cultures in
Guangdong were identified with major lineages in the Pearl River delta:
Huo Tao of the Huo lineage of Shitou near Foshan, He Xiongxiang of the
He lineage of Xinhui county, and He Wuzhou of the He lineage in Xiaolan,
Xiangshan county.[17] In fact, the names of the focal ancestral halls of the
He and Li lineages in Xiaolan were adorned with the highest official titles
of their lineage members. Xihuan tang, the focal ancestral hall of one of
the two He lineages, was also known as the Neige dazongci because He
Wuzhou, a member of the thirteenth generation, became a *Hanlin* scholar
and minister in the late Ming court. The focal ancestral hall of the Li lineage was named the Shangshu dazongci because Sunchen, a contemporary
of He Wuzhou, also became a minister.

The political privileges gained from shared status with the literati under
the Ming administration complemented the flourishing and consolidation
of the literati mode of lineage building in the Pearl River delta. In Xiaolan,
the proliferation of lineages was made all the more possible by the rapid
development of the sands from the eighteenth century on.[18] There were
many ways of accumulating wealth: claiming rights to turn river marshes
into polders and to collect a nominal "skeletal" fee (*shagu*), contracting
with the original claimants to reclaim the marshes, collecting rent in kind
from tenant farmers and then entering and controlling the grain trade, and
enjoying vast tax exemptions either by colluding with local officials or by
cheating them, since they had no way of recording the rapid growth of the
vast estates in the sands.[19] By using genealogies, He Yanggao, a local historian, estimates that the He lineage of Xiaolan started accumulating land
and building estates at the fifth generation (late fourteenth century). Most
of the 393 ancestral halls of that lineage were built during the nineteenth
century, when its members attained the height of their literati and official
achievements.[20]

There was a paradoxical development of the lineage complex. The easy access to wealth created a rapid "devolution" of the lineage, as practically every generation was able to establish an independent ancestral estate. On the other hand, developing the open "frontier" of the sands meant imposing territorial control with force and cultural exclusion over a class of laborers, tenants, and potential competitors. The maintenance of power by the town-based landlords necessitated a constant rebuilding of ties through focal ancestors in order to mobilize strength in numbers and in official ranks. In time the powerful landlords became "the major surnames" (daxing) in town, treated with due respect and awe; and their leading members constituted the core of a political alliance, the Lanxiang Gongyue. The focal ancestral halls, together with the halls of their lineage segments, were active patrons of religious rituals associated with the five major temples in town. They were also organizers of the community-wide chrysanthemum festivals from the early nineteenth century.[21]

As mentioned earlier, members of the two He lineages in Xiaolan jointly built an ancestral estate and hall for the grandfather of their focal ancestors in 1873. The new focal ancestor had been a minister in the Song court, and the hall was named after his title. To boost numerical power vis-à-vis other lineages, all male descendants of both lineages were included and were entitled to ritual pork after lineage ceremonies. But to highlight differentiated status and privilege within the lineage, only members of the segments who contributed to the new estate were given a share of the income.[22]

The third development came from thriving commerce associated with the grain from the sands and with the silk production in the neighboring Shunde county. By the twentieth century, Xiaolan had more than three hundred ancestral halls with estates. Some of these were set up by prosperous literati members, whose descendants also controlled the grain trade, the production of pigs, mulberry, and silk cocoons, and the distilling of liquor. There were two mulberry markets in Xiaolan, and merchants collected local cocoons to trade in specialized markets in Rongqi, a town midway between Xiaolan and the county capital of Shunde. Many were also bankers and pawnbrokers who collected rents in cash and in kind from their clients and supplied the grain wharves in Chencun (Shunde county). Rituals financed by or conducted in the ancestral halls highlighted the interconnections between the ancestral cult, lineage power, territorial control, literati politics, and commercial wealth.[23]

This complex of activities contrasted sharply with life in the sands. A kilometer or two outside the town, there was hardly a sizable village to be found. The area was worked by a mobile stratum of tenant farmers who lived in straw huts or on boats, were considered economically inferior, and were socially shunned. Their economic and social statuses were similar to the *shamin* or "Dan" in Tianma, who belonged to "mixed surnames" and had no settlement rights.[24] The political agenda beneath the labeling seems obvious. It was one of exclusion.

The Republican decades brought fundamental changes to the lineage complex and its associated social hierarchy. Its wealth and power were undermined by the rising bosses tied to the warlord government, and it collapsed completely during the Japanese occupation due to factors similar to those that operated in Huicheng. Local bosses from the surrounding sands took over rent and tax collection, broke trade blockades by smuggling, and established extortion rackets.[25] Many of their victims were the small landlords and the lineage estates in town.

In contrast to the situation in Tianma, in Xiaolan the local bosses did not stay in the villages. In fact, this recently reclaimed part of the delta had few sizable villages. The bosses moved their operations into town as soon as they secured the loyalty of their field functionaries. By the 1930s the area had seen a parade of military strongmen who tried to reach rural society directly in order to extract revenue. They did not belong to any of the major surnames in town.

Yuan Dai, one such strongman, was captain of a crop-protection force in the sands of Shunde and Xiangshan counties. During harvest, his men arrived in a fleet of motorboats and large sailboats to make sure that the fees were paid. In 1915, he clashed violently with another captain near a wholesale fish market in Shiqi, causing widespread civilian damage. He fought with the retreating county head, Li Jingyun, in 1922, and the conflict resulted in the looting of the merchants' quarters in Shiqi. Yuan Dai extended his control as far as Xinhui county and was given military titles by the warlord regimes in Guangzhou. In the 1930s he established his headquarters in Xiaolan and carved out spheres of control in the sands for his collaborators.[26]

The chrysanthemum festival of 1934 was illustrative of the rise of the local strongmen, which in turn corresponded to the demise of the lineage complex in Xiaolan.[27] Initially, the ancestral halls of the major lineages did not intend to hold the festival. Most of the cash revenues from their estates were lost to the excessive demands of the tax farmers. Their estates had been encroached upon by tenant contractors in the sands and their trading activities curtailed by the unstable monetary situation. However, the festival was organized with the initiative of a new stratum of local elites.

The head of the organization committee was one He Naizhong, a former title-holder and merchant. Although he belonged to a rich landowning family in Xiaolan, his prestige was largely based on his having been an adviser to the warlord Feng Yuxiang.[28] Liang Bingyun, who had been appointed head of the third district of Xiangshan county (renamed Zhongshan in 1925), of which Xiaolan was the administrative headquarters, gave the opening speeches. He also organized a trade fair at the site of the He Feng Academy, an institution set up decades before by the other surname groups in town with the intention of countering the power of the major lineages.

The headquarters of the festival was a study chamber belonging to a Liu family. Two nouveaux riches, Liu Rongjie and Gan Hanchen, who had made their fortunes by speculating in the financial markets of Shanghai, organized their own floral displays which became the talk of the town. Local temples were the unusual centers of these activities, financed by the bosses who had stationed their troops in them and used them as headquarters for tax collection. He Yanggao, a local scholar who was the head of the richest family in town, recalled that the major ancestral halls, which finally went along with the festivities, were so drained of resources that they had no ritual pork to distribute in the years that followed.

The Japanese occupation from 1938 to 1945 accelerated the demise of the lineage complex in Xiaolan. The major cities and county capitals of the Pearl River delta were controlled by the Japanese military and their collaborators, who maintained an uneasy truce with local strongmen. Some of the bosses had received titles of "captains of the self-defense corps" from the Nationalist government, which had retreated to the upper reaches of the Xi River system near Guangxi province. Yuan Dai and his cousin Qu Renze assumed the titles of commander and deputy commander of the Third Regiment of the Seventh War Zone (abbreviated to Ting San).[29] In the name of resisting Japanese aggression, they amassed a fleet of motorized gunboats. They smuggled war goods between Hong Kong, Macau, the occupied territories in the delta such as Guangzhou, Shunde, and Rongqi, and the Nationalist-controlled areas in the northwestern part of the delta. The commodities included grain, minerals, lumber, and herbs from the hilly regions and salt, kerosene, cloth, medicine, flour, cigarettes, and opium from Hong Kong and Macau.

The regiment was made up of eleven auxiliary troops, each headed by Yuan's collaborators, who were themselves local strongmen. Three of the troops were directly under Yuan and Qu, operating in the third district (the northern half of Xiangshan county). The troop centering on Xiaolan was headed by Qu Renze himself. He was helped by a captain (*da duizhang*), Xie Yunlong, nicknamed Xie the Tiger, and by a deputy (*zhong duizhang*),

Chao Tianlin. Together with Yuan, they were known as the *sida tianwang* (the four supreme bosses) and controlled a corporation known as the Min-sheng Gongsi. The other eight troops were organized in a corporation known as Minli Gongsi, which acted as a front for their activities.[30] These bosses monopolized money exchanges in native banks and owned opium dens and prostitution houses. They collected the "red tickets" in the name of resisting the Japanese military and the "black tickets" in the name of crop-protection.[31] As local residents recalled in 1986, "We paid the officials and the bandits; the revenue ended up in the same pockets."

Little was left for the ancestral estates. In fact, local bosses forcefully "bought" many of the estates whose managers were unable to pay taxes and surcharges in kind because the cash rent they had managed to collect became valueless during the turbulent decade. He Yanggao estimates that before the war, local strongmen owned about 400 mu in Sisha, a tract of diked fields southwest of Xiaolan. After the war, they owned about 5,000 mu. Twenty mu of He's land in Sisha were lost to the bosses. He and his family fled to Macau during the war and suffered great financial losses.

Li (Lai) Zhanquan was the head of the third district appointed by the Japanese during the war. An interview with him in Hong Kong in 1986 highlighted some revealing political dynamics among the local bosses in and around Xiaolan.[32] Li was a native of Nanhai county near Guangzhou. When he was appointed, he was a functionary of an important politician in Shiqi. He himself conducted some business in Xiaolan. Most of these bosses maintained elaborate mansions and businesses in Xiaolan. Securing a balance of power between the Japanese troops and the military bosses in the Xiangshan-Shunde region was essential for the stability of the town.

The Japanese army was the least of Li's problems. A lieutenant and his troops were stationed at Shakou, the eastern entrance of Xiaolan where Dan fishermen congregated in their boats. With the help of Qu's troops, Li was able to satisfy the Japanese with laborers and a small portion of the fees and taxes collected from the sands. His good relations with the Japanese military in Shiqi restrained the lieutenant. He was also in contact with the Communists in Shaping, a non-occupied town to the northwest that continued to use Chinese currency for business. He bought a house from Yuan Dai and organized a social club (named Siyou tang, "hall of four friends") with Xie Yunlong, Chao Tianlin, and a Liang Dingan.[33] Over dinners and games, they carved out territories for control, resolved conflicts of interest, mediated the kidnappings of the local rich and matters of troop discipline, and decided on the collection of taxes and fees (which he ac-knowledged never reached Guangzhou). With the bosses residing in Xiaolan and socializing among themselves, an uneasy peace was maintained. As Li recalled, "When we the bosses refrained from fighting and looting, who dared to make trouble?"[34]

According to He Yanggao and other old scholars in town whom I interviewed in 1986, local bosses did not claim ancestral halls outright; rather, they colluded with the managers in taking them over. A large ancestral hall of the Mai, the Qingyi tang, was dismantled in this manner. The focal ancestral halls of the major lineages remained, but over a hundred smaller halls were taken down and the materials sold.[35] Ordinary lineage members often went along willingly because they were desperately poor and hungry. The war had drastically reduced commercial activities in Xiaolan, which meant fewer jobs for the town residents. Laborers needed in the fields were drafted by both Chinese and Japanese forces, straining an already intensive agricultural production. While people were losing their livelihoods, grain prices maintained an all-time high because of war and blockades.[36] Single-surname neighborhoods gave way to mixed ones, as houses belonging to families who had fled the war or perished were sold to non–lineage members. Conflicts over the sale of this lineage property were reflected in the numerous announcements and lawsuits published in the county newspapers.

Strategies in pursuit of upward mobility also exacerbated the pain of demise for the lineages. Local bosses sought marriages with town families from among the major surnames whose fortunes had declined. They offered large dowries and practiced the delayed transfer of their daughters, customs that town lineages had used to distinguish themselves from the people of the sands and which town families found increasingly difficult to maintain. Among the poor in town, women settled with their husbands immediately after marriage because many family members had been killed or scattered during the war. There was little dowry to speak of. Instead, families began to ask for a bride price for their daughters, a marital payment they had earlier accused the sands people of shamelessly demanding.[37]

In sum, the cultural nexus of power that had once belonged to the lineage complex was undermined by a conjunction of pressures from within and without. Unlike the local bosses of Tianma, who constructed the lineage complex with their newfound wealth, those in Xiaolan built their power upon competing institutions in town and left the lineages to their own demise. The political campaigns in the Maoist period sealed the fate of the lineage complex and community rituals.[38] Furthermore, when the whirlwind of "modernization" swept the Pearl River delta in the 1980s, what remained of the ancestral halls were dismantled faster than ever to make way for factories and for the residences of the nouveaux riches.[39] For the young cadres and entrepreneurs alike, the halls belonged to an alien "feudal past" long faded from their lives.

Shawan, Panyu County

Shawan was a market town at the edge of the sands of Panyu county. These sands had been formed more recently than those surrounding Tianma and Xiaolan. The town and the power of its residents grew rapidly in the late Qing through active reclamation of land. In the early twentieth century, it was less commercialized than Xiaolan but much more prosperous and populous than Tianma. A He lineage dominated the town. As described in Liu Zhiwei's essay, their focal ancestor, He Renjian, was said to have settled in the area during the Song. With customary exaggeration and ingenuity, the lineage genealogy claimed that He Renjian had relied on the influence of the famous official Li Maoying to acquire vast tracts of river marshes from the Guangdong Ever Normal Granary Office (*changping si*) in 1233. The area claimed extended as far west as the borders of Xiangshan county, totaling over 30,000 mu. It was also said that by the early Ming, the He lineage had a population of "three thousand, subdivided into fourteen *fang*."[40] Its members formed a management committee, the Shuben tang, to run the expanding lineage estate. In time, lineage segments acquired another 35,000 mu. They also owned shops, landings, and land in Guangzhou. The Shuben tang maintained a fleet of boats, armed crop-watching forces, and employed technical functionaries (*daqing, yageng, tanjing, zhangshou*) to supervise the collection of grain and to repair the dikes.[41]

As in Xiaolan and Tianma, it was politically important for residents to trace descent from the focal ancestor, who supposedly had claims to vast territories. There was a rule which stipulated that only descendants of the He lineage were allowed to contract land from the ancestral trust. Although numerous lineage segments established independent estates, 116 in all, many of their members had prospered as tenant contractors of the focal ancestral hall.[42] Local historians estimated that over 40 percent of the He lineage members "rented" large plots from the Liugeng tang and then subcontracted them to cultivators.

Powerful lineage members also rented land from other surnames with estates in the region, such as the Su lineage of Bijiang, the Xie lineage of Shiqiao, the Wu lineage of Nancun, and the Han lineage of Guba. Occasionally they reclaimed the river marshes themselves. For example, one converted a 2,000-mu area named Xinsha in the 40th year of Qianlong (1775). Another member of the same lineage segment built nine diked fields in Qingjiaosha at the southernmost corner of Panyu county during the 60th year of the Qianlong reign.[43] Other fields were added in the later years, making up a total of 20,000 mu. Both sets of fields were registered with estate names other than Liugeng tang.[44] This spectacular rise to power of the He lineage and its corresponding cultural discourse is analyzed in detail by Liu Zhiwei in this volume. My essay concentrates on its fate in the twentieth century.

By the turn of this century, managers of the Liugeng tang and the segment estates controlled over 60,000 mu of cultivable land and its grain rent, which they traded with merchants in the neighboring market town of Chencun (Shunde county) where Hesheng Hao, a native bank owned by He Zhongshen, was the estate's banker. The proximity of Chencun, a long-established center for the financing and trading of grain and cash crops, dwarfed similar developments in Shawan. Unlike the commercialized Xiaolan, Shawan remained a place of residence for its elites, whose wealth was based almost exclusively on the control of grain.

Like Xiaolan, the claim of lineage power by town residents went hand in hand with barriers built against those in the sands. The sands people, referred to as Dan even today, did not belong to any major surname, were considered poor and uncouth, and were not invited to participate in any of the town's festivities. The Beidi parade and the *piaose* (floating colors) were two major festivities that required elaborate coordinated efforts of the town-based lineages, whose members lived in established neighborhoods (*fang, jia*). Those considered nonresidents, including the villagers at the southern edge of the town, were not involved. In this volume, Liu Zhiwei focuses on this discriminatory practice in Shawan, and Luo Yixing describes similar processes in Lubao.

Today, immigrants from the sands who have resided in town since the revolution continue to refer to themselves as being "people outside" (*kaimian ren*). Such is the case with a former Daoist priest who moved into town from the village of Da Congkou in the sands when a local boss in the 1940s tore down his father's shed in order to make room for a sugar refinery. I also encountered the case of a poor man who had moved out to the sands to build dikes. He married a "woman of the sands" and raised his family there. His daughter eventually came back to town for marriage but continues to be addressed by neighbors as *danjia po* (*danjia* woman) forty years later.[45] There are also many popular myths that delineate the history of settlement of the local residents. These explain how, through the centuries, the He conflicted with the Li over geomancy and territory, and why members of the He and the Wang lineage, another competitor, could not intermarry.

Although the dominance of the He lineage complex under the focal ancestral shadow of the Liugeng tang seemed unquestionable,[46] during the Republican era four families rose from within to become the *sida gengjia* (the four major tenant contractors). The founders were of humble origin. They made their fortunes by renting small parcels of the ancestral estates for a nominal rent of 60–100 catties per mu and then subleasing the land to their functionaries or directly to the farmers in the sands. They bought some land of their own with the profits and continued to expand their tenant-contracting enterprises in Panyu and Dongguan.[47] Few of them diked their own fields.

Their sons, who were mostly educated in modern schools, became the first agricultural entrepreneurs in the area. They expanded operations into large-scale grain milling. Responding to the call of the Guangdong warlord Chen Jitang to develop sugar cane as a cash crop, they established sugar plantations and refineries. Their fortunes were tied to tenant contracting in the sands and to specific ancestral trusts, but local residents remembered them as distinguished entrepreneurs. Their businesses, named Shengli, Xinhe, Liji, and Liuji, were labeled *pu* (shops). These entrepreneurs were powerful figures in Shawan. They competed and cooperated with militaristic local bosses in the 1930s and 1940s, maintained armed guards, and built fortified watch towers for defense. They nonetheless enjoyed a degree of legitimacy and goodwill in the community. Residents distinguished them from the bosses, *datian'er*, who were seen as preying on people by brute force.

He Houjiao, the founder of Xinhe Enterprises, was a hired hand in a social club for local elites. Some club members liked him enough to contract some land for him from the ancestral estates. Among his fifteen children, all of whom received modern education, He Shang, the sixth son, went to Lingnan University in Guangzhou. In the 1930s, He Shang set up experimental sugar plantations and the Xinxinghe sugar refinery in a village outside Shawan. He hired local foremen, known as *daqing*, to manage the sugar fields, paying them each a wage of about three *dan* of grain a month each.[48] When his father died in 1941, he took over the entire family enterprise. By that time, the Japanese military controlled Guangzhou and major cities in the delta.

To avoid spreading himself thin, he closed the native banks and jewelry shops in Guangzhou and Hong Kong that his father had bought, and concentrated on the agricultural enterprises in Shawan. He bid for ancestral land in the public auctions; he took the tax-farming quotas (the red tickets) imposed by the government on the estates, and negotiated with the local bosses for the payment of protection fees (the black tickets).[49] He built three watchtowers for self-defense and had a fleet of boats with armed men to supervise the harvests.

Two of He Shang's contemporaries took a much more active role in military affairs. He Shuheng was the eldest son of He Shengli and manager of Shengli Enterprises, the largest of the Liugeng tang's tenant contractors.[50] He organized a self-defense brigade equipped with two machine guns, and was on the front line of a battle in 1938 against Japanese troops at the southern edge of Shawan.[51] Both he and He Shang cooperated in military adventures with He Duan, known as "Duan the scholar," who had worked as a tutor-adviser for an old military boss in Panyu. At the beginning of the war with Japan, He Duan and his men were recruited by the Liugeng tang and the Shawan village office to head a self-defense force. They were responsible for guarding the central and northern parts of town. He stationed his troops in the Guangyu tang, one of the major ancestral halls of the He lineage. Some nationalist soldiers who had retreated from the East River area were given provisions by the village office and stationed in the focal ancestral hall of the Wang at the western edge of Shawan. The granary of the Liugeng tang, 30 meters high, was the main watchtower for this alliance of anti-Japanese forces.[52]

Although the rise of He Duan depended on his military adventures, he made himself more respectable by mingling in the local elite circles: competing in the Liugeng tang's public auction of tenant contracts and raising funds to support the local school.[53] He was known for his anti-Japanese stance in 1938–39, but he and He Shang were among the local notables who formed the *jianshe jiuji weiyuanhui* (war relief committee), the equivalent of the township government in 1940, which maintained an uneasy truce with the Japanese military who controlled Shiqiao, Panyu county capital. The committee centralized the resources of all the lineages in the community in the name of more effective defense and reconstruction of the community in a time of crisis.

Shawan did suffer damage during the seesaw power struggle among the local bosses and the Japanese military. When the latter attacked the delta, local bosses were given titles and arms by the retreating Nationalist government in order to put up a facade of resistance. There were skirmishes in 1938 that led to the Japanese bombing the town. When the Japanese military and Chinese collaborators established headquarters in the county capital, Shiqiao, they dealt with the committee organized by He Duan and others to keep public order. During the period of occupation, local bosses had rotated the headship of the town and acted as military captains for the Japanese and the Nationalists. They collected taxes and fees from the sands. At times, the power equilibrium was hard to maintain. In 1940, He Jian, an ally of a Chinese boss, Li Fuqun, in Shiqiao, occupied the town with his troops. While the local self-defense corps scattered to Xiangshan and Shunde, He's troops looted the town for three days.

Leading members of the four major tenant contractors were seldom regarded as the *datian'er*, especially if they were involved in managing ancestral estates. There is a local saying that "those who held guns would not be holding the keys to the ancestral chest." He Duan was close to being one of those who were feared and hated for having risen so precipitously during the war with the Japanese and identified as militaristic adventurers. In the eyes of local residents who lived off the income from lineage estates, the bosses had no redeeming qualities because "they made a living with their guns," and "ignored general moral persuasions." Their relationships with the established ancestral estates and the four major tenant contractors were tense. The lesser bosses seldom competed for tenant contracting at the public auctions because they did not command enough coercive means or prestige for the Liugeng tang to give them credit. But they demolished the estates belonging to smaller lineage segments. An old resident recalled that practically every family estate under their lineage segment (the third *fang*) was taken. After the estates were sold, the halls were dismantled.[54] These same bosses also led "crop-watching forces" to collect the "black tickets" from the tenant contractors as well as directly from tenant farmers.

The bosses' clash with the focal ancestral hall and its major contractors extended to the outlying areas of the sands, where they forcibly collected grain rent due to the Liugeng tang. At times, they colluded with the farmers to cheat the major tenant contractors. As a former functionary of Liji Enterprises recalled, "If these lesser bosses had a conscience, they should collect the rent from the farmers and give us 60 catties per mu. Even if we pressed hard, we might collect only 20 catties per mu. It was worse when they linked up with the Dan bandits of Minzong at the border with Xiangshan. As we say, the *danjia* is strong when the sea is wide."[55] These local bosses also dismantled temples and used the materials to build watchtower complexes in the villages, which were nicknamed "local bullies' mansions."[56]

Some military bosses in the sands became powerful enough to gain a foothold in town. They established their headquarters in the study chambers (private memorial halls) they bought from families who had lost their fortunes in the chaos of war.[57] He Cheng's father was unemployed all his life but managed to live off the income of several segment estates. He himself was literate but had made his living as a petty trader in Guangzhou. He was streetwise. When the Japanese came, he was the captain of a crop-watching force supported by the lineage segment to which he belonged.[58] At the height of his power, he had a following of a few hundred men and a study chamber in town as headquarters. He clashed with another powerful boss, He Rugen, over the latter's appointment as head of the township during the Japanese occupation. He had once linked up with Communist guerrillas in the Panyu-Shunde-Xiangshan border area and fought against the pro-Japanese forces of Li Fuqun and He Jian based in the county capital. He extracted surcharges from the segment estates. He also subcontracted land from those who had acquired vast areas of the sands from the Liugeng tang. His rapid rise was cut short in 1945 when competitors shot him in Guangzhou. He was 32. After his death, his younger brother, a lad of 16, regrouped He Cheng's followers, put himself under He Duan, and maintained a base in the southwestern tip of the county.

Other bosses of a similar kind included He Rugen, who assumed the post of *xiangzhang* during the war and had conflicts with He Cheng. The *xiangzhang* after the war, He Congbao, nicknamed Bao the Blind, trapped and shot He Shang and his bodyguard on the streets of Shawan during the power vacuum of 1949. According to the younger brother of He Shang, He Congbao was nervous about He Shang's willingness to compromise with the Communists. He invited He Shang to his house to discuss the issue of forming sharecropping arrangements with tenants in the sands, a project proposed by He Shang. At the time, the Communist troops had already visited the town and local bosses were giving up their guns. He Shang went unarmed with a bodyguard of his brother and was shot as soon as he left He Congbao's house.

The ambivalent relationship the bosses maintained with the ancestral trusts and the established elites in town can be illustrated by two other well-known incidents that occurred in the 1940s. During the Japanese occupation, the functionary of a local boss in Shawan had his gun confiscated by guards in a passenger boat running between Shiqiao and Guangzhou. In retaliation, he and his gang later shot at the ferry and accidentally killed a passenger. Unfortunately for them, the victim was the son of an official in the Shiqiao government. Han Shizhong, one of the bosses of that town, used the killing as an excuse to surround Shawan with his troops. He Duan acted as mediator. The Liugeng tang, representing the town, finally delivered the killer as well as 100,000 catties of rice to the group at Shiqiao as compensation.

The other incident took place after the war and involved disputes over the collection rights of the Liugeng tang itself. In the 1940s, the control of the trust had fallen into the hands of Liji Enterprises, in particular the fifth and seventeenth sons of Liji's founder. Among the four major tenant contractors of the Liugeng tang, Liji was the one whose wealth was most closely tied to the lineage trust. Its founder had maintained grain mills and native banks in Guangzhou, Foshan (Nanhai county), Chencun, Longgang (Shunde county), and Shilong (Dongguan county). After the collapse of the financial market in the early 1930s, He Tongzhi, the fifth son, refocused the business of Liji on tenant contracting under the Baozhuan *ci*, the ancestral trust and hall built by his father and his uncle. When the Japanese war broke out, He Tongzhi became the chief manager of the Liugeng tang. He held the position for two terms, a total of six years, and then passed it to his younger brother, known locally as He Shiqi (He the Seventeenth). The son of Shiqi, He Zhongxian, managed the grain trade and engaged in speculations for Liji. Any challenge to the Liugeng tang meant a challenge to Liji and the Baozhuan *ci*, and vice versa.

Two local bosses, He Gongba (once a *xiangzhang*) and He Diesheng, led crop-watching forces to patrol the estates of the Liugeng tang at Gaosha and Xinsha.[59] After the war, they cooperated with the bosses in Minzong of Xiangshan county (organized around Minli Gongsi) to collect rent and taxes, and ignored the claims of the Liugeng tang. He Shiqi, then the chief manager of the Liugeng tang, hired troops, cannons, and gunboats from a commander in Guangzhou in order to uphold the rights of the ancestral estate. The two forces fought intermittently until 1949, when He Shiqi's troops, together with He Jian's, defected to the Communists.

Unlike the situation in Xiaolan, where military bosses with mixed surnames accelerated the downfall of the major surnames in town, the upheaval in Shawan was viewed by villagers as infighting among members of the He lineage. The Liugeng tang continued to be the center of activities and its wealth a target of contention. Many of the local strongmen there subsequently fled the area or were arrested and shot by the Communists in the early 1950s. The lineage estates were redistributed to the poor residents of the sands. The Liugeng tang and the other ancestral halls were not torn down. As dilapidated storehouses, cow sheds, or village headquarters, they remain standing today, stubborn testimony to a glorious and contested past for those who would take a quiet moment to reflect. In the early 1980s, the Liugeng tang, symbolizing the wealth and power of the He lineage, was renovated and designated as a provincial-level historical monument. In Hong Kong, Xiaolan maintains a native place association that has taken on an increasingly active role in attracting investment from the town's successful émigrés, but Shawan relies on the He Lineage Association.

By comparing the fates of the lineage institution in Tianma, Xiaolan, and Shawan, I hope to have presented an account of cultural change that captures the breadth of historically lived experience in rural south China. Looking back to the late imperial period, one can see that the rise of the territorially based lineage complex in these towns was intimately tied to the development of the sands. In these towns, local populations at different points in time reclaimed river marshes that had been formed as the West River, a major tributary of the Pearl River, flowed in a southeastern direction. Improvising on the cultural resources of their patrons in the older parts of the delta, they established their own history and identity and built a unique range of social institutions. The self-aggrandizing agendas behind lineage genealogies and ancestral estates were blatant. The language of lineage and community was a means of acculturation and differentiation, representing shrewd political maneuvers on the part of upwardly mobile elements in these emerging communities who actively sought respective places in the expanding Chinese polity. These acts stretched tradition to the limits of local imagination.[60]

How did the process continue in the Republican era? In the twentieth century, lineage and communal institutions were the subject of much contest, because the authority of the imperial state on which they relied was shaken by fundamental changes in the economy and by powerful new elites with different territorial bases and claims to legitimacy. In the turbulent 1930s and 1940s, when the power bases of the former elites were disintegrating, the fates of these institutions in the Pearl River delta were determined by those who had formerly been marginalized. Be they tradition-bound expatriates, agricultural entrepreneurs educated by modern schools, or illiterate militaristic strongmen, all used the emerging ideologies of nation building to climb onto a local political stage they were creating for themselves.

To what extent was rural society transformed by their actions? The apparent persistence of lineage and community ideals in social life and in the popular mind made it difficult at first to argue that the imperial order was fundamentally shaken or that the "modernizing" state had successfully penetrated rural society. But the evidence suggests that underneath the surface these cultural complexes were undergoing a rapid recomposition in a variety of local guises. Changes were most evident in the Xiaolan, whose economy had been commercialized and diverse since the nineteenth century. The power of the lineage complex was no longer based on the direct control of land, and these ancestral estates were most vulnerable during the war. Local bosses from the sands took over their land, moved into town, and built alternative institutions without much need for negotiation. After the revolution in 1949, the Communists shot the militaristic bosses, turned the remaining ancestral halls into offices, warehouses, and factories, and divided the estates in the sands among those who were farming them. When, in 1963, the town was administratively separated from the rural commune surrounding it, any lingering ties signifying control of land in the sands were severed. The separation of the town (and its major lineages) from its former territorial identity was complete.

Village strongmen in Tianma were able to build ancestral halls because, during wartime, they forcibly took over the land and kept the rents that were due to their town-based patrons. But the flourishing of lineage estates in Tianma should not be seen solely as a resilient tradition regenerating itself on new soil. It also represented the emergence of new and uneasy relationships between the regional core and its periphery.[61] The rise of the Chen in the Republican period was particularly threatening to townships near the county capital because Tianma itself had been a sizable settlement. The original settlers were of other surnames. A careful reading of the Chen genealogy compiled in 1923 shows that they must have gained a foothold after much arbitration and struggle against the original settlers. Although they grew numerous by late Qing, they never gained a status as equals among the established lineages in the area. The building of the numerous lineage estates finally accorded them the recognition of their former patrons, even if it was given under the threat of a gun. Although the local bosses were eventually persecuted by Communists and peasants alike in 1950, the community was seen as one "legitimate" Chen lineage. The cultural frontier defining regional fringes was pushed further into the undiked river marshes where "mixed surnames" eventually formed a production brigade separate from the Chen of Tianma.

Underlying the persistence of the Liugeng tang in Shawan was a different political current. Buttressed for centuries by the language of lineage, which remained authoritative, its supremacy as landlord and symbol of community was not diminished but reinforced by the exigencies of war. Its domination over the area was so complete that even its most effective challengers from the sands had to work within the power structure of the lineage. After the Communist revolution, as in Tianma, many local bosses who had ruled with guns were killed. Others fled. The estates were divided among poor town residents who were He lineage members as well as their tenants in the sands. In a deliberate effort to break the power of the He lineage, the Communists recruited local cadres from among the "people of mixed surnames." Today, they occupy large neighborhoods and enjoy the political and economic security they built up during the Maoist era. But they continue to be referred to by residents as "the mixed surnames," as if they had hardly gained a foothold in town. Ironically, the stone stela erected in the Qing by the five major lineages to prohibit freed bondservants from building an ancestral hall remains standing today in the courtyard of an ancestral hall that has long been used as party headquarters.

The analysis of lineage, community, and politics in this essay illustrates some general concerns of historical anthropology, namely, how do historical events take into account inequalities of power, and how are social institutions and cultural perceptions understood in the spatial context of an evolving, differentiating political economy. In state agrarian societies where hierarchies of power and diverse bases of authority exist and are often contested, stability rests on the ways local elites anchor themselves in the community as well as within the larger polity. The evolution of local legitimacy involves the percolation of a state culture, be it imperial or revolutionary. In numerous arenas, the locally powerful and those they dominated were engaged in shaping this process. As in other times, discourses on lineage and community in the twentieth century were ways by which several generations of political actors created a new language by means of inherited words.[62]

Conclusion:
History and Anthropology

HELEN F. SIU

DAVID FAURE

IT IS well known that for those in southern China who claim to be
Han Chinese the home county and village are major markers of identity.
In this book, we have explored why this should be so. Our collective answer attempts to link regional identities, which are at once inclusive and
discriminating, to the ways the territorial bond interacted with lineage
building, the assertion of settlement rights, the creation of community and
ethnic boundaries, and the competing languages of power and authority,
during the late imperial and Republican periods. In the background was
the evolution of the imperial regime within which social groups vied for
legitimacy. We have argued that a close examination of the social interests
underlying the territorial bond is essential in an investigation of the dynamic evolution of local society within the context of the spread of an encompassing state order.

Cultural experiences, as they mature over time and space, are differentiating at one level and institutionalizing at another. Here lies the essential nature of what it means to be Chinese. The idea is not new. Scholars
have developed various paradigms to examine it. While appreciating their
insights, we question some of their functionalist and ahistorical assumptions. We would like to use a conceptual framework that highlights the
ways human agency, cultural meaning, and political economy interpene-
trated at crucial historical moments to shape local society. Anthropologists
have often argued that culture has two analytic dimensions—the objective
constituent that confronts individual initiative, and the subjective symbolics that individuals use to shape and give meaning to their circumstances and actions.

A parallel concern faces the historian. History is made up of an objective chronological sequence of happenings, but it is also a heuristic device constructed to show the patterns and impacts of events. The sense of the past, consequently, guides our understanding of the social process, and as such, it becomes a symbolic resource, contested, improvised, and manipulated by states and local agents with diverse agendas.[1] History is structured, therefore, to give meaning to culture, just as culture guides the historical interpretation. The intertwining of the two lies behind what defines Chineseness, a central issue for our collection of essays. And in the Pearl River delta, they coalesce around the issues of lineage and ethnicity.

The Nature of the Chinese Lineage

Maurice Freedman's seminal works on Chinese kinship and descent are so influential that many scholars have long taken for granted the lineage paradigm for understanding Chinese social life. Freedman stressed how the southeast coast provided the crucial material environment for kinship principles to blossom into aggressive lineage communities.[2] There was remarkable overlap between kin-based and territorially based organizations, both of which were reinforced by extensive corporate estates and public rituals. Although he focused on a far corner of the Chinese empire, he did not slight the power of the imperial state in shaping the development of these lineages. But he lamented that his lack of access to historical and ethnographic data prevented him from pursuing the issue. With new materials in hand, we hope to clarify how the evolution of lineage communities was anchored in local economies and in the imperial metaphor.

In an earlier article, David Faure downplays the structuralist assumptions of patrilineal descent in Freedman's works and argues that lineage has meant more than kinship to its members.[3] He cautions against the functionalist tendencies of later scholars such as Hugh Baker, Jack Potter, and, to an extent, James Watson and Rubie Watson, whose premise is that corporate estates, ancestral halls, and elaborate biannual rituals of kinship are constituting elements of Chinese lineages.[4] Instead, Faure argues that kinship and territory are related but must be treated as analytically separate, and that lineage formation involved their intertwining at particular historical moments of state-making. He calls attention to the crucial juncture of an organizationally expansive Ming bureaucracy, a rising class of high-ranking scholar-officials from southern China, the acceptance of degree holding as a status symbol, shrewd strategies of accumulating wealth through land reclamation and tax dodging, and the representation of a transformed mode of ancestor worship in specially designed ancestral halls. The process fundamentally changed the nature of local culture and society and created the particular forms of territorially based lineages we see in south China.

This historical view of Chinese lineage formation takes issue with Myron Cohen's notion of a basic, underlying principle of descent. Instead of typologizing lineage forms as belonging to a genealogical mode in north China or an associational mode in the south,[5] this volume suggests that their spread in space was linked to community and state building at the confluence of particular historical currents. Even within the Pearl River delta, lineages that established their roots on the older parts of the delta during the Ming and early Qing, as described by Freedman, and those that assumed dominance on the expanding sands during the Qing represented different forms of social organization and cultural significance for their members and neighbors. They require analytical tools that emphasize historical processes more than static functional typologies.

Although contact with the imperial bureaucracy by localized descent groups might only have been imagined and symbolic, higher-order lineage halls or academies based in regional cities and provincial capitals were arenas in which upwardly mobile local groups maintained direct dialogues with imperial officials. These groups were geographically widespread, but linked by the shared idioms of kinship and literati aspirations. Some academies (*shuyuan*) were organized according to visibly territorial principles, as were those in Guangzhou,[6] in the Xinhui county capital, and in the city of Jiangmen.[7] But their organization resembled that of lineages. The beneficiaries were limited to descendants of founding patrons whose tablets were permanently installed in the academies.

Gangzhou *shuyuan* and Xinan *shuyuan* represented large lineages in the southwestern part of Xinhui county, whereas Jingxian *shuyuan* in Jiangmen served those in the county's northeast. Started as gentry-led institutions to promote local education, they became centers of political networking. In times of relative peace, they created channels by which kinsmen could go through the civil service examinations. In times of dynastic decline, such as from the mid-nineteenth century on, they were commissioned by county officials to organize regional self-defense. They were also entrusted with rent collection for urban-based corporations that owned vast estates in the sands.

This model of the lineage suggests that even when the imperial bureaucracy was physically distant its impact was symbolically intense. Following this model, we opened this volume with the essay by Liu Zhiwei. He has analyzed the initial interface of state, territory, and lineage as the river marshes in Panyu county around the township of Shawan were converted to productive farmland under the auspices of agnatic descent groups. He traces the daunting growth of the He lineage and its ancestral trust in the last three centuries. It prospered on the reclamation of the sands among the numerous tributaries of the Pearl River, and subsequently on the rents it collected from tenants who were largely labeled as Dan and denied settlement rights. As its economic base expanded and diversified, lineage identity and ritual aggrandizement intensified for those residing in Shawan. A lineage genealogy was compiled and aggressively used to set clear boundaries against tenants and neighbors, even though the document contained blatant inconsistencies about the very founding of the lineage.

There was no doubt that the He was the most dominant and numerous surname in Shawan up to the socialist revolution. The power of the lineage was reinforced by an ancestral cult that was linked to imperial recognition. The interesting point was the process by which other surnames became "legitimate" settlers in the area. It was not by the strength of numbers, but by the groups' ability to trace their connection to a particular ancestral hall built during the time of settling in Shawan. The Li of Jingshu *li*, a neighborhood bordering the eastern side of the He settlement, fought with the He for three generations, inflicting casualties and bringing lawsuits, in order to build themselves an ancestral hall.

Apart from the annual ceremonies conducted in the ornate focal ancestral hall (Liugeng *tang*) and in a complex of segment halls, an elaborate arrangement was maintained for the annual parade of the Beidi, a deity worshiped in many parts of China but claimed by the "legitimate" settlers of Shawan as patron. The Beidi, in military gear, was claimed to be one of the four figures produced by the first emperor of the Ming dynasty in his own image. It had no temple. Instead, segment halls of the He lineage representing particular neighborhoods, and several of the ancestral halls of longtime settlers, received the Beidi image in a rotating order amid expensive celebrations. The ritual firmly bound kinship to territory. The study reveals the nature of social control as intertwined with kinship ties and territorial alliances. Furthermore, the symbolic authority of the state is intimately linked with the increasing power of a particularly localized lineage whose elites carved out their sphere of influence using the political nuances of literati pretensions.

Luo Yixing's study of Lubao township in Sanshui county in this book provides a contrast to Shawan. As in Shawan, communally based rituals underpin the complex interrelations of state, popular religion, and local groups.[8] In contrast to Shawan, in Lubao, where there was no single dominant lineage, the locus of territorial organization was the market, and intervillage alliances bridged the right of settlement at the village and the numerous rights of participation in the region. Similar to lineage bonds, these alliances were sanctified through religious rituals—in this case, rituals also focused on the Beidi, the deity that was recognized as the center of worship.

On the one hand Luo demonstrates that a sense of community, evolved over the Ming and the Qing periods, distinguished the settlements in the immediate vicinity of the Beidi Temple that played a full role in worship there from settlements some distance away that nonetheless participated in some ceremonies of worship, and from the outsiders, including the Dan boat people, who attended but were not recognized as having the right to participate. As Luo argues, a reflection of this process was the infiltration of the worship of the Beidi into indigenous local worship practices.

On the other hand, a process of gentrification also accompanied the growth of this sense of community through the Ming and the Qing, so that, in time, Lubao boasted of its own schools and literati leaders. From the movement to "destroy licentious temples," which established the position of the Beidi in the Ming, to the various revolts of marginalized groups—such as the Dan piracy in the early Qing, the red turban revolts of late Qing, and the usurpation of power by the local bosses of the Republican era—lineage and territorial identities continued to be reinforced and transformed.

Lineages, then, are complex historical constructions in which kinship and descent have come to serve as legitimizing labels for claims to settlement rights and territorial control concomitant with the downward percolation of dynastic prerogatives.[9] Integral to this treatment of lineage and territory is our belief that cultural meanings are not timeless principles with predetermining impacts. They are produced in social life and permeated by power relationships that are organized in time and space. Nor can the structuring of events be reduced to material forces of marketing resources, population pressure, and transport demands. Viewed dialectically, cultural institutions (in this case lineage) and political economy (in this case territorial control) never ceased to constitute each other through time.

Constructing the Ethnic Other

Central to the language of lineage pedigree was an intense process of entitlement for kin members and of exclusion of others. Those marginal-

ized were often labeled inferior and politically undeserving to the point of
not belonging to the same cultural universe. Like lineage membership,
these "ethnic" labels have long been ascribed a primordial nature in historical documents written from the point of view of the literati tradition.
We have highlighted this concern by focusing on the twin issues of native
place and ethnicity throughout the book, and we have concentrated on issues concerning the Dan and the Hakka.

The Dan have been characterized as a boat-dwelling ethnic group distinct from the agriculturalists. Although they speak a version of the local
dialects where they congregate, they maintain different styles in dress, hair,
living habits, and marriage.[10] As Ye Xian'en's essay shows, the relationship
of the Han to the Dan was legal as well as social, and the legal element to
a large extent concerned their right to hold land and their status. Despite
the numerous economic ties between the two groups, social distance was
maintained. It was widely believed that they seldom intermarried. Official
and unofficial abuses were heaped upon the Dan. They were said to be uncouth: they did not wear shoes and seldom sent their children to school.
They engaged in the mean trades and at times threatened the agriculturalists as pirates. Guo Podai, Zheng Yi, Zhang Bao and his wife—pirates
who defeated Qing troops numerous times with their fleets and plundered
established villages in the delta during the early nineteenth century—were
well-known figures in local folklore.[11]

Ye Xian'en's notes on the Dan touch on the issue of ethnic differentiation
and territorial domination. Despite repeated attempts to classify the Dan
by imperial edict as ordinary fishermen who were to be taxed and who
were worthy of social mobility through education, landed communities
that became established through the centuries used the Dan identity to
marginalize newcomers to the region and deny them settlement rights. One
may argue that on the sands of the Pearl River delta, the floating population
of Dan will exist as long as there are river marshes to be reclaimed.

In the market towns that were situated on the dividing line between the
older and younger parts of the delta, such as Xiaolan (Xiangshan county),
Shawan (Panyu county), and Chaolian (Xinhui county), where several major surnames built their ancestral estates and halls, we argue that most of
the agriculturalists did not necessarily originate from the central plains as
they claimed.[12] They were indigenous farmers and fishermen. Through the
centuries, they acquired and reconstituted the incoming Han culture to become part of the Chinese polity. From the mid-Qing on, the accelerated
reclamation of the river marshes triggered by the need for grain in an in-

creasingly commercialized delta allowed local and migrant populations to assimilate rapidly into the encroaching Han dynastic order.

Easy accumulation of wealth on the sands was reflected in the mushrooming of lineage-dominated market towns on the edge of the sands such as the ones we have examined. Town residents controlled land tenure as well as a lucrative grain trade. Their upward mobility entailed active involvement in the Chinese polity and shrewd strategies of political and cultural exclusion against those working the sands as laborers and tenants. Settlement history, the language of lineage, spectacular community rituals, elaborate marriage customs and religious practices, and ethnic labels were instrumental in this process of legitimizing status for the upwardly mobile. The Dan could have come from the same stock as the indigenous fishermen whose ecological niches were threatened by the accelerated reclamation of the sands. They were joined by poor lineage members and village outcasts who drifted to the sands.

However, domination was seldom total. Siu demonstrates that in historical Xinhui and Xiangshan counties, the vastness of the sands made it difficult for town-based lineage estates to extend their reach. They relied on tenant contractors who managed the outposts and secured harvests. These functionaries were mainly local "Dan" farmers who rapidly acquired enough power to carve out their own bases, to adopt the cultural strategies of their former patrons in order to became "Han," and to create another frontier in the more outlying sands where a new stratum of subjugated "Dan" would then emerge.[13]

Focusing on ethnographic cases in Hong Kong, we have continued the treatment the Han-Dan distinction less in terms of static ethnic categories and more in terms of intense relationships enacted over time. Inspired by the work of the late Barbara Ward on the fishermen in Hong Kong, and relying on historical and ethnographic fieldwork on the island of Cheung Chau, James Hayes and Choi Chi-cheung ask the crucial question of how diverse local groups consciously claim their respective places in an overarching "Chinese" cultural identity through the process of creating the ethnic "other."[14] In local political economies of the delta and Hong Kong in which social mobility was rapid, discriminating ethnic labels continued to be used by dominant lineage communities to keep latecomers socially and politically at a distance. But we see ethnicity as a fluid, artificial boundary drawn between groups whose economic and political interests are locked in competition.

James Hayes and Choi Chi-cheung thus examine ritual and political dynamics in the market town where local leaders, who did not belong to any physically dominant lineage, held the community together by constructing loyalties along territorial and ethnic lines. Situated on the southwestern coast of Hong Kong, Cheung Chau Island had been an important shelter for fishermen in the South China Sea as well as a regional fish market where they brought in their catch. Through credit arrangements, wholesale merchants controlled the buying and selling of fish and dried sea products. Although the merchants were under the shadow of a Wong lineage trust that had secured the right to collect land tax on the island for the colonial government in 1906, they claimed remote origins among various landed communities of Guangdong. Belonging to a variety of lesser surnames with no visible ancestral halls, they differentiated among themselves based on notions of native place. Native place reflects the drawing of boundaries more or less among equals—as defined by class as much as by position within the symbolic hierarchy of the imperial order.

But the merchants discriminated their suppliers by labeling them Dan and excluding them from community rituals. The distinctions between "people on the main street" who worshiped Beidi in an ornate temple in the center of town and "people from the boats" who worshiped Tianhou in a small temple on the eastern edge of the island were clearly marked in daily life. Ethnic labels in this circumstance were used to identify an underclass who occupied "mean" positions but whose livelihood was central to the merchants' prosperity. The labels were representations as well as an exercise of power.

The integration of an indigenous culture into Han written traditions and the identification of the resultant product as a cultural symbol is a process embedded in centuries of make-believe that can be unraveled only by skillful detective work. In this spirit, Chan Wing-hoi examines the ordination names in the genealogies of Hakka groups in the New Territories of Hong Kong. He unveils an active mutual borrowing of indigenous religious practices among local groups (the Yao, She, Hakka, and Punti) under the shadow of the imperial state. However reified ethnic categories become, custom itself is in flux. Popular religious practices, such as initiation ceremonies from which ordination names arose, continued among indigenous groups with different traditions. They can still be detected in community rituals in the New Territories of Hong Kong among groups who identify themselves as Hakka and Punti. The disappearance of divination names in genealogies does not mean that the popular practices had stopped. The documents were written at a time when the literati culture was expanding in the region, and the "Hakka" groups moved from one practice to the other as they became more acculturated to the orthodox "Han" tradition. Just as dominant territorial groups sought ways to marginalize weaker competitors, the latter actively used the same set of cultural metaphors to pursue their own agenda of gaining legitimacy and recognition.

Political Change and the Cultural Meaning of Territory

In stressing how cultural categories such as lineage and ethnicity are integral to the development of a regional complex, this collection attempts to go beyond the efforts of economic historians in refining the boundaries of regional systems set by G. William Skinner. In an earlier article describing the chrysanthemum festivals of a market town in the heart of the delta, Siu points to the crucial cultural resources—in the form of community rituals, pretensions of lineage pedigree, and literati achievements—that shaped the spatial structure of power between the town residents and those marginalized in the sands. She underscores the ways local populations in the sands anchored themselves by grappling onto a growing repertoire of state symbols. The language of the literati, adopted and refined by local strongmen, greatly shaped the changing political economic configurations on the ground. In the same spirit, almost all the essays in this volume treat popular beliefs and communal rituals not as reflecting a social order structured by the economic logic of material life, but rather as refining the complex, multilayered processes that simultaneously composed region and state as cultural systems.[15]

Our approach takes issue with the defense of Skinner's model by Joseph Esherick, Daniel Little, and William Lavely against the criticisms launched by Barbara Sands and Ramon Myers.[16] Our reading of Skinner, apparently different from Esherick, Little, and Lavely's, suggests that the claim of the regional system goes beyond its economic base, and that the interlocking of markets into regional structures is reflected in social interactions among the communities served by the market. It belittles the model to portray it as no more than a description of the flow of trade within the region. Sands and Myers's criticism that the regional differences in prices that should be implied by the model have not been empirically borne out is, to our minds, a valid one. We would add the observation that neither has the cultural unity within the regional system that should also be implied accorded with empirical data. The way in which meaning links human agency with geography goes beyond the economic logic of transportation costs and marketing needs. Instead, cultural concerns and political strategies enter into the picture to determine what the viable economic options will be.

If regional systems were constructed with cultural meanings made significant by the positions of the human agents within the imperial order, what happened when the Qing dynasty collapsed? How were regional systems reconstituted, and how were viable options renegotiated? The last three essays in the volume pursue this question. It will not suffice to claim, as a Skinnerian approach would, that regional systems reshaped themselves according to the demands of modern transportation. We explore how the languages of lineage, ethnicity, and territorial control were mixed with that of the modern nation to define new goals in the precarious political arenas of the Republican period.

In sum, this volume stresses the interpenetration of culture and history, of local society and an encompassing state. History is created and made significant by meaningful, purposeful actions. However compelled human actions and their unintended results may seem to be, social order and change are not guided by immutable laws. Our view of the human agent as the motive force of history treats culture not as an existing repertoire of values that generations learn and practice, but as a process produced in the flux of social life.

Moreover, social life is seldom neutral. It is permeated by relationships of power on the ground and their symbolic representations. The political context, therefore, mattered in the assertion of territorial claims. The essays by Hase, Faure, and Siu stress the new political environment after 1911, in which the communities struggled with territorial control. All three places studied bore the brunt of political upheaval. Hase's example, the market town of Sha Tau Kok, located within the New Territories, prospered within a cultural continuity protected under a colonial regime. In Faure's case, what linked the rebuilding of a lineage community in Tangang with overseas patrons was not modern transportation and market demands but a transnational cultural agenda manipulated by an unorthodox elite. In Siu's case, the most drastic reformulations of territorial boundaries and their associated social mobility strategies were conducted in the remote region of the sands by militaristic local bosses who neither ruled by imperial authority nor felt the exigencies of modern technology.

In his study, Hase emphasizes the fluidity of identity and custom as he meticulously reconstructs social and economic life in Sha Tau Kok from the founding of the market in the nineteenth century to the accommodations villagers made when the political boundary between Hong Kong and

China cut across the marketing community. Undoubtedly, the market was founded where it was because the river port was conveniently located along major coastal trading routes. It blossomed also because by then the Hakka villages using the market were able to form a political alliance (*yeuk*) that eventually asserted its independence from under the shadow of dominant Cantonese (Punti) lineages. As in Lubao, the village alliance centering around the market was headed by lineage elders and degree holders, and reinforced by community rituals.

The very interesting issue here is that the ethnic difference between Cantonese Lubao and Hakka Sha Tau Kok had no effect on the means by which the markets were managed, and that at Sha Tau Kok, while the Hakkas assumed their autonomy from the Cantonese lineages they created their own form of social exclusion. Certainly enough, other ethnic groups could trade at the market, but neither Punti or Hoklos dominated the town, and the Dan fishermen, who supplied the catches that were sold by wholesalers at the market, were required nonetheless to settle on sandbanks and islands off the coast of the town.

The irony of the story of Sha Tau Kok is that in this forsaken corner of the empire where imperial bureaucrats appeared only as remote entities, the Hakkas accumulated all the necessary cultural resources for social mobility and economic well-being. They continued in their extension along the East River and dominated local market towns, only to be interrupted when government officials, warlords, and armies descended upon them in the turbulent decades of the twentieth century.

The essays by Faure and Siu ask how lineage and community institutions survived or changed in the decades following the fall of the imperial order. Faure uses the records of a lineage association patronized by overseas merchants to highlight the difficulties of village management in the 1920s. He claims that the communal control of land—itself an ancient ideal—could exist only as an ideal, and that the strength of the lineage institution lay in maintaining the right of settlement for individual members together with an appearance of lineage solidarity. The frustrations of the overseas patrons arose from their failure to recognize the multiple meanings of lineage as well as the changing nature of leadership in the village. An ironic twist in Faure's case parallels that of Hase. It had been fine when lineage building in Tangang was but a serious pretense. It was only when zealots from outside the community wanted to rebuild it literally from the books that life in the villages became complicated.

Siu examines the fate of the lineage in relation to the redefinition of local power structures in the area a decade or so later when the country was experiencing civil war and military occupation by the Japanese. She describes the local bosses who rose precipitously from the sands of the delta in the 1930s and 1940s. They took over the management of lineage and community institutions. They subverted lineage power by encroaching upon ancestral land, serving as tax farmers for regional warlords, and, at times, collaborating with the Japanese army. Although they dominated vast territories for over two decades and in some instances revived lineage and community organizations, the bosses' power remained illegitimate in the popular mind, a fact reflected in the vengeance of the peasants against them during the land reform.

In the early twentieth century, the usual pattern of social mobility, based on acquiring the symbols of the larger state culture, was truncated by the disintegration of the imperial system. Local bosses in the 1930s and 1940s controlled vast areas of the sands at the expense of the town-based ancestral estates. Siu's essay analyzes their intricate manipulation of lineage resources in three closely situated communities. They maintained the lineage as an institution in various degrees, supported community schools, and patronized temples. They also adopted the more prestigious marriage customs of the town residents and, at times, successfully negotiated marriages of their children with those of town elites whose fortunes had declined. Town residents looked disapprovingly upon the efforts of these local strongmen to stage their own elaborate community festivals. Their harsh treatment by local people during the land reform (as compared to the leniency afforded members of "traditional" elites) revealed popular assumptions about their status. In the minds of those who suffered their abuse, these bosses remained "Dan," "bandits," "people outside," who dismantled ancestral halls and ruled with guns.

One might guess that if the imperial examination system had remained intact, or if there had been more time before the Communist revolution, these strongmen might eventually have acquired the necessary cultural means to become respectable.[17] One would need to rethink the underlying assumptions of the masses who struggled against the local bosses during the land reform. Were their actions governed by the lingering historical meanings of cultural categories (such as ethnic labels and interlineage hostility), which Communism mistook for class consciousness? In examining the diverse fates of lineage in three adjacent communities, the essay argues that the apparent bonds of kinship and territory the local bosses established in fact reflected authority and social relationships in crisis.

Culture and History

We hope this volume has shown that the assertion of territorial control was based on a time-space nexus and layered upon an evolving regional core where extraordinary wealth and cultural spectacle depended on a growing frontier founded upon lineage, ethnicity, and ideology. The concept of Dan as a derogatory ethnic label continued to be reinforced and perpetuated. But as populations, those branded as Dan rapidly converted themselves into Han. Furthermore, as each layer adopted the "established" Han institutions of the regional core at various historical junctures, the resultant cultural configurations carried their own uniqueness. This might explain why becoming Chinese could be a differentiating as well as a unifying experience.

At no time is cultural identity more relevant than at a time of flux, as when the process of territorial exclusion continued in the Republican and post-1949 periods. The politics of the Republican regimes drastically realigned power relationships between towns and villages and demanded that the realignment take account of the new Republican ideology. Lineage, ethnicity, and ideology were not static sets of traits within an all-encompassing cultural tradition. This collection moves away from structural analyses in the social sciences that have built on assumptions of neatly bounded social units frozen in time and space. Both modernization and Marxist theories describe change as a series of transformations from one discrete set of characteristics to another. But indicators of change are hard to pinpoint; persistence and reversals are often puzzling. Analytical concepts such as ethnicity and frontier can be historically contextualized to reflect fluid relationships that human agents rework through meaningful actions. These relationships are reproduced at one level, contested and transformed at another.

In a sense, we are echoing Fredrik Barth, who criticizes the assumption that an ethnic group maintains its cultural distinctiveness through "bellicose ignorance of its neighbors" in geographical and social isolation. Instead, ethnic labels "entail social processes of exclusion and incorporation whereby discrete categories are maintained despite changing participation and membership in the course of individual life histories. . . . Ethnic distinctions do not depend on an absence of social interaction and acceptance, but are quite to the contrary often the very foundations on which embracing social systems are built."[18] A critical reading of historical documents and "ethnographic texts" can point to inconsistencies in the historical narrative and unveil the power of inclusion and exclusion in the making of cultural identity.

We aim to integrate history and anthropology by means of a common agenda. Historians of Europe such as Natalie Davis and E. P. Thompson have highlighted the important role of subjective meanings in shaping historical events.[19] Anthropologists in the 1980s have increasingly recognized the creative use of the past and the invention of tradition by their ethnographic subjects.[20] A major aim of both historians and anthropologists is to understand the complex interactions of cultural ideas and experiences, social organizations, and material circumstances over time and across space. We hope to bring Chinese studies closer to this shared goal.

REFERENCE MATTER

Notes

Siu and Faure, Introduction

1. G. William Skinner, "Presidential Address: The Structure of Chinese History," *Journal of Asian Studies* 44, no. 2 (1985): 271–92.
2. See Dwight H. Perkins, *Agricultural Development in China, 1368–1969* (Edinburgh: Edinburgh University Press, 1969), pp. 16–17.
3. David Faure, "The Lineage as a Cultural Invention: The Case of the Pearl River Delta," *Modern China* 15, no. 1 (1989): 4–36.
4. For a brief history of Guangdong, see Jiang Zuyuan and Fang Zhiqin et al., *Jianming Guangdong shi* (A short history of Guangdong) (Guangzhou: Guangdong renmin, 1987); and for the historical geography, Ceng Zhaoxuan and Huang Shaomin, *Zhujiang sanjiaozhou lishi dimaoxue yanjiu* (Studies in the historical land forms of the Pearl River delta) (Guangzhou: Guangdong gaodeng jiaoyu chubanshe, 1987).
5. Quan Hansheng, "Songdai Guangzhou di guo neiwai maoyi" (The internal and external trade of Guangzhou in the Song), in his *Zhongguo jingji shi yanjiu* (Studies of Chinese economic history), vol. 2 (Hong Kong: New Asia Research Institute, 1976), pp. 85–158.
6. Foshan diqu geming weiyuanhui, *Zhujiang sanjiaozhou nongyeshi* bianxiezu, *Zhujiang sanjiaozhou nongyezhi* (A history of agriculture in the Pearl River delta), vol. 2 (n.p., 1976), pp. 8–11.
7. Helen F. Siu, *Agents and Victims in South China: Accomplices in Rural Revolution* (New Haven: Yale University Press, 1989), pp. 15–35; and Robert Y. Eng, "Institutional and Secondary Landlordism in the Pearl River Delta, 1600–1949," *Modern China* 12, no. 1 (1986): 3–37.
8. David Faure, *The Structure of Chinese Rural Society: Lineage and Village in the Eastern New Territories, Hong Kong* (London: Oxford University Press, 1986), pp. 30–44.
9. Examples may be found in ibid., pp. 166–72, and David Faure, *The Rural Economy of Pre-liberation China: Trade Increase and Peasant Livelihood in Jiangsu and Guangdong, 1870 to 1937* (Hong Kong: Oxford University Press, 1989), pp. 174–77, 188–93.

10. C. W. Howard and K. P. Buswell, *A Survey of the Silk Industry of South China* (Guangzhou: Lingnan Agricultural College, 1925), p. 50; and Maurice Freedman, *Chinese Lineage and Society: Fukien and Kwangtung* (London: Athlone, 1966), pp. 31–32.

11. Chen Han-seng, *Agrarian Problems in Southernmost China* (Shanghai: Kelly and Walsh, 1936), pp. 24–41.

12. Maurice Freedman, *Lineage Organization in Southeastern China* (London: Athlone, 1958), pp. 126–33.

13. David Faure, *Structure of Chinese Rural Society*, see especially pp. 30–44.

14. Ye Xian'en and Tan Dihua, "Lun Zhujiang sanjiaozhou de zutian" (A discussion of lineage land in the Pearl River delta), and "Fengjian zongfa xili dui Foshan jingji de kongzhi ji qi cansheng de yingxiang" (The control exercised by feudal lineage powers on the Foshan economy and its influence), in Guangdong lishi xuehui, *Ming-Qing Guangdong jingji xingtai* (Social and economic forms in Ming-Qing Guangdong) (Guangzhou: Guangdong renmin, 1985), pp. 22–64, pp. 114–64.

15. Hugh Baker, *A Chinese Lineage: Sheung Shui* (London: Frank Cass, 1968); and Rubie S. Watson, *Inequality Among Brothers: Class and Kinship in South China* (Cambridge, Eng.: Cambridge University Press, 1985).

16. Fu Yiling, "Lun xiangzu xili dui Zhongguo fengjian jingji de ganshe: Zhongguo fengjian shehui changqi chizhi de yige tansuo" (A discussion of interference by lineage village powerholders the Chinese feudal economy: An exploration of the long-term stagnation of Chinese feudal society), *Xiamen daxue xuebao* 1961, no. 3, reprinted in Fu Yiling, *Ming-Qing shehui jingjishi lunwen ji* (Essays on Ming-Qing social and economic history) (Beijing: Renmin, 1982), p. 81.

17. Sen Zhengfu (Mori Masao), "Weirao 'xiangzu' wenti: Cai Xiamen daxue gongtong yanjiuhui shang de taolun baogao" (On the question of the lineage village: Report of a discussion at the common research meeting at Xiamen University), *Zhongguo shehui jingjishi yanjiu* 2 (1986): 1–8.

18. Chen Zhiping, *Jin 500 nian lai Fujian de jiazu shehui yu wenhua* (Lineage society and culture in Fujian in the last 500 years) (Shanghai: Sanlian, 1991); and Zheng Zhenman, *Ming-Qing Fujian jiazu zuzhi yu shehui bianqian* (Lineage society and social change in Ming-Qing Fujian) (Hunan: Hunan jiaoyu, 1992).

19. Patricia Buckley Ebrey, *Confucianism and Family Rituals in Imperial China: A Social History of Writing About Rites* (Princeton, N. J.: Princeton University Press, 1991).

20. The papers presented at the conference were published in Patricia Buckley Ebrey and James L. Watson, eds., *Kinship Organization in Late Imperial China, 1000–1940* (Berkeley: University of California Press, 1986).

21. Harry J. Lamley, "Lineage and Surname Feuds in Southern Fukien and Eastern Kwangtung Under the Ch'ing," in K. C. Liu, ed., *Orthodoxy in Late Imperial China* (Berkeley: University of California Press, 1990), pp. 255–78; and Robert Eng, "Institutional and Secondary Landlordism in the Pearl River Delta, 1600–1949," *Modern China* 12, no. 9 (1986): 3–37.

22. Helen F. Siu, *Agents and Victims*, p. 67.

23. Prasenjit Duara, *Culture, Power, and the State: Rural North China, 1900–1942* (Stanford: Stanford University Press, 1988).

24. Muramatsu Yūji, *Kindai Kōnan no sosan* (The rent bursaries of Jiangnan in modern times) (Tokyo: Tokyo University Press, 1970).

25. David Faure, *Rural Economy of Pre-liberation China*, pp. 164–201.

26. Fei Hsiao-tung and Chih-i Chang, *Earthbound China: A Study of Rural Economy in Yunnan* (London: Routledge and Kegan Paul, 1948), p. 79.

27. Fei Hsiao-tung, *China's Gentry: Essays in Rural-Urban Relations* (1953), rev. and ed. Margaret Park Redfield (Chicago: University of Chicago Press, Midway Reprint Series, 1980); Fei Xiaotong and Wu Han, *Huangquan yu shenquan* (Imperial power and gentry power) (1948; repr. Hong Kong, n.d.); Philip A. Kuhn, "Local Self-Government Under the Republic: Problems of Control, Autonomy, and Mobilization," in Frederic Wakeman, ed., *Conflict and Control in Late Imperial China* (Berkeley: University of California Press, 1975), pp. 257–98; and "Late Ch'ing Views of the Polity," in Tang Tsou, ed., *Select Papers from the Center for Far Eastern Studies, No. 4, 1979–80* (Chicago: University of Chicago Press, 1981), pp. 1–18. The argument, as Kuhn duly acknowledges, draws heavily on Min Tu-ki's writings, which have been translated into English by Kuhn and Timothy Brook (*National Polity and Local Power: The Transformation of Late Imperial China* [Cambridge, Mass.: Harvard University Press, 1988]).

28. Fei Xiaotong, *Xiangtu chongjian* (Village reconstruction) (Shanghai: Guancha she, 1948; repr. Hong Kong, n.d.), p. 48; and Fei Hsiao-tung, *China's Gentry*, pp. 81–83.

29. Frederic Wakeman, *Strangers at the Gate: Social Disorder in South China, 1839–1861* (Berkeley: University of California Press, 1966).

30. Philip A. Kuhn, *Rebellion and Its Enemies in Late Imperial China: Militarization and Social Structure, 1796–1864* (Cambridge, Mass.: Harvard University Press, 1970).

31. James Hayes, *The Hong Kong Region 1850–1911: Institutions and Leadership in Town and Country* (Hamden, Conn.: Shoe String Press, 1977); and *Tsuenwan: Growth of a 'New Town' and Its People* (Hong Kong: Oxford University Press, 1993).

32. Guy S. Alitto, "Rural Elites in Transition: China's Cultural Crisis and the Problem of Legitimacy," in Susan Mann, ed., *Select Papers from the Center for Chinese Studies*, vol. 3 (Chicago: University of Chicago, 1978–79), pp. 218–75.

33. Joseph W. Esherick and Mary Backus Rankin, eds., *Chinese Local Elites and Patterns of Dominance* (Berkeley: University of California Press, 1990).

34. Mary Backus Rankin, *Elite Activism and Political Transformation in China: Zhejiang Province, 1865–1911* (Stanford: Stanford University Press, 1986).

35. Hsiao Kung-chuan, *Rural China: Imperial Control in the Nineteenth Century* (Seattle: University of Washington Press, 1960).

36. G. William Skinner, "Mobility Strategies in Late Imperial China: A Regional-Systems Analysis," in Carol Smoth, ed., *Regional Systems*, vol. 1, *Eco-*

nomic Systems (New York: Academic Press, 1976), pp. 327–64; and William Rowe, *Hankow: Commerce and Society in a Chinese City, 1796–1889* (Stanford: Stanford University Press, 1984).

37. Emily Honig, *Creating Chinese Ethnicity* (New Haven: Yale University Press, 1993).

38. See Barbara Ward, *Through Other Eyes* (Hong Kong: Chinese University Press, 1985); Fred C. Blake, *Ethnic Groups and Social Change in a Chinese Market Town* (Honolulu: University Press of Hawaii, 1981); Dian Murray, *Pirates of the South China Coast, 1790–1810* (Stanford: Stanford University Press, 1987), for ethnographic and historical studies of ethnic relations in Guangdong and Hong Kong.

39. Wolfram Eberhard, *Social Mobility in Traditional China* (Leiden: E. J. Brill, 1962), and *The Local Cultures of South and East China* (Leiden: E. J. Brill, 1968); Makino Tatsumi, "Chūgoku no ijū densetsu—tokuni sono sosen dōkyō densetsu o chūshin toshite" (Legends of migratory settlement in China, with focus on legends of common ancestry), in Ichiko Chūzō, Naitō Kanji, and Nakano Taku, *Makino Tatsumi chūsakushū*, vol. 5 (Tokyo: Ochanomizu shoba, 1985), pp. 54–83; Luo Xianglin, *Kejia yanjiu daolun* (An introduction to the study of the Hakkas in its ethnic, historical, and cultural aspects) (Guangdong: Xishan Library, 1933 and 1947) on the Hakka; Wu Ruilin, *Sanshui danmin diaocha* (An investigation of the Dan in Sanshui) (1948; repr. Taipei: Dongfang wenhua shuju, 1971); and Chen Xujing, *Danmin de yanjiu* (A study of the Dan people) (1948; repr. Taipei: Dongfang wenhua shuju, 1971).

40. The He lineages of Huicheng (Xinhui County), Xiaolan (Zhongshan County), and Shawan (Panyu County), three of the most powerful lineages in the delta, which owned vast estates in the sands since the Qing, claimed that they descended from brothers who had dispersed during their sojourn from Nanxiong.

41. Luo Xianglin, *Kejia yanjiu daolun.*

42. See Xu Songshi, *Yuejiang liuyu renmin* (The indigenous peoples of Guangdong and Guangxi), vols. 1 and 2 (1938; repr. Taipei: Dongfang wenhua shuju, 1973); Wu Ruilin, *Sanshui danmin diaocha*; and Chen Xujing, *Danmin de yanjiu*, for historical explanations of the origins and characteristics of the indigenous south China populations.

43. In fact Qu Dajun, a leading literati in the early Qing, loudly blamed the Qin dynasty general Zhao Tuo, who supposedly adopted "native ways," for unwittingly slowing acculturation processes in Guangdong. See Qu Dajun, *Guangdong xinyu* (New items relating to Guangdong) (1700; repr. Beijing: Zhonghua shuju, 1985); Xu Ke, ed., *Qingbei leichao* (A collection of unofficial writings in the Qing), vol. 5 (n.d.; repr. Beijing: Zhonghua shuju, 1984); and Huang Chaozhong, Liu Yaochuan, and Li Mo, *Guangdong yaozu lishi ziliao* (Historical materials on the Yao in Guangdong) (Guangxi: Guangxi renmin, 1984), on the historical materials on the Yao in Guangdong.

44. Helen F. Siu, "Where Were the Women: Rethinking Marriage Resistance and Regional Culture in South China," *Late Imperial China* 11, no. 2 (1990): 32–62.

45. Wu Yucheng, *Yuenan shenhua yanjiu* (A study of the folktales of southern Guangdong) (1932; repr. Taipei: Dongfang wenhua shuju, c. 1974); and Luo Xianglin, *Yuedong zhi feng* (Folksongs in eastern Guangdong) (1947; repr. Taipei: Dongfang wenhua shuju, 1974).

46. David Faure, "Lineage as a Cultural Invention."

47. S. T. Leong, "The Hakka Chinese of Lingnan: Ethnicity and Social Change in Modern Times," in David Pong and Edmond S. K. Fung, eds., *Ideal and Reality, Social and Political Change in Modern China 1860–1949* (Lanham, Md.: University Press of America, 1985).

48. See *Guangdong Taishan Shangchuan fang Ganshi zupu* (The genealogy of the Shangchuan branch of the Gan surname in Taishan, Guangdong) (n.p., 1935), p. 14b.

49. For comments on general processes of acculturation and modern transformations, see Myron Cohen, "Being Chinese: The Peripheralization of Traditional Identity," *Daedalus* 120, no. 2 (1991), pp. 113–34; and for similar treatment of the Yi, see Stevan Harrell, "Ethnicity, Local Interest and the State: Yi Communities in Southwest China," *Comparative Studies in Society and History* 32, no. 3 (1990): 515–48.

50. Morris Rossabi, *China and Inner Asia from 1368 to the Present Day* (London: Thames and Hudson, 1981); Pamela Crossley, "Thinking About Ethnicity in Early Modern China," *Late Imperial China* 11, no. 1 (1990): 1–35; and Dru Gladney, *Muslim Chinese: Ethnic Nationalism in the People's Republic* (Cambridge, Mass.: Council on East Asian Studies, Harvard University, 1991).

51. See James Watson and Evelyn Rawski, eds., *Death Ritual in Late Imperial and Modern China* (Berkeley: University of California Press, 1988), on official standardization and local improvisations; and Arthur Wolf, "The Origins and Explanation of Variation in the Chinese Kinship System," in Chang Kwang-chih, Li Kuang-chou, Arthur Wolf, and Alexander Chien-chung Yin, eds., *Anthropological Studies of the Taiwan Area: Accomplishments and Prospects* (Taipei: Department of Anthropology, National Taiwan University, 1989), pp. 241–60, for the importance of examining the ways native cultures influenced the Han.

52. Dru Gladney, *Muslim Chinese*, chap. 2, asserts that the very idea of a Han majority was "invented" by Sun Yat-sen in his efforts to mobilize opposition against Manchu rule.

53. There is a vast anthropological literature on the symbolics of power in a hierarchically structured space. For a representative piece, see Clifford Geertz, "Center, Kings, and Charisma: Reflections on the Symbolics of Power," in his *Local Knowledge* (New York: Basic Books, 1985), pp. 121–46. For various local patterns of dominance in China, see Joseph Esherick and Mary Rankin, *Chinese Local Elites*.

54. Philip Corrigan and Derek Sayer, *The Great Arch: English State-Formation as Cultural Revolution* (Oxford: Blackwell, 1985).

55. Etienne Balazs, *Chinese Civilization and Bureaucracy*, trans. H. M. Wright, ed. Arthur F. Wright (New Haven: Yale University Press, 1964).

56. For comparative analysis of the making of the modern state in Europe, see the concise statement by Bernard Cohn and Nicholas Dirks, "Beyond the Fringe: The Nation State, Colonialism, and the Technologies of Power," *Journal of Historical Sociology* 1, no. 2 (1988): 224–29.

Liu, Lineage on the Sands

1. The historical survey on which this paper is based is part of the Pearl River delta society and culture project conducted jointly by the author, David Faure, Helen F. Siu, and Ye Xian'en, and funded by the Institute of Chinese Studies, the Chinese University of Hong Kong, and the Wenner-Gren Foundation for Anthropological Research. Fieldwork was conducted by Helen F. Siu, Dai He, Chen Chunsheng, and myself. I would like to thank them for allowing me to use their materials and for their valuable input.

2. As in many parts of the Pearl River delta, local usage and administrative definition are different. During the Qing and the Republican periods, Shawan *si* was a subcounty administrative unit within Panyu county and what is now Shawan township was Benshan *xiang*. Today, the term Shawan *zhen* refers both to the township of Shawan and to the region that includes Shawan and seventeen neighboring villages. This article refers not to the administrative definitions of Shawan but to the customary understanding from the Qing, and includes, essentially, the four villages that made up the township formerly referred to as Benshan *xiang*.

3. The *Yuanhe junxian zhi* (Gazetteer of commanderies and counties in the Yuanhe period), ninth century (Beijing: Zhonghua, repr. 1983), chap. 34, p. 886, records, "To the south [of Guangzhou], the sea is 70 *li* away."

4. Zeng Zhaoxuan, "Zhujiang sanjiaozhou lishi hedao de bianqian" (The historical change of river routes of the Pearl River delta), in Institute of Geology of the Geography Department of the Huanan Shifan University, ed., *Redai dimiao* (Geography of tropical regions) 2, no. 2 (1981): 9–18, 14–15.

5. Shitu Tong, ed., *Panyu wenwu zhi* (Record of the historical artifacts of Panyu county) (Panyu: Panyu xian xianzhi bianzuan weiyuanhui, 1988), pp. 120–21, entry on "clear water well of Shawan" (*Shawan qingshui jing*).

6. From interviews with He Xingyao, June 23, 1989; and Feng Hua, July 19, 1989.

7. He Rugen and Er Yi, "Shawan Hezu Liugeng tang jingying guanli gaikuang" (An overview of the management of the Liugeng tang of the He lineage in Shawan), in *Panyu wenshi ziliao* (Literary and historical sources of Panyu county), vol. 2 (n.p., 1984), pp. 69–74.

8. Wu Qingshi, "Guangdong shatian zhi yimian" (One dimension of the sands in Guangdong), in *Wenshi ziliao xuanji* (Selected sources on history and literature), vol. 5 (Guangzhou, 1962), pp. 72–89.

9. Interview with He Rugen, Aug. 1, 1989. Also see He Rugen and Er Yi, "Shawan Hezu Liugeng tang," 69–77.

10. None of the documentary evidence I have examined on the Song origins of the He lineage's landholdings stands up to scrutiny. Locations of holdings in an

account purportedly written by the Song official Li Maoying are almost identical with the locations of plots that were granted in 1587 noted in the "Liugeng ge shatian zongzhi" (A complete record of the reclaimed land of the Liugeng tang), a manuscript record of the holdings of the He lineage ancestral trust, first written in August 1920 and now held by the town government of Shawan. There is also clear evidence of the corruption of an early Ming claim on lineage documentation in the account found in the *Shawan Heshi Lujiang zongpu* (The genealogy of the He surname of Shawan from Lujiang), dated in the Yongle reign of the early Ming. The same article is dated the *gengyin* year of the Yongli period (1650) in other genealogies, and also appears as "Shawan yuanzhi kao" (The original location of Shawan), written in the Yongli period, in *Panyu xian xuzhi* (1911), 43/9b–10b. The description in Zeng Zhaoxuan, "Zhujiang sanjiaozhou lishi hedao de bianqian," pp. 16–18, arguing that the delta at Panyu county was formed during the Song, is based on claims in genealogical records such as the He's.

11. See Matsuda Yoshirō, "Minmatsu Shinsho Kantō deruta no shadan kaihatsu to kyōshin shihai no kesei katei" (Rural gentry control and the development of the sands in the Pearl River delta in the late Ming and the early Qing), *Shakai keizai shigaku* 46 (1981): 54–81; and Nishikawa Kikuko, "Shindai Shukō deruta no shadan (The sands of the Pearl River delta during the Qing), *Tōyō gakuho* 63, nos. 1 and 2 (1981): 93–135.

12. See the "Liugeng ge shatian zongzhi." Ye Xian'en and Tan Dihua, "Lun Zhujiang sanjiaozhou de zutian" (On ancestral land in the Pearl River delta), in Guangdong lishi xuehui (Guangdong Historical Society), ed., *Ming-Qing Guangdong shehui jingji xingtai yanjiu* (Social and economic forms in Guangdong in the Ming-Qing period) (Guangzhou: Guangdong renmin, 1985), pp. 22–64, cites a similar source for a table on the holdings of the Liugeng tang. The earliest land grant made to the He lineage was in 1587, the grant consisting of over 1,200 mu of sands, and after litigations with the Wang lineage in 1616, another 906 mu was registered by local officials (pp. 33–34).

13. Long Tinghuai, *Jingxuexuan wenji* (Collected essays of the Jingxue study), *xu* dated 1832, 1/1b–2a, and Wu Qingshi, "Guangdong shatian zhi yimian."

14. "Jian Liugeng tang shimo zhi" (A brief history of the building of the He Liugeng tang), in *Shawan Heshi Lujiang zongpu*.

15. Ye Xian'en and Tan Dihua, "Lun Zhujiang sanjiaozhou de shatian," pp. 34–36.

16. See David Faure, *The Structure of Chinese Rural Society: Lineage and Village in the Eastern New Territories, Hong Kong* (London: Oxford University Press, 1986); and "The Lineage as a Cultural Invention: The Case of the Pearl River Delta," *Modern China* 15, no. 1 (1989): 4–36.

17. The early record of the He's scholarly achievements is too complex to be detailed here. The early ancestors were known, at one stage, by abbreviated titles only: the first generation was the *liu xueshi* (Sixth Scholar?), the second generation the *Sanjiu chengshilang* (Three-nine Gentleman for Managing Affairs), the third generation, the *niansan chengshilang* (Twenty-third Gentleman for Managing Affairs). At a later stage, the *liu xueshi* became a Hanlin *xueshi* (scholar of the Hanlin

Academy), and the second- and third-generation ancestors were also given refined titles.

18. "Shawan Heshi zupu," manuscript, n.d., appendix 2. The genealogies usually regard He Renjian as a fourth-generation ancestor, in which case He Zhihai would be eighth generation.

19. In the (*Heshi*) *Jishu tang pu*, the following is recorded in a note at the end of He Zihai's preface: "When Zihai *gong* wrote this preface there were only several tens of people in our lineage, which is why there was no written genealogy, and why Fupang *gong* of the fourth generation was venerated as the ancestor who credited our lineage with good deeds. From this we can see where lay his intentions."

20. "Shawan Heshi zupu," appendix 2.

21. He Zihai, "Shutian ji" (An account of book land), *Panyu xian xuzhi* (1911), 43/9a–b, *Panyu xian zhi* (1774), 15/ *renwu* 5a–6b, Ouyang Xiu, *Xin Wudai shi* (New history of the Five Dynasties) (Shanghai: Shanghai guji, 1986), pp. 5139–40.

22. "(Shawan Heshi) Shenxi tang xipu," manuscript, n.p.

23. "Shawan Heshi zupu," appendix 3.

24. "(Shawan Heshi) Shenxi tang xipu."

25. There were similar efforts at lineage myth-making for prestige purposes. He Li, of the Song dynasty, who is clearly documented in the *Song shi* (History of the Song dynasty) as a native of Sichuan province, was mingled with the myths surrounding He Chang and made one of three eminent officials arising from the lineage.

26. "Benzu chushi ershi bianyi heshi" (Verification of the first- and second-generation ancestors of our lineage), in "(Shawan Heshi) Shenxi tang xipu," citing as source the *Jishu tang pu*.

27. The preface of the He liugeng tang genealogy in "Shawan Heshi zupu."

28. "Shawan Heshi zupu," appendix 2.

29. Qu Dajun, *Guangdong xinyu* (New items relating to Guangdong), *xu* dated 1700 (Hong Kong: Zhonghua shuju, 1984), chap. 17, p. 464.

30. "Shawan Heshi zupu."

31. Ibid. See also Cai Dequan, "Shawan Liugeng tang shi jian yu henian?" (When was the Shawan He Liugeng tang first built?) *Guangzhou wenbo* (Guangzhou museum) (Guangzhou: Guangzhoushi wenwu bowuguan xuehui, 1987), no. 4, pp. 61–64.

32. "Shawan Heshi zupu," unpaginated entry.

33. For an example of private halls, see He Zihai, "Kengou tang zhi" (An account of the Kengou tang), in Wu Daorong, ed., *Guangdong wenzheng* (Collected works of Guangdong), vol. 4 (Hong Kong: Zhuhai shuyuan, 1977), p. 440.

34. "Lujiang Heshi zongpu," manuscript.

35. "Jian Liugeng tang shimo zhi" (An account of the construction of the Liugeng tang), manuscript; and He Pinduan, "Liugeng tang ji qi yishu tese" (The Liugeng tang and its artistic characteristics), in *Panyu wenshi ziliao*, vol. 3 (1985), pp. 157–64.

36. See Li Maoying, "Chengwulang Deming gong xiangzan" (Eulogy appended

to the portrait of the official in charge of affairs, the Venerable Deming), and an article entitled "Zhu Zhi kao," written in the early Ming, recorded in various editions of the He lineage genealogy. He Renjian's son married a niece of Li Maoying.

37. "(Shawan Heshi) Shenxi tang xipu."
38. *Panyu xian xuzhi* (1911), 43/9a–b.
39. "Shawan Heshi zupu."
40. Ibid., appendix 8.
41. *Panyu xian xuzhi* (1911), 19/6a.
42. "Shawan Heshi zupu," appendix 8.
43. Ibid., addendum.
44. "(Shawan Heshi) Lujiang zongpu."
45. Shitu Tong, *Panyu xian wenwu zhi*, (1988), p. 130.
46. Equivalent to *waimian ren* and *limian ren* in *putonghua*.
47. In the struggle for the control of the Wangqing *sha* in 1839 between the local gentry of Dongguan and the Wen lineage of Shunde, the two main defendants were Guo Jinxiang and Guo Yabao, both from Shawan. The charge states that Guo Jinxiang was a *danhu* (of a Dan household), *danfei* (a Dan bandit), and a *ji'an shagun* (a sands ruffian with a record). Guo Yabao was named as a *tuhao* (local boss) who had financially supported Guo Jinxiang's reclamation efforts. Those two were wealthy and powerful individuals of the sands who resembled the later *datian'er* (local bosses). However, even if they paid to reclaim the sands themselves, they had to rent the land from the Wen lineage of Shunde. From this we can see that even powerful people in the sands could not acquire outright ownership of the land. Instead, they were forced to acknowledge the ownership of the major lineages and to reclaim the sands under their protection. See *Dongguan xianzhi* (Local record of Dongguan) (1911), 99/5b–8a, 12b–14b. For the local bosses, see Helen Siu, *Agents and Victims in South China: Accomplices in Rural Revolution* (New Haven: Yale University Press, 1989), chaps. 3–5.
48. See Helen Siu, "Recycling Tradition: Culture, History and Political Economy in the Chrysanthemum Festivals of South China," *Comparative Studies in Society and History* 32, no. 4 (1990): 765–94, for similar processes of power.
49. "Shawan Heshi zupu," appendix 5.
50. Katayama Tsuyoshi, "Shinmatsu Kōtōshō Shukō deruta no zukohyō to sore o meguru shomondai: Zeiryō, koseki, dōzoku" (Some problems concerning the Tujia charts in the Pearl River delta in Guangdong province during the late Qing period: Taxes, household registration, and lineage). *Shigaku zasshi* 4 (1982): 42–81; Liu Zhiwei, "Ming-Qing Zhujiang sanjiaozhou diqu lijiazhi zhong 'hu' de yanbian" (The transformation of the "household unit" in the Lijia system in the Pearl River delta during the Ming and Qing periods), *Zhongshan Daxue xuebao* 3 (1988): 64–73; and "Qingdai Guangdong diqu tujiazhi zhong de 'zong hu' yu 'zi hu'" (The "Primary Household" and "Secondary Household" of the *tujia* system in the Guangdong region during the Qing dynasty), *Zhongguo shehui jingjishi yanjiu* 2 (1991): 36–42.
51. *Panyu xian xuzhi* (1911), 23/20a–b.

52. Panyu xian Shawan zhen jianshe weiyuanhui (The Developmental Committee of Shawan town, Panyu county), *Panyu xian Shawan zhen (Benshan xiang) jianshe zhi, 1930–1988* (1988), pp. 16–22.

53. On the Zidong boats, see Ou Ruizhi, "Zidong ting di laili" (On the origins of the Zidong boats), *Foshan wenshi ziliao* (Literary and historical sources on Foshan), vol. 5 (1985), pp. 110–13.

54. "Xinhai nian jingli xiangzu wenjian caobu" (A draft document of the management of the various lineages in 1911), manuscript.

55. Maurice Freedman, *Chinese Lineage and Society: Fukien and Kwangtung*, (London: Athlone, 1966), pp. 36–37.

56. Qu Dajun, *Guangdong xinyu*, p. 208.

57. Interview with He Yin, July 27, 1989. The incorporation of Li Maoying into this story was apparently due to a confusion on the part of the informant. According to another informant, the legend should be as follows: "When the Shawan native Li Luyuan served as a general in Yunnan during the Ming, a feud between two lineages broke out over the control of the image of Beidi commissioned by the Ming emperor. Because of the mediation of General Li, the lineages resolved their differences. In order to remember the upright character and the effective policies of General Li in preventing more conflicts, local people presented the image to Li, and he brought it back to Shawan" (Shitu Tong, "Shawan piaose" [Festival performances in Shawan], in *Panyu wenshi ziliao* [Literary and historical sources on Panyu] 4 [1986]: 156–60).

58. Interview with Wang Yaozu, July 31, 1989.

59. Interview with He Jinjua, July 26, 1989.

60. There were cultural activities comparable to local festivals and religious parades, such as the "autumn colors" (*qiuse*) of Foshan and the "water colors" (*shuise*) of Xiaolan.

Luo, Territorial Community at the Town of Lubao

1. *Sanshui xianzhi* (Record of Sanshui county) (1819), 1/43b.

2. Yang Wanli, *Chengzai shixuan* (Selected poems of Yang Wanli), in Chen Yu, *Song shiwujia shixuan* (Selected poems by sixteen Song poets) (1692), 20b.

3. According to genealogies and interview reports, the Liu surname at Liuzhai had come from Hubei province, the Hu surname at Lower Letang from Zhejiang province, the Cai surname at Dushugang from Fujian province, the Cao surname at Nan'an from Panyu county, the Ouyang surname at Ouyang Street from Heshan county, the Xie surname at Xie Street from Gaoyao county, and the Chen and Ye surnames at Fanluogang from Nanhai county.

4. *Yongle dadian* (The encyclopedia of the Yongle reign, i.e., 1403 to 1424), j. 11905, 11906, under "*guang*."

5. Wen Runeng, ed., *Yuedong shihai* (Sea of poetry in Guangdong) (Shunde, 1866), 15/9b.

6. Lun Wenxu, "Qingyun Qiao ji," *Sanshui xianzhi*, 14/47b.

7. Ibid. [Editors' note: For a discussion of the gentrification process, see David

Faure, "What Made Foshan a Town? The Evolution of Rural-Urban Identities in Ming-Qing China," *Late Imperial China* 11, no. 2 (1990): 1–31.]

8. *Guangdong tongzhi* (Record of Guangdong province) (1561), 13/17b notes that Lubao was well known for its wine, for which merchants from Qingyuan gathered.

9. The location of Lower Market that elderly people could point out to us was in front of the Beidi Temple; interview with Mai Gugong, July 17, 1989.

10. *Sanshui xianzhi* 1/45b, notes "The Xujiang upper market met on the 4th and 9th days, the Xujiang lower market met on the 2nd and 7th days, but now have been destroyed." Also, interview with He Liu, Aug. 8, 1989.

11. Interview with Chen Niu, Aug. 8, 1989, and *Sanshui xianzhi*, 1/46a.

12. Interviews with Huang Rengkang, July 22, 1989, and Lin Yangqing, Sept. 16, 1989.

13. Sanshui xian zhengxue wenshi weiyuanhui, ed., *Sanshui wenshi* (Literary and historical sources on Sanshui county) 1 (n.d.): 88.

14. *Sanshui wenshi*, nos. 18 and 19 combined issue (n.d.), pp. 88–100; interview with Pan Xiaohen, Aug. 9, 1989.

15. *Sanshui xianzhi* (1819), 1/20a.

16. Tablet found at Huashan Monastery, "Renovation of the Huashan Monastery and the rebuilding of the Dizang Hall" ("Chongxiu Huashan si fujian Dizang dian beiji"), dated 1791.

17. Ibid., and *Sanshui xianzhi* (1819), 16/1b, 2b, and 3b.

18. *Guangdong tongzhi* (1535), 1/14a.

19. "Liuzhai Liushi zupu" (Genealogy of the Liu surname at Liuzhai), Republican manuscript, copy retained by author.

20. *Sanshui xianzhi* (1819), 13/2a.

21. Tablet, "Renovation of the Huashan Monastery."

22. *Sanshui xianzhi* (1819), 14/49b.

23. On the *Beiyu ji*, see Gary Seaman, "The Divine Authorship of *Pei-yu Chi* [Journey to the North]," *Journal of Asian Studies* 45, no. 3 (1986): 483–97.

24. *Chongxiu Wuxian gumiao beiji* (n.d.).

25. Interview with Huang Rengkang, July 22, 1989.

26. *Sanshui xianzhi* (1819), 1/18a.

27. Ibid., 13/31a, 32b.

28. Interviews with Lin Yangtou, Fan Jiuntou, and Mai Gugong, July 6 and July 21, 1989, and poem in the Republican period in *Sanshui wenshi*, no. 12 (n.d.): 86–87: "The cattle boats mooring one after the other on the 3rd and 8th, / [while I] in the shade of the Longyan tree [enjoy] the cool breeze in the afternoon."

29. "Niulangang bianqian suoji" (Miscellaneous record of changes at Niulangang), in *Sanshui wenshi*, nos. 16 and 17 combined issue, pp. 99–101.

30. The term was used in opposition to the *fangunxu* (the rice-boiling market), meaning a market in which the trading hours were short.

31. *Sanshui xianzhi* (1819), 1/46a.

32. Interviews with Mai Gugong, July 17, 1989; Huang Rengkang, July 22, 1989; Ouyang Zuchang, July 31, 1989; and Tan Zhufang, Aug. 4, 1989.

33. We know of the following: Gong, Feng, Li, Huang, He, Ou, Xie, Li, Ye, Zhang, Liang, Zhu, Wang, Hu, Fan, Du, and Tan; interviews with Chen Niu, Aug. 8, 1989, and Peng Gen, Aug. 16, 1989.

34. Interviews with Peng Gen, Aug. 16, 1989; He Liu, Aug. 8, 1989; and Chen Niu, Aug. 8, 1989. The ancestor was Chen Zhongyi. We were told that Peng *jie* was like Fulu Road in Foshan, known for its shops in paper offerings. Selling these objects in the markets was known as *jiuxu*.

35. We were told in interviews that residents at Peng *jie* owned land at Shangtang, Caogang, and Liuyuan; that the Liu surname of Liuzhai owned land at Liuyuan in Xihe and rented it out to people of the Lue surname; that the Huang surname of Laogu *xiang* owned more than ten mu at Wosheng *kang* in Xihe; and that the Ouyang surname at Ouyang *jie* owned land at Caibian. Interviews with Peng Gen, Aug. 16, 1989; Liu Jiongyong, July 26, 1989; and Ye Guoxing, Sept. 18, 1989.

36. Dayigang is five kilometers from Peng Street.

37. "Dayigang Xieshi zupu" (Genealogy of the Xie surname at Dayigang), manuscript, copy retained by author.

38. Interview with Deng Zixuan, Aug. 25, 1989; the ancestor moved into Peng *jie* to work in the shops that cooked for travelers.

39. Tablet, "Temple Festival of the First, Second, and Third *pu*" ("Yi'ersan pu hedan beiji"), dated 1816; tablet remains in Huashan Monastery.

40. Ibid.

41. Tablet, "Commemoration of the Founding of the *Baiyi yinhui*" ("Juban baiyi yinhui bei"), dated 1822; tablet remains in Huashan Monastery.

42. Interview with Liu Jiongyong, Aug. 11, 1989.

43. *Sanshui wenshi* 13: 66.

44. Interview subjects described these activities in terms of "fighting for the pao" and paying for the "floats." From what is known about the practice in the New Territories of Hong Kong, it would seem quite clear that the two were related in that the pao consisted of the assignment of a representation of the deity that might be temporarily installed outside the temple (for instance, within the household), which was then returned, properly adorned as a float, in the following year. In the case of Lubao, it would seem that the floats were also paraded on the festival of the deity.

45. Described to us as their "longevity gowns" (*shoupao*, that is, funeral gowns).

46. Interview with Peng Gen, Aug. 16, 1989.

47. Interviews with Chen Niu, Aug. 8, 1989, and Ouyang Zuchang, Aug. 23, 1989.

48. *Sanshui wenshi* 8: 42. Prior to 1888, the temple was not repaired on a fixed schedule, and so the "great" and "small" gatherings must have started only then.

49. Interview with Huang Rengkang, Aug. 11, 1989.

50. Interview with Peng Gen, Aug. 16, 1989.

51. Sanshui xian wenwu pucha bangongsi bianshezu, *Sanshui wenwu zhi* (draft, n.d.), p. 38.

52. "Repayment of Accounts by the Wudi Temple to the Junyi *hui*" ("Erpu Wudi

miao wanzhang Junyihui xu"), dated 1896, stela found in a house adjacent to the Wudi Temple.

53. Interview with Huang Rengkang, July 22, 1989.

54. Interview with Huang Qiaoyong (female), aged 91, at Tanqi, Aug. 5, 1989.

55. Interview with Li Juwei, Sept. 21, 1989.

56. Interviews with Xie Kong'an, Aug. 19, 1989, and Xie Shaocheng, Aug. 19, 1989.

57. Interviews with Huang Hanming, Sept. 20, 1989, and Huang Jinyi, Sept. 20, 1989.

58. Interviews with Jiang Zhiliang and Jiang Hancai, Sept. 19, 1989.

59. Interviews with Mai Gugong, July 17, 1989; Huang Rengkang, July 22, 1989; Liu Jiongyong, July 26, 1989; Liu Jingyao, July 28, 1989; Ouyang Dacai, July 31, 1989; Cen Zeying, Sept. 19, 1989; Jiang Zhiliang, Sept. 19, 1989; and Liang Guanglin, Sept. 20, 1989.

60. *Sanshui xianzhi* (1819), 5/24b, 14/47b, 9/20a, and "Stela Record of the Yumen," dated 1808, found on the bank of the North River at Lubao.

61. Wang rose to be a teacher in calligraphy for the Guangxu emperor.

62. There were flags of Xie Yixi and Li Haunyao on the Longpo Community school then; interview with Tan Zhufang on Aug. 4, 1989. Also *Sanshui xianzhi* (1819), 9/26a, and interviews with Huang Rengkang, Aug. 5, 1989, and Wang Rujin, Aug. 4, 1989.

63. "Tablet at the Longpo Community School in Commemoration of the Spirit Tablets from the Villages" ("Longpo shexue labei jinian gexiang zhuwei ji"), dated 1936, found outside Huashan Monastery; and *Sanshui wenshi* 9: 98.

64. Interview with Huang Rengkang, Aug. 11, 1989.

65. Interview with Xie Kong'an, Aug. 17, 1989.

66. Interview with Cao Guodong, Aug. 16, 1989.

67. Interview with Huang Rengkang, Aug. 5, 1989.

68. Interview with Pan Xiaohen, Aug. 9, 1989.

69. Tablet, "Renovation of the Huashan Monastery."

70. The names listed in the "Longbo Community School in Commemoration" stela have been collated with the following records: interviews with Cao Xianling, Aug. 16, 1989; Cen Ziquan, Sept. 19, 1989; Li Jinhuai, Aug. 1, 1989; and Liu Jingyao, July 28, 1989; an inscription on the stone lintel at the Baiyi School operated by the Cen surname; "Tablet Commemorating the Repair of the Venerable Hu Xingquan Ancestral Hall" ("Xingquan Hugong ci chongxiu beiji"), at the Hu surname ancestral hall at Upper Letang; the "Liqu Lishi zupu" (Genealogy of the Li surname at Liqu); "Liuzhai Liushi zupu," the "Xialetang Wushi zupu" (Genealogy of the Wu surname at Lower Letang); and the *Sanshui xianzhi* (1819), 9/4a, 13a, 27b, 53b. The genealogies consulted are manuscripts, copies of which are in author's holding.

71. Liu Tongde, "Liushi zupu" (Genealogy of the Liu lineage) (draft, 1989), and *Sanshui wenshi*, nos. 18 and 19 combined issue, pp. 4–5. [Editors' note: The character sequence used for names among the Lius in this village includes the *ru* character. On character sequences in naming, see Patricia Buckley Ebrey, "The Early

Stages in the Development of Descent Group Organization," in Patricia Buckley Ebrey and James L. Watson, eds., *Kinship Organization in Late Imperial China, 1000–1940* (Berkeley: University of California Press, 1986), p. 47.]

72. Chen Zhoutang, ed., *Guangdong diqu Taiping tianguo shiliao xuanbian* (Selected historical documents on the Taiping Heavenly Kingdom in Guangdong) (Guangzhou: Guangdong renmin, 1986), pp. 198–99.

73. *Sanshui wenshi* 8: 42.

74. Jin Shixuan and Xu Wenshu, *Zhongguo tielu fazhanshi (1876–1949)* (History of Chinese railway development, 1876–1949) (Beijing: Zhongguo tielu chubanshe, 1986), pp. 327–28.

75. Interview with Liu Tongde, July 27, 1989; Liu Tongde, "Liushi zupu."

76. Interview with Wang Rujin, Aug. 4, 1989.

77. Interviews with Chen Niu, Aug. 8, 1989; Gong Jingbo, Aug. 9, 1989; and Peng Gen, Aug. 16, 1989.

78. Interviews with Mai Gugong, July 17, 1989; Pan Shaoyuan, Aug. 9, 1989; Huang Rengkang, July 26, 1989, and Aug. 11, 1989; Cai Huanquan, Aug. 17, 1989; Cen Ziquan, Sept. 19, 1989; and Li Jumei, Aug. 18, 1989.

79. Interviews with Cai Deyin, Cai Zanwen, and Cai Zhangwu, Aug. 17, 1989.

80. The Guangfang Pier was one of the main piers in Lubao; interviews with Huang Shaolun, Aug. 19, 1989; Peng Gen, Aug. 16, 1989; Ouyang Zuchang, Aug. 23, 1989; and Xie Zewen, Aug. 3, 1989.

81. Interview with Chen Niu, Aug. 8, 1989.

82. According to the *Guangdong quansheng difang jiyao*, entry on Sanshui, in the Republican period the temple contributed 400 silver dollars annually to the Sanshui county government.

83. Interview with Cai Huanquan, Aug. 17, 1989.

84. Interview with Cai Deyin, Aug. 24, 1989.

Chan, Ordination Names in Hakka Genealogies

1. My main sources are Luo Xianglin, *Kejia shiliao huipian*, vol. 1 (Hong Kong: Zhongguo xueshe, 1965), and genealogies from Hong Kong, most of which are listed in H. G. H. Nelson, "Preliminary List of the Baker Collection of New Territories Genealogies in the British Library," *Journal of the Hong Kong Branch of the Royal Asiatic Society* 16 (1976): 297–301 (hereafter referred to as the "Nelson list").

2. A study that draws attention to this stylistic difference is John Lagerwey, "The Fachang Ritual in Northern Taiwan," in Tsao Pen-yeh and Daniel P. L. Law, eds., *Studies of Taoist Rituals and Music of Today* (Hong Kong: Society for Ethnomusicological Research in Hong Kong, 1989), pp. 66–73. The Taiwanese collection published by Michael Saso under the title *Zhuanglin xu daozang* (Taipei: Chengwen, 1975) includes many manuals of the popular tradition. The shared stylistic features include a literary formula that begins by asserting the "root" or "origin" of a ritual object (*chuchu you genyuan*).

3. Takuji Takemura, a student of the Yao, draws attention to the similarity be-

tween the Hakka and the Yao ordination names in his "*Jaa-Fin-Taan* or Ancestor Registers: Fundamental Sources for Structural Analysis of Yao Ethnic Boundaries," *Bulletin of the National Museum of Ethnology*, Special Issue, no. 14 (1991): 433.

4. Jacques Lemoine, *Yao Ceremonial Paintings* (Bangkok: White Lotus, 1982), pp. 24–27.

5. See, e.g., Shi Lianzhu, *Shezu* (Beijing: Minzu, 1988), pp. 113–15.

6. Yang Chengzhi (team leader), Chen Fengxian, Huang Shuping, et al., "Guangdong Shemin shibie diaocha" (Field research on the identification of the She people in Guangdong), in "Zhongguo shaoshu minzu shehui lishi Diaocha zhiliao chongkan" Fujian shen bienji zu, *Shezu shehui lishi diaocha* (Field research on the social history of the She people) (Fuzhou: Fujian renmin, 1986), p. 282.

7. Yang Heshu, Li Anmin, and Chen Shulian, *Bapai wenhua: Bapai Yao di wenhua renleixue kaocha* (The culture of the Bapai Yao: Perspectives from cultural anthropology) (Guangzhou: Zhongshan daxue chubanshe, 1990), p. 69.

8. Yang Heshu et al., *Bapai wenhua*. Of the eight "ancestral lists" from Liannan in Li Mo and Fang Xianqing, *Liannan Bapai yanjiu ziliao* (Sources for the study of the Bapai of Liannan) (Guangzhou: Guangdong Shehui Dexue Yuan, c. 1988), only three contain names that do not conform to the formats of ordination names, and in all three cases, these names are found only toward the very end of the lists. One is tempted to ask if all ancestors were ordained, or if only those who had been ordained were remembered as ancestors.

9. Peter K. Kandre, "Passing Through the Countries, the Years and Life," in Jacques Lemoine and C. Chiao, eds., *The Yao of South China: Recent International Studies* (Paris: Pangu, Editions de l'A.F.E.Y., 1991), pp. 308–10.

10. See, e.g., Zhong Zhong, "Jiefangqian Shezu yuanshi shehui chanyu chutan" (Surviving practices of primitive society among the She before the Liberation), in Shi Lianzhu, ed., *Shezu yanjiu lunwenji* (Studies on the She people) (Beijing: Minzhu, 1987), p. 272. Two photographs of the dragon head cane are included in He Liankui, "Shemin de tuteng chongbai" (The She people's totemic worship), in his *Minzu wenhua yanjiu* (Studies of the cultures of national minorities) (Taipei?: n.p., preface dated 1951).

11. Luo Xianglin, *Kejia shiliao huipian*, p. 230.

12. Nelson list, vol. 69.

13. Luo Xianglin, *Kejia shiliao huipian*, pp. 97–98. In a genealogy of the Xu surname (Luo Xianglin, *Kejia shiliao huipian*, pp. 305–6), among those whose ordination names are recorded is a sorcerer or healer who lived during an unknown period between Wanli and Zhengtong in the Ming dynasty (that is, approximately the fifteenth and sixteenth centuries), who was widely respected among his kinsmen long after his death. The *Changle Gazetteer* of 1845 (repr. Taipei: Chengwen, 1968), 10/22b mentions without giving dates a Mao Qin'er, known "popularly" as Mao Qin Erlang, who together with a Hu Fawang and others, entered the mountains to learn magic, and acquired mystical powers. In the genealogy of the Tu surname of Jiaoling (Luo Xianglin, *Kejia shiliao huipian*, p. 351), one of the ancestors with a name in the *lang* format is said to have, together with another man of another surname and with a name in the *lang* style, harnessed a *sheguan* earth god.

The two were honored in a temple housing their images. This account may be compared with that of a battle between a *sheguan* earth god and a *sanggong* sorcerer in Zhang Zuji, *Zhonghua jiulisu* (Chinese old customs) (Taipei: Zhongyuan zazhi, 1980). The story is in vol. 3 under the entry *Sheguan doufa* (contest of power by officials of the earth) and concerns a temple at Qingyuan county in Guangdong province.

14. Luo Xianglin, *Kejia shiliao huipian*, p. 161.

15. *Shoufa* may be translated literally as "receiving the powers," but *dushui* is an impossible term to translate.

16. *Xingning xianzhi* (1552; repr. in *Tianyi Ge Mingdai fangszi xuankan xubian* [Selective reprints of Ming dynasty gazetteers in the Tianyi Ge Collection, second series], vol. 66, [Shanghai: Shanghai shudian, 1990]), 4/35b–36a.

17. These ranks resemble closely those found in the documents of the tradition known as the Tianxin zhengfa of the Song dynasty and the *Tianhuang zhidao taiqing yuce* manual of the Ming. See Chen Yonghai (Chan Wing-hoi), forthcoming, "Tianxin zhengfa di yuanliu he yingxiang" (The origins and influence of the Tianxin Zhengfa). Reference to a Daoist who had "returned from the performance of a *jiao* ceremony" in *Huizhou fuzhi* (1556; repr. Shanghai: Shanghai guji shudian, 1982), 15/14a–15b, may be additional evidence of Daoist presence in Xingning in this period.

18. Qu Dajun, *Guangdong xinyu* (Beijing: Zhonghua, 1985), pp. 302–3.

19. *Yong'an sanzhi* (1930 repr. of 1822 edition, repr. Taiwan: Chengwen, 1974), 1/207. For records of ordination in gazetteers, see also the *Changle xianzhi* (1845; Taipei: Xuesheng repr. 1968), 4/9a.

20. Zhang Zuji, *Zhonghua jiulisu*.

21. Untitled volume by Guangdong sheng xiju yanjiushi (Guangdong theater research unit) (n.p., prefaced 1980), pp. 132–38.

22. For the Yao, a small troop of *bingma* spiritual soldiers are assigned to an initiate according to his level of initiation (Lemoine, *Yao Ceremonial Paintings*, pp. 28–29). For the She a ceremony of *zhaobing* (recruiting soldiers) is held once every three or five years, but they see the soldiers as the spiritual generals and soldiers who helped Panhu in his mission to kill the "barbarian king." See Yang Chengzhi et al., "Guangdong Shemin shibie diaocha," p. 47.

23. Zhang Zuji, *Zhonghua jiulisu*, describes some celebrations as "*anlong* and *fengchao*" and shows that *anlong* includes rituals to maintain the celestial troops of the ancestors. The book includes a picture of a flag in the middle of which is written "Issued to the family altar of the Zhang surname to pay respect to ancestors, station troops, and distribute provisions." Hanging from the same pole is a strip of paper that notes the *anlong* and *fengchao*. According to Zhang, *anlong* was often part of the ritual to affiliate an additional ancestor with the incense burner in an ancestral hall.

24. Nelson list, vol. 66. It contains two or three separate genealogies of the Chen surname among which I cannot detect common descent. It seems that some pages are missing in the copy originally held in the Hong Kong University collection. The name Pujiao, if indeed an ordination name, does not follow the usual *lang* or *fa*

format. It is probably an ordination name from another, better-known "folk" religion, Luozu *jiao*, which used ordination names incorporating the character *pu*. See Fu Yiling, "Qing Qianlong Fujian ci laoguancai zhong qishi kao" (A study of the uprising of the people who ate the Laoguan vegetarian food in the Qianlong period in the Qing dynasty), in his *Fu Yiling zishi wushi nian wenbian* (Collected essays from Fu Yiling's fifty years of historical scholarship) (Xiamen: Xiamen daxue chubanshe, 1989), pp. 148–61. The Luozu *jiao* is not related to the tradition that is the subject of this article.

25. Nelson list, vol. 55. It is unlikely that the genealogy belonged to a *sang* specialist, for his repertoire would have taken up many volumes, rather than a few pages in a genealogy, as in this case.

26. See David Faure, *Structure of Chinese Rural Society* (Hong Kong: Oxford University Press, 1986) pp. 74–77.

27. *Dengke lu* (n.d.); included in vol. 3409 of *Congshu jicheng chubian* (Shanghai: Shangwu, 1939).

28. Yu Yue, *Chunzai tang suibi* (Essays from Chunzai tang) (Shanghai: Jinbu, n.d.), j. 5, pp. 3–4.

29. Zhao Yi, *Gaiyu congkao* (Research conducted during spare time while taking care of parents) (*xu* dated 1790; repr. Shijiazhuang: Hebei renmin, 1990), j. 37, p. 677.

30. Wu Han, *Dengxia ji* (Under the lamp) (Beijing: Sanlian, 1960), pp. 52–54.

31. Hong Mai, *Yijian zhi* (The record of the Listener) (Beijing: Zhonghua, 1981), p. 916.

32. Quoted in Rolf A. Stein, "Religious Taoism and Popular Religion from the Second to Seventh Centuries," in Holmes Welch and A. Seidel, eds., *Facets of Taoism* (New Haven: Yale University Press, 1979). Stein (p. 67) dates the compilation as from the Tang dynasty. The text is in the Daoist Canon, vol. 764.

33. "Haiqiong Baizhenren yulu" (The sayings of Bai Yuchan), in the Daoist Canon, vol. 1016, j. 1, pp. 8b–9a.

34. For Qujiang, see Jiang Yingliang, *Xi'nan Bianjiang minzu luncong* (Collected essays on the ethnic groups on the southwestern border) (repr. Taipei: Xinwenfeng, 1978). For Guangxi, see Hu Qiwang and Fang Honggui, *Pancun Yaozu* (The Yao at Pancun [Village]) (Beijing: Minzu, 1983). For Liannan, see Li and Fang, *Liannan Bapai yanjiu*, especially pp. 554 and 564 for King Asura, and p. 433 for Tou To Wang, Changsha Wang, and various Mowang (demons).

35. Michel Strickmann, "The Longest Taoist Scripture," in *History of Religions* 18 (1978): 349.

36. *Haiqiong Baizhenren yulu*, 1/11b–12b.

37. The Chen Jinggu legend is recorded under the title *Da'nai furen* (Lady of the big breasts) in the Qing reprint of that text reproduced in *Huitu Sanjiao yuanliu soushen daquan* (Shanghai: Shanghai guji, 1990), pp. 183–84. This account records that she went to Lu Shan to learn magic. Because of a misprint the name of her master is not given in this passage. That the master's name was Jiu Lang can be verified in a reprint of a Ming version of the same book, under the title of *Sanjiao yuanliu shengdi fozu soushen daquan*, reproduced in the series *Zhongguo minjian*

xinyang zijiao huibian (Taiwan: Xuesheng shudian, 1989). Compare also Shi shen, a Qing manuscript also reprinted in the same series, that quotes a *Zeng soushen*; the passage is otherwise identical with *Sanjiao yuanliu soushen daquan*.

38. In Wu Zhen, "Dashan li de guishen shijie: Zhe Xi'nan shanqu xinyang minsu diaocha" (The world of ghosts and gods in the mountains: A study of the beliefs and customs of the mountainous area of southwestern Zhejiang), p. 92, in *Zhongguo minjian wenhua* (Folk culture of China), no. 2 (Shanghai: Xuelin, 1991).

39. I am indebted to the late priest Mr. Leung On and his son Leung Chung, who allowed their copy of this text to be copied for the Oral History Project of the Chinese University of Hong Kong. The manual is among the Daoist ritual books in the collection of the project. For this collection, see David Faure, *Structure of Chinese Rural Society*, pp. 239–40, and Bartholomew Tsui, "Taoist Ritual Books of the New Territories," in Tsao Pen-yeh et al., *Studies of Taoist Rituals and Music*, pp. 136–43. In his *Taoism and the Rite of Cosmic Renewal* (Seattle: Washington State University Press, 1974), and *The Teachings of Taoist Master Chuang* (New Haven: Yale University Press, 1978), Michael Saso also makes brief references to a manual held by Taiwanese Daoist priests under the same title. From what can be learned from Saso's references, the content of the Taiwan manual is significantly different from that of the manual found in the New Territories of Hong Kong.

40. The title Xuanzhong Dafashi can be found in canonical Daoist literature as a Daoist deity who transmitted Daoist scripture at a time before Pangu, and also as the title of a Daoist who died in the year 569 or thereabout, approximately a century and a half before Emperor Xuanzong of the Tang. I know of no mention of his role in any supernatural trip taken by the emperor. See *Lishi zhenxian tidao tongjian* (Compendium of the immortals' paths to achieving the Dao in past dynasties) (vols. 139–48 in the Daoist Canon), j. 2, p. 1, and j. 29, pp. 4–5. I am similarly confused by some other passages in the manual.

Ye, Territorial Connections of the Dan

1. Huang Zuo, *Guangdong tongzhi*, 1561, 68/48a–b.
2. Gu Yanwu, *Tianxia junguo libingshu* (A book on the strengths and weaknesses of all parts of the empire), *xu* dated 1662, lithographic reproduction by Shenji shuzhuang (n.p., n.d.), 100/5a–b.
3. Qu Dajun, *Guangdong xinyu* (New items relating to Guangdong), *xu* dated 1700 (Hong Kong: Zhonghua repr., 1974), p. 486.
4. Quoted in Chen Xujing, *Danmin de yanjiu* (A study of the Dan people) (Shanghai: Shangwu, 1946), pp. 101–2.
5. "Yumiao hechong muya zengduo leixian deng fou shiyi" (On matters related to the use of portions of the shoreline for fish culture, rice worms, duck raising, stake-nets, and shellfish), in "Guangdong Qingdai dang'an lu" (Qing dynasty Guangdong archival documents) (manuscript, n.d., n.p., held in University of British Columbia library), unpaginated, vol. entitled "Shangchuan, duchuan, guanshui" (Commercial boats, ferry boats, and transit tariffs).

6. "Qianming toukao shijia daiwu tingqi congliang buxu zhicheng shibu reng-xing yajian" (Dan people attached to powerful families in the Ming are to be permitted to come clean and not to be pointed out as bondservants and demeaned), in "Guangdong Qingdai dang'an lu," vol. entitled "Shangchuan, duchuan, guan-shui."

7. Zhu Yun, *Yuedong cheng'an chubian* (First compilation of precedent cases in Guangdong), (n.p., 1832), 31/16a–17a.

8. Editors' note: Compare Qing dynasty documents found in the New Territories of Hong Kong discussed in David Faure, Bernard H. K. Luk, and Alice Ngai-ha Lun Ng, "The Hong Kong Region According to Historical Inscriptions," in David Faure, James Hayes, and Alan Birch, eds., *From Village to City: Studies in the Traditional Roots of Hong Kong Society* (Hong Kong: Centre of Asian Studies, University of Hong Kong, 1984), pp. 51–52.

9. Chen Xujing, *Danmin de yanjiu*, pp. 170–72.

Hayes, *The Cheung Chau Community*

The author remembers with gratitude and affection the many local leaders of the Cheung Chau Kaifong of the 1950s and 1960s, knowledgeable men who gave him their assistance and friendship: especially the late Messrs. Chau Li-peng, M.B.E., J.P.; Fung Pak-choi, B.H.; and Kwong Ping-yau, J.P. Many other Kaifong leaders and old persons put up with all his questions and did their best to provide the answers.

1. A brief statement is given at para. 48 of the officially published *Annual Departmental Report by the District Commissioner New Territories for the Financial Year 1954–55* (hereafter *Annual Departmental Report*), and at para. 523 in *Annual Departmental Report, 1955–56*. For more details see p. 116 of Austin Coates's *Summary Memorandum of the Southern District of the New Territories*, Spring 1955. Mr. Coates was district officer from May 1953 to July 1955. Although this document was not published, there is a copy in the Public Records Office, Hong Kong. For the new Rural Committee, see *Annual Departmental Report 1960–61*, paras. 121 and 126.

2. For the Fong Pin Hospital, see James Hayes, *The Hong Kong Region 1850–1911: Institutions and Leadership in Town and Countryside* (Hamden, Conn.: Archon Books, 1977), pp. 67–68, 69, and 219 n. 42.

3. Coates, *Summary Memorandum*, p. 42, recalls the chronic disagreements of the Residents Association in his day. "As one of its older members (in the days when it was a committee of seven) said to me: 'We're not a committee. We're seven warring states.'"

4. At the Hong Kong Colony Census of 1911, the land population of the Cheung Chau census district was recorded at 3,964; see *Sessional Papers* (Papers presented to the Legislative Council of Hong Kong) 1911, p. 103 (26) (hereafter cited as *SP*). At the 1921 census, it had risen to 5,037; see "Report on the Census of the Colony for 1921" in *SP* 1921, p. 152. The breakdown by sex was 2,390 males and 1,574

females in 1911 (*SP* 1911, p. 103 [26]), and 2,976 and 2,059 respectively in 1921 (*SP* 1921, p. 43).

5. The census breakdown in 1911 according to "dialect spoken in the home" was Punti, 2,443; Hakka, 564; and Hoklo, 957. See *SP* 1911, p. 103 (22).

6. The major work on Hong Kong's Tanka boat people has been done by Barbara E. Ward. See the collected papers in *Through Other Eyes: Essays in Understanding 'Conscious Models'—Mostly in Hong Kong* (Hong Kong: Chinese University Press, 1985); also her "Kau Sai, An Unfinished Manuscript," published posthumously in *Journal of the Hong Kong Branch of the Royal Asiatic Society* 15 (1985): 27–118. See also V. R. Burkhardt, "The Water People," in J. M. Braga, comp., *The Hong Kong Businesses Symposium* (Hong Kong: South China Morning Post, 1957), pp. 271–75.

7. *SP* 1911, p. 103 (26) and (38), and *SP* 1921, p. 42. In 1911, the respective figures for males and females were 2,601 and 1,841, and in 1921 they were reported to be 2,061 and 1,489.

8. *SP* 1921, p. 167.

9. In 1931 the count was much higher, at 7,045 (4,041 males and 3,004 females); see *SP* 1931, table at p. 106.

10. An entry in the British Admiralty's officially compiled *China Sea Pilot* advised sea captains that "The [Cheung Chau] bay . . . is generally so full of junks that there is little room for even a small vessel [to come in]"; see James Hayes, *Hong Kong Region*, p. 58. Another reliable source records that no fewer than nine hundred junks were in the harbor at one of the festival times in the 1890s (ibid., p. 58).

11. The harbor master's report for 1899 listed 123 vessels entering with cargo and 83 in ballast, with 23 and 3 local traders respectively; *SP* 1899. In 1899, 11,002 "licences, port clearances, permits, etc" were issued by the station, and 9,000 in 1905 (see the Annual Reports in *SP* 1899 and 1905).

12. *The Hong Kong Annual Report* (London: HMSO, 1939), p. 50.

13. See, e.g., the example given in James Hayes, *The Rural Communities of Hong Kong: Studies and Themes* (Hong Kong: Oxford University Press, 1983), pp. 68–69. The relationship described therein is similar to those I have encountered in other places where a long-established small group of Tanka boats occupied an anchorage close to a village, as at Shek Pik and Pui O on Lantau Island.

14. For the former, see James Hayes, *Rural Communities of Hong Kong*, and for the latter the description given at p. 592 of my paper "Stakenet and Fishing Canoe: Hong Kong and Adjacent Islands in the 19th and Early 20th Centuries: The Sea and the Shore in Social, Economic and Political Organization," in *Proceedings of the Eighth International Symposium on Asian Studies, 1986*, vol. 1, *China*, pp. 573–98, together with another paper (with Jack Tin), "Some Aspects of Traditional Life in Hong Kong: The Village Fisheries," in *Proceedings of the Ninth International Symposium on Asian Studies, 1987*, vol. 1 *China*, pp. 53–63.

15. See James Hayes, *Hong Kong Region*, p. 79.

16. The constitution approved by District Officer Islands on February 26, 1982, still contained these limiting provisions. Earlier, the constitution of the Cheung Chau Residents Association (before the disallowed revisions of 1954) had not pro-

vided for any representatives from the Tanka population. The old Kaifong committee did not have a written constitution, but by report its membership did not extend to any leader from the Tanka element either. However, beginning in 1960, those Tanka families living on land who met the residential qualifications for voting were able to vote in the rural committee elections, but as landsmen. I am grateful to Mr. Kim Salkeld, District Officer Islands, for showing me relevant papers.

17. It would seem from official papers that for the first term of the new Rural Committee in 1960 these representatives might have come from the Cheung Chau Joint Fisheries Organization and been put up for the district officer's consideration by it, but I cannot recall what actually happened. Like the Cheung Chau Residents' association, this body had been formed in response to a wartime Japanese initiative. It stood outside but alongside the fish-marketing cooperative societies formed after the war by the Hong Kong government, whose related department kept it at arm's length because of its unsatisfactory (unreformed) constitution, loose membership, and duplication of the new cooperatives. The later fishermen's representatives' appointment to the Rural Committee and the subsequent history of the Cheung Chau Joint Fisheries Organization are outside my knowledge; but the context is one of an ever-declining fishing fleet and the removal of more and more Tanka families to land, some of them later rehoused to new villages specially built for them by charitable bodies from outside the island; see, especially, *Annual Departmental Report 1967–68*, para. 140; and also *Annual Departmental Report 1963–64*, para. 149.

18. This is borne out by the lists of contributions made to the repair of temples in the area: see James Hayes, *Hong Kong Region*, pp. 97–102, for examples where the boat people's donations were larger than the landsmen's in joint funding exercises. Another commentary on the situation is that one of my Cheung Chau friends collected Tanka fishermen's money belts, which were waterproof and apparently of a special kind. In 1976, he told me that there were no more to be found in Cheung Chau and that he had to look for them in Macau.

19. Cheung Chau itself was part of the Xin'an District.

20. The Hoklos had named their association the Wai-Chiu Club, indicating that their fellow countrymen had come from the two prefectures of Chaozhou and Huizhou to the east of Hong Kong. The rest were named either for single counties (Dongguan and Bao'an) or for recognized groups (Siyi, or the Four Counties of Kaiping, Enping, Xinning, and Heshan).

21. See Hayes, *Hong Kong Region*, p. 70.

22. Ibid., p. 69 and note 43.

23. Ibid., pp. 78 and 220, note 59 for historical aspects. The *Hong Kong Standard*, May 2, 1971, recounts a major brawl at the *jiao* festival, albeit this was among outside lion dance teams.

24. In the 1860s–1870s, the local people had found it necessary to maintain a "Security Bureau"; see Hayes, *Hong Kong Region*, pp. 63 and 68. The full text of the commemorative tablet can be found in *Historical Inscriptions*, vol. 1, no. 55 (Hong Kong: Urban Council, 1986). As late as 1912 the police station was attacked by a robber band; see G. R. Sayer, *Hong Kong 1862–1919, Years of Discretion*

(Hong Kong: Hong Kong University Press, 1975), p. 113. A fuller account is given in the Captain-General of Police's annual report for 1912 in *Hong Kong Administrative Reports, 1912*.

25. In 1844, in British Hong Kong, it was reported that "a notorious nest of pirates was known to lurk" on the nearby island of Cheung Chau. The pirates had attacked passing British small craft three times in less than three months, and the governor had requested that the British naval commander send a force there to deal with them. By then, these pirates were reported to have 150 fighting boats and to be "in open defiance of the [Chinese] authorities and exacting blackmail from all passing native craft." They had "captured the official in charge of the Bogue, cut off his ears and carried away his seals." From Captain A. Cunynghame's *The Opium War* (Philadelphia, 1845), p. 208.

26. See James Hayes, *Rural Communities of Hong Kong*, pp. 26–31; and especially pp. 29–30 for the high rate of piratical activity in local waters reported by the officer in charge of the Chinese Imperial Maritime Customs post on Cheung Chau during the period 1893–99.

27. In the nineteenth century, salt and opium were government monopolies, farmed out on tender, which attracted smuggling. The smuggling of banned commodities into China was rife in the early 1950s. Coates, *Summary Memorandum*, p. 119, states, "As occasion offers, Cheung Chau makes large profits out of smuggling . . . Cheung Chau smugglers made a great deal of money out of fuel oil smuggling in 1950 and 1951, and many of the large European [style] houses on the [Cheung Chau] Peak rest on kerosene foundations." Some of the gains were also plowed back into community projects (ibid., pp. 119–20).

28. See the list of the four town area temples at p. 73 of Hayes, *Hong Kong Region*, and mention of the other three at p. 75.

29. In these regards the Cheung Chau situation was similar to that in many other places in the area. See Hayes, *Hong Kong Region*, pp. 46–53.

30. See the long note 22 to J. W. Hayes, "Cheung Chau 1850–1898: Information from Commemorative Tablets," *Journal of the Hong Kong Branch, Royal Asiatic Society* no. 3 (1963): 88–106, which provides details of the ranks and appointments of the 21 persons thus listed on the tablet. Although it cannot be ascertained how many of them were in residence on Cheung Chau, it is reasonable to suppose that some of them were living and doing business there. The fact that sixteen were surnamed Wong and likely to have been members of the Wong Wai Tsak Tong points to its important position on and in regard to the island. As stated at note 24 above, the text is given in full in *Historical Inscriptions*.

31. Coates, *Summary Memorandum*, p. 115.

32. *Historical Inscriptions*, vol. 3, pp. 790 and 824. Not included in these volumes is the inscribed headstone placed in the Siyi Association's premises to mark its repair in 1897. This was the work of a Wong Wai-sham (Huang Huaishen), said to have been a teacher in the association's school. However, it is also possible that the writer may have been the high official of this same name, a fellow Cantonese from Xiangshan county born in 1831 and once Governor of Guangxi with a rep-

utation as painter and calligrapher. See *Guangdong Calligraphy* (Hong Kong: Urban Council, 1981), p. 264.

33. See, e.g., Hayes, *Hong Kong Region*, pp. 69, 76–77.

Choi, Reinforcing Ethnicity

The author of this essay considers himself a native of Cheung Chau, even though his family were not indigenous villagers. Having been born there, having grown up and continued to live there for some years, and having elderly parents still living there, over the years he heard many stories about Cheung Chau that did not come by way of "fieldwork." However, since the late 1970s he has also supplemented his insider's knowledge with his academic interest in village society, and from 1978 to 1981, he observed closely, notebook in hand, the religious festivals celebrated on the island. An ethnographic paper on the *jiao* celebration of 1981 has been published as "Chi o arai ekibyō o harau taiheshinshō" (Jiao festival: To wash the land and to remove illness) *Kikan minzokugaku* (Ethnography quarterly) 40 (1987): 90–105.

1. *Tanka* is a discriminatory term for the boat people. They would prefer to be called *shuishang ren* or *shuimian ren* (literally meaning one who lives on the water), which are terms complementary to those referring to the land people. In addition to *Tanka* or its derivatives, such as *Tanka po*, meaning "floating woman" or *Tanka lo*, meaning "floating man," condescending terms like *shuilo*, meaning "water man," can be heard in conversation among the land people.

2. Because the boat people were not allowed to come up to land, fish brokers' houses in Cheung Chau in Hong Kong and Coloane Island in Macau had rear doors opening onto the sea or the river that were used by them (interview, Zhang Huobiao, aged 80, Dec. 20, 1989). According to Zhu Beisheng, an elder of Cheung Chau Island, "The boat people who were not allowed to come up to land could only sell their catch to the traders who went to their boats to haul in the catch" (interview, Zhu Beisheng, Mar. 19, 1985).

3. The land people–boat people distinction may be seen elsewhere. For instance, a notice issued in May 1992 announcing the dragon-boat race placed *yumin* (or fishermen) and *jumin* (or residents) under two separate categories (note taken on May 22, 1992, Cheung Chau, at the ferry pier).

4. An owner of a shop selling electrical appliances told me, in the summer of 1988, that the fishermen were so rich that they could afford to buy, for instance, air conditioners for their houses, and to leave them running until the house was like a refrigerator. For this reason according to him, air conditioners owned by the "boat people" ran down very fast. Such conspicuous consumption showed also in the number of gold teeth they had and the number of gold accessories they wore. Deep-sea fishing, and the export of seafood (to Japan) had helped to advance the boat people's prosperity.

5. Mr. Guo Daifu was elected a member of the rural committee in 1980. He was, until 1992, the only member of the committee with a boat-people origin. He lost

his seat on the District Council in 1991 to Mr. Kuang Guowei, whose late father was a fish broker and a justice of the peace. Mr. Kuang was a branch manager of a bank on Cheung Chau. In commenting on the reason for Mr. Guo's defeat, Mr. Kuang related it to his higher academic qualifications, although Mr. Kuang himself had completed only secondary school education (*South China Morning Post*, Mar. 4, 1991).

6. This incident happened in 1988, and the "rumor" was spread among the Chaozhou women of or above 50 years of age. I did not hear any favorable opinion that supported the young man, who happened to be one of my cousins.

7. *Nantou Huangshi zupu* (The genealogy of the Huang surname at Nantou), *shang*/8b (1872: repr. Hong Kong, 1972).

8. Ibid., *shang*/10a.

9. According to the 1911 census, the total population of the island was 7,686, including 3,244 land people and 4,442 boat people. See James Hayes, *The Hong Kong Region, 1850–1911: Institutions and Leadership in Town and Countryside* (Hamden, Conn.: Archon Books, 1977), p. 56.

10. According to the Hong Kong Government (*Hong Kong Blue Book 1906*, pp. V2–V11), there were 26 major manufacturers on Cheung Chau including 5 shipyards and 2 rope and sail works.

11. According to their genealogy, as early as 1779, the Huangs already held the ownership right of the island (*Nantou Huangshi zupu, shang*/8–9). They were then registered as the rightful owners of much of Cheung Chau when the British government took over the island in 1898 (James Hayes, *Hong Kong Region*, p. 60). In terms of Qing land law, the Huangs held the subsoil rights to the land. As registered landowners under the British regime, they have continued to impose a levy every five years on house owners in the town area of Cheung Chau. In 1989, leaders of the rural committee called a meeting to challenge the legality of the levy. The meeting divided into two opinions: there were those who accepted the Huangs' claim of ownership but objected to their levies, and those who denied outright their ownership claim. The meeting resulted in the filing of a lawsuit in the name of five members of the rural committee, which was subsequently settled out of court. Since then, house owners have claimed that the Huang surname has tightened its demand for payment in matters related to their properties. The issue remains unsettled as this essay is written.

12. The characters of "Cheung Chau *xu*" were carved on an incense burner in the Pak She Tianhou temple. See Ke Dawei, Lu Hongji, and Wu Lun Yixia, comps., *Xianggang beiming huipien* (The historical inscriptions of Hong Kong) (Hong Kong: Hong Kong Urban Council, 1986), p. 678.

13. See *Xiangshan xianzhi* (Gazetteer of Xiangshan county, 1879), 22/39ff. For a detailed analysis of the activities of "the water kingdom" from 1786 to 1810 in the South China Sea, see Dian Murray, *Pirates of the South China Coast, 1790–1810* (Stanford: Stanford University Press, 1987).

14. *Xin'an xianzhi* (Gazetteer of Xin'an county, 1819; repr. 1979), p. 32. The term implies that the market was established after 1688, when the previous edition

of the gazetteer was compiled. It was recorded on page 53 that many merchants came to the island.

15. Interview, Mar. 19, 1985. According to Mr. Zhu, during the Taiping Rebellion his male and female ancestors sought refuge in Cheung Chau with their young son. They settled in the place where the ancestral hall now stands. The male ancestor later left to search for the route to go back to Shanwei in Haifeng, from where they had come, but did not return. The wife and her son started their business first by making fishnets, and then became a fish dealer and goldsmith. The family fortune expanded. In about 1920, they established the second ancestral hall, the Zhu Yuande *tang* in Xinxing Back Street.

16. Shunshan's son Jinbang, together with Zhu Wenyan (ancestor of Mr. Zhu Beisheng, see n. 15) were two of the six elders who appealed to the Hong Kong government in 1905 for permission to pay taxes directly so that crown leases might be issued to them. The Luo family does not have an ancestral hall as do the Huang and the Zhu. However, the ancestral house, called Yuzhang *tang*, is in fact a prototype ancestral hall. The family also uses the name Luo Tong Yu to participate in various activities on the Island. For instance, Luo Tong Yu is a committee member of the jiao festival committee.

17. The same inscription lists 265 names of individuals who donated to the reconstruction of the public hospital. Out of the 265 names, 140 are described as relating to Cheung Chau. See Ke Dawei et al., *Xianggang beimeng*, pp. 380–83.

18. See Ke Dawei et al., *Xianggang beimeng*, pp. 146 and 879.

19. See Peter Wesley-Smith, *Unequal Treaty: 1898–1997* (Hong Kong: Oxford University Press, 1980) pp. 19, 49, and 137.

20. Hong Kong Government, *Hong Kong Administrative Report, 1912,* (Hong Kong, 1913) p. I-13.

21. These areas are regarded by local people as areas set aside for the inhabitation of spirits, for which reason graves are located there. This is perhaps why Westerners did not receive much resistance from the islanders when they established a resort at the southern hill and a Christian graveyard at the northern hill in 1930s.

22. In the 1920s, Hinton pointed out that there were four principal ethnic groups, Tanka, Hoklo, Punti, and Hakka, on Cheung Chau island. At the eastern end of the island was "a floating village of sampans, occupied by families of the Tanka tribe" and "to the west are the boats of the Hoklo tribe" (W. J. Hinton, "Cheung Chau—Long Island" [1929], repr. *Journal of the Hong Kong Branch of the Royal Asiatic Society* 17 [1977]: 134). Hayes in the 1970s also stated that "there was a general connection between location and dialect. . . . Hing Lung street . . . was mainly populated by Cantonese shopkeepers. Chung Hing, San Hing and Tai San streets . . . also attracted a predominantly Cantonese community. By contrast, the Pak She area near the Pak Tai [Beidi] temple was mainly Hoklo and rural" (James Hayes, *Hong Kong Region*, p. 70).

23. According to Mo Ruo-meng, *Changzhou Jinxin hui shilüe* (A brief history of the Baptist Church in Cheung Chau) (Hong Kong: Cheung Chau Baptist

Church, 1951; 2nd ed. 1972), p. 14, this area, especially the northern part of the eastern beach, was, in 1843, occupied by fishermen who spoke the Chaozhou dialect. By Chaozhou he meant those from Shantou, Shanwei, Haifeng, and Lufeng. He also mentioned that Rev. D. D. William was the first missionary who, using the Chaozhou dialect, preached in this area. Later, in 1872, Rev. Chen Shizhen from Chaozhou was sent to Cheung Chau to establish a Baptist Church. I am grateful to the Rev. Carl Smith for this information.

24. The only teahouse that is not located in this area today is the Haihui. However, this teahouse, originally named He Daxin, moved out from this area only in the 1970s.

25. Every street in the town area of Cheung Chau has another street parallel to it referred as the back street. For instance, the back street of Tai San street is called Tai San Back Street.

26. Interview, Feb. 19, 1989.

27. For example, two of the stone lions located outside the temple were donated in 1861 by Cantonese believers and two others by the Huizhou and Chaozhou people (Ke Dawei et al., *Xianggang beimeng*, pp. 866–68).

28. The Cantonese people are in charge of the opera performed on the birthday of Beidi, on the third day of the Third Month, the Chaozhou people the opera performed during a festival in the beginning of the Fourth Month, and the Huizhou people the one performed right after the jiao festival.

29. See "Guangxu erjiu nian Beidi miao chongxiu ji" (Record of renovation of the Beidi Temple in 1903) and "Changzhou Guang-Hui-Chao sanfu dizi zhongjian Beidi miao heyue" (Contract for the renovation of the Beidi Temple by Cantonese, Huizhou, and Chaozhou believers), reproduced in Tanaka Issei, *Chūgoku saishi engeki kenkyū* (Ritual theaters in China) (Tokyo: Institute of Oriental Culture, University of Tokyo, 1981), pp. 122–23.

30. See W. A. Taylor, "The Spirit-Festival," *Wide World Magazine*, Dec. 1953, reprinted in *Cheung Chau Bun Festival 1980, Special Bulletin*, pp. 39–41.

31. Messrs. Zhu and Luo were the most senior elders of their respective surname groups in 1991. Mr. Zhu was also chairman of the Cheung Chau Residents' Association.

32. The elders did not state clearly the year. They might be referring to the plague that occurred in 1854 or the one in 1894. See E. J. Eitel, *Europe in China* (Hong Kong: Kelly and Walsh, 1895), p. 278, and G. B. Endacott, *A History of Hong Kong* (Hong Kong: Oxford University Press, 1962; repr. 1988).

33. Tanaka Issei, *Chūgoku no sosoku to engeki* (Lineage and theater in China) (Tokyo: Institute of Oriental Culture, University of Tokyo, 1985), p. 284.

34. Despite this account, islanders also believe that Chaozhou Daoist priests were occasionally hired. However, dissatisfaction with the Chaozhou Daoist priests was common. For instance, on May 15, 1992, when I was talking to a group of middle-aged islanders, including a Mr. and Mrs. Lin who helped in the management of the jiao, I was told that the previous year had not been good for Cheung Chau because the chairman of the jiao festival had insisted on hiring Chaozhou Daoist priests. They complained that the Chaozhou Daoist priests did not know

the details of Hailufeng rituals. When I asked why they still hired the Chaozhou Daoist priests when they knew that the Chaozhou Daoist priests were not good, they replied that hiring them had been necessary because, having delayed making arrangements that year, they were unable to hire Hailufeng Daoist priests.

35. Interviews July 18, 1981, and July 29, 1981.

36. Interview with Mr. Zeng, about 30 years old, on May 15, 1992. Mr. Zeng claimed that he was one of Li's disciples, although Li, during our interview July 15, 1981, told me that he did not have any formal disciple and that his art could be transferred only to his son.

37. The location is near the present Sacred Heart School. See also Tanaka Issei, *Chūgoku saishi engeki*, pp. 93 and 97.

38. The police report, written in 1981, argued that the Triad groups, Fuk Yee Hing, Yee On (later San Yee On), and Hoi Luk Fung Mutual Aid Association, played a major role in the Bun festival until 1978.

39. The procession during the festival comprises mainly four kinds of voluntary associations. They are the clansmen's associations, the street associations, the schools, and the sports associations.

40. According to Hayes, the "Wai Chiu Club [Huizhou and Chaozhou Prefectures Association] elders claim 200 years for their association . . . as a private record in the possession of a long-established Hoklo family states that the Beidi temple was founded by the Wai Chiu natives in 1783" (James Hayes, *Hong Kong Region*, p. 62).

41. The organizing committee is always composed of about a hundred members. Though the chairmen and vice chairmen change every year, more than 90 percent of the committee members remain the same from year to year. Membership is recorded in the *Cheung Chau Bun Festival Special Bulletin*, issued by the committee. See also Tanaka Issei, *Chūgoku no sozoku to engeki*, pp. 148–49.

42. In 1992, I was told that the chairman now was expected to take vegetarian food for one month only. I also heard he was accused of not being sincere because he did not adhere to vegetarian food until the beginning of the festival.

43. According to the donation list posted on the wall of the temporary stage in 1992, a total of 70,400 Hong Kong dollars (approximately 10,000 U.S. dollars) was collected from members of the committee. Besides the chairmen, of the 96 committee members only 5 donated an amount of more than 600 Hong Kong dollars.

44. In 1981, the Chaozhou group presented one of the three large bun towers.

45. Interview, May 15, 1992.

46. The temple of the Hongsheng, though located near the center of the town area, is seldom visited by local residents. Unlike that of other temple deities, the birthday of Hongsheng is not celebrated. Casual conversations with the temple keeper, who happens to be a family friend of the author, reveal that most of the clients of the temple come from traditional fishing villages outside Cheung Chau, such as Aberdeen or Castle Peak. In fact, many boat people came to the temple to ask for "passing the crisis" (*guoguan*) rituals. Similar rituals can be seen on the island only during the *yulan* festivals held by the boat people every year in the Seventh Month.

47. Most of the jiao festivals celebrated in the New Territories of Hong Kong incorporate a strong territorial indication. They are either celebrated by a localized lineage such as the Peng surname of Fanling or by a village alliance such as Lam Tsuen. See Choi Chi-cheung, "Shō matsuri no jinmei risuto ni mirareru shinzoku han'i" (Kinship as seen in the name lists of jiao festivals), *Bunka jinruigaku* (Cultural anthropology) 5 (1988): 129–50.

48. About the "shares" seen in the jiao festivals, see ibid., pp. 133–34.

49. This temporary office was not seen in 1992.

50. The streets were washed, in 1992, in the early morning of the day before the festival started. In the afternoon, the Daoists, dressed in black, walked along the streets without their umbrellas after some argument as to whether they should bring them along. This ritual was carried out at the same time as the three deities were paraded.

51. In 1992, only three Daoist priests participated in this ritual. Moreover, some earth gods were not invited. My impression was that the purpose of inviting the earth god to the jiao area was forgotten. On the contrary, purification with incense sticks was enhanced. The child disciples had not been seen since 1985; I was told that no children wanted to shave their heads and be bound by the rituals for three days in return for the small amount of money paid. I was told that the disciples used to receive 20 Hong Kong dollars and a catty of meat after the festival (interview, May 15, 1992).

52. For the different types and functions of name lists in the jiao festival, see Choi Chi-cheung, "Shō matsuri no jinmei ritsuto."

53. See Tanaka Issei, "The Jiao Festival in Hong Kong and the New Territories," in Julian F. Pas, ed., *The Turning of the Tide* (Hong Kong: Hong Kong Branch, Royal Asiatic Society, and Oxford University Press, 1989), pp. 275–90 for a comparison of the three-day jiao in Cheung Chau and the jiao at the inland Punti village Lung Yeuk Tau. Unless otherwise mentioned, this section is based on field investigation in 1981.

54. In 1992, this ritual was conducted at 3:00 A.M. The name list was posted on the wall of the opera stage.

55. Four types of talismans are distributed to donors during the festival. According to Daoist master Mr. Yang, a large green talisman is pasted on the entrance of a house and a large yellow one in the kitchen, small green ones are carried on the person, and yellow ones are burned into ashes and drunk with water. According to him, the talismans have the power of protecting against evil and curing disease (interview, May 19, 1991). In 1992, after the ritual of "distributing talismans," I observed that at least one-third of the talismans were reserved for a Hailufeng group, and the others were collected by members of the Huizhou and Chaozhou Prefectures Association, the Chaozhou Regional Association, and the Pak She Kaifong (street) Association. In other words, the talismans were restricted to Huizhou and Chaozhou people regardless of whether they were living on the island or not.

56. I was told by the Daoist master at the jiao at Ho Chung on mainland New Territories that the cock symbolized the forces in charge of the beginning of the day (interview, Aug. 5, 1981).

57. "Each float consists of two children set up in a cunningly contrived tableau portraying some message or other of a topical or historical nature" (J. Chamberlain, *The Bun Festival of Cheung Chau* [Hong Kong: Studio Publications, 1990], n.p.). See also Tanaka Issei, *Chūgoku saishi engeki*, pp. 113 ff.

58. See description of "*zou* Hongsheng" above. This ritual was not seen in 1992.

59. In 1992, this "let-free" or *fangsheng* ritual was performed at the seacoast of the reclaimed land in front of the temple.

60. This part of the ceremony is called *zou pusa* (running the deities). In 1992, with the instruction of the police, the groups ran one after the other and not together.

61. At the festival he was referred to by participants as the "Dizang wang pusa," that is, Bodhisattva King Dicang. No villager knew his Indian name, but his role in opening up the underworld and salvaging and feeding the wandering spirits was widely known.

62. Tanaka Issei, "The Jiao festival in Hong Kong and the New Territories," and also David Faure, *The Structure of Chinese Rural Society: Lineage and Village in the Eastern New Territories of Hong Kong* (Hong Kong: Oxford University Press, 1986), pp. 85–86.

63. W. G. Lockwood, *Beyond Ethnic Boundaries: New Approaches in the Anthropology of Ethnicity* (Michigan Discussion in Anthropology 7, 1984), p. 4.

64. Marshall D. Sahlins, "The Segmentary Lineage: An Organization of Predatory Expansion," *American Anthropologist* 63 (1961): 342.

Hase, The Alliance of Ten

1. Place-names within Hong Kong are transliterated as in the *Gazetteer of Place Names in Hong Kong, Kowloon and the New Territories* (Hong Kong Government, 1969). Place-names in China are transliterated in their Cantonese form, with pinyin given on the first appearance of the name.

2. See David Faure, *Structure of Chinese Rural Society* (Hong Kong: Oxford University Press, 1986), p. 218, n. 24.

3. The dates of the reclamation can only, in most cases, be guessed at from village tradition, but the main phase of the Sha Tau Kok reclamation was probably completed in 1875 (David Faure, *Structure of Chinese Rural Society*, p. 217, n. 22), and the Luk Keng reclamation was in hand in 1887 (ibid., p. 204, n. 30). All the reclamations were completed before the British takeover, probably, in most cases, a generation or more before.

4. The missionaries of the Basel Mission, resident in Sha Tau Kok Market intermittently from 1847 to 1854, estimated the population of the villages formally "allied" with the market as about 6,000 in 1853. This would imply about 7,000 or a little less for the market district as a whole. This is a little lower than what is suggested here, i.e., 7,000 in 1800, 8,000 in 1825, and 11,000 or 12,000 in 1875, suggesting about 9,000 in 1850. However, the differences are within the range of error to be expected. See Basel Mission Archive, Doct. A1-1, Nr. 44. This document is printed in translation in the *Journal of the Royal Asiatic Society, Hong*

Kong Branch 30 (1990): 281–96. I am indebted to Rev. Carl Smith for drawing my attention to the importance of the Basel Mission documents to the history of Sha Tau Kok and for allowing me to make use of his notes and transcripts. I would also like to express my heartfelt appreciation of the unfailing courtesy and helpfulness of Mrs. W. Haas and the staff of the Basel Mission Archive in the preparation of this article.

5. Basel Mission Archive, Doct. A1-1, Nr. 44.

6. Documents in the Basel Mission archives are full of references to emigration out of this general area, starting from 1851 and going through the 1860s and 1870s. By 1880, the missionaries are speaking of "emigration fever" (Doct. A1-14, Nr. 42), and by 1894 of deserted villages and depopulated districts (Doct. A1-28, Nr. 47). By 1906 they describe villages with no adult males left at all (*Der Evangelische Heidenbote*, Feb. 1906, p. 9).

7. Ke Dawei (David Faure), Lu Hongji (Bernard Luk), and Wu-Lun Yixian (Alice Ng), comps., *Xianggang beiming huibian* (Historical Inscriptions of Hong Kong), vol. 1 (Hong Kong: Hong Kong Urban Council, 1986), pp. 262–80.

8. The *Report on the Census of the Colony for 1911* is in *Papers Laid Before the Legislative Council of Hongkong, 1911* (Sessional Papers), No. 17/1911 (Noronha and Co. Government Printers, 1911). It contains a very detailed breakdown of the population figures for the New Territories, on a village-by-village basis (tables XIX and XIXa). This shows a total population for that part of the Sha Tau Kok area lying within Hong Kong of 3,975 males, and 4,595 females, total 8,570. The census shows a general underrecording of young girls in the New Territories of about 5 percent. A more realistic figure for the females, therefore, would be about 4,825, making the overall total 8,800. That part of the total area lying in China was about a quarter of the whole, suggesting a total resident population in 1911 of about 11,733. If 1,200 males are added to this figure for those resident abroad—the figure suggested by the 1894 tablet—then the total of all the villagers of the area then was 12,933, or, say, 13,000. This should perhaps be raised as high as 13,500 to adjust for other suspected underreporting. It is unlikely that villager males aged between 15 and 45 could have numbered more than 3,500, and 3,000 is more likely. This implies that between 33 and 40 percent of young adult male villagers were living outside the village in this period.

9. The Basel missionaries estimated the population of the area as 15,000–20,000 in 1894 (*Der Evangelische Heidenbote*, July 1894, p. 53), but this must be too high.

10. Presumably San Tsuen ("New Village") is a little later than the others.

11. Detail on the reclamation is mostly taken from a study of the old maps of the area, especially the Demarcation District Sheets (about 1905), and the Old Survey Sheets. There has not been an opportunity for a detailed ground survey. The upper limit of reclamation coincides closely with a line at about 13 feet above Principal Datum (P.D.), which would not be far off highest storm surge levels. A level of 13 feet above P.D. for the upper limit of reclamation is also to be seen in most other reclamations in the Sha Tau Kok area, especially those near Wo Hang. The Sha Tau Kok area is particularly exposed to storm surges. The area of reclamation

coincides almost exactly with the area shown on the Hong Kong Geological Survey as "Terraced Alluvium"; Hong Kong Government, *Solid and Superficial Geology*, Map Series HGM 20, Sheet 3.

12. It is possible that the innermost part of the main reclamation, between Shan Tsui and Sheung Tam Shui Hang villages, was reclaimed earlier, in a private reclamation project involving only those two villages—the landowning patterns on this part of the reclamation seem quite different from those on other parts, with 78 percent owned by those two villages. Shan Tsui owned very little elsewhere on the reclamation.

13. At the time of the Block Crown Lease Survey (1905) 12.68 acres were recorded. However, the serious inadequacies of this survey led to another being conducted in 1912, when 17.31 acres were recorded. However, in 1912 two areas were left unclaimed—probably because storms had breached their bunds and ruined them. These two areas totaled about 3.3 acres. In addition, there were some 0.6 acres of houses, huts, and waste within the reclamation, which, therefore, totaled about 21.2 acres.

14. Both "commercial" and "communal" reclamation projects are known in the area, although "commercial" projects were probably the more common. Thus, the reclamation at Kuk Po was a commercial venture in which one Yim Tin family invested heavily (Ho Kei-hing of Yim Tin owned a fifth of the area at the date of the Block Crown Lease), while the Luk Keng reclamation was communal, being paid for by a rent charge on the village fields (David Faure, *Structure of Chinese Rural Society*, p. 204, n. 30).

15. The Tangs are invited to attend the annual New Year sacrifice at the Tai Wong Ye (*dawangye*) Superior Earth-God Shrine at Wo Hang. Kong Ha was regarded as being part of the Wo Hang Yeuk, rather than the Sam Heung Yeuk, in 1899, as the petition of the "Elders of the Wo Hang District" makes clear (Petition No. 13, under Report No. 18, in Item 204, p. 263, *Correspondence [June 20, 1898, to August 20, 1900] Respecting the Extension of the Boundaries of the Colony* [printed by the Colonial Office, London, Nov. 1900, from papers in the Colonial Office, file Eastern No. 66, hereafter cited as *Extension of the Boundaries of the Colony*]). This was a joint petition of the Wo Hang and Ma Tseuk Ling Yeuk, and the list of villages covered includes Kong Ha.

16. Copies are held in the Sha Tin Library, Regional Council Libraries Service, Hong Kong.

17. For the desertion of the market in the face of the Taiping rebels, see W. Schlatter, *Geschichte der Basler Mission, 1815–1915, mit besonderer Berücksichtigung der ungedruckten Quellen*, vol. 2 (Basel, 1916), p. 297. The Basel missionaries mention in 1853 the inappropriateness of the Chinese names adopted by saltworks (Basel Mission Archive, Doct. A1-2, Nr. 46) which suggests that there were saltworks in the Sha Tau Kok area then, although not necessarily in the immediate market area. The salt fields at the market were, however, well established by 1880—the missionaries mention a Tam Shui Hang man who had sold his salt business for several hundred dollars sometime before 1882 (Basel Mission Archive, Doct. A1-16, Nr. 45).

18. An old name for the street now known as Chung Ying Street ("China and England Street," the street along which the boundary runs) is also remembered— Lo Tsz Path ("Cormorant Path"), which probably refers to the period when the street was a path along the edge of an unreclaimed watercourse. See Shatoujiao quwei xuanchuanbu (Sha Tau Kok District Committee Propaganda Section), *Shatoujiaode lishi he xianzhuang: Aiguo zhuyi jiaoyu jianghua cailiao* (The history and present situation of Sha Tau Kok: Material for oral teaching of patriotism) (Sha Tau Kok, 1986). That this name is still remembered suggests that this reclamation was undertaken during the lifetime of people living when the current district elders were youths.

19. The 1911 census gives populations for the marketing districts of 21,670 for Yuen Long, 13,900 for Tai Po, 7,900 for Sai Kung, 10,706 for Kowloon City, 6,378 for Sham Shui Po, 8,570 resident within Hong Kong for Sha Tau Kok (representing, as noted above, about 12,000 resident in the marketing district as a whole), and 8,759 resident within Hong Kong for Sham Chun (Shenzhen), representing about a third of that marketing district. All these figures should be inflated by about 10 percent to reflect census underreporting. The markets in the Islands, and Tsuen Wan, had far smaller dependent populations, but their predominant business was with the coastal fishing and trading fleets, and they are thus not directly comparable with the landward towns in the north.

20. Where a clear physical boundary did not exist, as in the Yuen Long and Sham Chun areas, subordinated markets tended to appear within the primary marketing district; where such a boundary did exist, the primary market district seems to have tended to divide along the boundary when the dependent population beyond the boundary reached the necessary size. See G. Rozman, *Urban Networks in Ch'ing China and Tokugawa Japan* (Princeton, N.J.: Princeton University Press, 1973), and G. W. Skinner, "Cities and the Hierarchy of Local Systems" in idem, ed., *The City in Late Imperial China* (Stanford: Stanford University Press, 1977), pp. 275–351, for a general discussion of the factors influencing market foundation in traditional China: the local model seems to differ in detail from that postulated by Rozman and Skinner.

21. The Luk Heung (Luxiang, "Six Villages"—the intervillage alliance covering the area immediately east of Sha Tau Kok) certainly already existed in the early eighteenth century as the owner of the Tin Hau temple at Am King. The Sam Heung was sufficiently well established as a closed body by 1825 that the incoming Tangs of Kong Ha could not get admitted to it, but had to stay as members of the Wo Hang Yeuk from which they had come. The villages of the Yim Tin valley were already united before 1825—they had founded their own small market, probably about 1800. The village alliances of the Wo Hang Yeuk, Nam Yeuk Tung, and Hing Chun Yeuk, based on close lineage groupings, are likely to have existed before 1825.

22. A recently recovered genealogy of the Chan clan of Luk Keng includes a list of all the Hakka degree holders, and the villages from which they had come, from the first examination for which the Hakka in Xin'an County had a quota (1805) to 1813, and again from 1822 to 1825, plus those from one other examination

dated 1814–1821. Lin Ma Hang scored successes in 1813, 1822, and 1825, Yim Tin in 1814–1821 and 1822, and Luk Keng in 1814–1821. All these successes were in the civil examinations. Altogether, the Shap Yeuk provided 6 of the 22 civil examination successes in these years, or 27 percent of the total for the whole county. I am indebted to Mr. Chan Wing-hoi for drawing my attention to the documents in this genealogy. I understand that a copy of the genealogy will be incorporated into the collection of historical documents held at United College, Chinese University of Hong Kong.

23. The first comes from a genealogy of the Chan clan of Luk Keng. Of Ancestor Hip-tsun (1792–1864) it says, "The foundation of Tung Wo Market was undertaken at his initiative. He got all the people of the Yeuk together and secured unanimity." The second reference, which is to the foundation of the main temple at the market rather than to the market itself, comes from a genealogy of the Wong clan of Shan Tsui and Nai Chung. Of Ancestor Yin-fung (1779–1867) it says, "Throughout his life he was upright and firm; he took the lead in the first construction of the Tin Hau Temple at Sha Tau Kok." A copy of this genealogy is in the collection of New Territories historical documents at United College, Chinese University of Hong Kong. I am indebted to Dr. David Faure for drawing my attention to this reference. 1830–35 would seem to be the only period that would fit comfortably into both Chan Hip-tsun's and Wong Yin-fung's careers, with 1835 more likely.

24. *Jahresberichte der Basler Mission*, 1849.

25. *Xin'an xianzhi* (1688) 3/6.

26. *Xin'an xianzhi* (1979 repr. of 1819 edition), pp. 31–32.

27. The Yim Tin market did, however, have some significant trade in fish, which was carried over a "frequently used road" to Wong Kong (Henggang) a few miles away across the mountains. See Basel Mission Archives, Doct. A1-16, Nr. 52, Sept. 30, 1882.

28. *Xin'an xianzhi* (1688) 3/passim.

29. David Faure, *Structure of Chinese Rural Society*, p. 107.

30. These figures are implied by the surveys undertaken to assess likely rail traffic in the area in 1904 and 1910. See Colonial Office file 882 (Public Records Office, London, copy at Public Records Office, Hong Kong), dispatch No. 59, Sir Matthew Nathan to Mr. Lyttelton, received Feb. 13, 1905; and Colonial Office file 129/376 (Public Records Office, London, copy at Public Records Office, Hong Kong), dispatch No. 165 (page 582), from Sir Frederick Lugard to Rt. Hon. Lewis Harcourt, Apr. 28, 1911.

31. For a description of the market at Sha Tau Kok and its economic life between 1848 and 1941, see the author's "Eastern Peace: Sha Tau Kok Market, 1835–1941" in the *Journal of the Hong Kong Branch of the Royal Asiatic Society* 31 (1991) (forthcoming).

32. Tungfo is the Hakka pronunciation of Tung Wo, the formal name of the market.

33. *Jahresberichte der Basler Mission*, 1849 (first para.); and Basel Mission Archive, Doct. A1-1, Nr. 44 (second para.).

34. David Faure (*Structure of Chinese Rural Society*, p. 107), is incorrect in saying that the market was owned predominantly by the Wo Hang and Nam Chung people. This is true of the shops built *outside* the original market, on Wang Tau Street and Chung Ying Street, since the land there was mostly owned by Wo Hang and Nam Chung, especially Wo Hang. Since most of the shops in the 1920s were built there, oral references to owners of shops naturally refer mostly to Wo Hang people. But it seems likely that within the walls of the original market, land ownership was originally more broadly based.

35. Basel Mission Archive, Doct. A1-2, Nr. 46, 1853; *Jahresberichte der Basler Mission*, 1859.

36. Basel Mission Archive, Doct. A1-16, Nr. 45.

37. See Shatoujiao quwei xuanchuanbu, *Shatoujiaode Lishi*.

38. See *Jahresberichte der Basler Mission*, 1849. The school is also mentioned in the "Plan of the Mission House" (no archive number).

39. Ke Dawei et al., *Xianggang beiming huibian*, vol. 1, p. 279. The Sha Tau Kok pawnshop is probably also recorded on the Kwong Fuk Bridge tablet in Tai Po, also of 1896 (ibid., p. 300).

40. *Der Evangelische Heidenbote*, Apr. 1866; *Jahresberichte der Basler Mission*, 1859; and Basel Mission Archive, Doct. A1-2, Nr. 46.

41. See J. W. Hayes, "A Casualty of the Cultural Revolution," in *Journal of the Hong Kong Branch of the Royal Asiatic Society* 10 (1970): 196–97. For the date of foundation, see n. 23. The man who "took the lead" in the foundation was a villager of Shan Tsui who had "originally a few *shek tsung* of fields," but who later became wealthy enough to have four wives.

42. See David Faure, *Structure of Chinese Rural Society*, p. 200, n. 4.

43. See Ke Dawei et al., *Xianggang beiming huibian*, vol. 3, pp. 670–71.

44. See David Faure, *Structure of Chinese Rural Society*, p. 216, n. 20.

45. For alliances of "great families" nearby, see David Faure, *Structure of Chinese Rural Society*, for the Po Tak Temple and the Sham Chun Community School, and James Hayes, *The Hong Kong Region 1850–1911: Institutions and Leadership in Town and Countryside* (Hamden, Conn.: Archon Books, 1977), for the Kowloon Charitable School. The Basel missionaries made no bones about their contempt for the magistrate during the period of the Taiping Rebellion: "The San On Magistrate is a miserable, dirty fraud and hypocrite. He demands outward respect, but does no justice. Hence differences, by being denied a hearing, grow to quarrels, then to blows, then to war, while the Magistrate sits at home and does nothing" (*Der Evangelische Heidenbote*, Jan. 1862, from a report written by the missionary P. Winnes in 1861).

46. For the Yeuk in the New Territories, see David Faure *Structure of Chinese Rural Society*; James Hayes, *Hong Kong Region*; and James Hayes, *The Rural Communities of Hong Kong: Studies and Themes* (Hong Kong: Oxford University Press, 1983); and also P. H. Hase, "The Cheung Shan Kwu Tsz, an Ancient Buddhist Nunnery in the New Territories and Its Place in Local Society," in *Journal of the Hong Kong Branch of the Royal Asiatic Society* 29 (1989): 121–57, and "The Mu-

tual Defence Alliance (*Yeuk*) of the New Territories," in *Journal of the Hong Kong Branch of the Royal Asiatic Society* 29 (1989): 384–88.

47. The Yeuk were, in China, Yim Tin and Luk Heung (the villages around Kwun Lo Ha, Guanlouxia, just east of Sha Tau Kok), and, in Hong Kong, Sam Heung (the villages immediately west of Sha Tau Kok), Ma Tseuk Ling, Lin Ma Hang, Man Uk Pin, Wo Hang, Nam Luk (also known as Tai Tan; this Yeuk consisted of Nam Chung, Luk Keng, and the small villages nearby), Hing Chun (the villages near Lai Chi Wo), Kuk Po, and Nam Yeuk Tung, the area around Wu Kau Tang. The Yeuk of Man Uk Pin was rather anomalous, being also part of the next Yeuk alliance to the west, the Sze Yeuk ("Alliance of Four"). Which villages were in which Yeuk is discussed in David Faure, *Structure of Chinese Rural Society*, pp. 107–8, and 216–17, n. 21. Nam Yeuk (Tung) was not Nam Chung, but the correct name for the Wu Kau Tang Yeuk. The inscription at Fan Shui Au between Lai Chi Wo and Wu Kau Tang/Kuk Po (not included in Ke Dawei et al., *Xianggang beiming huibian*) from 1920 (it records the rebuilding of roads in the area) states that the old roads now rebuilt were those "which twist and turn worse than a goat's intestines through the mountains of the Nam Yeuk." The petitions translated under Item 204 in *Extension of the Boundaries of the Colony*, give lists of the villages of the Wo Hang Yeuk (including the villages of the Ma Tseuk Ling Yeuk) (Petition No. 13 in enclosure 18, p. 263), and of the Luk Keng/Nam Chung Yeuk (Petition No. 14, p. 264). Since in 1899 the Ma Tseuk Ling Yeuk petitioned together with the Wo Hang Yeuk, it is possible that these two Yeuk were, for some purposes, regarded as being only one. It may be for this reason that the area had the title "Alliance of Ten" instead of "Alliance of Eleven."

48. Basel Mission Archive, Doct. A1-1, Nr. 44.

49. David Faure, *Structure of Chinese Rural Society*, p. 218, n. 24, and p. 217, n. 22.

50. *Extension of the Boundaries of the Colony*, No. 204, Enclosure 18 (Petition No. 13, of Wo Hang) (petition No. 14, of Luk Keng), Enclosure No. 18A (petition No. 20, of Nam Yeuk Tung) (petition No. 27, of Ha Po) and petitions No. 21 (Kuk Po), 24 (Hing Chun), and 31 (Lin Ma Hang) mentioned in the table included in Enclosure No. 18A. Pages 263, 264, 266, 267. It will be noted that all the Yeuk of the Shap Yeuk within the New Territories presented petitions, except Man Uk Pin, which the Colonial Secretary presumably felt belonged more to the Sze Yeuk, with the Ma Tseuk Ling Yeuk joining in a single petition with the Wo Hang Yeuk.

51. Both the Wo Hang and Luk Keng petitions commit their respective Yeuk to grant land for erecting police stations without opposition. The Nam Yeuk Tung petition was signed "on behalf of their fellow villagers"; the Sam Heung petition is "the humble petition of the inhabitants," and the signatories speak for themselves and "the other villagers."

52. *Extension of the Boundaries of the Colony*, Enclosure No. 22, under No. 204, pp. 272–73.

53. *Jahresberichte der Basler Mission*, 1849.

54. Basel Mission Archive, Doct. A-1-2, Nr. 46.

55. David Faure, *Structure of Chinese Rural Society*, p. 107, says that control of the town scale was rotated around the Yeuk. My contacts doubt this. They say that often only one person would bid for the scale, and would then get it. If two people bid, then the one from a Yeuk different from the previous year's holder would get it. But only Shap Yeuk villagers operating shops in the market could bid.

56. W. Schlatter, *Geschichte der Basler Mission*, p. 294.

57. Ibid., p. 266.

58. *Der Evangelische Heidenbote*, April 1866: "Tungfo [Tung Wo] is a place where many scoundrels and ill-bred louts gather together. The missionaries received from all sides enmity and hate, attacks and robberies." *Jahresberichte der Basler Mission*, 1859: "I do not like taking a house in a market, for you always find wicked types there—thieves, opium smokers, gamblers—festering together, and leading to predictable outcomes."

59. See in particular James Hayes, *Hong Kong Region*.

60. Most were officially regarded as "literary clubs," and sponsored poetry competitions, etc. However, in all cases, dinners, drinking parties, and mah-jongg were important. It is not known whether the Shap Yeuk elders club sponsored poetry competitions, but it is clearly of much the same type as the "literary clubs."

61. See James Hayes, *Hong Kong Region*, for Kaifong in nineteenth-century towns in the area.

62. *Administrative Reports for the Year 1910*, appendix I, "Report on the New Territories," p. I6.

63. *Administrative Report for the Year 1937*, appendix J, pp. J7–J10.

Faure, Lineage Socialism and Community Control

1. The records were discovered by Dr. James Hayes in a Hong Kong secondhand bookshop. They were purchased jointly by Dr. Hayes and myself. The collection included, in addition to the minutes of the meetings of the board of directors, a record of lawsuits, a landholding record, and a pamphlet on moneys collected in 1919. Conveniently, duplicate copies of the minutes were included for most years. Dr. Hayes's arrangement with me was that I should keep a duplicate copy of all minutes, in addition to photocopies for all years for which duplicates were not available. Meanwhile, without knowing immediately that they formed part of the same collection, I managed to acquire the printed regulations of the Lineage Restoration Savings Association and a loose letter relating to Tangang, copies of which I presented to Dr. Hayes. Moreover, when I began reading the documents in 1989, Dr. Hayes discovered that he was in possession of numerous maps from Tangang, compiled by the *xiang* association. All of Dr. Hayes's collection of these documents have now been presented to the Hoover Institution at Stanford University. Mine are still in my holding.

2. For another study of the impact of expatriate villagers on the village in the 1920s and 1930s, see Yuen-fong Woon, *Social Organization in South China, 1911–1949: The Case of the Kuan Lineage in K'ai-p'ing County* (Ann Arbor: Center for

Chinese Studies, University of Michigan, 1984). K'ai-p'ing is located on the upper reaches of the Tanjiang River to the west of Xinhui.

3. *Xinhui Tangang xingzu jijuhui guizhang* (Regulations of the Tangang Lineage Restoration Savings Association), n.d., n.p.

4. *Tangang xiang xianghui dongshiju yi'an bu* (Minutes of the Tangang *xiang xiang* association; hereafter cited as "Minutes"), vol. 1, general meeting dated 6th Second Month, Republic 8.

5. Minutes vol. 3, meeting 35; vol. 4, meeting 37.

6. A biography of Yeying's father was published in the *Tangang xiang zazi* (Tangang xiang magazine) 19, no. 3 (1938), section "Xiangzhong jishi" (Record of events in the xiang), pp. 3–4.

7. Unfortunately, neither the accounts nor the budgets for most years after 1931 are included in the minutes.

8. The records do not specify what currency was used. Presumably it was the Guangdong silver dollar.

9. One might ponder whether the presentation of the regulations in writing was necessarily a novelty of the Republican period. Such practice must have varied from village to village, but from the proliferation of written manuals in the New Territories I would be inclined to think that village regulations in Guangdong in the late Qing were quite often written down.

10. Minutes, vol. 3.

11. Minutes, vol. 3, mtg. 26.

12. The xiang association minutes refer to clusters of houses in the vicinity of an earth-god shrine as li. In 1924, the xiang association numbered the li from 1 to 8 (Minutes, vol. 6, mtg. 73). However, as the Third li was made up of four separate li, it is possible to think of the xiang as being made up of eleven house clusters. The minutes do not record any reference to the xiang population, but some idea may be formed from two sources. First, two plans are available of two of the eight li, and they show a total of approximately 300 house plots of 4 units each. These plans were prepared for the distribution of house plots in 1925 and 1926 (Minutes, vol. 7, mtg. 75, and vol. 8, mtg. 93), and such plots were claimed not only by villagers at Tangang but also by expatriate villagers resident in the cities. The number of house plots, therefore, must have exceeded the number of houses that were eventually built, but it may not be unreasonable to think that Tangang was made up of several hundred houses. More telling than the number of plots, however, is that the two plans bear 680 names. Because one would expect these names to include also male minors, a figure three to four times this total must be the upper limit of the male population of the xiang. Against such a high estimate must be weighed the second source, that is, a list of schoolchildren at the Tangang village school in 1938 published in the *Tangang xiang zazi* 19, no. 2 (1938): 5–6, under section entitled *xiangzhong baogao* (report on the xiang). The list consists of 221 names, of which 9 are not of the Ruan surname. One should expect the school population to be predominantly, even if not exclusively, male, and it should be well below the total of all children at school age. A population of 2,500, which would allow perhaps 600 to 700 children at school age, would perhaps not be unreasonable.

13. Minutes, vol. 9, mtgs. 105, 107, and 108. The village manager had ruled in favor of the plaintiff on the evidence of what he perceived to be the similarity of the signature on the loan contract to various correspondence received. Such evidence must be considered quite tenuous.

14. Minutes, vol. 5, mtg. 61. The signing of a pledge by both parties in dispute was common practice in legal disputes in the Qing dynasty.

15. The involvement of the village leadership in the trial process in the late Qing is documented with material on Xinhui county in David Faure, "Custom in the Legal Process: The Inheritance of Land and Houses in South China," *Proceedings of the Tenth International Symposium on Asian Studies* (Hong Kong, 1988), pp. 477–88.

16. Minutes, vol. 13, mtgs. 152 and 156.

17. See note 8 regarding currency.

18. Minutes, vol. 6, mtgs. 67, 68, 72, 73; vol. 8, mtg. 94; vol. 9, mtg. 107; vol. 12, mtgs. 136, 146, 147; vol. 13, mtg. 155; and vol. 14, mtg. 166.

19. The ultimate penalty for the violation of a law based on membership, as may be expected, was banishment, and in Tangang, at least two villagers were banished from the village. One villager was banished for five years for conspiring against the village office (Minutes, vol. 5, mtg. 56), and the other, apparently for perpetuity, for being adopted outside the surname (Minutes, vol. 9, mtg. 110).

20. Such aspirations may be expressed in terms of the ideals of the communal family or the charity work of the lineage estate. See Patricia Buckley Ebrey, "The Early Stages in the Development of Descent Group Organization," in Patricia Buckley Ebrey and James L. Watson, eds., *Kinship Organization in Late Imperial China, 1000–1940* (Berkeley: University of California Press, 1986), pp. 16–61. In the Pearl River delta, such aspirations may be found in Huo Tao, *Huo Weiya jiaxun* (Family regulations of Huo Weiya) (1529; repr. Hanfenlou *miji*).

21. Minutes, vol. 1, mtg. 3.

22. Minutes, vol. 5, mtgs. 50, 51, and 52.

23. In its 28th mtg., the board of directors of the xiang association decided that spies should be dispatched to see if any tenant whose rent was in arrears had been able to accumulate a stock of grain at home (Minutes, vol. 3, 1921). One detects in this kind of decision the closeness of the village community and the feeling that few secrets could be kept.

24. Minutes, vol. 3, mtg. 29.   25. Minutes, vol. 3, mtg. 31.
26. Minutes, vol. 3, mtg. 34.   27. Minutes, vol. 3, mtg. 35.
28. Minutes, vol. 3, mtg. 35.

29. These figures are summarized from the *Tian guohu zongce* (Complete record of land transfer), a record of landholdings of Tangang villagers. It does not seem to include their holdings on the *shatian*, which in the one case we know of (Minutes, vol. 13, mtg. 156), at 653 mu, were substantial.

30. Minutes, vol. 21, mtgs. 259, 260, and special mtg. 4.

31. Minutes, vol. 22, mtg. 269.

32. Minutes, vol. 3, mtg. 30.

33. Chen Xiangheng, "Chen-Lin xiedou jishi" (A true record of the armed feud

between the Chen and the Lin surnames), *Xinhui wenshi ziliao* (Sources on Xinhui literature and history) 1 (1963?): 11–20.

34. Minutes, vol. 11, mtg. 129 for quote, mtg. 127 for discussion.

35. Minutes, vol. 1, mtg. 4.   36. Minutes, vol. 5, mtg. 52.

37. Minutes, vol. 6, mtg. 66.   38. Minutes, vol. 1, mtg. 5.

39. Minutes, vol. 6, mtg. 67.   40. Minutes, vol. 19, mtg. 234.

41. On the crop-watching litigation, Minutes, vol. 13, mtgs. 152 and 155; on the "duckports," Minutes, vol. 11, mtg. 138, vol. 15, mtg. 180, and vol. 16, mtg. 191; and on the dispute with the Zhao surname, Minutes, vol. 13, mtg. 156, vol. 18, mtg. 217, and vol. 26, mtg. 231.

42. Minutes, vol. 19, mtg. 229.

43. Minutes, vol. 18, mtgs. 220, 221; vol. 19, mtgs. 229, 233.

44. The *Xinhui xian xiangtu zhi* (Local history of Xinhui *xian*) (1908) does not list the Ruan surname in its chapter on lineages; Liang Zaoquan, *Xinhui xi'nanfang shenshi renminglu* (Record of names of the *shenshi* of the southwest area of Xinhui) (Xinhui: Xi'nan shuyuan, 1919), which gives a list of the *shenshi* of the southwest district of Xinhui county, includes only one person of the Ruan surname, and this was a resident of Jiangmen and not of Tangang.

45. The records give the impression that such laws of morality were more rigorously enforced in the early years of the restoration of Tangang. At one stage, the xiang association compiled a list of all opium smokers, 35 individuals in all, and gave them deadlines to give up the habit. See Minutes, vol. 8, mtg. 95.

46. Minutes, vol. 1, mtg. 1.   47. Minutes, vol. 1, mtg. 2.

48. Minutes, vol. 11, mtg. 133.   49. Minutes, vol. 9, mtg. 99.

50. Minutes, vol. 20, mtg. 241, 1938. Although no explicit reference is made here to worship of the earth gods, it should be clear that their lack of relationship with the incomer is the reason why he may not give birth or die in the lane, i.e., house cluster.

51. *Tangang xiang zazi* 16, no. 3 (1935), section "Xiangzhong baogao," pp. 2–3. Note the precise timetable as another departure from traditional practice: traditional celebrations made use of timetables determined by the propitiousness of the two-hour *shichen*, and finer divisions in time were not made.

52. Minutes, vol. 20, mtg. 211; *Tangang xiang zazi* 19, no. 3 (1938), section *xiangzhong jishi*, pp. 1–3.

53. Minutes, vol. 3, mtgs. 31, 32; vol. 4, mtg. 37; and *Tangang xingzu jijuhui Biaoji jingli zhi qingce* (A clear record of Biaoji's management in the Tangang Lineage Restoration Savings Association) (1921).

54. Minutes, vol. 8, mtg. 96, and see also *Gangzhou xingqi bao* (The Gangzhou weekly) 1925, no. 12, pp. 16–17.

55. Minutes, vol. 8, mtg. 97.

56. Minutes, vol. 9, mtg. 101, 102, 105; vol. 11, mtg. 131.

57. For background, see Fernando Galbiati, *P'eng P'ai and the Hai-Lu-feng Soviet* (Stanford: Stanford University Press, 1985), pp. 203–5 and 230–31; and Yuenfong Woon, *Social Organization in South China*, pp. 62–65.

58. Minutes, vol. 15, mtgs. 176, 178; vol. 16, mtg. 194.

59. On organizing the militia, see *Xinhui xianzheng yuekan* (Xinhui xiang administration monthly) 1933, no. 12, pp. 6–8. On abolition of the *sishu*, see Minutes, vol. 11, mtg. 126.

60. The quote is from Minutes, vol. 12, mtg. 138.

61. Minutes, vol. 13, mtg. 152.

62. Minutes, vol. 13, mtgs. 160, 161, and vol. 14, mtg. 167.

63. Minutes, vol. 14, mtg. 169; vol. 19, mtg. 226.

64. Minutes, vol. 14, mtg. 169; vol. 19, mtg. 226.

65. Minutes, vol. 12, mtg. 146.

66. Minutes, vol. 15, mtg. 184; vol. 18, mtg. 219.

67. *Tangang xiang zazi* 19, no. 3 (1938), section "Xiangzhong jishi," pp. 1–4.

68. Chen Xiangheng, "Chen-Lin xiedou jishi," p. 20.

69. Minutes, vol. 24, general meeting.

Siu, Subverting Lineage Power

1. For summaries of this literature on south China, see Maurice Freedman, *Lineage Organization in Southeastern China* (London: Athlone, 1958), and *Chinese Lineage and Society: Fukien and Kwangtung* (London: Athlone, 1966); David Faure, *The Structure of Chinese Rural Society: Lineage and Village in the Eastern New Territories* (Hong Kong: Oxford University Press, 1986), and "The Lineage as a Cultural Invention: The Case of the Pearl River Delta," *Modern China* (1989): 4–36; Rubie Watson, "The Creation of a Chinese Lineage: The Teng of Ha Tsuen, 1669–1751," *Modern Asian Studies* 16 (1982): 69–100; and Patricia Ebrey and James Watson, eds., *Kinship Organization in Late Imperial China, 1000–1940* (Berkeley: University of California Press, 1986). For comparisons in north China, see Myron L. Cohen, "Lineage Organization in North China," *Journal of Asian Studies* 49, no. 3 (1990): 509–34.

2. This view was presented at the panel on Lineage Power and Community Change in Republican South China, Association of Asian Studies Meetings, Chicago, April 5–8, 1990. Part of the research was conducted in 1986 under the sponsorship of the Committee for Scholarly Exchanges with the People's Republic of China. Subsequent research was made possible by funds from Social Science Faculty Research Fund of Yale University and the Wenner Gren Foundation for Anthropological Research. The research on Shawan was conducted with Liu Zhiwei, David Faure, Dai He, and Chen Chunsheng in the summer of 1989. Liu Zhiwei and I have returned there for short research trips since then.

3. Scholars have debated how much the town-based estates were collecting rent from the tenant farmers and how much more directly local bosses at Tianma extracted rents and taxes. It is generally believed that the local bosses were harsher, but at the same time, their wealth remained in the community. I have dealt with the issue in Helen Siu, *Agents and Victims in South China: Accomplices in Rural Revolution* (New Haven: Yale University Press, 1989), chaps. 4 and 5.

4. Tianma *xiang* was about an hour from the county capital by boat. Villagers interviewed in 1987 acknowledged that most of their 35 halls were built in the

twentieth century, and that at least two were built during the Japanese occupation period by militaristic local bosses.

5. In the sands surrounding the town of Xiaolan, there were hardly any sizable villages. Most of the dwellings were straw huts strung out on the dikes.

6. Over a hundred of the town's 393 ancestral halls and study chambers were torn down during the Japanese occupation. The focal ancestral halls of the three major surnames remained.

7. At the Modern China Seminar at Columbia University, 1985, Rubie Watson commented on similar situations in the New Territories.

8. A document from the land office of the post-1949 town government lists 116 ancestral halls that can be identified. He Liugeng tang topped the list with an area of three-quarters of an acre on the northern part of the town. It was followed by Li Jiuyuan tang with half an acre and Li (Lai) Yongxi tang with a quarter of an acre, both on the eastern part of town, and a Wang focal ancestral hall with a third of an acre on the western side of town. The He lineage had 85 halls; only one was distinctly identified in this document as having been dismantled during the Japanese occupation. Many were torn down after 1949 when they were given to the poor from the sands, who took the materials back to their villages for building houses and cattle sheds. Fifty-nine halls remained in 1989. See Panyu xian Shawan zhen jianshe weiyuanhui, "Panyu xian Shawan zhen (Benshan xiang) jianshe zhi 1930–1988" (A record of the constructions in Shawan town of Panyu county), manuscript, 1988.

9. The Liugeng tang, the focal ancestral hall of the He in Shawan, survived the forty years of socialist revolution and was renovated in the early 1980s as a provincial-level "cultural unit" to be protected. Other ancestral halls had been the headquarters of brigades and neighborhoods. An ancestral hall adjacent to the Liugeng tang was converted to a temple for Beidi, the community patron of Shawan.

10. See *Chen zu jiapu* (Genealogy of the Chen lineage) compiled in 1923.

11. See Helen Siu, *Agents and Victims*, chap. 3.

12. The building of permanent houses signified settlement rights. These residents were finally grouped together to form a brigade in 1971.

13. See the essay by Ye Xian'en in this volume.

14. See Barbara Ward, *Through Other Eyes* (Hong Kong: Chinese University of Hong Kong Press, 1985), on how a culturally subordinated group like the Dan perceive themselves. I find similar allegations by villagers in the older sands of Zhongshan municipality and Panyu county against those living in the more recently reclaimed sands.

15. For the general theoretical argument, see David Faure, "The Lineage as a Cultural Invention," and "The Written and the Unwritten: The Political Agenda of the Written Genealogy," Institute of Modern History, Academia Sinica, ed., *Family Process and Political Process in Modern Chinese History* (Taipei: Institute of Modern History, Academia Sinica, 1992), pp. 259–96. He stresses the importance of a cultural definition of class and argues that Marxists are too preoccupied with a materialist definition.

16. This applied to the *minzhi* households. Members of the military colonies,

junzhi households, were given land through the eighteen *weisuo*, each having a ritual headquarters at a Guandi temple. By the late Ming and early Qing, the boundary between the two types of households had blurred somewhat. Li Sunchen, who rose to be a minister at the Ming court, had his household registration switched to a nonmilitary one. His agnatic kin formed the prominent Li lineage in town. For an early history of lineage building in Xiaolan, see also Choi Chi-cheung, "Descent Group Unification and Segmentation in the Coastal Area of Southern China" (Ph.D. diss., University of Tokyo, 1987).

17. See David Faure, "The Lineage as a Cultural Invention."

18. On the development of the sands in the Zhongshan-Shunde border, see He Yanggao, "Ju wo suo zhi Zhongshan Xiaolan zhen He zu lidai de fajia shi ji qita youguan ziliao" (What I know of the history of the growth of the He lineage in Xiaolan of Zhongshan, and other materials), manuscript, 1964, copy held by author; and Wong Wing-ho, "Qingdai Zhujiang sanjiaozhou shatian, xiangshen, zongzu yu zudian guanxi" (The relationship between the sands, local gentry, lineage and land tenure in the Pearl River delta during the Qing) (M.A. thesis, Chinese University of Hong Kong, 1986). On the development of the He Wenyi *gong* estate (He Xiongxiang of Xinhui) and He Liugeng tang in Shawan, see Ye Xian'en and Tan Dihua, "Lun Zhujiang sanjiaozhou de zutian" (On the lineage land of the Pearl River delta), in Guangdong lishi xuehui, ed., *Ming-Qing Guangdong shehui jingji xingtai yanjiu* (Social and economic forms in Ming-Qing Guangdong) (Guangzhou: Guangdong renmin, 1985), pp. 22–64.

19. See Helen Siu, *Agents and Victims*, chap. 2, which summarizes existing literature on the development of the sands in the Pearl River delta.

20. See He Yanggao, "Zhongshan Xiaolan zhen He zu lidai de fajia shi," on the rise of the He lineage in the 19th century. Yuexi, a member of the sixth generation, registered in a tax account as having 208 mu in 1381. He was 26 years old. By 1422, land under his account reached 21,909 mu (p. 37). He Yanggao also points to the building materials used in these halls. Before this period, red stone (from quarries in Panyu) and oyster shells were used. From the mid-nineteenth century on, granite from quarries in Hong Kong was used.

21. See Helen Siu, "Recycling Tradition: Culture, History and Political Economy in the Chrysanthemum Festivals of South China," *Comparative Studies in Society and History* 32, no. 4 (1990): 765–94; and Tanaka Issei, *Chūgoku kyōson saishi kenkyū: Chihōgeki no kankyō* (Village festivals in China: Backgrounds of local theaters) (Tokyo: Tōkyō daigaku shuppankai, 1989). For more theoretical discussions on the underlying structures in lineage segmentation and fusion, see P. Steven Sangren, "Traditional Chinese Corporations: Beyond Kinship," *Journal of Asian Studies* 43 (1984): 391–415, and Emily Ahern, "Segmentation in Chinese Lineages: A View from Written Genealogies," *American Ethnologist* 3, no. 1 (1976): 1–16.

22. This was obtained through an interview with He Yanggao in 1989. See also He Yanggao, "Zhongshan Xiaolan zhen He zu lidai de fajia shi," p. 33, on the background of this focal ancestor.

23. See Helen Siu, *Agents and Victims*, and "Recycling Tradition." Merchants

invested a great deal in community religious rituals in the name of either trade guilds or lineage trusts. They contributed to the renovation of the town's temples and sponsored groups for parading temple deities.

24. See David Faure, *The Rural Economy of Pre-Liberation China: Trade Increase and Peasant Livelihood in Jiangsu and Guangdong, 1870 to 1937* (Hong Kong: Oxford University Press, 1989), chap. 8, on the plight of those who were landless and who had no settlement rights.

25. See *Zhongshan wenshi ziliao* (Sources on the history and literature of Zhongshan county), vols. 1, 2, and 3.

26. See Wu Ruisheng, "Shiqi dangnian xiao junfa diexue ji" (The fighting among small warlords in Shiqi in years past), *Zhongshan wenshi ziliao*, vol. 2 (n.d.), pp. 49–50; We Gen, "'Shiba jian' jiehuo" (The looting of 'the Eighteen Shops'), *Zhongshan wenshi ziliao*, vol 2. (n.d.), p. 51.

27. For the details of the festivals, see original documents collected in *Zhongshan wenxian* (Historical documents on Zhongshan county) (Taipei), or Tanaka Issei, *Chūgoku kyōson saishi kenkyū*, which reproduces part of the original documents and provides maps of the festival sites.

28. See He Yanggao, "He Naizhong xiaozhuan" (A brief biography of He Naizhong), *Zhongshan wenshi* 11 (1987): 71–72. He wanted to reform the management of the ancestral estates by adding new, younger managers. However, he finally left for Beijing disappointed because the younger managers were just as corrupt.

29. See *Zhongshan wenshi ziliao* 3: 66–71.

30. See "Ting San zongdui and Minli gongsi" (The Third Regiment of the Seventh War Zone and the Minli Company), *Zhongshan wenshi ziliao* 2: 18–21.

31. See "Ting San zongdui yu Minli gongsi." The red tickets meant the peasants had to pay the corporation 30 to 200 catties of grain per mu in order to harvest the rest of their crops. "Black tickets" were payments for protection. Registration fees were also extracted from boats that transported goods and passengers along the numerous waterways. For a brief description of the monetary situation in Xiaolan during the war, see He Yanggao, "Zhongshan Xiaolan zhen He zu lidai de fajia shi," pp. 25–26.

32. I was introduced to Li Zhanquan by He Yanggao, who wanted to give another side to Li's history of being a "Japanese collaborator." Li died in 1989, but was allowed to visit Xiaolan a year before.

33. Liang was later shot by the Communists.

34. Li maneuvered so well that in the wake of the Communist takeover, an underground CCP military leader in Shiqi invited him to mediate the problems of the local bosses. He fled to Hong Kong on the eve of the land reform in late 1950.

35. Newspapers in Zhongshan during this period were filled with public announcements disputing the illegal sales of ancestral properties. See He Yanggao, "Zhongshan Xiaolan zhen He zu lidai de fajia shi," p. 28, on the dismantling of ancestral halls.

36. The famine of 1943, when one Chinese dollar could buy only four *qian* of grain, was still very vivid in the minds of some old people.

37. On the evolving customs of marital payments in Xiaolan and the surrounding villages, see Helen Siu, "The Reconstitution of Brideprice and Dowry in South China," in Deborah Davis and Stevan Harrell, eds., *The Family in Post-Mao China* (Berkeley: University of California Press, 1993), pp. 165–88.

38. See Helen Siu, *Agents and Victims*, and "Recycling Rituals: Politics and Popular Culture in Contemporary Rural China," in Richard Madsen, Perry Link, and Paul Pickowicz, eds., *Unofficial China: Essays in Popular Culture and Thought in the People's Republic* (Boulder, Colo.: Westview, 1989), pp. 121–37.

39. See Helen Siu, "Socialist Peddlers and Princes in a Chinese Market Town," *American Ethnologist* 16, no. 2 (1989): 195–212.

40. See He Rugen and Er Yi, "Shawan Hezu Liugeng tang jingying guanli gaikuang" (An overview of the management of the Liugeng tang of the He lineage in Shawan), *Panyu wenshi ziliao* 2 (1984): 69–77. Lineage members refer to four segments: *jia* (first), *yi* (second), *bing* (third), and *ding* (fourth) *fang*. The first *fang* was subdivided into two segments. See also "Heshi shixitu" (The genealogical chart of the He lineage), manuscript (n.d., probably Republican), which documents that by the fourth generation, the lineage had branched into four. The fourteen *fang* were headed by grandsons of the focal ancestor.

41. The estate of the He Liugeng tang is listed in Ye Xian'en and Tan Dihua, "Lun Zhujiang sanjiaozhou de zutian," p. 33. The records show that the estate acquired the first tract of land in the fifteenth year of Wanli's reign. See conflicting descriptions in *Panyu xian xuzhi* (Supplementary record of Panyu county) (1911); the earliest record in a manuscript locally compiled, "Liugeng ge shatian zongzhi" (A complete record of the reclaimed land of the Liugeng tang), dates from the reign of Kangxi; see also He Rugen and Er Yi, "Shawan Hezu Liugeng tang jingying guanli gaikuang," pp. 69–77.

42. Local informants said that there were 139 ancestral halls. I counted only 116 in the government document. For the holdings of the Liugeng tang, see Ye Xianen and Tan Dihua, "Lun Zhujiang Sanjiaozhou de zutian," pp. 34–36. See also "Liugeng ge shatian zongzhi" (manuscript, 1920).

43. The name was registered in local history as He Daoheng.

44. See He Rugen and Er Yi, "Shawan Hezu Liugeng tang jingying guanli gaikuang," p. 76.

45. The low position of the sands people becomes an embarrassing issue for the cadres in Shawan and in the surrounding villages. From their surnames, one can tell that the cadres do not belong to the major lineages in town, which means that they are probably sands people who were recruited into the party after the revolution. One time, I drew only puzzlement and blank stares from them when I asked about the "double toenail," a myth used by the town people to distinguish themselves from the Dan.

46. See the management of daily affairs of the community in "Xinhai nian jingli xiangzu caobu" (A draft record of lineage affairs in 1911), manuscript, and also "Tianfu zazhi" (An informal record of the land tax), manuscript. These documents are kept at the Panyu township government office.

47. In an interview with He Xuan, one of the sons of the founder of Xinhe, he

said that his brother He Shang, the manager of the enterprise, contracted with the Wu lineage of Nancun in Panyu and with the Minglun tang of Dongguan.

48. At the time, there were four refineries. The biggest was the one operated by the He of Shengli, with a press of 70–80 horsepower and ten furnaces. He Shang's Xinxinghe owned a 50-horsepower press and six furnaces. The enterprises were most prosperous during the period of Japanese occupation. One of the supervisors of He Shang was a native of Shunde who was shot as a local boss during the land reform.

49. In an interview, He Shang's younger brother confirmed that the big tenant contractors often paid a rent of 60 catties per mu to the Liugeng tang and then rented the land out to peasants or smaller tenant contractors for 80–100 catties per mu. I think the rent paid to the Liugeng tang included the government taxes.

50. Local residents referred to him as the largest of the four tenant contractors. See Wu Lipeng and Yang Shipan, "Panyu shatian fengjian dizu zongzong" (Types of feudal landlords on the reclamation of Panyu county), *Panyu wenshi ziliao* 3 (1984): 187–91. Shengli Enterprises is listed as having hired 100 long-term foremen (*daqing*) and 80 grain collectors (*yageng*) and having received an annual income of 123,400 *shi* of grain.

51. See He Zhichiang and Er Yi, "Shawan zuoji reting ji" (An account of skirmishes with the Japanese military), *Panyu wenshi ziliao* 1 (1984): 33–35.

52. See He Zhichiang and Er Yi, "Shawan zuoji reting ji."

53. According to some of his contemporaries, He Duan came to the auctions with a group of followers carrying machine guns. In 1939, he took over the Mingde school, named after the founder of the He lineage in Shawan, and renamed it after himself. After the townwide committee was formed in 1940, the school was renamed Xiangxian Middle School. See He Pinduan, "Xiangxian zhongxue xiaoshi" (A short history of the Xiangxian Middle School), *Panyu wenshi zilaio* 3 (1985): 115–30. In 1989, I interviewed several of He Duan's former staff.

54. Public ancestral halls were not meant to be used as living quarters. The new bosses took apart the halls in order to build themselves large houses. The study chambers and private memorial halls were sometimes used as residences.

55. This was related to me by He Rennong, whose father was the ninth son of the founder of Liji.

56. A former head of a temple in Shawan, He Zhengheng, alleged that it was the temples, not the ancestral halls, that were dismantled and seriously damaged. Large statues of deities were cut up and sold. The temples taken apart were Puti Temple, Guanyin Temple, and Banshan Nunnery. The seven-story pagoda was also taken apart layer by layer.

57. He Qianwen was the younger brother of a powerful local boss nicknamed Zhouchang Cheng, who was killed in Guangzhou by rivals in 1945. He stationed himself in the sands at the southwestern edge of Panyu county but kept a home in a study chamber in Shawan bought by his brother. The ancestral hall was nicknamed by residents as the "Yiding *ci*" because the family had very few male heirs.

58. He Cheng's younger brother, whom I interviewed, said that he received payments from Shenxi, Xianqing, and Kongan, all large segment trusts.

59. At the beginning of the war, He Gongba was a manager and township head. For his mismanagement of the estate, he was actually tied up by a crowd and beaten in front of the ancestral hall. See He Pinduan, "Liugeng Tang jiqi yishu teshi" (The artistic style of the Liugeng tang), *Panyu wenshi ziliao* 3 (1985): 157–64.

60. See David Faure, "The Written and the Unwritten."

61. In his preface to Anton Blok's *The Mafia of a Sicilian Village, 1860–1960: A Study of Violent Peasant Entrepreneurs* (New York: Harper and Row, 1974), Charles Tilly points to a situation not unlike that of Republican rural China. The persistent bonds of kin and territorial enclaves were powerful political tools in a society in flux. Although Charles Tilly was describing the violent basis of rural leadership in Sicily in the same period, his words are remarkably applicable to the situation in Republican China. See also Prasenjit Duara, "State Involution: A Study of Local Finance in North China, 1911–1935," *Comparative Studies in Society and History* 29, no. 1 (1988): 132–61, on "state involution," and Michael Gilsenan, "Domination as Social Practice: Patrimonalism in North Lebanon: Arbitrary Power, Desecration, and the Aesthetics of Violence," *Critique of Anthropology* 6, no. 1 (1986): 17–37.

62. In his *Peasant Intellectuals: Anthropology and History in Tanzania* (Madison: University of Wisconsin Press, 1990), Steven Feierman describes a similar problem for analyzing social change in Tanzania in the following: "The difficult task in actual historical analysis is to create a method and a form of ethnographic description which can capture the cultural categories as both continuous and in transformation, and the actors as both creating new language and speaking inherited words, all at the same time."

Siu and Faure, Conclusion

1. See Sherry Ortner, *High Religion: A Cultural and Political History of Sherpa Buddhism* (Princeton, N.J.: Princeton University Press, 1989). She explores the concepts of agency and practice in the history of the founding of temples in Nepal. We find the concepts useful in understanding the cultural strategies of local elites in the Pearl River delta. See also Eric Hobsbawm and Terence Ranger, eds., *The Invention of Tradition* (Cambridge, Eng.: Cambridge University Press, 1983); Arjun Appadurai, "The Past as a Scarce Resource," *Man* 16 (1981): 201–19; and William Kelly, "Rationalization and Nostalgia: Cultural Dynamics of New Middle-Class Japan," *American Ethnologist* 13, no. 4 (1986): 603–18, and "Finding a Place in Metropolitan Japan: Postwar Transpositions of Everyday Life," in Andrew Gordon, ed., *Postwar Japan as History* (Berkeley: University of California Press, 1992).

2. See Maurice Freedman, *Lineage Organization in Southeastern Kwangtung* (London: Athlone, 1958), *Chinese Lineage and Society: Fukien and Kwangtung* (London: Athlone, 1966), and *The Study of Chinese Society* (ed. G. William Skinner) (Stanford: Stanford University Press, 1979) on his various contributions to the study of Chinese lineage.

3. David Faure, "The Lineage as a Cultural Invention: The Case of the Pearl River Delta," *Modern China* (1989): 4–36.

4. See Jack Potter, "Land and Lineage in Traditional China," in Maurice Freedman, ed., *Family and Kinship in Chinese Society* (Stanford: Stanford University Press, 1970), pp. 121–38; Hugh Baker, *A Chinese Lineage: Sheung Shui* (London: Frank Cass, 1968); and James Watson, "Chinese Kinship Reconsidered: Anthropological Approaches on Historical Research," *China Quarterly* 92 (1982): 589–627.

5. Myron Cohen, "Lineage Organization in North China," *Journal of Asian Studies* 49 (1990): 504–34.

6. Tilemann Grimm, "Academies and the Urban System in Kwangtung," in G. W. Skinner, ed., *The City in Late Imperial China* (Stanford: Stanford University Press, 1977), pp. 475–98.

7. Helen Siu, *Agents and Victims in South China: Accomplices in Rural Revolution* (New Haven: Yale University Press, 1989).

8. In addition to James L. Watson, "Standardizing the Gods: The Promotion of T'ien Hou' (Empress of Heaven) Along the South China Coast, 960–1960," in David Johnson, Andrew Nathan, and Evelyn Rawski, eds., *Popular Culture in Late Imperial China* (Berkeley: University of California Press, 1985), pp. 292–324, see Stephan Feuchtwang, "School Temple and City God," in G. William Skinner, *The City in Late Imperial China*, pp. 581–608, and *The Imperial Metaphor: Popular Religion in China* (London: Routledge, 1991); and Hugh Baker and Stephan Feuchtwang, eds., *An Old State in New Settings: Studies in the Social Anthropology of China in Memory of Maurice Freedman* (Oxford: Journal of the Anthropological Society of Oxford Occasional Papers No. 8, 1991).

9. For a historical treatment of Chinese kinship, see David Faure, *The Structure of Chinese Rural Society: Lineage and Village in the Eastern New Territories* (Hong Kong: Oxford University Press, 1986); and also Patricia Buckley Ebrey and James Watson, eds., *Kinship Organization in Late Imperial China, 1000–1940* (Berkeley: University of California Press, 1986).

10. See Chen Xujing, *Danmin de yanjiu* (A study of the Dan people) (1948; repr. Taipei: Dongfang wenhua shuju, 1971); Guangdong sheng renmin zhengfu minzu shiwu weiyuanhui, *Yangjiang yanhai ji Zhongshan gangkou shatian danmin diaocha ziliao* (An investigation into the Dan people in the sands around the Zhongshan port and along the coast of Yangjiang) (n.p., 1953); Barbara Ward, *Through Other Eyes* (Hong Kong: Chinese University Press, 1985).

11. See Dian Murray, *Pirates of the South China Coast 1790–1810* (Stanford: Stanford University Press, 1987).

12. There were military colonies during the Ming, and many of the descendants retained military household registration.

13. See Helen Siu, *Agents and Victims*, chap. 3, on such a process.

14. See also Fred C. Blake, *Ethnic Groups and Social Change in a Chinese Market Town* (Honolulu: University Press of Hawaii, 1981).

15. We appreciate the work of James L. Watson ("Standardizing the Gods," pp. 292–324; and "The Structure of Chinese Funerary Rites: Elementary Forms, Rit-

ual Sequence, and the Primacy of Performance," in James L. Watson and Evelyn S. Rawski, eds., *Death Ritual in Late Imperial China* [Berkeley: University of California Press, 1988], pp. 3–19), which clarifies the standardizing impact of rituals on cultural identity, particularly the significance of Tianhou to the different social groups that promoted her along the coast through the centuries. The contemporary relevance of this mode of analysis is demonstrated in David Faure's work on the New Territories of Hong Kong (*Structure of Chinese Rural Society*), P. Steven Sangren's work on the Ma-tsu cult of Taiwan ("History and the Rhetoric of Legitimacy: The Ma Tsu Cult of Taiwan," *Comparative Studies in Society and History* 30, no. 4 [1988]: 674–97), and Prasenjit Duara's on North China (*Culture, Power, and the State: Rural North China, 1900–1942* [Stanford: Stanford University Press, 1988]).

16. Barbara Sands and Ramon H. Myers, "The Spatial Approach to Chinese History: A Test," *Journal of Asian Studies* 45, no. 4 (1986): 721–43; Daniel Little and Joseph H. Esherick, "Testing the Testers: A Reply to Barbara Sands and Ramon Myers's Critique of G. William Skinner's Regional System Approach to China," *Journal of Asian Studies* 48, no. 1 (1989): 90–99; William Lavely, "The Spatial Approach to Chinese History: Illustrations from North China and the Upper Yangzi," *Journal of Asian Studies* 48, no. 1 (1989): 100–113; Barbara Sands and Ramon Myers, "Economics and Macroregions: A Reply to Our Critics," *Journal of Asian Studies* 49, no. 2 (1990): 344–46.

17. On the functions of the civil service examinations for political, social, and cultural reproduction, see Benjamin Elman, "Political, Social and Cultural Reproduction via Civil Service Examinations in Late Imperial China," *Journal of Asian Studies* 50, no. 1 (1991): 7–28.

18. See the introduction to Fredrik Barth, ed., *Ethnic Groups and Boundaries: The Social Organization of Cultural Difference* (Boston: Little, Brown, 1969), pp. 9–38.

19. See also the works of Jacques Le Goff for medieval Europe, David Sabean for early modern Germany, Carlo Ginsberg for Italy, and Natalie Davis for early modern France.

20. The works of Bernard Cohn, William Kelly, Arjun Appadurai, Sherry Ortner, and Nicholas Dirks are prime examples of such scholarship.

Character List

An asterisk (*) indicates a vernacular pronunciation.

an 庵
anlong 安龍
anshang ren 岸上人

Bai Yuchan 白玉蟾
baiguan 拜官
baiyi yinhui 百益銀會
banfu 頒符
bang 榜
banshisuo zhuren 辦事所主任
banzuo 頒胙
bao 堡
Baochang 保昌
baolan 包攬
baoshan 包山
baozhang 保長
Bapai 八排
Beidi (Pak Tai) 北帝
Beiji 北極
bendi (Punti) 本地
bingma 兵馬
bo 箔
bu 埠

Cao-Pan *di* 曹潘地
chalou 茶樓
chang 廠
changping si 常平司
Changzhou *she wei* 長洲社圍

chao 朝
chaodie 朝牒
Chen Jinggu 陳靖姑
Chen Lin Li *nai* 陳林李奶
Cheung Chau* 長洲
chicai shimo 吃菜事魔
chongxin 重新
chongxiu 重修
chuhui 出會
ci 祠
Cui 崔

da duizhang 大隊長
dajiao 打醮
Dakui *lou* 大魁樓
dan 担
Dan 蛋
dangjia 當甲
danhu 蛋戶
danjia (Tanka*) 蛋家
Daode *tianjun* 道德天尊
Daodian Lun 道典論
Daojiao Yuanliu 道教源流
Daotong *yongchuan* 道統永傳
daowu 道巫
daoxue 道學
daozu 道祖
daqing 大青
Dashi *gong* 大士公

datian er 大天二
Dawang miao 大王廟
dawangye (Tai Wong Ye*) 大王爺
daxing 大姓
dazong ci 大宗祠
dazong guan 大宗館
di 第
dian 店
Dingfeng ji 定風基
disha 地沙
Dizang 地藏
dong-xi fang 東西坊
Dongping ju 東平局
dongxi cunci 東西襯祠
dongxi liangwu 東西兩廡
du 渡
du 都
dugong 都功
duming 度名
duo 多
dushen 度身
dushi 度師
dushui 度水

fa 法
fa hua* (faming) 法名
fa zhaobing pai 發招兵牌
Faguang 法廣
fan 幡
Fan Gui 范規
fang 房
fang 坊
fangsheng 放生
fashi 法師
fazhang 法章
fengchao 奉朝
fengshui 風水
fu 符
fuhu 富戶

gang 筶
gaodou 告斗

gengjia 耕家
genglian 更練
gongming 功名
gongsuo 公所
gongtong* 降童
gu 姑
gu 罟
guahua 掛花
guan 館
guan 管
Guandi 關帝
guan'gao 官誥
Guangxu erjiu nian Beidi miao
   chongxiu ji 光緒二九年北帝廟重修記
Guanyao 官窯
Guanyin (Koon Yam*) 觀音
guoguan 過關
gusao fen 姑嫂墳
gutun 古屯

Hailufeng 海陸豐
haixian 海鮮
Han Yin 韓殷
he 合
He 何
hebosuo 河泊所
hegeng 禾耕
Hengshan Shilang 橫山十郎
heshang tian 和尚田
Hoklo* (Helao) 鶴佬
hongchao 洪朝
Hongsheng (Hung Sheng*) 洪聖
houqin 後寢
Houwang 侯王
Huaguang 華光
huahong 花紅
huajia yinhui 花甲銀會
Huang Weize tang 黃維則堂
huangbang 黃榜
huapao 花炮
Huashan 華山
huazhao 花朝

Huicheng 會城
hunyuan 混元

ji dayou 祭大幽
ji shuiyou 祭水幽
ji'an shagun 積案沙棍
jia 甲
jiamiao 家廟
jianchao 監朝
jianshe jiuji weiyuanhui
   建設救濟委員會
jiao 醮
jiaoming 醮名
jiaopeng 醮棚
jiashou 甲首
jiatian 甲田
jiazhang 甲長
jiazu 家族
jie 街
jiefang (Kaifong*) 街坊
jietouxu 街頭墟
jiju 寄居
jindu 津渡
jingxiang 淨香
Jiulang 九郎
jizu 祭祖
juding 局丁
jumin 居民

kaiguang 開光
kaimian ren 開面人
Kejia (Hakka) 客家
kuatang * (*kwa tang*)* 掛燈

Lam Pui* 林培
lang 郎
langhao 郎號
langming 郎名
lao dengpeng 老燈棚
Laogu *xiang* 老古巷
Li 李
Li (Lai*) 黎

Li Maoying 李昂英
liangzhang 糧長
lianhe banshichu 聯合辦事處
lichang 釐廠
lingbao 靈寶
Linshui furen 臨水夫人
Liulang 六郎
lizhang 里長
*lo** (*lao*) 佬
Longmu *miao* 龍母廟
Longpo *shexue* 龍坡社學
Lubao 盧苞
Lun Wenxu 倫文敍
Luobei 羅陂
Lüshan Jiulang 閭山九郎
lushang jumin 陸上居民
lushang ren 陸上人

maimian ren 埋面人
Maoshan 茅山
Mengshan Qilang 蒙山七郎
mengwei 盟威
menxia 門下
Miao 繆
miao 妙
miaozi miaosun 廟子廟孫
mifeng 迷奉
ming 名
Mingzhen Ke 明真科
mintian 民田
mintuan 民團

nainiang 奶娘
nanmo (*nammo**) 喃嘸
nanmo peng 喃嘸棚
Nanxiong 南雄
niang 娘
nonghui 農會

paiwei 拍圍
paixing 排行
Pangu 盤古

pao 炮
piaose 飄色
po* (*po*) 婆
pu 僕
pu 舖
putan 舖壇

qianchuan 遣船
qiangpao 搶炮
qianpan 僉判
Qibao 七堡
qidi 企地
qingbai 清白
qingfu 請福
Qingluo *zhang* 青蘿嶂
Qingtang *wei* 青塘圍
Qingyun *qiao* 青雲橋
qu 區
Qu Dajun 屈大均
quxie zhi yuan 驅邪之院

rangzai 禳災
Renran *gongju* 仁讓公局
renyuan bang 人緣榜
rulu 入籙

san maliang 散馬糧
sanchao sanchan 三朝三懺
sang* 覡
Sanhe *gongsi* 三合公司
Sanjiang 三江
sannai 三奶
sanwang peng 三王棚
sanwei furen 三位夫人
Sanxiang (Sam Heung*) 三鄉
sanxing miao 三姓廟
Sanyi *yinhui* 三益銀會
Sanyuan 三元
se 色
sha 沙
Sha Tau Kok* 沙頭角
shagu 沙骨

Shajiao 沙滘
shalan 沙欄
shamin 沙民
shang renyuan bang 上人緣榜
shangzu 上祖
shatian 沙田
shatou 沙頭
Shatou 沙頭
Shawan 沙灣
she 社
she 畬
hen peng 神棚
sheng citang 盛祠堂
shengong 神功
shenjia qingbai 身家清白
shetan 社壇
shi 士
shipu 世僕
Shiqi 石歧
shiren 士人
shiwu 師巫
shiyu 侍御
Shiyue (Shap Yeuk*) 十約
shuilao 水佬
shuiliu chai 水流柴
shuimian ren 水面人
shuishang ren 水上人
shuliang 薯莨
Si Gong 嗣恭
sida tian wang 四大天王
sida gengjia 四大耕家
sienpo* 仙婆
sili jian siku 司理兼司庫
simin 四民
Sishan 寺山
sishu 私塾
Siyi 四邑
Sun Fen 孫賁
Suotan* 娑坦

taigong 太公
taigong shu 太公數

taigong fen zhurou 太公分豬肉
Taiping shan 太平山
Taishang *hunyuan jiaozhu daode
   tianjun* 太山混元教主道德天尊
Taishang Laojun 太上老君
tang 堂
Tangang 潭岡
tanjing 灘精
Tianhou (Tin Hau) 天后
tianjing (tin-tseng*) 天井
tiaogui 跳鬼
toumen 頭門
tousai* 度師
Toutuo 頭陀
tu 圖
tujia 圖甲
Tung Wo* (Donghe) 東和

wancan 晚參
Wangmu 王母
Wangtaimu 王太母
Wei Tuo 韋陀
Weitai 惟泰
Weituoshi 維陀始
Wenwu erdi 文武二帝
wosong* (heshang) 和尚
wu 巫
Wu Tingju 吳廷舉
wu daxing 五大姓
Wudang xinggong 武當行宮
wuhua qihao 五花旗號
Wulang 五郎
wuben zhi ren 務本之人
wushi 巫師
Wuxian 五顯
Wuyi 五邑
wuzhe 巫者

xiahu 下戶
xianghuo 香火
Xianglai 香來
xiangmin 鄉民

xiangyue 鄉約
xiangzhang 鄉長
Xiaolan 小欖
xibo jing 洗鉢井
xiefan 謝幡
xiejiao 邪教
xinggong 行宮
xintian 心田
xipeng 戲棚
xiu 秀
xu 墟
Xu Liu 許六
Xu Xun 許遜
Xuantian *shangdi* 玄天上帝
Xuanzhong *dafashi* 玄中大法師
Xuanzong 玄宗
Xueshan 雪山
Xueshi *xuan* 學士軒
Xujiang 胥江
xulang 墟廊

yabu 鴨埠
yageng 押耕 (or 押更)
yanjing 演經
Yao 徭
yaowu 妖巫
yasheng hui 迓聖會
yeuk* (yue) 約
yezhu 業主
yichu xiangcun yichu li 一處鄉村
   一處例
Yijian zhi 夷堅志
yimen 儀門
Yin Shan 尹善
yingsheng 迎聖
yingsuo 營所
yipin dafu 一品大夫
Yong an 永安
youfen 有份
Yu 禹
yuanbu 緣部
yuke 漁課

yulan 盂蘭
Yumen 禹門
yumin 漁民

zaxing 雜姓
zeng 瞻
zengmen 瞻門
Zhang Sanlang 張三郎
Zhang Zhao Erlang 張趙二郎
zhangshou 丈手
Zhao Tuo 趙陀
Zhao Hou Sanlang 趙侯三郎
zhaobing pai 招兵牌
zhaobing 招兵
zhaojiang 召將
Zhendu 鎮都
zhengdao 正道
zhengjiao 正醮
zhengtan 正壇
Zhengyi 正一
Zhenren 真人

zhili 值理
zhong duizhang 中隊長
zhongyuan 中原
zhongzuo 中座
zhu 主
zhupeng 主棚
Zidong 紫洞
zizhihui 自治會
zong 宗
zonggu lou 鐘鼓樓
zongli 總理
zongzi 宗子
zou Hongsheng 走洪聖
zou wuchao 走午朝
zou pusa 走菩薩
zouming 奏名
zu 族
zuchao 祖朝
zugong 祖公
zuoju 坐局
zushi 祖師

Index

In this index an "f" after a number indicates a separate reference on the next page, and an "ff" indicates separate references on the next two pages. A continuous discussion over two or more pages is indicated by a span of page numbers, e.g., "57–59." *Passim* is used for a cluster of references in close but not consecutive sequence.

Library of Congress Cataloging-in-Publication Data

Down to earth : the territorial bond in South China / edited by David
   Faure, Helen F. Siu.
      p.   cm.
   Includes bibliographical references (p.   ) and index.
   ISBN 0-8047-2434-2 (cloth : alk. paper). — ISBN 0-8047-2435-0
   (paperback : alk. paper)
   1. Kinship—China—Chu River Delta—History. 2. Ethnicity—China—
   Chu River Delta—History. 3. Land tenure—China—Chu River Delta—
   History. 4. Land use, Rural—China—Chu River Delta—History.
   5. Right of property—China—Chu River Delta—History.
   6. Inheritance and succession—China—Chu River Delta—History.
   7. China—History—Ming dynasty, 1368–1644. 8. China—History—
   Ch'ing dynasty, 1644–1912. 9. Chu River Delta (China)—Genealogy.
   I. Faure, David. II. Siu, Helen F.
   GN635.C5D66   1995
   305.5′23′0951—dc20   94-48410
                                                                  CIP

Original printing 1995
Last figure below indicates year of this printing:

04 03 02 01 00 99 98 97 96 95